John Siko is head of the Africa business intelligence practice at the Risk Advisory Group. He previously spent 15 years as an analyst and diplomat with the US government, specializing in Southern Africa and serving in Pretoria and Cape Town. John has taught African politics and security at Georgetown and George Washington Universities in Washington DC, and he is a term member of the US Council on Foreign Relations.

'Through meticulous research John Siko has produced a masterful comparative analysis of the dark arts of foreign policy making in the old and new South Africa. For sensitive readers the similarities between the two eras might be disconcerting, whereas seasoned foreign policy analysts will find authoritative confirmation of their presumptions about the inner workings of the "black box" of democratic South Africa's foreign policy formulation.'
Deon Geldenhuys, University of Johannesburg

'When it comes to understanding South Africa, John Siko has few equals. His book is a valuable addition to the canon of South African foreign-policy literature, particularly given his five years experience as a diplomat in the country. It is a must read for anyone – whether South Africans or outsiders – trying to understand how the foreign policy making process really works. Incoming diplomats in particular should put this at the top of their reading lists.'
Donald Gips, US Ambassador to South Africa, 2009–13

'John Siko has written the finest and most comprehensive account of South African foreign policy to date. It is an irony that the foreign policy of an apartheid era was more active internationally, beyond Africa, than South African foreign policy is today. At the same time, Thabo Mbeki's painstaking "African diplomacy" within Africa is captured by Siko in a compelling fashion, especially in its Zimbabwean dimension. The various think tanks and interest groups, some public and others secret, are all represented here in a valuable and important book.'

Stephen Chan OBE, SOAS, University of London

'Dr Siko has produced an innovative and perceptive study of the varying impact of key South African elites on the foreign-policy decision-making process. It is closely argued, based on a formidably wide range of sources including productive interviews with many of the key actors. The tone and substance of the book demonstrates a commendable scholarly detachment; it will certainly be a valuable text for those interested in a variety of fields including foreign-policy analysis, democratic theory and practice and transitional politics.'

J.E. Spence, King's College London

INSIDE SOUTH AFRICA'S FOREIGN POLICY

Diplomacy in Africa from Smuts to Mbeki

JOHN SIKO

I.B.TAURIS

LONDON · NEW YORK

New paperback edition published in 2016 by
I.B.Tauris & Co. Ltd
London • New York
www.ibtauris.com

First published in hardback in 2014 by I.B.Tauris & Co. Ltd

ISBN: 978 1 78453 736 4
eISBN: 978 0 85773 579 9

A full CIP record for this book is available from the British Library
A full CIP record is available from the Library of Congress

Library of Congress Catalog Card Number: available

Typeset in Garamond Three by OKS Prepress Services, Chennai, India

To Romy and Carl ... may you inherit your parents' love of learning.

CONTENTS

Acknowledgments   viii
List of Acronyms   x

1. Understanding South African Foreign Policymaking   1
2. A Brief History of South African Foreign Policy   14
3. Public Opinion and Pressure Groups   47
4. The Press   70
5. Academia   91
6. Business   134
7. Parliament   160
8. Ruling Parties   181
9. Government Departments   200
10. The Prime Minister and President   229
11. Conclusion—Room, But Not Willingness,
    for Engagement   254

Appendix: List of Interviews   263
Notes   267
Bibliography   309
Index   325

ACKNOWLEDGMENTS

Many thanks are in order for this book. First off, my sincere thanks go out to Thabisi Hoeane, my advisor at the University of South Africa, for all of his guidance and meticulous review of the drafts of my doctoral dissertation, from which this book is derived. His assistance was invaluable in tightening my argumentation and improving the draft. Dirk Kotze of the Politics Department also provided valuable assistance in the early stages of the process and, most importantly, helped convince me to undertake the daunting task of a doctoral dissertation.

Two books, cited liberally in this text, gave me the inspiration to tackle the topic of South African foreign policy through the Mbeki period: Ned Munger's 1965 *Notes on the Formation of South African Foreign Policy* and Deon Geldenhuys' 1984 *Diplomacy of Isolation*. My thanks go out to both authors. I never got the opportunity to meet Dr Munger, an American who passed away in 2010, but I did have the good fortune to talk with Dr Geldenhuys, who was extremely gracious in sitting for an interview.

My interviewees, all 113 of them, deserve tremendous thanks for taking time out of their busy schedules to meet in person (more than 100 of them), talk on the phone, or consider my questions by email. Their insider inputs and anecdotes provided me a wealth of information about the foreign policy decision-making process, past and present, which greatly enriched my analysis. While all interviewees were a huge help, I want to particularly thank Niel Barnard, Pik Botha, Pallo Jordan, and Aziz Pahad, each of whom gave me more than three hours of their time in one-on-one personal interviews.

Huge thanks go out to Todd Johnson, who read every chapter of this book and provided excellent feedback. Scott Hamilton and Jonathan Smallridge also read selected chapters and gave useful comments. Brendan Dabkowski, my oldest friend, meticulously edited the manuscript, making it far better in the process. Tomasz Hoskins and Allison Walker, my editors at I.B.Tauris, deserve huge thanks for guiding me through the process of publishing this manuscript. Last but not least, I have to thank my wife Yolaine for putting up with my research, writing, and editing over the past three years. She never complained about my long nights at the computer or my spending vacations trekking around South Africa to do interviews and research. *Je t'aime tres fort, mon coeur!*

LIST OF ACRONYMS

ACCORD	African Center for Constructive Resolution of Disputes
AISA	Africa Institute of South Africa
ANC	African National Congress
BEE	Black Economic Empowerment
BLSA	Business Leadership South Africa
BOSS	Bureau of State Security
BUSA	Business Unity South Africa
CCR	Center for Conflict Resolution
CIA	Central Intelligence Agency (USA)
CONSAS	Constellation of Southern African States
COSATU	Congress of South African Trade Unions
CPS	Center for Policy Studies
CSAS	Center for Southern African Studies
DA	Democratic Alliance
DEA	Department of External Affairs
DFA	Department of Foreign Affairs
DIA	Department of International Affairs (ANC)
DIP	Department of Information and Publicity (ANC)
DONS	Department of National Security
DPLG	Department of Provincial and Local Government
DTI	Department of Trade and Industry

FAK	Federation of Afrikaner Cultural Organizations (translated)
FRELIMO	Liberation Front of Mozambique (translated)
G-8	Group of 8
G-77	Group of 77
IDP	Institute for Defense Policy
IGD	Institute for Global Dialogue
IMF	International Monetary Fund
IRA	Irish Republican Army
IRPS	International Relations, Peace, and Security
ISS	Institute for Security Studies
ISSUP	Institute for Strategic Studies-University of Pretoria
MDC	Movement for Democratic Change (Zimbabwe)
MI	Military Intelligence
MK	Umkhonto we Sizwe (ANC armed wing)
MPLA	People's Movement for the Liberation of Angola (translated)
MRG	Military Research Group
NATO	North Atlantic Treaty Organization
NCOP	National Council of Provinces
NEC	National Executive Committee
NEPAD	New Economic Partnership for Africa's Development
NIA	National Intelligence Agency
NIS	National Intelligence Service
NP	National Party
NWC	National Working Committee
OAU	Organization of African Unity
PAC	Pan-Africanist Congress
PCAS	Policy Coordination and Advisory Services
PCFA	Portfolio Committee on Foreign Affairs
PLO	Palestinian Liberation Organization
PRAU	Policy, Research, and Analysis Unit (DFA)

RAU	Rand Afrikaans University
RENAMO	Mozambican National Resistance (translated)
RI	Republican Intelligence
SACBC	Southern African Catholic Bishops' Conference
SACC	South African Council of Churches
SACP	South African Communist Party
SACU	Southern African Customs Union
SADC	Southern African Development Community
SADF	South African Defense Force
SAIIA	South African Institute of International Affairs
SANDF	South African National Defense Force
SASS	South African Secret Service
SSC	State Security Council
SWAPO	Southwest African People's Organization
UDI	Unilateral Declaration of Independence (Rhodesia)
UNISA	University of South Africa
UNITA	National Union for the Total Independence of Angola (translated)
UWC	University of the Western Cape
WTO	World Trade Organization
ZANU-PF	Zimbabwe African National Union-Patriotic Front

CHAPTER 1

UNDERSTANDING SOUTH AFRICAN FOREIGN POLICYMAKING

Every day, governments around the world make decisions, small and large, about their bilateral or multilateral external relations. Their sum results in what can be broadly termed as a country's 'foreign policy,' best defined by American academic Marijke Breuning as 'the totality of a country's policies toward and interactions with the environment beyond its borders.'[1] Usually, these policies are relatively clear, characterized by such outcomes as trade and mutual defense pacts, foreign assistance packages, embargoes, or declarations of war.

While the 'what' of foreign policy is easily discerned, the question of 'why' can pose a more difficult question. Another definition of foreign policy comes from Nigerian scholar Adewale Banjo, who describes it as a 'framework outlining how the country will interact, relate and do business with other countries and with non-state actors in mutually beneficial ways and within the context of a country's national interest and economic prosperity.'[2] Implicit in this definition is the assumption that state priorities are unambiguous and that 'national interest' and 'economic prosperity' would be clear to a country's policymakers and populace. Any citizen of a democratic society knows this is not the case; ask ten Germans about whether

European Union membership is in their national interest or ten Americans about the wars in Afghanistan and Iraq, and one is certain to receive an array of replies.

If one accepts that the foreign policy orientation of states (or non-state actors, players ignored by the definitions above) is open to interpretation, then the question turns from 'why' to 'who matters' in making policy. As Joseph Frankel noted in his seminal 1963 study on foreign policymaking, "'State decisions" are not made by states but on their behalf, by individuals and by groups of individuals.'[3] From a legal and constitutional standpoint, responsibility for most of these decisions resides with the head of state or head of government, while ministries like foreign affairs, trade, defense, and others handle more mundane issues. In democratic societies, however, government entities are not necessarily the only actors that matter. Legislatures in many democracies have foreign policy competencies, such as the ratification of treaties. Business leaders seek policies that will improve their export possibilities and limit import competition. Academics, journalists, and civil society organizations will stake out positions on various external issues based on their beliefs and interests. At the base of the pyramid of actors is public opinion, which, while not always voluble on foreign policy, can assert itself at the ballot box if government actions stray too far from society's norms and values.

Assuming that one accepts the hypothesis that actors beyond the executive branch matter in making foreign policy, one must turn to the final question of 'how' they engage in the foreign policymaking process. For example, let us assume a situation whereby a business association wants its government to pursue entry into a free trade area. What means would it use to build its case that such a policy was in the country's national interest? How would the association seek to lobby the president and foreign minister? Would it use public pressure, private cajoling and financial contributions to the ruling political party, or a combination of tactics, to achieve its aims? Conversely, how would the government determine whether an association's position deserves consideration or can be safely ignored? This is perhaps the most complex question of them all, given the multiplicity of factors that must be considered.

The goal of this book (adopted from a doctoral dissertation done with the University of South Africa) is to apply the questions raised above to South Africa—both pre- and post-1994—through the broad theoretical lens of foreign policy analysis to better understand how foreign policy *really* gets made, with an eye toward determining whether the country's democratic transition has also made the foreign policymaking process more open and participatory. The African National Congress (ANC) government of post-transition South Africa made a distinct break with many policies of its apartheid-era National Party (NP) predecessor, but it is less clear—and little explored—whether the new government heeded calls before and during the transition to 'democratize' the country's foreign policy apparatus, both by law and by custom, to give outside actors more influence in the process.

Framing the Question

To examine the degree to which the foreign policy debate was opened up after 1994, one must first ask what, exactly, constitutes 'democratic' foreign policymaking, a theoretical construct that has received so little attention to date in academic literature that it remains open to interpretation. Alexander Johnson in his chapter in the 2001 compilation *South Africa's Foreign Policy: Dilemmas of a New Democracy* enunciates three different models for conceptualizing democratic foreign policy:

- A liberal or 'good citizen' model that emphasizes states as bearers of individual rights and freedoms, focusing on the promotion of 'democratic' rights within nations.
- A model that views democratic foreign policy as seeking to transform the international collective mindset of democracy, seeking to make the global system more 'democratic.'
- A third model that is more concerned with procedural democracy in the domestic political system and the priority of domestic obligations and duties of government over the discharge of international commitments.[4]

Much has been written about South Africa's application of the first two models in its foreign policy, such as its promotion of 'democratic values' like respect for human rights and its efforts to reform global governance systems to give poor countries more influence.[5] In this book, however, we will focus on the third model, which asks, basically, to what extent the broader electorate and other appropriate actors are able to weigh in on and influence a country's foreign policy. This model is predicated on a conceptualization of 'democracy' broader than that proposed by Samuel Huntington, who argues that 'the central procedure of democracy is the selection of leaders through competitive elections by the people they govern.'[6] Rather, we will use the more inclusive definition proposed by Larry Diamond, Juan Linz, and Seymour Lipset:

- Meaningful and extensive competition among individuals and organizational groups (especially political parties) for positions of government power through regular, free, and fair elections.
- A highly inclusive level of political participation in the selection of leaders and policies such that no major (adult) social group is prevented from exercising the rights of citizenship.
- A level of civil and political liberties—freedom of thought and expression, freedom of the press, freedom of assembly and demonstrations, freedom to form and join organizations—sufficient to ensure the integrity of political competition and participation.[7]

Diamond, Linz, and Lipset emphasize the mechanics of feedback between election cycles, ensuring that through continual participation in governance and the personal freedom necessary for citizens to provide honest and regular feedback to their elected representatives, citizens (and groups) can influence policy debates, including those about foreign affairs. It is this framework that will help answer the key question of this book, which is how did South African leaders from the dawn of Union to the end of the Mbeki era take into account domestic inputs in South African foreign policy issues?

Obviously, the question of whether the process was made more democratic is highly subjective and rooted in perception; decisionmakers may claim (and truly believe) they considered outside inputs in the policy process, while those attempting to weigh in may feel their participation was ignored. Policy pronouncements seldom mention the means by which they were reached, how the metaphorical 'sausage' was made. Hence, the best the analyst can do—and the aim of this book—is to canvas a broad spectrum of opinions and insights by participants in the process, seek their impressions, compare their insights with those of others and existing literature, and draw conclusions.

Selecting the Actors for Examination

South Africa's 1996 constitution—like that of many democracies—gives significant power to the head of state in the foreign policy sphere, although this does not mean he or she acts in a vacuum. A range of actors, inside and outside government, has throughout the country's history attempted to influence South Africa's external orientation. It is therefore necessary to examine a host of actors to see whether they have had an impact on making policy, or if they have been largely ignored. Chapters 3 through 10 will examine the influences of various actors on the policy process and their interactions with the executive. Each chapter will give a brief historical overview of each entity and the degree to which it has influenced past South African administrations before turning to their relative influences post-1994.

Public Opinion and Civil Society

Foreign policymaking in democracies tends to receive far less popular interest than that related to domestic issues, given that with the exception of military deployments, such issues have little day-to-day impact on voters and their families. Political scientist Ole Holsti's model of foreign policy interest among populaces, for example, argues that citizens can be grouped into three categories—attentive and informed; moderately interested and with limited knowledge; and totally disinterested.[8] Holsti puts the informed top layer at generally no more than 15 percent of the population, with the bottom, disinterested tier accounting for as much as 70 percent. Other models differ slightly from Holsti's in terminology and percentage categorizations, but most have similar principles. While applying Holsti's model to South Africa is difficult and inexact, this chapter will examine the available data and use interviews with policymakers to gauge public interest and better understand how (and whether) it was taken into account.

This chapter will also examine the role of civil society and pressure groups on the foreign policy debate, paying specific attention to the roles of organized labor and religious organizations. In the pre-1994 context, the role of the Broederbond will be examined in depth. After 1994, the ANC's tripartite alliance partners, the Congress of South African Trade Unions (COSATU) and the South African Communist Party (SACP), will be the chief focus. They are of particular interest since, despite their alliance with the ruling party, both groups have espoused distinct foreign policies from the ANC and butted heads with ANC leaders—and Mbeki in particular—on occasion, notably regarding Zimbabwe and Swaziland policies. In addition, the role of religious groups after 1994, given their lobbying efforts on such issues as Zimbabwe and the Middle East, merit attention.

The Press

In South Africa and around the world, the press—specifically the print press, the focus of this chapter—is the means by which citizens are kept informed of their government's foreign interactions and policymaking. After examining the degree to which South Africans are engaged on foreign policy, it is worth exploring further to what degree the press is able (and willing) to drive the foreign policy debate in South Africa. Hence, a major focus of the chapter will be on the relationship between the reader and the media, with an eye toward better understanding how the demands of readership influenced foreign affairs coverage, and whether the press has ever been able to influence public opinion on external issues. In addition, the relationship between the press and government will be explored, particularly how it did or did not change after 1994.

Think Tanks and Academia

Think tanks and universities generate some of the most sophisticated foreign policy thinking and analysis worldwide, and South Africa is no exception. Foreign policy academics have been present in South Africa since the 1960s, and since 1994 have proliferated, fueled by the end of South Africa's isolation. Despite the fact that South African academia has for years produced high-quality analytic products, it is less clear the extent to which the South African Government—especially during Mbeki's administration—considered their inputs in shaping foreign policy or simply seeking diverse opinions on external issues. Did South African leaders consult broadly or rather use a small crop of 'trusted' academics? Did they consider these inputs when making decisions or just pay them lip service? This chapter will seek to answer these questions, fleshing out whether academia has been an influential player.

Business

South Africa's business community, from conglomerates like Anglo-American to small- and medium-sized enterprises, is a force that cannot be ignored in the South African political arena, particularly given its ability to use party funding to lobby for or against policies. Given the growing interest of South African firms on the rest of the continent and the way in which events like the crisis in Zimbabwe affect corporate bottom lines, one would imagine that companies and groupings like Business Leadership South Africa or Business Unity South Africa would actively seek to engage the government on foreign policy. This study will henceforth seek to better understand how much influence the business community—broadly and in individual parts—had on Mbeki and his predecessors in the external realm.

Parliament

Legislatures in most democratic countries are empowered to provide a necessary check on executive foreign policy decisionmaking, particularly in terms of controlling the purse strings for defense and foreign affairs departmental budgets. That said, legislators also generally do not prioritize foreign policy issues, since they rarely have a direct impact on voter behaviors and tend to generate little legislation. This chapter will examine the degree to which South Africa's parliament, both pre- and post-1994, has had the ability and shown the willingness to stand up to the executive in regard to foreign policy. Of particular interest will be the differences between ruling and opposition party legislators in their manner of dealing with external affairs.

The Ruling Party

Evaluating the roles of ruling parties and governments in policy formulation, both domestic and foreign, is tricky given the difficulty drawing distinctions where one ends and the other begins, particularly given the NP's post-1948 and ANC's post-1994 dominances of the political sphere. Foreign policy is generally not viewed as a factor of great dispute within the ANC, but this study will explore the means by which Thabo Mbeki—the Party's dominant foreign policy figure from 1994 to 2008—solicited and processed inputs from within the Party, most notably from the ANC's Department of International Relations, the National Executive Committee (NEC) subcommittee on International Relations, and other NEC subcommittees that play a role in the foreign policy debate. The interactions of Mandela and Mbeki with the ANC on foreign affairs will be compared with that of pre-1994 leaders with the NP, determining whether NP structures played any significant role on that front. In addition, this chapter will examine the foreign policymaking of the exiled ANC, with an eye toward understanding how its foreign policy structures influenced those of the post-1994 government.

Government Departments

Although nearly every government department in South Africa has some sort of external affairs competency, four departments since 1994—Foreign Affairs (International Affairs and Cooperation since

2009), Trade and Industry, Defense, and Intelligence—have been the primary players. Chapter 9 will explore the interactions between departments; between these departments and the Presidency; and with external actors in the making of policy to determine what departments have played dominant roles in the foreign policymaking process and how such influences have ebbed and flowed. The role of the now-abolished Department of Information on foreign policy in the 1960s and 1970s also will be examined. Chapter 9 will focus in particular on the role of department principals (ministers, directors-general, generals, ambassadors, and the like) in influencing policy.

The Prime Minister/President

The last actor to consider is the national leader (prime minister until 1984; president thereafter). While studies of the other actors will seek to determine to what extent they influenced the decisionmaker, it would be remiss to not examine the decisionmaking characteristics of the national leaders to better understand how they made decisions. Mbeki, for example, has been widely painted as a president whose intense interest in foreign policy issues, as well as his years as one of the ANC's leading foreign policy mavens, led him to keep his own counsel to the point that he gave short shrift to what outsiders told him, particularly on issues where he had some experience.[9] This chapter also will examine the decisionmaking styles of Mbeki's predecessors as president/prime minister, as well as that of Oliver Tambo, the ANC's *de facto* prime minister in exile and Mbeki's mentor. This examination will seek to unravel the extent to which South African leaders have been open to outside influence and advice, which voices mattered, and how executive openness to outside inputs has changed through the years.

Research Methodology: Getting at a Difficult Question

Researching a study on the 'nuts and bolts' of foreign policymaking (or government policymaking in any sphere) is a difficult task for several reasons. As one scholarly work noted, 'data are notoriously hard to come by because governments are prone to suppress many things which the scholar must know and wants to know. Diplomatic records and memoirs are published years after the events occurred. Negotiations are held in secret or semi-secret. Security regulations—necessary and otherwise—hide many vital facts. Busy administrators have been known to have little sympathy for the scholarly curiosity of the academic man.'[10] Even when available, primary data, like diplomatic cables or policy pronouncements, generally do not delve into the process by which the decisions were reached; the finished products do not reflect the debates that shaped them. Given these difficulties, notes Breuning, 'It can be quite difficult to figure out whether a foreign policy decision was based on sound analysis and careful thought.'[11]

Another problem in analyzing decisionmaking is that published academic and journalistic works on foreign policy (particularly in South Africa) focus on analyzing the outputs rather than examining the policymaking process. Most accounts, past and present, have avoided the decisionmaking aspect of foreign policy, focusing instead on state-centric conceptualizations of international relations theory (such as post-1994 characterizations of South Africa as a 'regional hegemon' or 'global middle power').[12] Before 1994, there were relatively few academic accounts of the foreign policymaking process in South Africa, with the notable exceptions of American academic Ned Munger's 1965 *Notes on the Formation of South African Foreign Policy* and Deon Geldenhuys' 1984 *Diplomacy of Isolation*. These two books will be referenced often throughout the text.

There is as yet no definitive work on post-1994 foreign policymaking, specifically the process by which Thabo Mbeki—the dominant foreign policy actor of the 1994–2008 period—made decisions. Mbeki revealed little about the decisionmaking process during his presidency, and while observers had some insights into the identities of the 'inner circle,' the nature and character of their interactions was largely opaque. Esteemed political analyst Richard Calland in his book *Anatomy of South Africa: Who Holds the Power?* presented a revealing vignette about the inner circle's foreign policy debates:

An informal subcommittee, hastily pulled together the previous evening by Frank Chikane, Director-General in the Presidency, to discuss the worsening crisis in the Middle East in 2003. 'So' began Mbeki. 'What position do we take on this?'

There was silence from the collection of ministers and advisors. Then one of the advisors raised his hand and began to speak.

'Mr. President, I think . . .'

'No,' interrupted Mbeki, 'you speak last.'

On this issue, Mbeki knew the advisor's position already. Moreover, he knew that the two of them shared the same view, and he wanted to avoid a phenomenon known as 'groupthink'—a psychological concept adapted by an American political scientist in the 1960s to explain the failure of President John F. Kennedy's Cuban policy at the time of the Bay of Pigs. This phenomenon occurs when a small group of like-minded people meet to make a key decision and, instead of testing hypotheses or fundamental assumptions and analyses, end up simply affirming each other's preconceived views, thus promoting a poor decisionmaking process.[13]

This is an illuminating account, and one made far more interesting by the dearth of similar reports over a nearly decade-long administration. Now that Mbeki has been out of office for more than five years, however, the time is ripe for a closer examination of these processes. Mbeki and his closest advisors are no longer bound by the strictures of office, and outsiders who sought to influence the president no longer have reason to hold back their accounts of proceedings. So an overarching aim of this book is to provide an 'insider' account about how the process actually unfolded, during both Mbeki's presidency and the administrations of his predecessors, which also are poorly studied.

To address this opacity and shed light the decisionmaking process, this book relies heavily (albeit not exclusively) on interviews with the various participants in the process. Between January 2010 and August 2011, I interviewed 113 people involved in South African foreign policy, dating back to the pre-1948 era.* The interviewees represent a broad cross-section of the 'foreign policy community,' including members of each of the subsets of domestic actors identified. Several interviewees were representative of two or more foreign policy actors during their careers (such as academia and government), and these interviews proved particularly insightful. These interviews will be quoted extensively in the forthcoming chapters, allowing the individuals to tell the history of the foreign policymaking process in their own words. Nearly all of the interviews were conducted face to face, ranging in length from 20 minutes in to more than four hours; a few were by telephone or email. All interviews were 'on the record,' and in only two instances was I asked to turn off my recorder (both times on issues not germane to this study). That said, I have anonymized some quotes under the rubric of 'Author's private archive' if I felt the interviewee might experience negative repercussions as a result of his or her statements.

One must acknowledge up front that an interview-based approach provides a subjective view of the foreign policymaking process. Government principals have axes to grind and reputations to uphold; principals close to Mbeki were particularly keen to portray themselves and their political master in a good light. Other interviewees, particularly older ones, struggled to recall certain details, or confused historical facts. To address these challenges, I took a 'trust but verify' approach to the process, cross-referencing interviewee anecdotes, whenever possible, against other recollections or published accounts. While not all anecdotes and opinions related could be verified independently, I made a good-faith effort to do so. Obvious cases of 'axe-grinding' were excluded or properly caveated.

Another challenge was access to principals, particularly those from the Mbeki administration. I sought an interview with President Mbeki for more than 18 months, and communicated with the former president via his personal assistant, but unfortunately these efforts were unsuccessful. Attempts to interview other members of Mbeki's 'inner circle'—like Frank Chikane, Mojanku Gumbi and Joel Netshitenzhe—also were unsuccessful, although they and others graciously responded to emails and cited time constraints, rather than an unwillingness to speak, as the reason for declining interviews. That said, the overall success rate in seeking interviews was more than 80 percent; only a handful of those contacted rejected an interview out of hand or did not respond. Many Mbeki-era principals—Aziz and Essop Pahad, Smuts Ngonyama, Mosiuoa Lekota, Pallo Jordan, and others—agreed to interviews that were tremendously illuminating. In addition, I had success in interviewing pre-1994 principals—including Pik Botha, Niel Barnard and Jannie Geldenhuys—as well as lower-ranking but nonetheless influential figures. The interview success rate of those outside government—academics, civil society figures, journalists, business-people and so on—was greater than 90 percent.

Conclusion

As noted earlier, unpacking any public policy decisionmaking process is a difficult task owing to a dearth of source material until long after the fact, differing accounts of the process, desires to conceal debates and arguments for political or personal purposes, and a whole host of other reasons. In addition, on foreign policy matters in particular, decisionmakers occasionally pin decisionmaking opacity on national security grounds. Such excuses can sometimes hold water in the immediate term, but democratic governance rests on the principle that citizens have the right to understand why their governments make decisions. While no book can explain all facets of decisionmaking, I hope that this volume provides some insight into the South African policymaking process and illuminates it somewhat for the nation's citizens.

CHAPTER 2

A BRIEF HISTORY OF SOUTH AFRICAN FOREIGN POLICY

Before examining the role various actors have played through the years in shaping South African foreign policy, I will provide a brief overview of South Africa's foreign relations, pre- and post-1994. To this end, this chapter is subdivided into six parts covering the foreign policy priorities of the South African Government and the ANC during the past century, albeit with a focus on the post-1948 period:

– *Pre-1948 Foreign Policy.* This section will briefly discuss the origins of South African foreign policy, both pre-Union and in the 1910–48 period. This will cover South Africa's involvement in the two World Wars and the impact of the Balfour Declaration on developing South Africa's independent foreign policy competency.
– *The Diplomacy of Defiance, 1948–90.* The NP's rule until the unbanning of the ANC was characterized by South Africa's efforts to counter its growing international isolation and find friends wherever possible. Key issues include withdrawal from the Commonwealth; growing international isolation; strained ties with the United Nations (UN); increasing estrangement from the United States and traditional allies in Europe; growing ties with other global pariahs; and Pretoria's efforts to build ties with African states.

- *ANC Foreign Policy to 1990.* ANC foreign engagement goes back to the organization's foundation in 1912, although this section will focus on its post-1960 attempts to bolster its international legitimacy. This section will examine the ANC's attempts to establish representation around the world, raise money, turn international opinion against apartheid, and isolate the government in Pretoria.
- *The Foreign Policy of Transition.* This section will discuss the dominant issues of the 1990–4 transitional period, particularly attempts by the ANC and government to build international support for their positions. It also will examine how the Transitional Executive Council and other discussion fora helped shape South Africa's future foreign policy priorities and diplomatic infrastructure.
- *The Mandela Era.* Nelson Mandela's 1994–9 administration saw the country, still basking in the afterglow of its successful transition, play an active and outsized role in the international arena. Despite this, South African foreign policy during this period also was marked by significant difficulties in balancing idealist aims with realist considerations.
- *Mbeki and the African Agenda.* Lastly, this section will examine Thabo Mbeki's efforts to bring peace, democracy and prosperity to the rest of Africa while positioning Pretoria as an influential actor, both globally and on the continent. It will scrutinize South Africa's prioritization of the developing world in its foreign relations; its global diplomatic expansion; Pretoria's efforts to 'punch above its weight' in the international arena; and its shift from a human rights focus in the early period to more 'pragmatic' policies in the late 1990s. South Africa's policy toward Zimbabwe, probably the most prominent foreign policy issue since 1994, will merit particular examination, both here and in chapters to come.

South African Foreign Policy to 1948

Although the Boer republics of the Transvaal and Orange Free State from the 1840s had limited foreign policy competencies and sent diplomatic representatives to Europe and the United States, South Africa had no independent foreign policy decisionmaking competency until the Balfour Declaration of 1926 granted Great Britain's dominions equal and autonomous status under the new Commonwealth.[1] Although the declaration stated that most foreign policy responsibility would remain in London, it allowed for autonomous dominion diplomatic services; South Africa's Department of External Affairs (DEA) was set up later that year. External affairs were generally a low priority for South Africa for most of the 1920s and 1930s, but this changed with the coming storm in Europe. The march to war raised questions about the country's autonomy in the event of war, with the two main governmental leaders—Prime Minister JBM Hertzog and Deputy Prime Minister Jan Smuts—divided over South Africa's obligation to back Great Britain in a conflict with Germany.[2]

Matters came to a head with Germany's September 1, 1939 invasion of Poland, which brought Great Britain into the war two days later. A neutrality motion put forth by Hertzog was defeated by 80 votes to 67, while a Smuts motion urging cooperation with Great Britain passed by the same margin. South Africa was at war. Despite inheriting a small military unprepared for conflict, Smuts—who emerged as prime minister after Hertzog's resignation—turned the South African force into a valuable partner for the Allies. In all, 334,000 men volunteered for service in the South African Army (including 123,000 non-white members of support units); nearly 9,000 were killed in action. At war's end, Smuts served as South Africa's representative at the San Francisco conference that established the UN, drafting the preamble to the UN Charter. Smuts' heightened international profile, however, did him few favors at home. In the run-up to 1948 elections, the NP attacked Smuts and his United Party for being soft on racial segregation and more focused on global statesmanship than problems at home. Although the NP and its Afrikaner Party allies only took 42 percent of the vote to the United Party's 49 percent, their support in smaller rural constituencies allowed them to win 79 of 153 seats. DF Malan assumed the premiership, and the era of apartheid and isolation began.

The Diplomacy of Defiance, 1948–90

The NP government's resistance to majority rule underscored South Africa's foreign relations between 1948 and 1990. As a former director of the South African Institute of International Affairs succinctly observed, 'The South African Government's policy abroad is to seek to maintain apartheid at home.'[3] To this end, Pretoria engaged in an increasingly sophisticated, multi-headed approach that used legal tactics, diplomatic overtures, and economic incentives to win friends and rebuff enemies. As anti-South Africa attitudes hardened by the mid-1960s, these policy options expanded to include covert action, the development of a nuclear deterrent, and the use of conventional and unconventional military force—all elements of the 'Total Strategy,' a comprehensive plan that aimed to use political, economic, and military levers to maintain white rule—to show South Africa's opponents that it had no intention of capitulation. The Nationalists effectively played up the communist threat to South Africa from the Soviet-backed ANC to maintain consistently high levels of domestic support and win anti-communist friends abroad.

The Foreign Policy of Malan and Strijdom: A Balancing Act

South Africa's foreign policy during the premierships of DF Malan (1948–54) and JG Strijdom (1954–8) was characterized by attempts to maintain close ties with the West and establish South Africa as a player in a rapidly decolonizing Africa, all the while showing voters that Pretoria would not be cowed by external pressure.[4] Pretoria achieved some success in regard to the first two goals. The escalation of the Cold War helped South Africa maintain good standing with the West, as did the South African Air Force's participation in both the 1948 Berlin Air Lift and the Korean War, although Malan's efforts to make South Africa an 'auxiliary' of NATO in the Southern Hemisphere came to naught.[5] For avowed republicans, Malan and Strijdom also retained surprisingly strong relations with Great Britain and dismissed calls for withdrawal from the Commonwealth. Economics was key to this; Commonwealth trade preferences, security cooperation, and access to British capital all made continued membership highly desirable.[6]

Efforts to improve South Africa's standing in Africa, however, had less success. In the run-up to decolonization, Malan was taken with the idea of an 'African Charter' aimed at preserving colonial rule by stopping Asian immigration, keeping out communism, and ensuring that the continent remained non-militarized.[7] South Africa would play a central role in this charter, offering assistance and cooperation to African colonies, but European powers paid it no heed.[8] Malan's attempt to acquire control from Great Britain of the British Protectorate states—Bechuanaland, Basutoland, and Swaziland—on South Africa's borders, the independence of which he found abhorrent, similarly found no success. Strijdom, in contrast, took a more pragmatic approach toward the continent, with a focus on maintaining white rule where tenable but recognizing that independence for much of the continent was a reality. He emphasized the need for cooperation and the 'hand of friendship' between South Africa and black-ruled states, and to that end established several organizations to advance technical and agricultural cooperation.[9] Strijdom even sent senior officials to Ghana's independence ceremony, although he drew the line at exchanging diplomats with a black-ruled country. Unsurprisingly, Ghana and other new states showed little outward enthusiasm for close ties.

Verwoerd and the Politics of Withdrawal

Hendrik Verwoerd's ascension to the premiership in 1958 after Strijdom's death marked a significant shift in the tone of South Africa's external relations. While Malan and Strijdom had tried to maintain ties to South Africa's traditional allies and remain a respected member of the international community, Verwoerd was far more comfortable with a 'go it alone' mentality, one that would permeate the foreign relations of his eight-year tenure. Verwoerd was firmly committed to the establishment of a South African republic, although this republicanism was not necessarily based on the assumption that South Africa would leave the Commonwealth.[10] Despite this, Verwoerd's refusal to offer any concessions on its racial policies—or even accredit diplomats from newly-independent African Commonwealth members, calling them a potential 'center of agitation' for attacking apartheid—raised tensions to the point of South Africa's 1961 withdrawal. The pullout was met by great consternation among English-speaking South Africans and business-men, who feared the loss of Commonwealth trade preferences, although economic fears proved unfounded.

Pretoria's relations under Verwoerd with the increasingly vocal UN, however, proved more difficult. Ties to the UN were by no means cordial under his predecessors; perceived meddling in South Africa's affairs led Malan and Strijdom to suspend South African participation in various UN bodies at points during their tenures.[11] Nonetheless, relations worsened notably under Verwoerd, with both the 1960 Sharpeville massacre and the explosion of independent African states—16 in 1960 alone—leading South Africa to face unprecedented pressure. The General Assembly in 1962 for the first time called on a trade and diplomatic boycott of South Africa, and the following year it voted in favor of a voluntary arms embargo.[12] Verwoerd responded with open contempt of the UN, blaming a 'Communist bloc' for attacks on South Africa, although he stopped short of total withdrawal. Verwoerd skillfully used the bugbear of communism to maintain solid ties with the West, but he was unafraid to upset potential allies over matters of principle. Despite rapidly increasing American investment in South Africa, particularly in the mining sector, Verwoerd scrapped the planned 1965 visit of the *USS Independence* aircraft carrier to Cape Town because its racially mixed crew was unacceptable.[13] He also blocked US plans to open a satellite tracking station in South Africa on the same grounds.

In Africa, Verwoerd's policy reiterated Strijdom's partnership rhetoric but also emphasized binding newly-independent states in the region to South Africa. Although he expressed concern about the rapidity of African decolonization, Verwoerd was clear that he did not begrudge African states choosing independence and emphasized the 'civilizing' potential of South Africa in regard to technological and economic cooperation.[14] Although he sought at first, like Strijdom, to incorporate the protectorates, Verwoerd by 1964 abandoned these efforts and focused instead on binding them closely to South Africa through economic cooperation.[15] He showed no qualms about meddling in the political affairs of South Africa's soon-to-be independent neighbors. Seeing a potential ally in Basutoland chief Leabua Jonathan, Verwoerd allowed him and his Basuto National Party (but not other parties) to campaign among Basuto resident in South Africa before the 1965 elections, and South Africa later that year donated 100,000 bags of grain to alleviate famine gripping the newly-independent state. Verwoerd later spent three and a half hours with Jonathan on December 3, 1966—four days before his assassination—discussing prospects for closer ties.[16]

Vorster and the Uphill Struggle for Engagement

Taking office after Verwoerd's death, new Prime Minister John Vorster inherited a government coming under increasing attack in the UN, with few meaningful links to newly-independent African states. Pretoria was also starting to come under pressure from the political 'left' in Western countries over its racial policies. Vorster, a pragmatist at heart, was determined to address this situation, and his 'outward policy' was crafted as a means to build relationships on the continent, keep doors open in Europe and the United States, and bolster trade and diplomatic links around the world.[17] Although opposed by certain *verkrampte* (conservative) elements within the NP—who viewed any accommodation with black Africa as a betrayal of apartheid principles—this movement was supported by an increasingly wealthy and urbanizing Afrikaner community that recognized the danger of international isolation.[18]

Building ties in Africa was paramount to Vorster's foreign policy, with James Barber and John Barratt describing it as being conducted outward on the basis of three concentric circles—'greater South Africa,' southern Africa, and the rest of the continent—with different motivations and tactics for each.[19] Closest to home, Vorster sought to bind the newly-independent protectorates—Botswana, Lesotho, and Swaziland—tightly to South Africa to ensure that they would remain dependent on South African assistance for their economic development and political survival. He used a 1969 renegotiation of the Southern African Customs Union and 1974 creation of the Rand zone to tie these states more closely to Pretoria.[20] In the region, Vorster's chief focus was to ensure the security of white-ruled states. Although Portuguese frostiness toward Pretoria limited South African assistance in Angola and Mozambique, Vorster—with support from the white electorate—maintained consistent military and economic support for the breakaway Rhodesian government until the mid-1970s.

With regard to black-ruled states, Vorster engaged in a continent-wide charm offensive that primarily used economic incentives to try to win political support in African capitals. These efforts met with some success. Provided significant economic aid, Malawi went so far as to establish formal diplomatic ties with Pretoria in 1967 and would remain one of the apartheid government's most reliable defenders for the next two decades.[21] Pretoria's approaches also were well received in several Francophone countries—notably Ivory Coast, Senegal, Gabon, Madagascar, and the Central African Republic—while Liberia, Ghana, and Kenya were Anglophone states that showed a willingness to hear out South African approaches.[22] This diplomacy, conducted by Pretoria in utmost secrecy and spearheaded by the Bureau of State Security and Department of Information, culminated with Vorster visiting Ivory Coast President Houphouet-Boigny and Senegalese President Senghor in 1974, as well as Liberian President Tolbert the next year.[23] Although Pretoria's 'wins' were more symbolic than substantive, South Africa's liberation movements, particularly the ANC, viewed them with concern; one ANC diplomat in 1975 said that the organization feared exclusion from every sub-Saharan state because of Pretoria's outreach.[24]

With memories of Sharpeville fading and the anti-apartheid movement still nascent in the United States and western Europe, Pretoria in the 1960s and early 1970s was able to maintain strong ties in the West. Pretoria's sophisticated (and well-funded) lobbying and propaganda efforts helped paint South Africa as a useful bulwark against communism, which appealed particularly to conservative governments eager to cooperate on defense matters. Pretoria tied itself more closely to NATO with its 1973 construction of the Silvermine surveillance center near Cape Town, which provided invaluable coverage of Soviet naval operations in the South Atlantic.[25] Pretoria also built ties to other 'pariah' states around the world, such as military governments in Brazil, Argentina, Paraguay, and Uruguay, although neither side received many tangible benefits.[26] Relations with Taiwan and the Shah's Iran were more substantive, with South Africa benefiting from access to Iranian oil—making up to 90 percent of its imported crude by 1979—and Taiwanese military technology and training.[27] Most important, however, were South Africa's burgeoning ties with Israel from 1973 onward, resulting in military cooperation that was essential to developing South Africa's nuclear weapons program.[28]

Vorster's limited progress began to disintegrate, however, with Portugal's April 1974 coup that brought down the Caetano government. Initiated largely by military disgruntlement over being forced to fight unwinnable wars in the country's African colonies, the coup and subsequent shift to democratic rule led to the 1975 independence of Angola and Mozambique, putting hostile governments on the borders of South Africa and Rhodesia. Although Vorster tried to maintain his *détente* efforts with black-ruled states, including by gradually pulling back support for Salisbury, South Africa's August 1975 invasion of Angola—undertaken to support Jonas Savimbi's National Union for the Total Independence of Angola (UNITA) movement against the Soviet and Cuban-backed People's Movement for the Liberation of Angola (MPLA) prior to that country's November independence—scuttled any chance that it would succeed. Operation Savannah saw approximately 3,000 South African Defence Force (SADF) troops move to within 200 km of Luanda, turning over captured territory to UNITA en route. By November, the invasion led to the insertion of Cuban troops and Soviet materiel that ultimately repulsed the South African advance. Most importantly, South Africa's intervention irreparably damaged its standing on the continent, forcing all but the most slavishly devoted countries (like Malawi) to turn their backs (at least publicly) on Pretoria.[29]

The 1974–8 period also saw Pretoria lose support further afield. The UN General Assembly suspended South Africa in 1974, a ban not lifted for 20 years, while the June 1976 Soweto massacre and

1977 death of Black Consciousness leader Steve Biko in police custody had even more crippling effects, galvanizing global opinion against South Africa and ushering in UN adoption of a 1977 mandatory arms embargo. This growing international isolation had the effect at home of bolstering the position of the defense establishment in the foreign policy arena. Whereas the Departments of Foreign Affairs, the Bureau of State Security, and Information focused on winning friends, Defense under Minister PW Botha was oriented toward intimidating and undermining enemies. Infighting among departments reached fever pitch by the late 1970s, but Vorster—ailing and faced with mounting political pressures—was unable to address it, leading to a lack of policy coordination and coherence. However, the 1977 breaking of the 'Muldergate' information scandal—which revealed political malfeasance in the Information Department's secret operations—quickly brought down Vorster and his allies, opening the door to Botha's ascension to the premiership. Henceforth, the military's primacy in the foreign policy field would be unchallenged.

The PW Botha Era

The cantankerous PW Botha assumed the premiership in September 1978, determined to bring a new muscularity to South Africa's foreign engagement, if no significant shifts to the policy aims. While still using 'carrots' to incentivize greater regional and African cooperation with Pretoria, Botha's avid use of 'sticks' like regional military intervention, continued development of nuclear weapons, and covert action was meant to show the region and the world that South Africa did not intend to be bullied. The Prime Minister (state president from 1984) mustered state resources behind his 'Total Strategy,' in the process giving the military and defense establishment a predominant position in foreign policy formulation. Perhaps even more so than his predecessors, Botha was avowedly anti-communist and quick to use the 'red menace' to ameliorate Western pressure. Botha's finger-wagging isolationism, however, would prove unsustainable by the end of the 1980s. Once-sympathetic Western governments, banks, and businesses—under pressure from electorates increasingly aware and critical of apartheid—enacted sanctions, withdrew investment, and refused to roll over loans. Meanwhile, huge increases in state spending, particularly on the military, combined with external economic pressure left the South African economy on the brink of collapse by 1989.

Botha entered office committed to taking forward Verwoerd and Vorster's ideas of promoting greater partnership in southern Africa and on the continent. In 1979, for example, Botha proposed the creation of a Constellation of Southern African States (CONSAS) that would provide up to ten regional states with 'a common approach in the security field, the economic field, and the political field.'[30] Robert Mugabe's victory in Zimbabwe's 1980 election killed the concept, however, before it could get off the ground; instead nine states formed the Southern African Development Coordination Conference later that year in an effort to oppose South African imperialism and reduce economic dependence on South Africa. Botha continued earlier efforts to use economic incentives to win over hostile African states, but these met with limited success. Given the failures of these overtures and growing concerns about ANC presence on South Africa's borders, Pretoria increasingly turned to outright military destabilization in the region to intimidate its neighbors. South African incursions and attacks were to have a devastating economic effect on the region, causing an estimated $90 billion in damage between 1975 and 1988.[31] These included periodic incursions into Angola through to 1988; cross-border raids on Botswana, Lesotho, Mozambique, Swaziland, and Zimbabwe; support for RENAMO rebels in Mozambique; and economic pressure throughout the region.[32] Pretoria also ramped up its use of unconventional operations during this time, to include often-successful assassination attempts against ANC leaders and supporters. South Africa also continued work on developing its nuclear weapons program—in close cooperation with Israel—and in 1983 initiated its chemical and biological weapons program, Project Coast.[33]

Building the capacity to carry out these operations was extremely costly. Upon Botha taking office in the 1978/9 fiscal year, South Africa spent R1.5 billion on defense; in 1988/9, his last year, this had reached R10 billion.[34] In 1982/3, defense spending accounted for 22.7 percent of the national budget and more than 5 percent of the gross domestic product (GDP); it would account for at least 15 percent of the budget and 4 percent of GDP through 1990. This is merely the defense budget, however; if including non-military internal security, intelligence, and secret projects (like the nuclear program), some estimate 'real' security spending to have represented as much as 30 percent of the budget and 9 percent of GDP by 1990.[35] Given that economic growth dropped to just 1.5 percent per year on average during the 1980s, this spending was unsustainable.[36]

International pressure also began to exert meaningful economic pressure on the government. Western governments and banks continued to deal with South Africa through the early 1980s—US support was crucial to South Africa receiving a $1.1 billion loan from the International Monetary Fund (IMF) in 1982—but by 1985 public pressure to disengage from South Africa was mounting in the United States and throughout Europe.[37] Botha's August 1985 'Rubicon' speech—which disappointed after being hyped by Foreign Minister Pik Botha and others beforehand as a significant step toward ending apartheid—led Chase Manhattan Bank to cease rolling over South Africa's short-term debt and stop further lending, causing a collapse of the rand and a government moratorium on taking on further international debt. Moreover, Western investors were disinvesting in droves, driven by mounting anti-apartheid sentiments at home; between 1984 and 1989, as many as 555 foreign multinational firms left South Africa. Botha's fervent anti-communism could no longer be counted on to preserve South Africa's standing among even conservative governments. The 1986 US Comprehensive Anti-Apartheid Act, a sanctions regime Congress passed over the veto of President Reagan, was perhaps the clearest sign that the tide of international opinion had turned irrevocably against Pretoria.

This growing pressure, in addition to fatigue from the military stalemate in Angola, finally brought Angolan, Cuban, and South African parties together in London in 1988 to settle the future of Southwest Africa/Namibia. They agreed to the Brazzaville Protocol that December, an agreement that led to the withdrawal of Cuban troops from Angola and South Africa, turning over Southwest Africa to UN control, before elections and independence in 1990. PW Botha, however, would not remain in office to see it. In January 1989, the 73-year-old Botha suffered a stroke and the following month resigned as leader of the NP. Although the President in his final months showed he could make hard decisions on issues like Namibian independence, he could not make the ultimate tough call. Although he had met with Nelson Mandela and National Intelligence was talking with the ANC in exile, Botha could not to pull the trigger on the only decisions that mattered: releasing Mandela, unbanning the ANC, and finishing off apartheid. With the Berlin Wall falling and the Soviet Union collapsing, those decisions would fall to a colorless, chain-smoking lawyer from Potchefstroom.

ANC Foreign Policy to 1990

The ANC's pre-1990 foreign policy can be divided into two phases. The first, from its founding until its 1960 banning, consisted of constant—if disjointed—attempts to win friends abroad. The second phase spanned from its entry to exile to its 1990 return, which saw the organization fight for survival and, later, bring increased pressure on the apartheid government through lobbying governments and by raising popular support in the West.

An elitist organization with little broad popular support for its first two decades, the ANC had a strong internationalist component from its 1912 foundation. The ANC sent a delegation to Great Britain in 1914 to voice dissatisfaction with the 1913 Native Land Act, which restricted black land ownership, but its protests were ignored.[38] A subsequent delegation to Great Britain and to the Versailles Conference in 1919 that demanded an end to the color bar in South Africa was similarly ignored, despite ANC support for the war effort.[39] Efforts to form ties with the Soviet Union, forged through the congress' relations with the Communist Party of South Africa, showed more promise. In 1927, ANC Natal leader Josiah Gumede followed a European tour by traveling to Moscow, where he was received by Stalin and toured the republics. He came away convinced that the Soviet Union—with its multinational citizenry, rural poverty, and underdeveloped capitalist system before the revolution—offered a model for South Africa's political and economic development. He returned to South Africa energized, telling crowds, 'I have seen the world to come [. . .] I have been to the new Jerusalem,' and later that year won the leadership of the ANC on the grounds that the party must take a more militant stance against white rule and work in concert with communists.[40] This cooperation, however, would prove short-lived; a conservative faction skeptical of Soviet ties ousted Gumede as president-general in 1930, and relations with Moscow were uneven through the 1950s.[41]

The 1939 outbreak of war saw latent tensions between radicals and conservatives in the ANC come to a head over whether to advise blacks to support the war effort. The latter strategy ultimately won the day, with the movement supporting the war effort but calling for all South Africans to be given equal rights of citizenship. The unstated hope was that this loyalty would pay benefits after the war, but these were quickly dashed; a lobbying effort by ANC president (1940–9) AB Xuma to the newly-formed UN's stance against the proposed incorporation of Southwest Africa into South Africa embarrassed Smuts but paid no discernable material benefits. Still, the post-war period saw a more internationally active ANC, especially with regard to its ties with global anti-colonial movements. The 1955 Freedom Charter spelled out the Congress' foreign policy tenets, notably a commitment to African self-determination and to peacefully settling international disputes. The movement also was able to send its activists abroad, where leaders like Walter Sisulu and Duma Nokwe were able to build the organization's international profile, although not necessarily material support.

The ANC's foreign orientation and tactics changed with its April 1960 banning, as now its external wing would have to carry the burden of keeping the organization alive and building international support.[42] This Herculean task was given to Deputy President Oliver Tambo, who was snuck out of the country in 1960 to establish the external mission tasked with raising international awareness of the South African situation, fundraising, prosecuting the armed struggle, and establishing links to newly-independent African governments and other liberation movements.[43] Tambo had to do this with no existing support structures and limited guidance from the movement in South Africa, particularly after the 1963 Rivonia arrests led to the detention of the movement's internal leadership.

This was a difficult task, and Tambo found limited success through the mid-1970s. Western governments and populaces showed little enthusiasm for the anti-apartheid movement, and even in those Western capitals where the ANC was able to establish a presence, it made little impact. African governments provided it with little material support, generally focusing on liberation movements with more near-term potential, as in Rhodesia and the Portuguese colonies.[44] Even allies like Zambian President Kaunda, who hosted the ANC's headquarters from 1967, were subject to South African Government pressure that limited the extent of their support.[45] In addition, its efforts at armed struggle were almost nonexistent, with the sole significant effort—the 1967 Wankie campaign, in which Umkhonto we Sizwe (MK) unsuccessfully tried to infiltrate a handful of military operatives into Rhodesia—a disaster that led, at the ANC's 1969 Morogoro conference, to one of the most serious attacks on Tambo's leadership.[46] A sole bright spot during these years was the ANC's ability to attract Soviet backing, fostered by its South African Communist Party (the Communist Party of South Africa assumed this new name after it was banned and went underground in 1953) allies. This support—which included funding, educational and military training, and military materiel—was crucial to keeping the movement alive during this period.[47]

Several events in the mid-1970s provided the movement with a much-needed spark. First, Angolan and Mozambican independence in 1975 opened up two invaluable fronts to the ANC. Then, in June 1976, the Soweto riots opened the world's eyes to the human rights abuses of the South African Government and galvanized global opinion against apartheid. The ANC was quick to take advantage of both events. The movement established diplomatic and military presences in Angola and Mozambique, using the former primarily for military training camps and the latter for infiltrating cadres into South Africa. Tambo leveraged Soweto to address the UN

General Assembly in October 1976 on apartheid; this was the first time an ANC leader had been afforded that opportunity. The UN thereafter, even in the face of Western truculence, would prove forward-leaning in seeking to isolate the apartheid government and aid the liberation movements, even voting in 1979 to provide the ANC and Pan-Africanist Congress (PAC) funds for their New York offices.[48]

From the late 1970s, the ANC saw its international support blossom on all fronts. Although many African states showed affinities toward the more radical PAC, African support for the ANC grew after Zimbabwe's 1980 independence left only one white government on the continent; in 1983 the Organisation of African Unity (OAU) recognized the ANC as the 'vanguard of the national liberation movement.'[49] The Non-Aligned Movement, once cold toward the ANC, gave Tambo a prominent speaking slot at the 1979 Havana Conference, and the ANC expanded its ties in places like Southeast Asia and Latin America.[50] Fundraising also took off, to the point that the ANC's budget topped $50 million per year by the end of the 1980s.[51] Support from the Soviet Union and its Warsaw Pact allies remained key, particularly for military training and arms.[52] However, the movement diversified its sources of support in the 1980s, with Scandinavian governments—Sweden in particular—becoming major donors and eventually accounting for half of its non-military aid.[53]

The ANC's major coup in the 1980s, however, was its expansion and deepening of its ties with Western governments, particularly the United States and Great Britain. Recognizing the 'fantastic possibilities' that could result from American support, Thabo Mbeki—then *aide-de-camp* to Tambo—prevailed on ANC leaders to allow a US television program to shoot a documentary on the ANC in 1978. The program portrayed the ANC as a responsible movement with viable grievances.[54] This effective image management helped the ANC in the early 1980s begin to engage regularly with Western elected officials on both the left and right; by the end of the decade Tambo had met with both US Secretary of State George Shultz and British Prime Minister Margaret Thatcher.[55] The ANC was also effective in building grassroots opposition to apartheid in Europe and the United States; the latter's African-American community emerged as a support base. ANC lobbying efforts were effective in effecting unofficial boycotts of South African goods, corporate disinvestment, and government sanctions. The growing international profile of the imprisoned Nelson Mandela also helped the cause raise money and attention.

By the late 1980s, the ANC—through sheer survival but also the skilled international outreach of its leadership—had come to be viewed as a government in waiting, its ultimate success inevitable.[56] Already engaged in secret talks with proxies of the South African Government, the movement was starting to prepare for this transition, even producing a paper called 'The Foreign Policy of the Future South Africa' that elucidated a strongly anti-imperialist foreign policy in concert with the ANC's socialist allies.[57] As Mbeki and many senior party leaders have recounted, the ANC was nonetheless caught off guard by FW de Klerk's February 2, 1990 speech that unbanned it. The next four years would prove some of the most challenging in South Africa's history, and shaping a new foreign policy—and new foreign policy architecture—for a democratic South Africa would prove particularly vexing.

The Foreign Policy of Transition: Competition and Convergence

De Klerk's speech and Mandela's release nine days later sparked a period of negotiation toward a new, democratic dispensation that would last to the eve of South Africa's April 27, 1994 elections. While the focus of these talks was South Africa's future domestic dispensation, South Africa's future foreign policy was also a topic of debate and discussion. The two sides, particularly until 1993, engaged in divergent, competitive international outreach aimed at winning support for their respective domestic positions. De Klerk during this period took advantage of his newfound stature and the global attention being paid to South Africa to travel the world and push for a repeal of sanctions, build support for free market principles, and advocate minority rights.[58] These efforts met with some success; the European Community started rolling back restrictions in late

1990, while President Bush agreed to rescind the Comprehensive Anti-Apartheid Act the following July. De Klerk's 1989 decision to end South Africa's nuclear program and South Africa's 1991 accession to the Nuclear Non-Proliferation Treaty also were praised by the West, both for ending Pretoria's nuclear pariah status and—more quietly—for ensuring an ANC government would not have a nuclear option. Even Russia showed a surprising willingness to deal with Pretoria.[59]

These successes galled the ANC, which opposed early rollback of sanctions. Nevertheless, despite its slow start, the ANC also engaged in robust diplomacy, using Mandela's celebrity status to raise money and support. Mandela visited 49 countries from his release through 1992 (compared to de Klerk's 32), where he was met with massive public acclaim and largely afforded the same honors as a head of state.[60] Visits by Mandela and other top ANC officials helped slow the pace of sanctions rollback, tying them to continued progress from Pretoria, and limited visits from foreign leaders to South Africa. Most important for the ANC, however, was Mandela's ability to raise money, which was in short supply following the withdrawal of Eastern Bloc support and a drawdown of Scandinavian funding— 90 percent of its $27 million budget in 1990 came from foreign sources.[61] These big donations—$10 million from the Taiwanese and Indonesian governments, $5 million from Malaysia, several million from India, and countless more from private Western sources— helped the party stay afloat and later finance its 1994 election campaign.[62] The ANC's Department of International Affairs— headed by Mbeki since 1989—also began plotting a post-transition foreign policy based on multilateralism and demilitarization in accordance with South Africa's domestic interests.[63]

Foreign policy initiatives and discussions between the government and ANC began to see greater convergence in late 1993, when the Transitional Executive Council was established to bring the ANC and government together formally for discussions on post-transition policy formulation. While most of the Transitional Executive Council's activities dealt with the domestic arena, three sub-councils— foreign affairs, intelligence, and defense—dealt with external issues.

While it did not have the power to make or implement policy, the Foreign Affairs Sub-Council was through conferences and regular meetings able to start shaping South Africa's new foreign policy architecture, in particular the integration of ANC, PAC, and homeland foreign affairs infrastructures into the Department of Foreign Affairs (DFA).[64] Ultimately, this transitional period—which came to a close with Mandela's May 10, 1994 inauguration as president—was a time of reassessment of South Africa's foreign policy priorities and reengagement with the outside world. In the words of Deon Geldenhuys, the 'diplomacy of isolation' was replaced by the 'diplomacy of participation.'[65]

The Mandela Years: All Things to All People

Nelson Mandela's inauguration ushered in South Africa's re-admittance into the global community of nations. By the end of 1994, South Africa joined or was re-admitted to 16 multilateral organizations (including the Commonwealth, G-77, OAU, Southern African Development Community (SADC), Non-Aligned Movement, World Trade Organization (WTO) and several specialized UN agencies), concluded 86 bilateral treaties, and acceded to 21 multilateral treaties and conventions. In 1990, Pretoria had only 30 diplomatic missions around the world; by 1996, this had mushroomed to 124, while governments worldwide flocked to open embassies in Pretoria. Pretoria also established bi-national commissions with several countries from both the global 'North' and 'South,' including the United States, Germany, China, India, and Nigeria. However, this reengagement meant South Africa, so long insulated from these global realities by its isolation, now had to make hard choices and take sides, a process complicated by the complex post-Cold War environment and divergent views on policy direction within the country. Mandela and his under-capacitated foreign affairs team, led by now Deputy President Mbeki, were forced to balance a highly 'idealist' foreign policy platform—undergirded by an explicit commitment to human rights—with political realities and loyalties to old friends that ran counter to these principles. This would prove a delicate balance throughout Mandela's presidency, and it was not fully resolved when Mbeki left office in 2008.

Principles of a Post-Apartheid Foreign Policy

As previously noted, the ANC from the late 1980s deliberated internally and engaged with academics and other actors in debating a post-apartheid foreign policy for the country. In foreign policy documents issued in 1991, 1993, and 1994—as well as a late 1993 article in *Foreign Affairs* credited to Mandela—the ANC laid out a foreign policy vision based on principles of multilateralism, human rights, promotion of democracy, international law, peace, and African interests.[66] These broadly 'idealist' goals were balanced by 'realist' considerations, however, particularly on the economic front. While Pretoria sought to expand its trade linkages with the global 'South,' its main trading partners remained the United States and Europe. To balance these considerations, Pretoria adopted a position of 'universality,' best summed up by Deputy Foreign Minister (1994–2008) Aziz Pahad in saying South Africa's policy was 'being very nice to the rich and powerful, nice to the potentially rich and powerful, and kind to old friends who are neither.'[67] While associating itself with the global South, and calling for an overhaul of the global economic system, Pretoria at the same time operated within the neoliberal constructs of the WTO, accepting the so-called 'Washington consensus' and seeking out trade and investment from the North.[68]

The Ups and Downs of Pretoria's Nascent African Agenda

Africa, and especially the countries of the SADC, were the main focus of South Africa's foreign policy during the Mandela administration, particularly with regard to regional peacemaking and expanding economic linkages. As the ANC's 1994 foreign policy document noted, 'We have a special relationship with the peoples of southern Africa, all of whom have suffered under apartheid.'[69] What Pretoria needed to do, however, was to move the relationship forward without being seen as a regional 'bully' like the apartheid state; as Aziz Pahad noted in 1996, 'We must carry our relations with the region in a way that is not a big brother relationship. This means that because of our relative strength we don't simply impose ourselves.'[70]

This would prove easier said than done, particularly in the African conflict-resolution realm, where South Africa was often viewed as an unwelcome interloper. Angola—galled by Pretoria's decision to invite UNITA rebel leader Jonas Savimbi to Mandela's inauguration—paid little heed to Mandela's efforts to mediate the conflict there, preferring to resolve the situation through force (which it successfully did in 2001).[71] In 1997, Mandela's efforts to avert war in Congo-Kinshasa (which joined SADC that year) were similarly thwarted by Laurent Kabila's judgment that he could take power in Kinshasa by force. Its peacemaking efforts after full-blown civil war broke out the following year were again ignored, with SADC members Zimbabwe, Namibia, and Angola all readily intervening against Uganda- and Rwanda-backed rebels. Mandela's sole notable success—in concert with Zimbabwe's Mugabe and Botswana's Ketumile Masire—was in peacefully returning the democratically-elected government of Lesotho to office in August 1994 after it was illegally ousted by the King. This success, however, would be overshadowed by a less successful intervention in that country four years later.

Mandela's attempts to promote democracy and human rights in Nigeria displayed the difficulties South Africa would face on the continent in projecting its influence. After taking power, Mandela focused intently on getting military dictator Sani Abacha—who had seized power the previous year—to release his political prisoners and make democratic reforms.[72] These efforts bore some fruit, such as the commutation of death sentences for top political opponents (including once and future President Olusegun Obasanjo), although Abacha avoided additional reforms. In October 1995, the Nigerian Government arrested environmental and political activist Ken Saro-Wiwa and eight others on trumped-up murder charges, allegedly fomented by the Shell Oil Company; they were quickly found guilty in a sham trial and condemned to death, igniting a global uproar. Despite South African efforts to free them, Abacha had them executed on November 10. Mandela, upon hearing the news, was furious, saying that Abacha was 'sitting on a volcano, and I'm going to blow it up under him.' Mandela called for Nigeria's immediate suspension from the Commonwealth, demanded economic sanctions, and recalled South Africa's high commissioner from Lagos.[73]

The muted African response to Mandela's call demonstrated clearly how little political capital South Africa had on the continent. The OAU dismissed Mandela's call for sanctions as 'not an African way to deal with an African problem,' while a December SADC meeting to discuss the problem determined the region would take no further action on Nigeria.[74] This lack of support forced Pretoria to back down; by June 1996 Foreign Minister Nzo announced that South Africa was abandoning its hard line against Nigeria, saying it breached 'the norms of African solidarity.'[75] While continuing to engage on Nigeria through Abacha's 1998 death and the country's 1999 return to civilian rule, South Africa shifted its efforts to the multilateral—and specifically African—arena, liaising with the OAU and SADC on common positions. As Mbeki, then deputy president, later noted, 'This issue [Saro-Wiwa's execution] high-lighted the potential limits of our influence as an individual country [. . .] and the need to act in concert with others and to forge strategic alliances in pursuit of foreign policy objectives.'[76]

An even more striking example of South Africa's inability to project influence, even on its borders, came with its botched 1998 intervention in Lesotho, which further laid bare shortcomings in South African policy-coordination mechanisms and displayed the perils of underinvestment in the security sector. After failed attempts to mediate a political crisis, South Africa sent 600 troops (alongside 200 from the Botswana Defense Force) to stabilize the country, at the invitation of Lesotho's prime minister. The intervention, the first foreign military excursion of the post-apartheid government, was a disaster; underestimating Basotho resistance, 11 South African National Defense Force (SANDF) troops were killed. Interagency coordination, particularly between the Department of Defense and DFA, was almost nonexistent; a failure to inform Home Affairs of the intervention even resulted in the brief detention of Botswana's troops at the South African border on their way to Maseru. Although they defended the rationale, Mandela and Nzo subsequently acknowledged that the intervention had been poorly handled and planned.

Pretoria had more success in expanding its economic influence in the region, although it too was met with limited enthusiasm by its neighbors. Between 1994 and 1999, South Africa invested R3.5 billion in the region, with an emphasis on the construction and retail sectors, a figure that accounted for nearly 30 percent of all foreign direct investment into SADC.[77] By 2001, total South African investment in SADC was estimated to be close to R15 billion, dwarfing runner-up Great Britain, at just R4 billion.[78] This picture was repeated further afield on the continent, with total African trade rising from R11 billion in 1994 to more than R28 billion by 1999.[79] Despite the benefits of this investment, however, other African states bristled at what they characterized as aggressive South African business intervention that crowded out local entrepreneurs and positioned South Africa as an economic hegemon.[80]

Balancing Principles, Old Friends, and Finances

Nigeria epitomized South Africa's broader difficulties in translating its stated human rights agenda into action; as Aziz Pahad stated, there had to be 'interaction between theory and practice' in translating a human rights emphasis into diplomatic relations, something that was easier said than done.[81] Even a relative 'idealist' like Raymond Suttner, chair of parliament's Portfolio Committee on Foreign Affairs (PCFA), in 1997 wrote, 'The promotion of human rights and democracy in foreign policy is easy to state as an aspiration. It is however, difficult to implement. There are no easy answers as to how it should be done.'[82] Weapons sales were a thorny topic in this regard. Armaments manufacture was (and remains) a big business in South Africa, which in 1994 was the world's tenth-largest arms producer, with an industry employing 50,000 people, and boomed after the transition.[83] Although government policy was that South Africa would act as a 'responsible arms seller,' the country in the late 1990s sold weapons to human rights abusers and countries waging wars in Africa and elsewhere.[84]

The ANC government backing 'old friends' who supported the ANC during the struggle and the transition—including those with less-than-stellar human rights records—was another contentious issue. Mandela made clear that South Africa had no intention of abandoning long-time allies like Libya's Muammar Gadhafi, Cuba's Fidel Castro, or the Palestinian Liberation Organization's Yasser Arafat.[85] These friendships sometimes undermined Pretoria's effort to act as an honest broker in negotiations, such as in its efforts to intervene in the Middle East peace process.

Of course, even friends could be jettisoned if Pretoria's conception of national interest so dictated, as with the South Africa's late 1996 decision (enacted in 1997) to recognize China instead of Taiwan. Despite its longstanding support for the old government, Taipei donated R35 million to the ANC's 1994 election campaign, invested heavily in South Africa—both in terms of aid and business interests—and intensively lobbied the ANC to retain recognition during the transition.[86] Moreover, Taiwan was also undergoing a period of democratization in the mid-1990s and had a respectable human rights record, two factors that should have aligned it with South Africa's stated foreign policy principles, particularly in comparison to post-Tiananmen China. However, the prospect of trade relations with a blossoming China, after it took control of Hong Kong in 1997, was too alluring to dismiss. China's potential to assist South Africa in seeking a permanent UN Security Council seat was also a consideration in its favor.[87]

Mbeki and the African Agenda, 1999–2008

Thabo Mbeki's assumption of the national presidency in 1999 meant little change to South Africa's foreign policy priorities, given that he had dominated ANC foreign policymaking from the early 1980s and had played the role of *de facto* prime minister under Mandela. A focus on Africa under the auspices of an 'African Renaissance,' a push to reform global governance institutions, and a preference for extended dialogue to resolve conflict, all remained at the forefront during Mbeki's administration. He also emphasized the need for solidarity among developing countries, as such unity was necessary to reform global financial and governance institutions like the UN, IMF, and World Bank.[88] This period was marked by greater interagency coordination driven by the Presidency, a translation of domestic priorities into foreign policy action, and pragmatism in terms of what could be reasonably achieved. As Department of Foreign Affairs Director-General Jackie Selebi noted in 1999, Pretoria sought to make South Africa's foreign policy more 'predictable,' ensuring that it was proactive and not 'colliding with events.'[89] Nonetheless, South Africa did collide with one notable event—Zimbabwe's political and economic crisis—that Mbeki would prove unable to address.

Deepening African Engagement

Africa, as before, was the overarching focus of South Africa's foreign policy thrust. Originally mentioned by Mandela at a 1994 OAU summit, Thabo Mbeki first used the term 'African Renaissance' in a 1997 speech near Washington DC to potential investors in the continent, and the term would in time come to dominate any discussion of the country's foreign policy priorities.[90] While South African leaders had long emphasized the importance of Africa rhetorically, Mbeki was the first to devote significant financial resources toward promoting good governance, economic development, peace, and security on the continent. For Mbeki, promoting the African Renaissance was no hollow assertion; in the words of one of his confidantes, the president was 'emotionally and intellectually committed to prove Afro-pessimism wrong.'[91] Mbeki was clear about the need to improve governance on the continent and broadly critical of African elites who acted like a 'parasite on the rest of society,' calling them the source of the continent's underdevelopment and calling for governments to be accountable to their populaces.[92] In another speech, Mbeki said Africa had 'no need for petty gangsters who would be our governors by theft of elective positions, as a result of holding fraudulent elections, or by purchasing positions of authority through bribery and corruption.'[93]

To promote his good governance agenda, Mbeki was a leading proponent of sweeping pan-continental initiatives, such as the 2002 formation of the African Union, its African Peer Review Mechanism, and the Pan-African Parliament, set up in 2004. However, Mbeki's New Economic Partnership for African Development (NEPAD), unveiled in 2001, was his crown jewel. Designed as a compact between Africa and the developed world, NEPAD would compel African states to commit to good governance, conflict resolution, and sound economic policies. In exchange, international donors would accelerate debt relief, increase assistance levels, bolster African peace support capacity, and open their markets to African imports.[94] Implicit in NEPAD and Mbeki's broader vision for the continent was that Africa had no hope of economic development without good governance and stability. He also pushed for African states to hasten regional economic integration initiatives to boost development, although Pretoria's propensity to go it alone in trade negotiations, South Africa's skewed balance of trade with the continent, and the growing footprints of South African firms in Africa roused suspicions and allegations of South African hypocrisy across the continent and especially in the region.[95]

Mbeki was unafraid to put South African money on the table for his African initiatives. South Africa footed a sizable portion of the bill for NEPAD and the African Union, for instance, and Pretoria also emerged as a donor on the continent; in 2004, its external assistance to Africa (including peacekeeping expenditures) reached $1.6 billion, more than the 0.7 percent of GDP targeted for developed countries.[96] Nowhere, however, was this commitment of resources more notable than in Mbeki's pledge of South African forces to African peacekeeping. By the time of Mbeki's September 2008 resignation, South Africa had—largely at its own expense—close to 3,500 troops deployed across the continent, mostly in Congo-Kinshasa, Sudan, and Burundi. It also played a leading role in establishing the African Standby Force and provided most of the required financial and logistical support to the SADC Brigade. This is striking in that South Africa had almost no troops engaged in peacekeeping operations when Mbeki took office, and Department of Defense planning documents oriented the SANDF toward domestic operations, with few resources devoted to peacekeeping.[97]

South African involvement in African peace processes was not just through deployment of peacekeepers; Mbeki and his team also sought to solve some of the continent's most intractable conflicts. There were notable successes. In 2001 in Congo, Mbeki pushed President Joseph Kabila to the negotiating table alongside rebel leaders to seek a peace settlement, culminating in the March 2003 signing of the Inter-Congolese Dialogue that led to 2006 elections. Pretoria was closely involved throughout the dialogue. Although Mbeki had little personal involvement in Burundi, former President Mandela and Deputy President Jacob Zuma were able to see through an often-difficult peace process, drumming up Western support for it and facilitating civil society efforts to train and reintegrate combatants.[98] Mbeki also sought to resolve conflicts in the Ivory Coast and Sudan, although a lack of commitment to peace processes by combatants in those countries hindered South African efforts.[99]

Pretoria's Diplomacy Less Effective Beyond Africa
South Africa during Mbeki's administration continued its efforts to reform global governance institutions and promote conflict resolution worldwide, but these efforts met with little success. Pretoria's attempts to promote its dialogue-driven transition as a model for solving other global conflicts largely failed, with actors it was seeking to influence viewing South Africa as either unwelcome or irrelevant.[100] Despite Pretoria's efforts to resolve the Israel–Palestine conflagration, Israel showed little interest, viewing South Africa as an unwelcome interloper that viewed the issue through the lenses of apartheid and anti-imperialism.[101] South Africa's 2007 abstention in the UN on a US-led motion to investigate political killings in Lebanon further undermined Pretoria's attempts to portray itself as an unbiased, honest broker. Pretoria's efforts to avert the 2003 Iraq invasion were even more quixotic and similarly futile.

Pretoria's controversial tenure as a non-permanent member of the UN Security Council in 2007/8, the first term in the country's history, was a clear demonstration of Pretoria's difficulties in projecting its influence on the global stage. Pretoria struggled to balance its stated human rights agenda and desire to be a global normative leader with its efforts to rebalance relations between the developed and developing world. Pretoria was quick to reject what it viewed as inappropriate (and hypocritical) pressure from the West on human rights issues, which Mbeki framed as a pseudo-imperialist 'tool' by Western countries to achieve their own political aims. This, in turn, prompted domestic and international criticisms that it was ignoring legitimate issues to please old friends and allies.[102] Pretoria during its tenure on the council voted against a Security Council resolution urging Burma's junta to free political prisoners (alongside only Russia and China); voted to discontinue scrutiny of human rights abuses in Iran; and blocked efforts to raise discussions of sanctions against Zimbabwe and Sudan.[103] Even on the Human Rights Council—which Pretoria claimed was a more appropriate venue for such discussions—South Africa opposed resolutions condemning abuses in Uzbekistan and Iran.[104]

Zimbabwe and 'Quiet' Diplomacy

Mbeki's inability to make progress toward solving the political and economic crisis in Zimbabwe will go down in history, rightly or not, as the dominant foreign policy issue of his tenure, given that none of his other initiatives—many of which were successes—generated the same sort of international and domestic attention. While the roots of Zimbabwe's crisis date to the early 1990s, growing public discontent over corruption, misgovernment, and poor economic conditions gave rise to growing labor-led protest later in the decade. This anti-government coalition of urbanites, labor, civil society, and white business interests in 1999 coalesced into the Movement for Democratic Change (MDC) opposition party. In a shock to the government, the MDC and its allies successfully defeated a draft constitution in February 2000 that would have consolidated power under the president, a result that foreshadowed the results of parliamentary elections that June, in which the MDC took 57 of 120 elected seats, decimating the ruling Zimbabwe African National Union-Patriotic Front (ZANU-PF) hold on that body.

The referendum loss and near parliamentary upset set off a wave of government-instigated violence against MDC supporters that would leave hundreds dead—and thousands more tortured or displaced—between 2000 and 2008, peaking in the run-ups to the 2002 and 2008 parliamentary elections and the 2005 presidential poll. It also sparked Harare's policy of expropriating land from white commercial farmers, which destroyed the agricultural sector (one of Zimbabwe's biggest export earners), undermined food security, and forced farm workers out of jobs. This helped set off the country's spectacular economic collapse; the IMF estimates that the country's economy contracted by 40 percent between 2000 and 2007.[105] With a mass exodus of skilled workers (up to 3 million Zimbabweans are estimated to have left the country) and withdrawal of foreign investment in the face of nationalization threats, Zimbabwe's tax base withered, forcing Harare to survive by simply printing more money, leading to hyperinflation that reached an unfathomable 89.7 sextillion percent before the US dollar was adopted in early 2009.[106]

Zimbabwe's economic collapse also had a significant impact on the region; one 2003 report estimated the loss of potential investment in the region at close to $36 billion.[107] The direct economic impact on South Africa, however, is more difficult to measure. South African parastatals Eskom and Sasol lost hundreds of millions of rand on unpaid bills for electric and fuel supplies to Zimbabwe, while Pretoria also has been forced to deal with the cost of processing, deporting, and securing its borders against millions of refugees.[108] These refugees also increased social pressures, sparking periodic outbreaks of xenophobic violence against foreign workers, Zimbabwean and otherwise. There were, however, also benefits. Despite fears of a trade collapse, South African exports to Zimbabwe in 2009 topped R13 billion, up from less than R5 billion in 2000, and Pretoria maintained a massive trade surplus.[109] The influx of Zimbabwean farm workers benefited commercial farmers, who used them (often illegally) for cheap labor, while the influx of skilled Zimbabwean workers to South Africa helped address the domestic skills shortage. One 2007 report estimated the impact of these immigrants was at worst neutral and perhaps slightly beneficial to South Africa's economy.[110]

The Roots of 'Quiet Diplomacy'

Given this economic and political collapse, Mbeki and his government came under intense pressure at home and abroad to address the Zimbabwe situation. A broad swath of domestic actors—including the political opposition, churches, press, and civil society—spoke out loudly against what they viewed as inaction by Pretoria toward the situation in Zimbabwe.[111] The Congress of South African Trade Unions (COSATU), the ANC's partner in the ruling tripartite alliance, was a particularly vociferous critic, with union leaders condemning Mugabe's land redistribution program from the beginning and backing its Zimbabwean labor allies. Although they did not couch their public arguments in such a way, concerns about the government's inability to address the influx of cheap Zimbabwean labor clearly were an area of concern to the federation. Even within the ANC, prominent figures like Defense Minister Mosiuoa Lekota and PCFA Chair Pallo Jordan broke with Party practice in publicly calling for a firmer line in Zimbabwe, although they were quickly reined in and warned not to buck the consensus, at least in public.[112]

By most accounts, Mbeki had no great affinity toward Mugabe, who—jealous of the attention paid to South Africa—continually sought to undermine South African initiatives on the continent and dismissed Mbeki's African Renaissance vision as 'political nonsense.'[113] Mbeki opted not to take a confrontational approach toward Zimbabwe, however, choosing instead a behind-the-scenes process that came to be known as 'quiet diplomacy' in order to cajole Mugabe toward reform rather than publicly attack him. The roots of the policy date to South Africa's failure in 1995 in Nigeria, where overt criticism—in Mbeki's view—hindered South Africa's ability to influence Abacha. As Mbeki himself noted in 2002, 'We could have invaded Zimbabwe as some people suggested—but what would this have achieved? [...] You must remember what happened to us [at the Auckland Commonwealth meeting in 1995] We suddenly found that we were the only ones who condemned the planned hanging. As a result we learnt a valuable lesson that, especially in Africa, you cannot act alone because you will find yourself isolated and in a position similar to that of the apartheid government.'[114]

The reasons and justifications for 'quiet diplomacy' were myriad. Resignation was part of it; there was a simple understanding that no one could force Robert Mugabe to make changes he did not want to make. Mbeki admitted as early as 2001 that Pretoria's strategy was not yielding results, while Pahad acknowledged the following year that South Africa had run out of ideas on how to move things forward.[115] Strategic concerns clearly played a role. Mbeki's 2002 comments reveal one of the more significant reasons behind his refusal to take a 'harder line' on Zimbabwe, namely that a tough stance there could undermine his efforts to reshape continental political and economic governance.[116] Despite Zimbabwean antagonism toward his African Renaissance ideals, Mbeki was actively seeking continental and regional support for NEPAD when Zimbabwe's crisis arose as well as pushing his neighbors for a reform of SADC's security organ.[117] Maintaining stability at home was another justification for not pushing harder. Any push toward sanctions because of the belief that such a move would make the political and economic problems in Zimbabwe worse, thereby exacerbating refugee flows.[118] Hence, as Aziz Pahad acknowledged to a group of academics in 2004, quiet diplomacy may not have been a perfect option, but it was the one most conducive to ensuring stability in Zimbabwe.[119]

There also were ideological reasons for this stance. While these have been overstated in the press, Mbeki and the ANC were also motivated to an extent by struggle-era loyalties to ZANU-PF, which did assist the movement in the 1980s. In addition, many in the ANC did not care for the MDC alternative. Mbeki did not rate Tsvangirai's leadership acumen highly, and ANC leaders were critical of the MDC's confrontational approach with ZANU-PF and suspicious of its ties with the West and its labor roots.[120] Zimbabwe policy also was shaped by an anti-imperialist worldview that shone through in Mbeki's public statements. Mbeki appeared to believe that the only reason Western countries and white South Africans cared about Zimbabwe was because white people were affected. 'A million people die in Rwanda and do the white South Africans care?' he asked in 2002, further stating that everyone wanted to talk about Zimbabwe 'because 12 white people died.'[121] South African decisionmakers frequently stated that they would not be dictated to by the West in how they dealt with their northern neighbor; as spokesman Bheki Khumalo noted, 'We'll do things because we believe they're correct and right,' and not to 'appease the G-8 leaders.'[122]

Whatever the motivations behind it, Pretoria's stance toward Zimbabwe changed very little throughout Mbeki's administration. The South African Government endorsed elections in 2002 and 2005 as free and fair despite criticisms of their conduct by local and international observers, but Mbeki and his deputies—notably Pahad and Local Government Minister Sydney Mufamadi—remained involved with shuttle diplomacy there throughout Mbeki's second term. South Africa, through SADC, criticized the June 2008 second round of the Zimbabwean presidential election—boycotted by the MDC in the face of government intimidation—as not representing the will of the Zimbabwean people, but it remained engaged behind the scenes. South African mediation proved essential to the September 15, 2008 signing of Zimbabwe's Global Political Agreement, which held until elections in July 2013. The Global Political Agreement proved a fitting coda to Mbeki's presidency—just five days later, Mbeki, under fire at home, announced his resignation.

The Perils of a Foreign Policy Presidency

Thabo Mbeki's ouster as ANC president at the December 2007 Polokwane conference and his subsequent resignation as national president cannot be tied specifically to his handling of foreign policy; such issues generated little heat within the ruling party. However, the widespread view that Mbeki was a 'foreign policy president' and criticisms of his frequent travel did not help bolster the Mbeki's populist credentials, especially in the face of a challenge by someone like Jacob Zuma. Although Mbeki from the start of his term tasked his foreign policy team with reconciling domestic and external priorities, his government was never able to translate his foreign agenda— particularly his continental good governance agenda—into something that made sense at home.[123] Public opinion polling consistently showed issues like unemployment, crime, service delivery, and HIV as the public's main priorities; nothing in the foreign affairs realm generated that sort of interest.[124] Mbeki's affinity for the 'high' politics of the international scene perpetuated and deepened the stereotype that he was out of touch with South African realities. This alone did not lead to his ouster, but it certainly contributed.

CHAPTER 3

PUBLIC OPINION AND PRESSURE GROUPS

The first actors whose role in the foreign policy process will be examined constitute the broadest swathes of society: public opinion and pressure groups. For purposes of this study, public opinion refers to the South African electorate's views on foreign affairs and the degree to which voters have made external issues a priority at or between elections. It will examine whether South African voters—white before 1994 and the multi-racial electorate thereafter—have ever made foreign policy an electoral issue and whether government has taken the electorate's views into account when crafting foreign policy.

As for pressure groups, these are organizations that in many ways represent the vanguard of the electorate, the 'attentive public' noted in Chapter 1. Broadly, these groups—which include organized labor, churches, advocacy groups, cultural organizations, and others, often broadly characterized as 'civil society'—consist of citizens who have banded together to push for their government to pursue certain policies. This chapter will focus on attempts by South African pressure groups to influence foreign policy, specifically their methods for pressuring government, their success in doing so, and government receptivity to those efforts. Relatively few of these groups in South Africa have a specific foreign focus, but many have weighed in on foreign policy because it has an impact on domestic concerns.

Academia and political party structures—which also are types of pressure groups—will be covered in separate chapters.

It should be clarified that this chapter's focus is on these groups' influence on South Africa's 'foreign policymaking,' not its 'foreign relations.' During the 1980s, for example, South African church and labor leaders played an essential role in turning global opinion against apartheid as well as pressuring the government for *domestic* reforms that, in turn, affected international views. Such advocacy is not the focus here; rather it is on whether groups were able to change Pretoria's policies toward the rest of the world.

Public Opinion's Pre-1994 Impact Almost Nonexistent

Although polling data were nonexistent until the 1970s, contemporary accounts suggest mass interest in foreign affairs and foreign policy was low.[1] South Africa's entrance into the First and Second World Wars aroused popular interest, but foreign policy was not a factor in parliamentary elections during the inter-war period.[2] As late as 1941, *The Forum* journal was able to claim, 'No sort of public opinion on world affairs has ever been created in South Africa.'[3] According to late MP Japie Basson, who entered parliament in 1950, '[Foreign affairs] didn't excite the public. There was no wide discussion on the issues.'[4] Here, Basson is referring to white voters, as non-white voices had negligible impact on foreign policy before 1994.

Even after the onset of the Cold War and myriad changes to the global governance system, few issues raised much public interest. One exception was Rhodesia's 1965 Unilateral Declaration of Independence, which was cheered by most white South Africans despite being met with chill by Verwoerd, whose measured response was calculated to not unnecessarily antagonize Great Britain.[5] Despite the formation of (short-lived) voluntary aid organizations across South Africa, the Rhodesia issue was never a 'make or break' electoral issue for the NP, evidenced by Vorster's correct calculation in the late 1970s that he could abandon Ian Smith's government with few recriminations at home.[6]

Interviews with participants in the foreign policy process indicate they saw little in the way of inputs or interest from the populace on external affairs. Public interest was periodic, related to specific events, and generally not sustained. As former Deputy Foreign Minister (1991–4) Renier Schoeman notes, 'The breadth of awareness from *vox pop* would only come around some sort of crisis, where PW or Vorster or someone would say "Stuff off," or there was a perceived attempt at interference in our policies. Ordinary people didn't really care, because it was quite simple—there was no choice in terms of what side you're on. Everyone was quite happy with how it was dealt with, because there was no other real response.'[7] Former DFA Deputy Director-General Derek Auret is even more blunt, saying, 'The entire citizenry of this country was neutered as far as foreign policy was concerned; they didn't know what was going on.'[8] Members of parliament, even those with a personal interest in foreign affairs, note that foreign policy never received attention in campaigns or between elections; local issues took priority. 'Foreign policy never played a part in my constituency,' says longtime MP from Randfontein Boy Geldenhuys. 'It's a mining constituency, so all people cared about were blasting certificates, which dominated their lives. They're not interested in Europe or America, they're interested in blasting certificates.'[9]

Even if there were public interest, few mechanisms existed during this period by which government could measure it. Munger wrote in 1965 that the concept of public opinion polling on foreign policy was so alien to white South Africans that 'the [white] European public would be confused and uncertain if asked.'[10] Limited opinion polling began in the mid-1970s, but it was not until 1982—when the South African Institute of International Affairs began its 'What Do We Think?' series—that the pulse of (white) South Africans was taken on external issues. The series, which was conducted biennially through to 1992, polled between 1,500 and 2,000 whites, disaggregating the results by age, language, gender, income, politics, and geographic location to give the best look to date at white opinions on foreign policy. The polls revealed several trends—such as a preoccupation with domestic affairs and a suspicion of the outside world—that reinforced the anecdotal recollections of limited public engagement.[11] Even when polling became more common, the government made little use of it in relation to foreign policy. Government communications director (1985–92) Dave Steward notes that his department from 1986 commissioned large-scale (up to 8,000 respondents of all races) surveys on South African domestic political opinions but included no foreign policy questions.[12]

One notable exception where public interest—and government attentiveness—was high during the pre-1994 period was in regard to South Africa's regional military incursions, particularly ensuring white casualties were kept down. Former SADF/SANDF officer Henri Boshoff recalled that, 'I know that during the 1980s when I was in Angola, priority number one was no casualties.'[13] This was an important consideration during Operation Savannah in 1975, when the SADF planned to invade Luanda on the eve of Angola's November independence. Planners estimated that such an attack, by 1,500 South African troops, would result in casualties of up to 40 percent. 'Even the vague possibility,' writes author Peter Stiff, 'that they might end up having to explain to the electorate how some 600 young, mostly white Afrikaans-speaking national servicemen had come to be killed in action or mutilated on a remote field of battle near Luanda frightened the hell out of Vorster and cabinet.'[14] The attack was called off, and operations over the next 15 years were designed to minimize casualties. There were exceptions, such as heavy losses during the 1987–8 battles of Cuito Cuanavale, but in general, as former Minister Dawie de Villiers recalls, 'It was a distance war in Angola.'[15] That Angola never turned into a killing field for white South Africans *a la* Vietnam for the United States allowed Pretoria to maintain broad support for its border operations through to their late 1980s conclusion.[16]

Pressure Groups' Pre-1994 Involvement in Foreign Affairs

Few pressure groups before 1994 focused on foreign affairs, even as a secondary concern. The few exceptions came from immigrant or religious groups, such as Jewish groups like the Israel–South African

Friendship League, which was founded in 1968.[17] South Africa's Jewish community from 1948 emerged as vocal advocates of supporting Israel, and the Nationalist government's granting of permission to South African Jews to send funds to the new country represents a rare example of the government using a foreign policy decision to win support from a domestic constituency.[18] None of these groups, however, had a broad base in white South African society. Despite this, some influential extra-governmental groups—notably the Afrikaner Broederbond—dealt with foreign affairs in a secondary capacity.

Influence of the Broederbond on Policy

Few pre-1994 South African entities were subject to as much discussion and debate—nearly all of it uninformed—about its influence on the political scene as the Afrikaner Broederbond. Founded as Jong Suid Afrika in 1918 (it was renamed in 1920) by 37 professional Afrikaner men committed to protecting their language and culture, it grew steadily, topping 1,000 members by 1933, 8,000 by 1968, and reached an estimated 20,000 in the mid-1980s.[19] Its membership was elitist, focused on recruiting the cream of the crop of Afrikanerdom. The Bond and its junior affiliate the Ruiterwag were secret organizations, but the Bond's public arm, the Federasie van Afrikaanse Kultuurverenigings (FAK), dictated the political direction of more than 200 public cultural, youth, religious, and civic organizations.[20] Although the Bond's constitution mandated that the organization separate itself from party politics and dictated that members of cabinet could not serve on the Bond's 16-member executive council, every prime minister from 1948 to 1994 and the vast majority of NP MPs and senior officials were members, at least until the rise of the *verligte* (politically liberal) generation of NP politicians in the 1970s.[21] Most of the top ranks of the military and intelligence community were also members.[22]

The above is related as fact. Less clear to this day is the degree of influence that the organization had over the NP and government from 1948 onward. The Bond's secrecy and hand-in-glove relationship with the NP made it journalistic catnip for the

English-speaking press, which from the 1940s onward closely scrutinized the organization. Books like Hennie Serfontein's *Brotherhood of Power: An Expose of the Secret Afrikaner Broederbond* and *The Super Afrikaners* by Ivor Wilkins and Hans Strydom further hyped the Bond's influence in the 1970s and 1980s, using limited documentary information to paint a picture of an organization that acted as a 'hidden hand' guiding government policy direction.

Others are more skeptical of the Bond's influence. As early as the mid-1960s, Munger dismissed the Broederbond as a 'jobs for pals' organization with little political clout beyond the local level, despite its ability to 'furnish eye-catching headlines.'[23] The Bond, he argued, took a back seat after the NP took power in 1948; its caché as a debating chamber diminished once the NP controlled parliament.[24] Historian Herman Giliomee, one of the leading experts on the Bond, calls its influence on policy 'greatly overrated,' particularly in comparison to cabinet.[25] Longtime Finance Minister Barend du Plessis, who was not a Bond member, also downplays the organization's influence: 'People say the Broederbond played a major role; I say nonsense.'[26]

The Broederbond's real impact and influence appears, as is often the case, to be somewhere in between these two streams of opinion. While sensationalist claims that the Broederbond tail wagged the government dog are overstated, the Bond did play an important role as a parallel structure for debating policy. In its role as a think tank, the Bond was a place of 'molding and sharpening members' views [...] where people pool their resources to think through the affairs of the day.'[27] While class and rank distinctions never completely disappeared, Bond meetings were places where members could interact outside accepted governmental hierarchies. Former Bloemfontein *Volksblad* editor Hennie van Deventer, who chaired the Bond's communication committee during the 1980s, described intra-organizational discussions as 'another way of communicating, with another hat on our heads.'[28] Bond members could query ministers at these meetings, where, as van Deventer notes, 'We didn't quiver in their sight.'[29]

The Bond's earliest forays into foreign policy debate date to the 1926 Balfour Declaration, the acceptance of which by Hertzog angered republicans in the Bond and elsewhere who felt this acquiescence undermined their goals of an independent republic.[30] In 1933, the Bond included the republican goal in its formal statement of purpose.[31] After 1948, the organization's inputs did have an occasional, if small, impact on foreign policy. The 1960 formation of the government-funded Africa Institute of South Africa, for example, stemmed from a discussion in the Broederbond executive eight years prior, and Bond members played a key role in setting up the think tank.[32] Vorster skillfully used the Bond to defend his Rhodesia policy against *verkrampte* attacks, while the government also passed information to the Bond executive about the 1975 Angola invasion to reassure the body's membership that the government had a strategy for the operation.[33] Later, the government used the Bond and its overt institutional allies, particularly in academia, to disseminate and defend the anti-communist underpinnings of its 'Total Strategy.'[34]

Overall, however, the Bond's impact on foreign policy direction was limited.[35] As NP spokesman Johan Steenkamp, a Bond member and FAK leader, remembers, foreign policy was never a hot-button issue within the organization: 'External policies were not a main focus. They focused almost exclusively on the internal.'[36] Although two committees—'Africa' and 'Africa and the World'—dealt with foreign policy and commissioned studies on foreign affairs topics, both ranked among the smallest Broderbond groups, with less than a dozen members each (although the latter included intelligence chief Hendrik van den Bergh).[37] All three post-1948 foreign ministers— Eric Louw, Hilgard Muller, and Pik Botha—were Bond members, although none of them appear to have been active in the organization's limited foreign policy debates.[38] While the Bond certainly had value as a parallel debating structure and disseminator of information, its independent organizational impact on foreign affairs was negligible.

Negligible Church and Labor Impact on Foreign Affairs

Prior to 1994, churches in South Africa played at best a negligible role in influencing foreign policy. Munger in 1965 noted that while the family of Dutch Reformed Churches—essentially the state religion of Afrikanerdom—would be expected to have some influence on foreign policy, its influencing role as an entity was nonexistent.[39] Boy Geldenhuys, who has a doctorate in theology and was a Dutch Reformed minister for 11 years before entering politics, echoes this view, noting that churches never engaged seriously on foreign affairs despite becoming key actors in the domestic arena.[40] If there was any role taken on by the Dutch Reformed Churches, it was, as with the Broederbond, as a disseminator of policy messages to members.[41] Although they made significant strides isolating the apartheid government internationally, reformist religious elements—both dissident Afrikaners like Beyers Naude and non-white leaders like Desmond Tutu, Frank Chikane, and Allan Boesak—also, unsurprisingly, had almost no influence upon the government's foreign policy.

South African labor groups also generally did not play a role in the foreign policy process before 1994, although the anti-fascist stances of such groups in the 1930s were a notable exception.[42] For example, after Italy invaded Ethiopia in 1936, black and white labor groups organized an effective 'Hands Off Ethiopia' campaign and refused to offload Italian goods at the ports of Cape Town and Durban. The following year, the Cape Federation of Labor Unions and South African Trades and Labor Council took similar stances toward Japan after its invasion of China, calling (albeit unsuccessfully) on Prime Minister Hertzog to close South African ports to Japanese goods.[43] Labor groups were also early opponents of neutrality in the run-up to World War II, providing a boost to their longtime antagonist Jan Smuts.[44] After the war, however, labor's foreign policy influence on government more or less disappeared until 1994.

High Hopes Unmet for Greater Post-Transition Impact

South Africa's political transition brought hope that policymaking, foreign and domestic, would be a far more participatory process than in the past. The ANC at its first post-unbanning conference in 1991, for example, resolved to use its Department of International Affairs to boost public awareness and participation in the discussion of foreign policy questions, and subsequent conferences iterated this aim.[45] The DFA in its 1995 foreign policy discussion document resolved to 'actively stimulate debate on international affairs and foreign policy,' while then-DFA Director-General Jackie Selebi noted in 1999 an 'urgent need in this country to broaden the interest in and understanding of foreign relations issues and how directly these impact on the attainment of domestic priorities.'[46] The government invited public comment on discussion documents in the late 1990s—including those covering foreign affairs, defense, and peace missions—with a goal of seeking 'national consensus' on these issues. Academics like Philip Nel proposed the possibility of open forums on foreign policy to create room for 'counter-hegemonic' voices to emerge and challenge elite opinions.[47]

Similarly, pressure groups entered the post-1994 dispensation believing the new government would take their views seriously in the policymaking arena, foreign and domestic, particularly given the important role played by the United Democratic Front—a coalition of ANC-aligned civil society groups that emerged as the leading mass democratic movement opposed to apartheid from its 1983 founding—in challenging the apartheid regime at home during the 1980s. United Democratic Front activists, many of whom joined the ANC, expected a system in which inputs from pressure groups, broader civil society, and the public would be continually sought and carefully considered during the decisionmaking process.[48] ANC conference resolutions in 1991 supported this notion, emphasizing the ruling party's commitment to seeking input from civil society in the policy process.

Public Apathy and Government Disinterest Continues After 1994

Government efforts to engage the public and take into account its inputs on foreign policy did not match the high-minded rhetoric of the early 1990s. Efforts to open up the foreign policy debate among the public were unsuccessful; as Gerrit Olivier reflected in 2006, South African foreign policy 'is noticeably undemocratic, a situation sustained by lack of public enlightenment, interest or participation [. . .] Lacking sufficient democratic control, the policy is essentially bureaucratic-elitist and top-down.'[49] The dearth of foreign policy discussion documents during Mbeki's administration limited the public's ability to comment on policy direction, and the lack of a formalized system of soliciting public inputs meant that DFA public education efforts—like its 2006 *izimbizo* program of public meetings—were haphazard and inconsistent.[50] Thus, as Garth le Pere and Brendan Vickers have argued, 'Government increasingly does not appear to be consulting about its foreign policy objectives and certainly is not explaining them to the country.'[51]

The public's lack of impact is clear; the reasons for it are less so. Was the public actively cut out of the foreign policy process by a government bent on asserting its predominance in this domain? Were its inputs ignored? Or rather, did the public simply not care enough about external issues to prioritize them in the broader political debate? Quantitative and interview data shed some light on the last question. Polling data from the 1994–2008 period is relatively limited on the foreign policy question, particularly in measuring prioritization of foreign issues vis-á-vis those of the domestic arena, but what data there are suggest South Africans are overwhelmingly focused on domestic rather than external issues. The first and still most comprehensive survey was conducted in 1997 by Philip Nel and Anthoni van Nieuwkerk, who polled 3,500 South Africans of all races on their attitudes toward foreign relations. The survey found that the public considered domestic concerns— employment, crime, housing, and education—far more important than external issues like trade policy, peacekeeping, and land mines; only a handful of respondents (almost all from high-income groups) considered external issues important.[52] Nel attributed these findings to the facts that South Africa had no culture of public debate of foreign policy and, more pressingly, that most citizens 'are denied the security of existence that is a precondition for an outward orientation.'[53] Day-to-day survival took precedence over less-pressing foreign concerns.

Interviewees broadly supported the findings of the Nel/van Nieuwkerk poll, particularly members of parliament asked to reflect upon the concerns of their constituents. 'Foreign affairs has never been a front burner issue, not at the point at which we are,' claims longtime ANC MP from KwaZulu-Natal Albertina Luthuli, raising a point echoed by several MPs. 'People are more concerned with things like social grants; it's very remote to them. But we're trying to involve people in the process.'[54] MPs also cited a rural/urban split in discussing public awareness of foreign affairs, with constituents from the latter generally more cognizant of the outside world. Former Gauteng MP and PCFA Chair Job Sithole says that in his Alexandra constituency in Johannesburg, constituents had an awareness of the outside world, but it was centered on recognition of long-term relationships from the liberation struggle with movements like FRELIMO, MPLA, and the Palestinian Liberation Organization (PLO). 'When you talk to South Africans about Israel, they only know Israelis are killing Palestinians. Things like Fatah, Hamas, they won't register. They'll only know PLO.'[55] Former Minister in the Presidency Essop Pahad, who did extensive ANC politicking in the Free State and Northwest provinces, said he would always try to address a foreign policy issue in his speeches there, telling attendees, 'Listen, sitting here in this bloody corner of the Free State, you have to understand what the world is, not just Lesotho.'[56] Pahad said rural listeners were receptive but lacked a sophisticated understanding of the issues.

Other interviewees said interest in foreign affairs would ebb and flow in relation to world events. Longtime KwaZulu-Natal MP and former Deputy Foreign Minister (2008–9) Fatima Hajaig recounted the following: 'I remember going to a huge wholesaler around 1990, and the people working there were wearing Saddam Hussein tee shirts. I asked why they were wearing them, and they all knew, it was to protest the might of America and the Arab world in fighting the Iraq. It symbolized standing up to America.'[57] Sithole echoes the point: 'I've learned that foreign policy is event driven. You come home, and Israel has attacked Palestine. Everyone's angry; they're prepared to listen to you. But three months down the line [. . .] there's no consistency to say how we as ordinary citizens contribute to our country's positions. You don't get South Africans marching about a UN vote.'[58]

Foreign affairs has not factored into any South African election since 1994, with party platforms of the ANC and opposition parties hardly mentioning external issues. 'Where people see relevance for their own situation, they show an interest,' notes Stellenbosch political science

professor Scarlett Cornelissen.[59] Several interviewees emphasized the
need to raise public awareness that foreign policy is relevant in their
daily lives. As Sithole notes, 'It's your foreign policy that commits your
troops. Those troops are your kids, brothers, sisters. Why would they go
to Burundi if I have no understanding of what he's going to do in
Burundi? As an ordinary person, I need to be able to relate with
government's decision to go to Burundi.'[60] Henri Boshoff questioned to
what extent mass casualties on a peacekeeping mission would raise
public awareness of foreign policy. 'We have been lucky that we haven't
brought back a lot of body bags,' noted Boshoff, drawing a parallel to
South Africa's pre-1994 Angola experience, during which the military
was similarly lucky.[61*]

With the consensus view that foreign policy is generally a low
priority for South African voters, the question turns to whether the
government actively sought out public opinion on foreign policy and
took it into account. On the former question, little appears
to have been done under Mbeki. Former Government Communication and Information System official Baby Tyawa notes that while
the information service after 1994 continually commissioned focus
groups and public polling from reputable polling firms to take the
country's pulse on various policies, Government Communication and
Information System questioning did not address foreign policy,
although she added that the Defense Force commissioned polling on
attitudes toward Pretoria's peacekeeping presence in the region.[62]
Longtime Minister Sydney Mufamadi also said the focus of government
polling tended to be on domestic matters.[63]

Government decision-makers also showed little inclination to use
available polling data in taking the pulse on foreign policy views of
South Africans. Academic Anthoni van Nieuwkerk's account of a
presentation on his 1997 survey findings made to an audience
including then-Foreign Minister Nkosazana Dlamini-Zuma shortly
after she took office provides insight into government attitudes
toward such polls:

I start to talk about South African perceptions of foreign policy,
and looked at how different ethnic groups view foreign policy

priorities, and she stops me and asks where I got my information. I respond that it was a Markinor survey with 3,000+ people, and she says, 'I can't stand academics like you. I'm a trained doctor; I know methodology. There's nothing you can tell me. Everything you say is nonsense. All of this is rubbish. We know what the people think and what they want, because they have elected us to rule the country. So we know what they want. We are them, they are us, and I run foreign affairs. So I know what they want.' So, she put me in my place, and I realized this is how the heavyweights view democratic participation in foreign policymaking, meaning the branches of the ANC. Don't talk Markinor or middle class households.[64]

Former Deputy Foreign Minister (1994–2008) Aziz Pahad provides a similar, if less hostile, perspective on the government view of public opinion:

You know, in reality, public opinion was not sufficiently informed to influence policy [...] Outside of some of the think tanks, I felt the public was not sufficiently informed to make an informed input. Except for the Middle East, where you had some Muslims make inputs. But it did not impact on policy. I find it now more as I'm out of government that you've got a very unenlightened public opinion on foreign affairs [...] There was not great influence on policy.[65]

More Active, but Similarly Powerless, Pressure Groups

While public opinion from 1994 was accorded little weight in policymaking, pressure groups during the early Mandela years had some impact on foreign policy discussions. The DFA in 1996 invited civil society organizations to weigh in on its draft foreign policy discussion document, and in September of that year held a workshop to discuss and debate elements of the document, such as the definition of 'national interest.'[66] Civil society organizations also helped develop the agendas for multilateral summits, to include the

Commonwealth and UN agencies.[67] Pressure groups had their most striking impact, however, in efforts to seek a ban on the use, production, and trade of anti-personnel landmines by the South African Government. These efforts, begun in 1995, brought together more than 100 organizations—including community, student, and religious groups—under the banner of the South African Campaign to Ban Landmines.[68] It mobilized the public behind the issue, organizing a write-in campaign that saw 5,000 postcards sent to Mandela urging a total ban.[69] Despite early opposition from the Departments of Defense and Foreign Affairs—the latter of which supported the continued use of 'smart mines'—the government in February 1997 announced a ban on the production, sale, and use of mines as well as a decision to destroy existing stock.

The anti-landmine campaign would prove pressure groups' last hurrah in the foreign policy realm until the tail end of Mbeki's administration. The government continued to formally (if unevenly) consult with certain groups, but participants recounted such talks as being largely *pro forma*, with the government already seemingly settled on its course of action. Mbeki saw no need to consult outside groups prior to his NEPAD program, while civil society blasted Mbeki for his administration's 'self-congratulating and self-legitimating' handling of the country's African Peer Review Mechanism process after it was launched in 2005.[70] Civic groups also blasted Mbeki after being shut out of 2005 discussions on South Africa's Millennium Development Goals. The experiences of two such groups under Mbeki, the churches and organized labor, provide excellent insights into how his administration consulted with non-governmental actors and, in most instances, chose to ignore them.

Church Largely Shut Out of Foreign Policy Debates ...
Churches and religious organizations had little impact on foreign policy during the Mandela and Mbeki administrations, although there was some engagement. In 2001, Mbeki and Dlamini-Zuma stopped state-owned oil firm Soekor from investing in Sudan after the South African Council of Churches (SACC) and the Southern African Catholic Bishops' Conference (SACBC) condemned human rights

abuses there, but this was an isolated instance, and Mbeki would reverse this decision before the end of his term.[71] Mbeki met with religious leaders twice a year under the banner of the National Religious Leaders' Forum; these discussions mostly focused on domestic matters, although foreign policy issues—like the Middle East—occasionally arose.[72] Mbeki also sought to cultivate church leaders for support on foreign policy issues with some success, like SACC Secretary-General Molefe Tsele's endorsement of NEPAD.[73]

Zimbabwe, however, was the key bone of contention between government and the church during Mbeki's presidency, and one that brought him extensive criticism from the likes of Cardinal Wilfrid Napier of Durban and Archbishop Njongonkulu Ndungane of Cape Town. Tutu was another strong critic, in 2003 saying, 'What has been reported as happening in Zimbabwe is totally unacceptable and reprehensible and we ought to say so.'[74] Father Richard Menatsi, secretary-general of the SACBC from 1999 to 2005, noted that during the religious leaders' biannual meeting with the president, they persistently brought up Zimbabwe for discussion, and each time it was removed from the agenda. According to Menatsi, 'I was in a working group to draw up the agenda for these meetings, but the Director-General [Frank Chikane] would strike it off. Or we would get it on the agenda, and we'd find a different agenda when we got into the meetings. It was crazy.'[75] Every once in a while the president would raise the topic, but his responses were unsatisfactory. 'From time to time, the president would say, "These issues are very complicated, we're working on it behind closed doors,"' notes Menatsi, who adds, 'You could see that foreign policy was rather closely held.'[76] In time, the formal engagement petered out; as Aziz Pahad remembers, 'There was a time we were in close touch with the SACC, but as time and dynamics changed, less and less.'[77]

... while Alliance Partners Feel Ignored

Defining the ANC's alliance partners—COSATU and the South African Communist Party (SACP)—as pressure groups is a debatable proposition; one might argue that their proximity to the ANC and participation in government since 1994 should lead them to be considered as part of the system. Since 1994, many top leaders of COSATU and the SACP—dual-hatted as ANC members—have been brought into government as civil servants, MPs, and ministers. The impact of this move is widely debated; proponents of such close ties argue that having alliance members involved in decisionmaking ensures that their organizational voices are considered, particularly with regard to domestic economic policy. Critics, however, have argued that such moves represent more a cooptation of alliance partners than a true partnership, with participants in government bent to ANC orthodoxy. They have also decried that moves into government from alliance representatives have weakened the leadership pool of the SACP and COSATU, leaving them ill-equipped to formulate policy positions independent of the ANC.[78]

On foreign policy, however, COSATU and the SACP since 1994 have acted as independent pressure groups rather than as junior partners of the ANC, espousing views that are at times sharply different from those of the government and indicating they are unafraid to criticize government foreign policies with which they disagree. The two entities each have separate (if small) international affairs departments that organize campaigns around issues important to the movements. As former COSATU International Affairs Secretary Simon Boshielo notes, 'We would use the *Shop Steward* [COSATU's monthly publication] to publicize these issues. We tried to publicize these issues for COSATU members who would not necessarily have the background on them.'[79] Although these were not frequent, COSATU during the Mbeki administration was effective at organizing marches and protests at diplomatic missions, picketing the Moroccan embassy over its occupation of Western Sahara; the Zimbabwean embassy for abuses there; and the US embassy on American Middle East policy.[80]

The SACP and COSATU had some success interjecting themselves into the government's foreign policy debate during Mandela's administration. As SACP International Affairs Secretary Chris Matlhako remembers, 'In the period of Mandela, it was very consensus driven. The SACP could make significant inputs, such as on our policy toward China.'[81] The SACP and COSATU were active proponents of the 'one China' policy that was eventually announced in 1996. Raymond Suttner, chair from 1994–7 of parliament's PCFA and a prominent SACP member, argued in 1994 that the alliance had independent foreign policy potential, given its partnerships around the world, and should not shy away from lobbying in the foreign policy arena, particularly on issues where the government was seen to be acting contrary to its stated policies or dragging its feet on implementing them.[82] The alliance's ability to 'make essential interventions that may be too sensitive or unsuitable for the government' meant that it could engage in 'second track' diplomatic efforts that would advance the government's foreign policy aims but outside of traditional channels of state-to-state engagement.[83]

The alliance and government differed on several issues during Mbeki's administration; the two most notable were the government's approaches toward Swaziland and Zimbabwe. COSATU from the late 1990s has worked with civil society and labor elements in Swaziland in their efforts to open up political space in that absolute monarchy, and the movement has criticized Pretoria for ignoring the monarchy's perceived repression of its political opponents.[84] The movement repeatedly called for Swaziland's political isolation, and in 2002 demanded Swaziland's suspension from the African Union and from Mbeki's NEPAD due to a lack of democracy, good governance, and transparency.[85] More visibly, COSATU in August 2003 and April 2006 engineered effective, if brief, blockades of the South African–Swazi border.[86] SACP General Secretary Blade Nzimande also was particularly vocal about the need for reform in Swaziland.

While Swaziland was a chief priority for the ANC's alliance partners, their efforts pale in comparison to those made in influencing South African policy toward Zimbabwe. COSATU engagement on Zimbabwe dates to late 1999, when then COSATU President Willie Madisha visited the increasingly restive country to meet with Zimbabwean counterparts, including the then-secretary general of the Zimbabwe Congress of Trade Unions, Morgan Tsvangirai. The following year, National Union of Mineworkers President James Motlatsi condemned the invasions of commercial farmland by Mugabe proxies as creating conditions of 'anarchy' there.[87] COSATU and SACP strongly and repeatedly criticized the Mugabe government's attacks on political activists, particularly trade unionist supporters of the new MDC party—helmed by Tsvangirai—which won nearly half of the elected legislative seats in the June 2000 parliamentary elections.[88] COSATU and the SACP frequently called upon President Mbeki to alter Pretoria's policy of 'quiet diplomacy' toward the Mugabe government through the 2008 conclusion of his presidency, but to little avail.

Alliance/Government Interaction Under Mbeki: The Alliance View . . .

There was regularized contact between alliance partners and ANC foreign policy decision-makers during the Mbeki period. SACP and COSATU representatives sat on the ANC's NEC Subcommittee on International Relations during its monthly meetings, for example, while their representatives also were allowed to weigh in on foreign policy concerns at the party's policy and elective conferences.[89] Matlhako cites this as the key arena for engagement between the ANC and alliance partners on foreign policy.[90] COSATU and SACP representatives frequently made submissions to the parliament's PCFA, and they were in regular contact with DFA, particularly Aziz Pahad.[91]

Despite the regular nature of the meetings, alliance interviewees bemoaned what they viewed as the poor quality of the dialogue with the ANC. As COSATU International Affairs Secretary Bongani Masuku notes, 'The biggest problem for us was not the differences in approaches, it was the lack of space to engage,' with foreign policy decision-makers. Although the meetings occurred, he was less sure if his positions were taken seriously—'Even if my view was not taken, was I listened to?'[92] In addition, alliance leaders claim President Mbeki had little time for discussion with them on foreign policy issues; according to Madisha, such discussions were usually at the end of meetings on domestic issues and consisted of Mbeki 'briefing us that [the government] has moved in a certain way.'[93]

The view of COSATU and SACP leaders is that while government and the ANC were happy to listen to them on issues where there was broad agreement, they were shut down on contentious topics.

As Madisha notes, 'When it came to Cuba, Palestine, and many other areas, Mbeki would listen when you spoke to him.'[94] Policy toward Western Sahara and African peacekeeping were other areas of confluence. 'We supported those [peacekeeping] initiatives. No one rejoices in the wars that go on in Africa,' Masuku notes.[95] Contentious issues—particularly Zimbabwe—were more problematic. 'Giving advice on Zimbabwe was very difficult,' Boshielo remembers. 'When engaging with government, they felt they and they alone were capable of making policy on this or that issue. Our advice was ignored under Mbeki, despite being the best-organized element of civil society.'[96] They partly ascribe this to Mbeki's enmity toward organized labor. 'I can't take away the fact that Mbeki didn't like the trade union movement very much,' Boshielo claims. 'Not just the movement, but the people in the movement [. . .] he didn't treat them with respect.'[97]

... and that of Government

Top government and ANC foreign policy decision-makers dismiss the notion that alliance partners were ignored on foreign policy. 'Everybody, including COSATU, was taken into account on foreign affairs,' said Presidency NEPAD Advisor Cunningham Ngcukana.[98] They expressed disappointment with what they described as unrealistic demands by the partners, particularly by COSATU. 'For example, on Swaziland, we would tell them, you can't just have a blockade and then forget the issue [. . .] you have to have a systematic program. And government can't call for an overthrow of the monarchy or send troops to overthrow the monarchy,' Aziz Pahad contends.[99] Longtime minister and Mbeki point man on key foreign policy concerns Sydney Mufamadi echoes this point, using Swaziland as an example. 'If COSATU comes to us and says there is no democracy in Swaziland, we must have a big demonstration about that. But you can't expect government to be party to that, because we have other ways of dealing with the situation. We have to be sensitive about how South Africa deals with neighboring countries.'[100] On Zimbabwe, longtime PCFA Chair Pallo Jordan adds that COSATU's inability to 'look at the larger picture' made it difficult to work with.[101]

Another criticism of alliance partners was the contradictory nature of some alliance demands, particularly in relation to China. Although an avid and early advocate of a 'one China' policy, organized labor later came to rue this position once the implications of competition with Chinese labor became clearer.[102] Mufamadi notes that 'I must say that on matters related to China, COSATU was taken seriously. But there was debate of double standard even there, where you find that COSATU would call for this very important relations with China but at the same time, when China's encroaching at the textile level, they'd say, "No, we can't do this, we can't open our exchange controls, we must protect our industry."'[103] In addition, alliance partners keen to criticize the West over issues like the Middle East did not seem to appreciate the potential economic implications of attacking South Africa's biggest trading partners.

If anything is clear, it is that communication between the two sides—particularly on tough issues—failed under Mbeki. Both sides claim in retrospect to understand the need for a delicate balance in discussing sensitive foreign policy issues, like on Zimbabwe. Masuku explains that he and COSATU fully understood that there was a need to keep the practice of South African diplomacy in Zimbabwe quiet to avoid being compromised as a mediator. Despite this, 'There must be a level of openness; it's a people's process, it's not all closed. The delicate balance is needed.'[104] Jordan echoes this point, noting that taking key pressure group leaders into confidence could have paid significant benefits. Although Jordan acknowledges dangers in revealing too much and having it leaked, he contends, 'One way or the other you have to convey your thinking to these people; Tutu throwing stones at your foreign policy is not very helpful. Even if the day after he does throw stones, perhaps he throws smaller ones.'[105]

The Chinese Arms Saga—Pressure Groups get it Right

Despite the weaknesses and disadvantages of non-governmental organizations in the foreign policy arena, these groups did show in 2008 that they could have an impact on government policy through concerted effort. In April 2008, the Chinese cargo ship *An Yue Jiang* arrived at Durban harbor with 77 tons of weapons—including ammunition, rockets, and mortar bombs—bound for overland delivery to Zimbabwe. The National Conventional Arms Control Committee, the cabinet-level organization tasked with approving such shipments, issued a permit for the shipment to proceed.[106]

The shipment did not go undetected by local and international media outlets, which jumped on the story, sparking civil society organizations to action. Religious leaders—including Tutu and the Anglican Bishop of KwaZulu-Natal Ruben Phillip—and non-governmental organizations like the Open Society Initiative for Southern Africa demonstrated at Durban harbor, while a COSATU affiliate announced it would not offload weapons at the port.[107] The Southern Africa Litigation Center assembled a legal team to challenge the legality of the permitting. Within days of the application, the Durban High Court ruled in the Southern Africa Litigation Center's favor that while the arms could be unloaded, they could not be transported overland to Zimbabwe.[108] The ship departed shortly thereafter, ultimately offloading its cargo in Pointe Noire, Congo-Brazzaville, from where they were shipped to Zimbabwe.

One should not make too much of this incident's significance. Pressure groups did not force a wholesale change in broader government policy toward Zimbabwe, nor did they stop the arms from arriving there. However, by uniting, raising public awareness of the shipment through effective use of the media, and focusing on a specific issue where they were able to influence the situation, pressure groups were able to interject themselves into the conversation and force the government to make a tactical retreat on its policy.[109]

Conclusion: Why so Weak?

Ultimately, it is clear that public opinion has never had any discernable impact on foreign policy formulation in South Africa. Before 1994, the white voting public showed little interest in foreign policy, and even when the public was energized about certain issues (like Rhodesia), government largely ignored its inputs. After 1994, the now-broadened South African electorate was, if anything, less engaged on international affairs than before 1994, with domestic issues based around day-to-day survival taking priority for the vast majority, particularly non-white voters. Foreign policy issues also had no impact on election outcomes, before or after the transition, giving the government little incentive to take public inputs into account. As one analysis from 1999 stated, 'Since the experts do not have popular backing or a significant constituency, the formulators of foreign policy can afford to disregard their advice.'[110]

Pressure groups have fared just as badly, owing to a lack of focus on foreign affairs and the government's refusal to take their inputs seriously, particularly before 1994. Munger in 1965 said that, unlike in the United States, pressure and lobbying groups were not important in South Africa, noting that such efforts were 'viewed at best as basically incompatible with good government and, at worst, as something evil.'[111] Growing centralization of decisionmaking within the executive after 1948, particularly during Verwoerd's adminis-tration, was another factor that reduced the influence of outsiders.[112]

Pressure groups had similarly limited impact post-1994. Although the Chinese arms saga showed that non-governmental organizations could organize around a particular foreign policy issue, few issues elicited enough attention and support for their advocates to have any real influence. Meanwhile, more broadly influential groupings—especially churches and organized labor—were ineffec-tive in the foreign policy arena owing to the elitist nature of the debates, a lack of focus on the issues, and limited resources:

- *Elitism.* As elsewhere in the world, South African civil society's efforts to influence foreign policy suffer in that its involvement comes from a 'small stratum of the public whose occupational responsibilities require them to pay attention to the international scene, or whose self-image of their role and interests lead them to feel involved in foreign affairs.'[113] Despite a profusion of civil society organizations in South Africa—more than 100,000 by 2000—only a handful focus to even a limited extent on foreign affairs.[114] As Mufamadi notes, 'Foreign affairs tends in one sense to be a relatively insulated, specialized area. Elitist [. . .] it doesn't generate the same interest as economic policy or local government. Those are issues that people deal with on a day to day basis at the ground level.'[115] Hence, decision-makers know they can discount the vast majority of pressure group inputs on foreign affairs, given the lack of consequences at the ballot box.

- *Prioritization.* Even for groups like the churches, SACP, and COSATU that speak out frequently on foreign policy concerns, external issues are not a chief priority. Father Peter John Pearson, head of the SACB's parliamentary liaison unit, notes that although the SACBC follows foreign affairs, faith communities tend to focus on domestic issues first and foremost, particularly those related to poverty.[116] As for the unions, 'I think collectively, we have not put foreign policy at the center of engagement with government,' Masuku notes.[117] Given that foreign policy 'is not an ordinary worker issue,' the unions have focused most of their engagement with government on the domestic arena.[118] Although COSATU tried, through campaigns and editorials in its *Shop Steward* journal, to raise the profile of foreign policy issues, alliance leaders acknowledge this has yielded only limited and inconsistent results.

- *Resources.* Given foreign policy's low prioritization, pressure groups with an interest in foreign affairs—forced to balance tight budgets and competing demands—did not allocate much funding to international issues. Religious groups have only a handful of staff working on foreign affairs. COSATU during this period only had three people, while Matlhako has solely handled the portfolio for SACP. As he notes, 'Since the unbanning, the majority of those doing international relations for SACP gravitated into the state, which meant the rolling back of the international relations of the party.'[119] Budgets are also limited, meaning pressure groups have been unable to carry out effective advocacy work among its members or maintain solidarity campaigns. Madisha says that while workers will happily 'yell *amandla* and *viva* for Zim trade unions, but there are differences between supporting through action and supporting through *vivas*,' they are far less interested in contributing part of their salaries to support such action.[120]

CHAPTER 4

THE PRESS

Since accounts of the 1853–6 Crimean War in British newspapers raised awareness of that deadly conflict, the press has played an important role in influencing public opinion and decision-maker attitudes on foreign policy issues.[1] For the former, particularly in the developed world, the media determines what is 'newsworthy' and dictates the parameters of policy debates, writes public policy expert Wayne Parsons.[2] Of course, media outlets—at least those that are profit-making enterprises—must ensure that their content resonates with consumers, or else they will find other sources of information more in line with their thinking.

The media has a more complex relationship with government; the two need, but in many instances detest, one another. For government officials, the media provides an outlet to sell their policies and actions to voters. In addition, according to academic Christopher Hill, 'The press has long been used to launch diplomatic trial balloons, and not infrequently information is released which has only the most tenuous relationship to the truth.'[3] He adds that members of the media can in some cases also have direct contact with decision-makers and other influential members, providing journalists with an opportunity to influence the policy discourse.[4] Public perception of this 'insider' access can prove valuable for selling newspapers or luring listeners, but for the journalist it also carries the risk of painting the press as a government stooge that pushes the party line. On the flip side, government officials can freeze out outlets viewed as unsympathetic or overly critical of policy, potentially inviting more criticism but possibly pushing readers toward more sympathetic reportage and better access.

Media outlets everywhere, therefore, have a difficult calculus—how to make money, friends, and news simultaneously. This has been no different in South Africa, before and after 1994. South Africa has since the nineteenth century had a vibrant, multilingual print press, followed in the twentieth century by radio, television, and, more recently, the Internet. It is easily the most media-saturated country in Africa. The country's 23 daily newspapers, 25 weekly newspapers, and countless community newspapers are read by an estimated 20 million of the country's 50 million citizens every week.[5] Radio access is ubiquitous, while cable television and the Internet have seen significant growth since 2000. These outlets provide significant coverage (from local and international outlets) of South African politics and policies, meaning that any citizen, rural or urban, can easily find out what is happening at home and abroad.

The goal of this chapter is to explore the impact of the print press on foreign policy, both in swaying the opinions of its readership and influencing decision-makers. For the former issue, this chapter will probe whether press coverage of foreign affairs has resonated with readers to the extent that it has helped alter public opinion in the external sphere. For the latter, the chapter will examine press relationships with South African decision-makers to determine whether journalists have been able to exert influence 'upward' on the policymakers themselves, due to personal relationships or political expedience. The mainstream print press, consisting of newspapers and news magazines, is the focus of this chapter because it has through the years devoted the most time and resources to serious consideration of foreign affairs and been the primary destination for readers interested in external issues or South African foreign policy, serving as the 'media of record.' Although radio and television have more penetration in the country, their coverage of foreign affairs has tended to be cursory. In addition, the print press is by far the most established entity in the South African media—television was only introduced to the country in 1976—making it convenient for making comparisons over time.

The Origins of the South African Media

South Africa's print media dates to 1800, when the Cape Colony government established the *Cape Town Gazette and African Advertiser* to print administrative notices and other news. The first Afrikaans newspaper, *Die Afrikaanse Patriot*, was founded in 1876, although most newspapers tended to be in English and located in the Cape until the end of the century. The *Cape Argus*, founded in 1857 as a tri-weekly paper, was the first newspaper to receive news stories from abroad by telegraph.[6] The *Cape Times*, founded in 1876, was the country's first daily newspaper, and its success soon forced the *Argus* to become a daily. The Johannesburg gold rush of 1886 meant that the media would no longer solely be a Cape affair, with the Johannesburg *Star* founded that same year, the *Rand Daily Mail* in 1901, and the *Sunday Times* in 1906. These English papers, both in the Cape and elsewhere, were strongly pro-British and almost exclusively owned by mining interests.[7] These interests consolidated their media holdings over time into a handful of publishing companies, most notable of which was the Argus Group, established in 1888 and owner of the *Star* and *Argus*, among others.[8]

While the print press in the early twentieth century was dominated by English-language publications, the period also saw the advent of Afrikaans-medium publications. Coinciding with the rise of Afrikaner nationalism and that community's quest for political power, these Afrikaans-medium newspapers were more overtly political than their English-language counterparts, focusing on promoting the Afrikaans culture and language as an element of the country's political life. Although Bloemfontein's *Volksblad*, founded in 1904, was the country's first Afrikaans daily newspaper, the dominant Afrikaner newspaper of the era was Cape Town's *Die Burger*, founded in 1915. Nasionale Pers (now Naspers), a media company operated by the new NP (formed the previous year) to publicize its events, published *Die Burger*; it later became the Party's official organ in the Cape.* After the

Party split in 1933 between backers of fusion with the South Africa Party and the 'Purified' wing, led by *Die Burger* editor DF Malan, the paper stayed loyal to Malan, who was appointed to Nasionale Pers' board in 1935.[9]

The Press and Foreign Affairs Before 1948

The newspapers of the nineteenth and early twentieth century focused mostly on domestic concerns, although foreign news was not ignored. In describing the *Rand Daily Mail* at the turn of the twentieth century, Joel Mervis writes, 'On a given day the commentary would deal with a variety of subjects ranging from the Brussels Convention and sugar bounties to labor problems in France; negotiations between Britain and India over an exclusively British-controlled cable between the two countries; the marriage of the British Secretary of State, Mr. Broderick (who was a widower), to a titled lady; and Japan's evacuation of Shanghai.'[10] The biggest barrier to increased coverage was the cost of acquiring foreign stories. Describing the same period, Benjamin Pogrund writes, 'The reaching for foreign news lasted only as long as it took for the bills to come in—at ten shillings and three pence a word for cables from Tokyo, and six shillings and two pence a word from Buenos Aires. Those were huge amounts. Lunch in a Johannesburg café could be had for one shilling and sixpence.'[11] It was not until the formation of the South African Press Association—the country's first centralized news service—in 1938 that gathering foreign stories became more cost effective.[12]

The start of World War II in 1939 brought foreign issues to the front pages of both English and Afrikaans newspapers, which flew their political colors in covering the conflict. English newspapers almost universally supported Smuts' decision to enter the war and for its six-year duration consistently supported South African involvement.[13] In contrast, Afrikaans papers—especially *Die Transvaler*, the Johannesburg paper edited by future Prime Minister Hendrik Verwoerd—virulently opposed the conflict. Verwoerd was quick to gloat early in the war over British setbacks; after the retreat from Dunkirk and during the bombing of London in 1940, Verwoerd wrote in *Die Transvaler*, 'Britain has lost the war. This is not only my opinion; it is my wish.'[14] Even

Hitler's invasion of Holland, which troubled many Afrikaners, did nothing to change the newspaper's stance.[15] Verwoerd's anti-British sentiment did not stop after the war, with *Die Transvaler* notably refusing to cover the British royal family's 1947 visit to southern Africa.

The Changing Face of Government–Press Relations, 1948–94

The NP's stunning win in the 1948 election radically altered the government–press relationship. Not only did the Afrikaans press heartily support the new government, but they were also part and parcel of the ruling party, with the major publishing houses— Nasionale Pers, Voortrekker Pers, and Afrikaanse Pers (the latter two would merge into Perskor in 1971)—having extensive direct linkages to the NP political elite. New Prime Minister DF Malan's connections to Nasionale Pers are well documented, while successors Strijdom, Verwoerd, and Vorster all chaired the board of directors at Afrikaanse Pers while serving as head of government.[16]

The Afrikaans Press and Government: Birds of a Feather
Former *Beeld* editor Schalk Pienaar best described ties between the Afrikaans press and the NP government through the 1980s as 'independence in commitment, friendship in tension.'[17] While opposing the Party's underlying principles—such as dedication to the Afrikaans language and Afrikaner cultural values—was verboten, seeking to influence its policies, particularly on racial issues, was not.[18] As longtime (1954–77) *Die Burger* editor Piet Cillié noted during his tenure, 'We support the Nationalist Party. We criticize it, but to make it better. By and large, its battles are our battles.'[19] The Afrikaans press, it should be noted, was not a monolithic entity by any means, with the various publishing houses divided on regional and, later, ideological lines. Cape Town-based Nasionale Pers was notable for promoting the 'Cape line' of NP thought, one that through the 1970s favored, in the words of Hermann Giliomee, a 'softer, more liberal implementation of apartheid' that attacked its discriminatory elements, such as the disenfranchisement of coloured

voters.[20] The northern papers—exclusively controlled by Perskor and its precedents until the 1965 establishment of *Beeld* in Johannesburg by Nasionale Pers—were far more supportive of the *baaskap* (white supremacy) principles of Strijdom and Verwoerd, and through the 1980s they would take largely *verkrampte* positions on issues ranging from reform of apartheid institutions to negotiations with the ANC.[21]

By the 1980s, Afrikaans newspapers—even the traditional 'party organs'—began to show increasing editorial independence from the NP line, with most taking an increasingly *verligte* stance.[22] *Beeld*, from its founding, had emerged as the leading 'dissident' newspaper, and in 1980 editor Ton Vosloo went so far as to suggest the government would have to negotiate with the ANC.[23] 'Shreds were torn from my back by PW,' recalls Vosloo about that occasion.[24] PW Botha also took a significant step toward undoing the relationship between government and the Afrikaans press when he resigned as a director of Nasionale Pers after becoming prime minister in 1978 and asked his cabinet to resign their directorships as well.[25] It was not until 1990, however, when Ebbe Dommisse took over as *Die Burger* editor, that the decision was finally made to end the newspaper's formal relationship with the Cape NP. 'There was opposition from the party,' notes Dommisse, 'but if a newspaper wanted credibility, how could it be a party organ?'[26]

The Afrikaans Press Opens the Door to the National Party Government

Contacts between Afrikaans editors and ruling NP politicians were generally, although not universally, frequent and close. Premiers through Vorster would meet with Afrikaans editors before the opening of parliament to cue them in to legislative priorities for the forthcoming year.[27] DF Malan would go so far as to invite *Die Burger* editor Phil Weber to the NP's weekly parliamentary caucus meetings, although this ended under Strijdom.[28] Verwoerd, despite being a former editor himself, was an exception in that he did not enjoy close ties with the Afrikaans press during his tenure, rarely granting newspaper interviews nor meeting with parliamentary correspondents.[29] He tended to dictate to editors, telling them what policy would be rather than considering their inputs.[30] Vorster, in contrast, was more open to the inputs of Cillié and other editors, and he enjoyed close personal ties with some journalists, notably *Die Burger* political correspondent Alf Ries.[31] Ries travelled with Vorster on several of his trips to African countries, getting the inside scoop, and their closeness was such that veteran journalist Peter Fabricius says Ries was 'jokingly referred to as a secret member of the cabinet' in journalistic circles.[32]

At a provincial level, editors of the provincial Party mouthpieces— *Die Burger* in the Cape, *Die Transvaler* in the Transvaal, and *Volksblad* in the Orange Free State—were considered part of their provincial NP structures and participated in federal party congresses, allowing them to shape policy outside the pages of the newspapers. 'All of the editors had a place on the provincial organs,' remembers longtime *Volksblad* editor Hennie Deventer. 'I was not a fully fledged member of the NP executive, but I had a secure position on the committee in the province.'[33] In the Cape, recalls Vosloo, 'the editor of *Die Burger* [Piet Cillié] would be invited on a permanent basis by the head of the provincial party to attend their monthly caucuses.' There, editors like Cillié 'could influence the cabinet ministers on various policies. These guys were hand in hand with government on formation of policy, but they rarely criticized publicly.'[34]

Encounters between journalist and politician could be bruising, particularly between Cillié (who chaired the Nasionale Pers board of directors from 1977–85) and PW Botha. 'Oh my gosh ... they had clashes! Especially at the federal congresses,' recalls Dommisse. 'At the parties, when the drinks started flowing, there would be clashes. PW was a difficult customer; if he flew into a rage, you got out of the way. But he listened.'[35] *Die Burger* political journalist Theuns van der Westhuizen recalls another encounter between the two men during a party congress in the mid-1980s:

One evening in Port Elizabeth, they were discussing some issue, I believe group areas, and Piet Cillié said that no one could defend them any longer. And PW said, *'Piet, jou moer.'*

(loosely, 'Go to hell') And Piet Cillié, a short stocky little guy—and PW was fairly tall—and Piet went up to PW, stood in front of him, looked up, pointed his finger at him in PW's style, and said, with great decency, '*Eerste Minister, U se moer ook.*' ('Prime Minister, respectfully go to hell yourself.')[36]

This exchange exemplifies the complexities of the NP–Afrikaans press relationship through the 1980s. As much as Botha may not have appreciated Cillié's inputs, *Die Burger* was a key backer of his 1978 push to become Party leader against Connie Mulder. Cillié, according to Vosloo, also was the key driver behind Botha's 1978 decision to remove himself and his cabinet from newspaper boards of directors.[37] They could bruise each other inside the caucus, but they kept their disagreements in house.

In recalling their relations with PW Botha, Afrikaans journalists note his tempestuousness but also his attentiveness to what was written. Theuns van der Westhuizen recalls one incident involving former *Beeld* political reporter Freek Swart: 'Freek and I were walking down Roeland Street to parliament, and a police car pulls up to us. We didn't know what was happening, but then the next minute another car pulls up, and it's PW. He got out and walked up to Freek and said, "Listen, Freek, why did you write that piece?"'[38] That said, both Vosloo and van der Westhuizen said Botha would take calls from journalists and would listen to their arguments, particularly on domestic policy issues. Botha's relations with the Afrikaans press were in sharp contrast with those of de Klerk; while he would respond to their questions and interview requests, editors say he had no close ties with any of them.[39]

The Other Side of the Door: The English Press and Government

The NP's victory in 1948 largely relegated the English press to the political wilderness for much of the next 46 years.[†] English papers largely supported the United Party and, later, the progressives, although they never developed the hand-in-glove ties with opposition parties such as those seen between the Afrikaans papers and the NP. English newspapers, the circulation of which were always far greater than Afrikaans papers, were tenacious in their critiques of government policies, leading the government to ignore them or, in Gordon Jackson's words, regard them with 'a mix of wariness, anger, or outright hostility.'[40] NP politicians generally talked down to the English press, if they talked at all. Eric Louw, South Africa's first minister of external affairs, was a noted government attack dog during its early years; in 1959, he blamed the English press for 'a great deal of South Africa's internal trouble' as well as for damaging South Africa's image abroad.[41] When he did interact with the English press, it was with contempt. Longtime Johannesburg *Star* editor Harvey Tyson, remembering his early career as a political journalist with the Natal *Mercury*, recalls meeting the 'overweening and vain' minister in parliament: '[Louw said] "Ask me the following question . . . and I shall give you an interesting answer." "Consider the question asked," I said. And he then proceeded to give me at length his views on some international issue unrelated to South African affairs. It was so rare—an "exclusive interview" with the Nat Government—that our papers published his non-story.'[42]

One key exception was John Vorster, who understood the value of cultivating the English press. Although he once told English journalists at a press conference, 'You hate me and I hate you,' Vorster also understood that the international press largely relied on copy from the English newspapers, hence influencing them could burnish South Africa's image abroad.[43] As *Cape Times* deputy editor Gerald Shaw recalls, 'Vorster had been the most approachable of cabinet ministers, and he remained so after becoming prime minister. Representing the *Rand Daily Mail* in the parliamentary press gallery, I found him to be friendly and accessible, remarkably so, for the *Mail* was fiercely hostile to his policies.'[44] Vorster went so far as to give *Cape Times* editor Tony Heard a lengthy off-the-record interview at the Union Buildings confirming South Africa's invasion of Angola in 1975—although the Defense Act barred Heard from printing any of it.[45] The enmity toward the English press returned, however, under PW Botha, especially toward Heard and the *Cape Times*. Botha attacked the newspaper in parliament in 1983 for its coverage of Pretoria's regional destabilization efforts in the region, and specifically called out Heard—whom he described as 'not quite normal'—for printing 'common lies.'[46] Two years later, Botha had Heard arrested and charged under the Internal Security Act (although the charge was later dropped) for printing his interview with Oliver Tambo in London, as Tambo was a banned person who could not be quoted.

Operation Savannah and the Perils of Defense Coverage

Pretoria's 1975 invasion of Angola—codenamed Operation Savannah—and its subsequent military operations in the region forced the press, English and Afrikaans, to figure out how to cover the fighting without contravening secrecy legislation. Pretoria officially denied its involvement in Angola to the press despite its troops being well inside Angola.[47] The truth—from overseas coverage and inside briefings like that received by Heard—came out quickly, but printing it was more difficult. The Defense Amendment Act of 1967 made it illegal to publish information without the government's permission on defense force operations and composition; information that would damage South Africa's foreign relations; or any classified information on defense matters.[48] The government, under the Official Secrets Act of 1956, had the power to censor such information.[49]

Newspapers, therefore, had to find a balance between respecting the law—contravention of which could mean criminal prosecution or even closure of the newspaper—and providing readers with coverage of events, leading papers (especially the English press) to use creative means to convey information. South African newspapers, for example, cited foreign sources like the BBC and *New York Times*, which were actively covering the Angolan invasion.[50] Semantics were also key: 'You could not report about the movement of troops, so what we did was report about advances of the "allied forces,"' Dommisse recalls.[51] Prominent *Cape Times* defense correspondent Willem Steenkamp notes that parliamentary privilege was another useful tool: 'If there was a piece of information that we could not use, we'd ask a friendly MP to state it in parliament.'[52] Lastly, the *Rand*

Daily Mail adopted a tactic from the Rhodesian press: blank space. As Harvey Tyson recalls:

> I vividly remember the first time the *Rand Daily Mail* used blank space. The first victim of the war in Angola was a guy called Christopher Robin, whose death notice appeared in a paper without any explanation. The editor of the *Mail*, Ray Herbert, said we could not publish how or where he died, because that would contravene the Defense Act, so he took the death notice and put it on the front page with blank space and a note at the bottom saying we cannot say how he died or the circumstances.[53]

Over time, the SADF took steps to try to win over the press, such as flying journalists and editors to the front and providing them with regular briefings. Some journalists enjoyed exceptional access, none more so that Steenkamp, who also served as a reserve officer while writing his weekly column on military matters, 'On Parade.'[54] Steenkamp recalls his access to the military top brass as excellent, and found them receptive to dissenting opinions: 'I had dealings with everyone [Generals] Geldenhuys, Viljoen, Liebenberg, all these people. They were quite open to that, and they wouldn't shout you down if they disagreed. I could say that I was hearing something on the ground different than what they thought, and they'd listen.'[55]

Steenkamp's experience, however, was an outlier. Relations with top security sector officials were, in general, chilly for English and Afrikaans editors and journalists. Fabricius remembers that outside of Pik Botha, few principals of the State Security Council (which will be discussed in Chapter 9) kept frequent contact with journalists.[56] Van der Westhuizen describes intelligence chief Niel Barnard as 'pretty closed,' a characterization with which Barnard himself agrees.[57] 'We never had a good relationship with the media,' he recalls. 'Let me say very openly that we never aspired to have good relations. They took an extremely negative view when I was appointed head of the service [...] in *Rapport* on the Sunday after I was appointed, the headline was, "Everybody's Laughing About Our

New James Bond.'"[58] However, Barnard claims relations were closer with some than they would appear: 'There's no doubt they were well informed. One of your biggest challenges was that the media in Africa often had better contacts than our agents. Relations with them existed at an operational level [. . .] I hate to say they were being handled, but several were paid sources. They'll vehemently deny that.'[59]

While most coverage of the military and Pretoria's foreign interventions by the English press was unhesitatingly critical, the Afrikaans press tended toward 'softer' coverage, something that rankles some of its editors and journalists to this day. 'We allowed government to lead us by the nose on the whole bush war,' van Deventer says. 'They allowed us to stay in the dark. They invited us to the front, and we had jolly parties, and when I see the criticism of the present generation, it pains me, because we went with those people and partied with them.'[60] Vosloo agrees with van Deventer's sentiments—'It was a tough time, and I'm not proud of what happened then'—although he adds that the potential repercussions of abrogating the Defense Act were a significant consideration. 'You risk your whole group by breaking the rules; otherwise you become a Bram Fischer,' he notes, referring to the noted Afrikaner lawyer who was imprisoned for his membership in the Communist Party and association with the ANC.[61] Dommisse seconds this sentiment, noting press group lawyers were very concerned with following the act, given the implications. Hence, 'The raids in the region, our reporting depended on what the Defense Force told us.'[62]

The Media and Foreign Affairs Before 1994: Little Impact Up or Down

Overall, press coverage of foreign affairs before 1994 took a back seat to domestic issues. 'By and large we failed to cover foreign events and foreign policy in any significant sense,' claims Rex Gibson of the *Cape Times* and *Rand Daily Mail*. 'Foreign affairs has always been relegated to a left hand page, inside the paper.'[63] English papers generally had more robust coverage of foreign issues, although this started declining by the 1970s. One reason for this was that South Africa's growing isolation and the growing affinity of white voters for the NP started to diminish their historical connections to Great Britain.[64] 'The *Star* had an ethos that front page news was foreign, with one core reason being that many readers regarded England as home,' recalls Tyson. 'That changed when I was editor, in the 1970s, and it had to change. That was old fashioned.'[65]

A handful of foreign issues were of interest to South African readers during this period. Rhodesia from its 1965 UDI was widely covered in the press, especially in English newspapers more strident in pushing support for the rebel government than their more cautious Afrikaans counterparts, which reflected the government line.[66] The war in Angola also was of great interest to readers, particularly when there were South African casualties. Occasionally, events in Europe—like the Prague Spring of 1968—would also generate readership, but these stories failed to hold reader interest for long. Overall, 'There wasn't a very robust foreign policy debate,' Dommisse says.[67]

The extent to which foreign policy stayed in the picture had a great deal to do with the openness of Foreign Minister (1977–94) Pik Botha, who enjoyed close personal ties to the media, both English and Afrikaans. Botha described both Cillié and *Rapport* editor Willem de Klerk as 'great friends of mine.' Botha was also close to Ries and Gerald Shaw, both of whom were university friends from the 1950s.[68] In general, the media loved Pik—as his biographer notes, 'Pik was always good for a story, and those stories often made the front page.'[69] 'He was an unusually accessible person,' remembers Fabricius. 'We in our office would ring Pik at home at 6 am, and he would take the call.'[70] Fabricius and Vosloo remember that Pik had few qualms about being quoted anonymously or leaking inside information.[71] That said, journalists from both sides of the linguistic divide understood that Pik's accessibility was about winning support for his political ambitions and, particularly for the English press, disseminating the government line internationally. 'Pik was sophisticated enough to try to court us, as he realized the way to get the message to the world was through the English press,' Fabricius notes.[72]

Despite Pik Botha's efforts to shape the media's foreign affairs reporting, however, it had little impact on a largely disinterested public. 'Foreign policy doesn't sell newspapers,' claims Ken Owen.[73] Van Deventer adds: 'I can't really think of foreign policy issues that got people interested. When local young lads were killed, that would be a lead story, but there wasn't really an uproar. It was a way of life [...] We'd always go for the local story over the foreign story.'[74] The stories that did boost circulation, he notes, tended to be 'soft' news—'things like the [British] royal family and Wimbledon.'[75] Given this lack of interest—and the expense of covering international stories—South Africa before 1994 had few foreign correspondents posted abroad, generally in Washington, New York, or London. Owen recalls that he was more or less alone during his 1969–77 tenure as a correspondent in Washington: 'The Afrikaans papers for most of the period I was in DC didn't have anyone.'[76]

Despite a system whereby Afrikaans editors were part and parcel of NP structures, their influence on foreign policy also was limited. Within the Party, while Cillié and others weighed in on domestic affairs, such as reform of the apartheid system, foreign policy issues were generally not raised in these venues.[77] With the possible exception of journalists working for the intelligence apparatus, communication between government and the press on foreign affairs issues was largely a one-way street. Although Owen and several other journalists said they had good relations with DFA principals like Pik, 'He didn't pick my brain,' Owen says.[78] Owen also cites what he describes as amateurish coverage of foreign affairs as another reason for this lack of impact: 'I used to go bonkers in Washington over the sheer lack of professionalism in publishing what I wrote, in putting smart assed Fleet Street headlines on serious stories. The result was that the bureaucrats didn't take you seriously.'[79]

The Press and Government after 1994: All Gloves Off

South African journalists were hardly unfamiliar with the new ANC government when it took power in April 1994. Liberal English and Afrikaans journalists had established contacts with the ANC in exile from the mid-1980s, and leaders like Thabo Mbeki were assiduous about keeping in touch with these journalists to ensure ANC policies were characterized properly in the press.[80] Familiarity, however, did not necessarily mean trust. The major press organizations remained largely white, and Afrikaans papers felt they were particularly distrusted by the ANC owing to their close relationship with the previous government. 'There was a great sensitivity about any kind of criticism, which was viewed as racist,' notes van Deventer, who retired in 1998 as chief executive officer (CEO) of Naspers' newspaper division.[81]

Nelson Mandela was an exception to this rule. 'Nothing can compare to the Mandela years,' says *Sunday Times* editor Mondli Makhanya. 'He would say, "Slam me, criticize me, whatever." There was much, much better access. When you went on trips with him, he always made time to say something for the journalists.'[82] Makhanya further recalled that Mandela would almost always brief the local press corps after receiving a foreign head of state. Mandela was open to interaction with all sorts of journalists and editors, no matter age, race, or language; Vosloo, by then managing director of Naspers, recalls traveling with the president several times and having him visit the group's Cape Town headquarters on a couple of occasions.[83] *Business Day* journalist and foreign editor Hopewell Radebe, who broke into journalism in 1994, said Mandela frequently gave access to junior writers like himself, much to the dismay of the bigger names.[84] Mandela also made sure that this openness filtered downward to his ministers and MPs. 'During the Mandela period, you could grab a minister in parliament in the concourse. You could just stand there and wait long enough,' Makhanya recalls.[85]

Mbeki's Deteriorating Relations with the Press

By all accounts, the tentative good will—or at least mutual tolerance—established between press and government during the Mandela years disappeared quickly under Mbeki.[86] Most journalists viewed Mbeki as genial and accessible to the press during his tenure as deputy president. 'I met Mbeki quite a few times,' Vosloo recalls. 'Mbeki was always very affable; he loved talking to editors. We reached out to him and he responded, but he became more remote over time.'[87] *Sowetan* and *Sunday Times* editor Mathatha Tsedu recalls traveling as part of a group of journalists with the then-deputy president on a 1998 trip to Asia. 'I flew with him, stayed at the same hotel, and in the evenings, there would be off the record briefings on the day, and what would happen tomorrow. Stuff that would not be for use was identified. It was great [...] we all had unlimited access.'[88] On another occasion that year, Mbeki put in front of journalists an organogram—possibly originating from the intelligence services—on the linkages between Zimbabwean businessman Billy Rautenbach and the ZANU-PF regime. 'He said, "You can't re-sketch this, but you can copy the information you can use,"' Tsedu says.[89]

The Asia trip, however, included an incident that foreshadowed the breakdown in Mbeki's relationship with the media. After one briefing, explains Tsedu, 'One guy took the information that was three times emphasized as off the record and filed the story. So, first thing, the rest of us got calls from our offices, "How could we miss the story?" And Mbeki blew his top, and he decided not to have any more evening sessions.'[90] Mbeki relented later in the trip, but the damage was done. Mbeki would never again show much trust for the local media, nor offer it much access. Tsedu says Mbeki and ministers would meet periodically with the local media under the auspices of the South African National Editors Forum, but these meetings were largely perfunctory and, aside from the first in 2001, poorly attended by cabinet.[91] Makhanya described a 2002 state visit to Cuba where, on the last day, Mbeki turned down an interview request by the handful of local media who had accompanied him on the trip. 'We were very pissed off, because we've traveled halfway across the world at great cost, and you at least want that appreciation that we're being taken seriously. If there was a time constraint, that's one thing, but the visit was over. He could have done it in 15 minutes.'[92] Several journalists chafed at the fact Mbeki was much more accessible to the foreign press than he was to them.

Interviewees raised several possible reasons for Mbeki's inaccessibility:

— *Hypersensitivity.* Several journalists speculated Mbeki's aversion to criticism pushed him away from the press; at one point in his administration, Mbeki simply stopped reading the local press for a time because he could not abide their critiques of his policies.[93] This hypersensitivity resembles that of PW Botha's, but whereas Botha would fire back at his critics, Mbeki ignored them altogether.

— *Micromanagement.* Another issue cited for Mbeki's hostility to the press was his desire to manage information and control the government's messaging much more tightly than did Mandela. Jan-Jan Joubert of *Die Burger* recalls the unsuccessful 2003 attempt to establish an official presidential press corps as an example of this desire to control the message; its creation would have used secrecy legislation to restrict the ability of its members to report on issues on which they'd been briefed on 'deep background,' much like Heard and Vorster.[94] Press opposition ultimately scotched it.

— *Mistrust.* In addition to issues around the unauthorized revelation of information, 'There was a view that the white liberal press was the mouthpiece of the opposition,' Tsedu notes. 'So, consequently, whatever you would say on, for example, the position on Myanmar, Thabo would say, "I don't have to listen to that, that's the DA's [opposition Democratic Alliance] view."'[95] Both black and white journalists suffered from this view.

— *Disrespect.* Particularly with regard to foreign affairs, journalists observed that Mbeki did not respect the judgment of journalists, especially given that newspapers devoted so little attention to foreign affairs. Tsedu recalls about Mbeki, 'He would say, "Under normal circumstances, you would assume the agricultural reporter has a background in agriculture, but when it comes to politics, people don't understand what they're trying to do" [. . .] that was Thabo's line.'[96]

— *No need.* Lastly, several journalists raised the issue that Mbeki simply had no need to cultivate a close relationship with the press. Whereas 72 percent of the (white) electorate in 1968 read a daily newspaper, that number today in a multiracial electorate is just 31 percent.[97] In addition, there was no publishing house or newspaper considered part of the ANC structure in the way that some Afrikaans newspapers were to the NP before 1994.

Whatever the reasons, space for the press to engage with government closed under Mbeki, from the Presidency on down. Whereas ministers were once accessible in parliament, 'The only time that happens now is after the budget or State of the Nation,' Makhanya notes.[98] Several journalists, of all races, noted that ministers, MPs, and other ANC politicians largely refused to go on the record in discussing government or Party business during Mbeki's time in office; 'They were shit scared of being quoted,' one says.[99]

The Foreign Affairs Freeze Out

Although officials in the Presidency recognized of foreign affairs coverage in newspapers like *Business Day* and the *Mail & Guardian*, Mbeki largely froze out journalists regarding foreign affairs.[100] Vosloo notes that: 'For foreign policy, what we get and what we report comes from leaks, from officials or contacts, that such and such is happening. They do briefings for the press, but it's what they want you to know. Pretty useless.'[101] This attitude filtered downward. Foreign Minister Nkosazana Dlamini-Zuma had, in the words of one journalist, a 'don't irritate me' mindset and had little time to interact with the press, thereby setting the tone for the rest of the department.[102] Deputy Minister Aziz Pahad was a saving grace for journalists, however, establishing a weekly briefing for the press that he usually delivered. 'Aziz was great,' says Makhanya, although he adds that Pahad 'was very careful about pushing the line' in these generally unenlightening press conferences.[103] Still, 'You always showed up; you didn't want to not be there the one time something juicy came out of it!'[104] Fabricius says Pahad, unlike the minister, would take journalists' phone calls and, on occasion, invite them to off-the-record briefings on various issues.[105] Journalists describe Presidency Director-General Frank Chikane and DFA Director-General Ayanda Ntsaluba as two other candid officials, although more off the record than on.

In the view of journalists and editors who covered foreign affairs, the government's lack of interaction with them on foreign policy represented a missed opportunity. 'They did not get out their story on Zimbabwe,' says Makhanya, who adds, 'Every official you spoke to had a different story about why we took our position on Zimbabwe.'[106] Everyone would speak off the record about it, but the government struggled to formally frame its message. One journalist recalls Mbeki saying in an off-the-record briefing around 2003 that Zimbabwe was a very difficult situation; another notes that a senior cabinet minister told him (also off the record) Pretoria's strategy was to wait for Mugabe to die.[107] Makhanya argues that government missed an opportunity to sell its success stories: 'Their work on the continent, that was a story they never got to tell. Burundi was an incredible achievement. DRC, I don't think it will ever be a success, but the relative stabilization was something on which they played a massive role. But it could have been done a hell of a lot better, not just with the South African media but internationally.'[108]

Reflecting on his department's communication with the press, Pahad admits that the DFA and the government writ large could have done a better job keeping the doors open but expressed frustration with the quality of press coverage of foreign affairs, particularly by younger reporters. 'The young ones are learning. You'd do a briefing, and they can't conceptualize what you are saying. We'd start sending transcripts, including the Q&As. But, even then you found they didn't understand, and the few who understood would give a twist to what you were saying,' he notes.[109] He singled out as notable exceptions in the print media Fabricius and Radebe, who were able to analyze and dissect external issues.

Selling Foreign Affairs to a (Still) Disinterested Public
Despite—or perhaps because of—the end of South Africa's international isolation, foreign affairs remained a tough sell for newspapers that, due to broadly declining circulation, faced increasing pressure to cut costs. 'You'll never sell your front page story on foreign affairs unless it's the collapse of Zimbabwe,' Makhanya says. 'People aren't really engaged.'[110] Vosloo echoes this sentiment, broadening it to political issues on the whole: 'A big

scandal may get you a few [extra sales], but sensation and sport sell. If the [Pretoria rugby] Blue Bulls win, you'll sell 30,000 more papers.'[111] Tsedu adds that the often slow-moving nature of foreign developments is another strike against their marketability: '[Sales] would peak when there were horrendous chapters of Mugabe's rule, and with each tick you would have huge increases. But now, until Mugabe's dead, there won't be great demand. Generally, it's just more of the same thing [. . .] a story on Myanmar will never sell on a front page.'[112]

Given that lack of focus, newspapers in the past decade have devoted fewer resources to covering foreign affairs, cutting already limited coverage to the bone. Only a few newspaper groups have foreign editors, the most prominent of whom is Independent's Fabricius, who adds, 'I don't know if they'd replace me when I retire.'[113] He adds that the Independent Group—which publishes the *Cape Times* and *Star*, among others—currently has no full-time person abroad, meaning, 'We've lost the South African perspective on things.'[114] Naspers had only a correspondent in Brussels during Mbeki's tenure. This lack of a unique perspective means foreign editors are left with wire services, making the position, in the words of former *Die Burger* foreign affairs editor Jannie Ferreira, 'largely a cut and paste job.'[115] Nevertheless, print journalism remains where the action is on foreign affairs. Despite its decreasing attention, notes Tsedu, 'The print press gives you the real coverage. With radio, you get headlines. Stations like SAFM may choose to make it an "After 8" debate, bringing in a few of the experts to analyze the issues with some level of intelligence. But if you want to find something that covers an issue with some level of sophistication, then it's only the print press.'[116]

Conclusion: Press Never a Foreign Policy Player

Specifically regarding foreign policy, South Africa's print press—past and present—has had little impact in influencing public opinion or convincing policymakers to change policy tacks. As noted in the previous chapter, the South African public generally does not care much about the country's foreign policy or events beyond its borders. The press, in an effort to sell newspapers and advertising, takes note of this and adjusts its coverage accordingly. For government, because the press does not provide much coverage of foreign affairs and has little influence on the reading public, the media voice is muted, allowing government decision-makers to ignore calls from the media to pursue particular foreign policies. This was as much the case before 1994 as it was under Mandela and Mbeki. This press influence was even further limited after 1994 by South Africa's openness to the world. Unlike Vorster, Mbeki had no need to cultivate the local press (particularly the English-language press) to sell South African policies to the world; his willingness to prioritize talking to foreign journalists before local ones clearly displays the South African media's marginality.

The media's influence post-1994 was also circumscribed by the lack of a 'loyal' press, particularly in the print sphere. The NP always had its stable of 'party organ' newspapers that it could use to sell its policies, but also take the pulse of Afrikanerdom. The ANC has no such thing, and this was reflected by the deep-seated suspicion of the press by Mbeki and others within the ANC. Private access to the president and senior officials has been severely limited, and there was no development of an 'insider' relationship between certain journalists and senior ANC officials; even personal connections between some black journalists and ANC leaders appear to have been tempered by their affiliations with media groups viewed as white and opposition-aligned. Ultimately, on all matters of policy, foreign and domestic, the press has never been an influential body, and looks to be even less so in the future.

CHAPTER 5

ACADEMIA

One might regard the inclusion of subject matter experts—either independent or affiliated with a university or think tank—in a discussion about participatory foreign policy as out of place. Few entities could be considered more elite and unrepresentative of a populace, given the specialized nature of academic study and debate. Such experts however constitute a voice that cannot be ignored, in terms of 'downward' influence on the populace and other non-government actors and 'upward' impact on the policymakers themselves. They find themselves called upon not only by government, but also by the press, pressure groups, and business interests to advise and educate.

This chapter will explore how academics, pre- and post-1994, have influenced the foreign policy debate in South Africa, especially among principal foreign policy decision-makers. Specifically, it will seek to answer whether these principals consulted subject matter experts and, if so, the mechanisms by which this consultation occurred. It also will identify influential policy experts, under Mbeki and his predecessors, and why they had access and consideration. For purposes of examining this question, this chapter will examine academic influence on foreign policy during three specific epochs: pre-1990, the 1990–4 transition period, and post-1994.

Academic Impact on Foreign Policy Until 1990

The study of 'international affairs'—a mix of academic disciplines that includes political science, history, economics, geography, and military strategy—received scant attention in South Africa before the mid-1970s. University academic departments offered some courses dealing in history, geography, and politics, but these were heavily Eurocentric. Africa, in particular, was ignored, with not more than a dozen South African academics studying Africa north of the Limpopo in the mid-1960s.[1] The University of the Witwatersrand, through its Jan Smuts Chair in International Relations, was the first tertiary institute to offer a separate course in international affairs, although this did not come until 1962.[2] The first chair, British academic Ben Cockram, designed the curriculum, which former student—and later leading strategic studies scholar—Deon Fourie remembers as focused more on military and strategic issues than diplomacy.[3] Given inattention, it is unsurprising, as Ned Munger noted in his seminal 1965 work *Notes on the Formation of South African Foreign Policy* that intellectuals were 'well removed from the formation of (foreign) policy.'[4]

Key Institutional Actors

Before the mid-1970s, only two non-academic institutions, or 'think tanks,' focused on external affairs. The Africa Institute of South Africa (AISA) was established by parliamentary statute in 1960 to promote the study of African affairs as well as public awareness of the continent. This status provided it with government funding (which continues through Mbeki's administration) and, to an extent, government business through the commissioning of reports. As Munger noted, however, these services during AISA's early years were 'primarily fact producing and not policymaking,' such as its compilation of the country's finest African studies library.[5] As former Executive Director (1994–9) Denis Venter—who joined AISA in 1979—remembers, the Institute was 'more or less a government mouthpiece' until the late 1970s, when it began to hoe a more independent road.[6]

Founded in 1934 in Cape Town by a group of (predominantly English-speaking) politicians, journalists, and academics, the South

African Institute of International Affairs (SAIIA) was the only independent body devoted to the study of foreign affairs. It operated, however, more as an elite club and library than an academic body in its early years, not producing a paper until 1945.[7] The quantity and quality of its production improved significantly after 1967, when former Foreign Service officer John Barratt took over as national director. Funding came almost exclusively from the English business community, and in particular from Anglo-American; SAIIA's liberal, and increasingly progressive, worldview was much in sync with that of its patrons.[8]

South Africa from the late 1960s saw significant growth in the number of scholars and institutions focusing on aspects of international affairs, particularly from a defense and security optic. The perception of a military threat from the Soviet Union helped bolster government demand for academic outputs, particularly from the SADF, as well as interest by students. Centers dealing with 'strategic studies' were established at the University of South Africa (UNISA), Rand Afrikaans University (RAU), and the University of Pretoria (with its Institute for Strategic Studies (ISSUP), established in 1977, the most prominent and long lasting), while Potchefstroom set up a Center for International Politics.[9] A burgeoning interest in the Soviet Union helped launch the Institute for the Study of Marxism (renamed the Institute for Soviet Studies in 1983) at Stellenbosch, as well as the Russian Studies department at Wits.[10] Even less strategically important parts of the world merited institutes, such as UNISA's Center for Latin American Studies, founded in 1984.[11]

The relationship between these institutions and government is not entirely clear, even now. Some observers said that they were little more than government fronts, designed to endorse South African policies with a veneer of scholarship in exchange for government funds.[12] After the 'Muldergate' Information Department scandal broke in 1978, it was revealed in parliament that the centers at Potchefstroom and Pretoria had both received covert funding from the Department of Information.[13] Covert financing continued, however. Philip Nel, head of the Stellenbosch Institute for Soviet Studies from 1983 to 1992, admits that his institute received funding from Military Intelligence (MI). 'MI approached us and said they would fund us to the tune of R50,000 a year for three years, because we wanted to appoint another analyst,' Nel recalls. 'The university top brass knew about the MI funding and blessed it; it was to pay for an academic, not any sort of propaganda.'[14] Funding for institutions from National Intelligence also was widely rumored, although never proved. Niel Barnard said that the National Intelligence Service (NIS) had 'an operational understanding' with 'centers of excellence with knowledge on threats to our national security,' but did not elaborate further.[15]

That said, academics at these centers bristle at allegations that their government funding compromised their independence. Nel—who like many political scientists served his military obligation in MI and maintained contact through his reserve duties—maintains that his work at the center allowed him to influence the debate in a way that otherwise would not have been possible as an outsider.[16] Furthermore, the funding received was small compared with what was necessary for operating budgets, and it dried up after the early 1980s. The institute at Pretoria, longtime director Mike Hough recalls, ran on fumes from the time he started in 1979, surviving on fees from conferences and journal articles; even his directorship of ISSUP was a part-time job in addition to departmental duties. 'For funding,' he claimed, 'we were on our own.'[17] Nearly all of the centers and academic departments with an international focus during this period were small affairs; none had more than a handful of researchers.

By the time of the transition, South Africa had developed a small, but capable, group of academics devoted to the study of international affairs and strategic studies. SAIIA during this period was a particularly fertile ground for developing experts, turning out leading analysts like Deon Geldenhuys, Andre du Pisani, and Peter Vale, while other bright stars (notably Deon Fourie at UNISA and Gerrit Olivier at Pretoria) were dotted around the academic landscape. Journals like ISSUP's *Strategic Studies* and the South African Association of Political Studies publication *Politikon* included articles on various aspects of international affairs, including

South African foreign policymaking. While the quality of work on issues and regions of the world with minimal strategic interest for South Africa was a mixed bag, work focusing on the southern Africa sub-region tended to be high quality.

Limited High-Level Interaction, but more at Working Level

Academics—individually and institutionally—had varying degrees of access to the government before 1990, owing to a mix of factors including seniority of officials, personal relations, utility of the interaction for the officials, and ethnicity. At the most senior levels of the Presidency and DFA, however, this access was limited. The only head of state before 1990 who paid even some attention to academic outputs was PW Botha, who occasionally met with groups of academics (albeit not solely focused on foreign policy), approvingly cited the work of Wits professor (and Jan Smuts Chair) Dirk Kunert, and found time to excoriate Deon Geldenhuys in parliament for perceived inaccuracies in his work. Otherwise, interviewees say neither Foreign Ministers Hilgard Muller (1964–77) nor Pik Botha (1977–94) had much interaction with foreign affairs experts. Pik in an interview vaguely implied that he met with academics, but offered no specifics.* Others were outright dismissive of academic inputs; Deputy Foreign Minister (1984–6) Louis Nel bluntly stated, 'I never paid attention to academics. You know what I read? Newspapers, and telexes from our missions around the world.'[18]

At the working levels of government (specifically the DFA), there was more back and forth with outside experts, although it was haphazard and slow to develop. Munger noted in 1965, for example, that the head of AISA, a government-funded body, had not met the DFA's Africa section head, even after the latter had been on the job for two years.[19] This lack of interaction appeared to stem largely from disinterest by the DFA in what academics had to say. As longtime diplomat Donald Sole remembers, 'In my time at head office [in the 1960s], there was no great confidence in any of the institutes.'[20] Interviews with academics and diplomats trace the origin of semi-regular contact to the mid-1970s, when the DFA began calling on experts for training purposes and, in some instances, for individual consultations on specific issues. However, such outreach was more the exception than the rule, dependent on personal initiative and relationships (such as with former professors from university).

By the late 1970s and through the 1980s, these interactions became more regular. Nel remembers attending semi-regular ('maybe once a year') conferences between academics and the DFA; even Director-General Neil van Heerden would attend.[21] Barnard's sudden elevation from political science professor to NIS chief in 1979 also sparked more regular interaction between the civilian intelligence service and academia: 'We would have a conference at the time on something like the fighting in Angola, and we'd invite people from Stellenbosch and the Africa Institute to discuss it with us,' he remembered.[22] Such sessions could be contentious. 'There was one session [around 1988] that even NIS invited a bunch of academics to give talks on Marxism, revolutionary politics, and the like,' recalled Nel. 'It was Willie Esterhuyse, myself, Anton van Niekerk, the current head of philosophy at Stellenbosch. I remember saying that the SACP should be unbanned, and several NIS guys got up and walked out.'[23]

Overall, however, these interactions led to more dead ends than breakthroughs. Several academics recounted submitting papers to the DFA for comment and never hearing back; others would attend seminars or hold seemingly productive meetings with DFA contacts, but have them come to nothing.[24] Both Olivier and Deon Geldenhuys recall making submissions to the DFA in the early 1980s on the idea of creating an academic advisory council on foreign affairs; nothing came of it. For academics, government was a black box—after making their inputs, they had no insights into whether their ideas were given any consideration.

Academic Engagement with the Military: A Sharp Contrast
While academic interaction with executive decision-makers, the DFA, and NIS was inconsistent, the SADF and Department of Defense provided more fertile ground for engagement. Defense interaction with academics, particularly those studying military strategy, dates to the mid-1960s, after the 1961 declaration of

republic forced the SADF—still at that stage a semi-professional military—to take on responsibility for defense strategy and planning.[25] Much of the credit for this enhanced interaction can be ascribed to Lieutenant General Allan 'Pop' Fraser, who served as army chief (1966–7) and joint operations commander (1967–73). Fraser in the early 1960s authored a document, *Lessons Learnt from Past Revolutionary Wars*, which was one of the first serious treatments of counter-insurgency to come out of the Defense Force and one that would inform military leadership's thinking on the subject through the 1980s.[26] Fraser, who had recently returned as defense attaché to France, drew heavily upon the writings of French military theorist Andre Beaufre, who originally coined the term 'Total Strategy' to explain the multi-faceted nature of combating revolutionary insurgency.[27] Beaufre—who visited South Africa in the late 1960s—emphasized that military force was not enough to combat insurgency; psychological, diplomatic, and economic levers had to be used as well.[28] Furthermore, these actions had to be complemented by government reforms that addressed combatant grievances.[29]

Seeing the need for greater exposure of established and emerging SADF leaders to Beaufre's concepts of military strategy, Fraser in 1968 called upon Ben Cockram from Wits and his former student, UNISA professor and reserve officer Deon Fourie, to undertake a series of seminars on counter-insurgency strategy. Fourie's 1968 work *War Potentials of the African States South of the Sahara* was one of the first academic applications of Beaufre's principles to Africa, and he would be a frequent contributor to the SADF journal *Paratus* through the 1970s.[30] The first lecture at the Defense Staff College, in October of that year, was to a select group of officers from around Pretoria and Johannesburg, including the chiefs of Defense Staff, Army Staff, and MI, as well as the Director of Plans.[31] The commandant of the college, then Colonel Constandt Viljoen—SADF Chief from 1980–5—was also in attendance.[32] The lecture—which in Fourie's words broke down Beaufre's principles into 'digestible and usable chunks'—was a success with the top brass, and led to a more in-depth seminar the following December attended by nearly all of the top military leadership.[33]

Fourie's seminars morphed over the next decade into what became a regular interaction between officers at the services' staff courses, as well as the Defense College staff course for officers aspiring to brigadier. These courses continued to focus heavily on counter-insurgency strategy, invoking the works of Beaufre alongside those of American Colonel John McCuen and British expert Sir Robert Thompson, although they consequently branched out beyond military strategy, covering political and economic issues as well, such as US and Soviet foreign policy.[34] Almost all lecturers came from outside the military, although South African diplomats taught certain segments.[35] According to Fourie, by the end of the 1980s there were more than 300 lecturers cleared to teach military courses.[36] Many came from Afrikaans-medium universities like Stellenbosch and RAU or think tanks like the Terrorism Research Center and ISSUP.[37]

Relations were not always smooth. Fourie recalls being dropped from the lecture circuit for several years for disagreeing too strongly with the military brass, failing to acknowledge the bureaucratic politics that drove the leadership's decisionmaking.[38] Another problematic issue was the vein of anti-intellectualism that flowed through certain segments of the service, particularly skepticism of theoretical models and their applicability to local conditions.[39] Fourie remembers a particular chief of defense staff being skeptical of his seminars. 'I remember General van der Reit, who was a decorated officer, said, "Cockram's wasting our time." Soldiers wanted a drill book, an answer, and that's why they can't win insurgency wars, because they have to think. Fraser said, "He's educating us," and van der Reit said, "We don't have time to be educated."'[40]

Eventually, this exposure to academics helped develop openness to outside expertise and new ideas that were not seen in other parts of government. Some senior officers could be considered *bona fide* intellectuals, notably former Director of Strategy Major General John Huyser, author of the military's voluminous strategy document dubbed the 'Green Monster.'[41] While the majority did not have the same intellectual skills, most recognized the gaps in their knowledge and actively sought out those who could fill them, no matter what the rank or experience. Author, analyst, and longtime reserve officer Helmoed Heitman remembers being asked by SADF chief (1985–90) General Jannie Geldenhuys whether he thought there was a conventional threat to South Africa; his 140-page response was turned into a training document for the SADF. 'They often went out and would say, "OK, we don't know a lot about this subject, let's find the expert and bring him in,"' he notes.[42] Geldenhuys in particular was open to outside interaction with academics, notably using Soviet expert Jan du Plessis to strategize on how to counter the perceived Soviet military threat in the region. Although he is careful not to overstate their influence on policymaking, Geldenhuys said that unless the issue was controversial, he encouraged his officers to use outside expertise whenever they could.[43]

At the top levels—with the exception of Geldenhuys—however, the military leadership seldom consulted with academic outsiders informally. Fourie was privy to some conversations, but as a Reserve Force officer (retiring as a brigadier general) he was considered inside the circle of trust. Hough remembers occasionally being invited to some meetings with other academics and being asked about some aspects of policy, but not often.[44] ISSUP otherwise would provide a platform for military leaders to give speeches or publish in its journal, but this was an outward flow of information from them rather than an openness to academic inputs.[45] That said, the access to officers from a relatively junior level helped facilitate a unique relationship between academics and the military brass. They may not have always operationalized their coursework, but they at least knew it was out there, and those who reached top leadership positions, in particular, had sufficient external exposure to know where to go for advice.

The Importance of Who You Are and Who You Know

In terms of interacting with government, not all academics were created equal—much depended on one's personal connections, politics, and ethnicity. SAIIA's government interactions are an excellent case in point. Munger famously wrote in 1965 that SAIIA's political worldview gave it the same influence on the Verwoerd government as the ultra-conservative John Birch Society had on Lyndon Johnson's Democratic administration in the United States.[46] From an institutional standpoint, this view held more or less true through the 1980s—SAIIA was largely excluded from organized government symposia and did not have research commissioned by government departments, as did the Africa Institute. The latter was a moot point, as SAIIA under John Barratt steadfastly refused to take government (or foreign) money, a stance that made it heavily dependent on its business funders.[47]

Barratt's personal connections within the DFA—not to mention respect for SAIIA's products within the department—allowed the Institute to retain a foothold of access with working-level officials.[48] 'Barratt had come out of the service, and he had a close personal relationship with these people,' close friend Peter Vale remembers. 'They were dinner-party pals. Informal networks were crucial to the work of Barratt and the Institute. It seemed to me that he never crossed the road between one world and the other. With academics he saw himself as a diplomat, and vice versa. He kept this dual personality his whole life.'[49] These connections allowed Barratt entrée to certain segments of the department throughout the 1970s and 1980s, although these were not necessarily the parts that mattered. As Vale notes, 'He was close to [senior DFA official Jeremy] Shearer and [veteran diplomat] Don Sole and people like that, but I don't think he had an influence on policy.'[50] As for the real powers in the Department, Vale notes, 'He didn't have a good relationship with [longtime Director-General] Brand Fourie. He was not close to Pik.'[51]

As Barratt's case illustrates, a mixture of personal ties, ideology, institutional affiliation, and ethnicity was a key determinant of whether an academic would be included in discussions. Barratt was a rarity in that his personal connections helped him overcome his detriments. Few other academics had such luck. As Vale notes, 'I was considered by many in DFA to be sympathetic to, if not a member of, the ANC. From the time I returned from the UK as a student in 1977, even though I was at the International Institute of Strategic Studies, they never tapped into me [...] I was never once even invited to a cocktail party.'[52] With regard to academic institutions, professors from Afrikaans-medium institutions had a leg up on their English colleagues. According to Garth Shelton of Wits, 'You'd find scholars divided into Afrikaans and English speaking universities, the former tending to be sympathetic and the latter critical. I can never remember being invited to anything before 1994, and I was at Wits ten years before that. You would see DFA folks at general conferences, but they would never ask our opinions. Most of the time they just expected it to be critical.'[53]

Meanwhile, academics at Stellenbosch, RAU, Pretoria, and Free State had more privileged access. As with certain privileged institutes, such access led to questions in many contemporary accounts about the independence of their academic views, although Afrikaner academics interviewed for this study contested such allegations. While the Africa Institute was alleged to have changed its views to suit government orthodoxy, Venter cited several examples where government departments complained that the Africa Institute's work was not suitably sympathetic.[54] He also contends that longtime director Erich Leistner consistently backed his researchers in conducting independent research.[55] Not all Afrikaner academics were sympathetic to government views, and many were unafraid of voicing such opinions. Nel, for example, said he would use the access given to him to provide a counterpoint to orthodox views on Soviet expansionism, a line his government interlocutors did not always want to hear.[56]

Overly dissident academics, English and Afrikaans alike, were subject to government harassment, petty and otherwise. In one egregious case, Vale—then president of the South African Political Science Association—had his passport cancelled in the 1980s.[57] England-born Sara Pienaar, a Soviet expert who later served as SAIIA national director, was told that her request for a security clearance was refused, preventing her from lecturing at a military course.[58] Promotion prospects could be limited for being overly outspoken in public.[59] The state-owned media could also blackball academics if they spouted analysis countering that of the government. Deon Fourie recalled the following anecdote:

Once, there was a rumor that the USSR was selling MiG-29s to
Zimbabwe, and I told an interviewer from SABC that the
USSR never gave new stuff to the 3rd World, so I doubted it
was true. That evening I listened to the news at five, and it said
Malan said this kind of sale was typical. The only thing they
used from my recording was a section on what happens if it
really does eventuate, nothing that gave my opinion. Then I
was dumped by the SABC entirely. A year later around
Christmas, the USSR invaded Afghanistan, and the same guy
phoned me, and said, 'I'm sorry to use you, but no one else is in
town!' He actually confessed that I was blackballed.[60†]

Were Academics Useful for Government?
While several former government officials noted that they
appreciated the specialized knowledge and expertise of academics,
they also said that general academic incomprehension of how
government works limited their utility.[61] While Barnard said
academics were useful in exposing his people to different views,
ensuring NIS did not succumb to 'tunnel vision' in its analysis, he
further complained that professors 'tend to talk too long, have an
academic view of things, and don't understand the challenges of
government. They believe that if you analyze the situation, the
solution will come down from the heavens. They don't understand
that mortal people are involved in the decisions.'[62] Former UN
Permanent Representative and Director-General in the Presidency
Dave Steward shared another anecdote highlighting academic
disconnection from government:

I remember going to a lecture presided over by one of the
luminaries in the academic sphere on international relations.
He had a chart—inputs here, bureaucrats here, business, all
feeds into policy formulation, being fed back to parliament,
then to the DG, and then the minister, cabinet, gets
reformulated and comes out as policy! I stood up and said,
'Do you know how policy is made in DFA?' He looked at me
aghast. And I said, 'It's like this. I'd been working with some of

the top structures while down at parliament, Brand Fourie and them. The way it works is that the secretary, Fourie, is very difficult to find. He speaks only to the next echelon, and he doesn't like any of them. But he's the only one who takes decision. So the real way policy is made is that anyone who wants anything done will try to butter up his elephantine secretary to see if you can get an appointment. Inevitably he cannot. So what he does is to wait in an anteroom with his pet project until the secretary wants to go to the loo. And he follows him down the passage. While the secretary is peeing, foreign policy is made. I'm not joking; this is what happens.'[63]

Several academics acknowledged that their lack of access to classified information and facts on breaking developments limited their contributions. Despite this, they bemoaned perceived diplomatic arrogance in not using them in a more systematic way. While acknowledging that 'ivory tower academics are too far removed to make a difference,' Deon Geldenhuys also opined 'the flip side is that some bureaucrats could become very self-satisfied and arrogant and think they knew the ways of the world because they were at the coalface.'[64] Both academics and government officials bemoaned the lack of a 'revolving door' system, as exists in the United States, which would have allowed academics the opportunity to enter government for a period of time.

Overstating Influence: The Case of Deon Geldenhuys

Several accounts written during the 1980s ascribe to certain academics and institutions significant influence on foreign policy, but in retrospect these articles—often written by non-South African analysts with little firsthand knowledge—appear to have overstated their impact. The case of SAIIA analyst and longtime RAU (now University of Johannesburg) political science professor Deon Geldenhuys is an illustrative case in point. Geldenhuys during the early 1980s published two articles on South Africa's strategic options in the region, 'Some Strategic Implications of Regional Economic Relations for the Republic of South Africa' (1981) and 'The

Destabilization Controversy: An Analysis of a High-Risk Foreign Policy Option for South Africa' (1982), both of which received wide notice outside South Africa given that they coincided with Pretoria's burgeoning cross-border military operations. Geldenhuys in 1984 then published his book, *The Diplomacy of Isolation*, which remains the gold standard for studies of South Africa's pre-transition foreign policy.

These publications brought Geldenhuys notoriety in academic circles outside South Africa. One 1985 piece (co-written by future Trade and Industry Minister Rob Davies, then attached to Mozambique's Eduardo Mondlane University) called Geldenhuys 'one of the Botha regime's leading consultants on foreign policy issues.'[65] British academic Joseph Hanlon in his 1986 book *Beggar Your Neighbors: Apartheid Power in Southern Africa* referred to Geldenhuys as a 'major theoretician of destabilization' and claims that the professor was 'close to at least some of the National Party strategists and ideologists.' Hanlon further postulated that Geldenhuys could emerge as 'a future Henry Kissinger or [US Assistant Secretary of State for Africa, 1981–8] Chester Crocker,' emerging from academia to make policy.[66]

A quarter century later, Geldenhuys can laugh at the allegations that he 'more or less single-handedly devised the destabilization of Africa from the Limpopo to the Mediterranean.' It was less of a laughing matter during the 1980s, however, when—fearing ramifications for his academic career—he sought legal advice in Great Britain on how to refute the allegations, backing off only due to the prohibitive price. In reality, according to Geldenhuys, 'I was never, not once, asked by someone in DFA or the military or intelligence or any organ of state to come talk to them, much less advise them on any aspect of foreign policy,' with occasional lecturing at the military staff college his sole government interaction.[67] As for the senior leaders he was supposedly advising, Geldenhuys claims he only met Magnus Malan and Pik Botha once each during the 1980s, when he interviewed them (fruitlessly) for *Diplomacy*, and never met PW Botha. Geldenhuys asserts that he was never told by anyone in government that his writings were in any way influential.

To back up his assertion that he had no inside track, Geldenhuys cites the flak he received from PW Botha and others over his publications. 'When *Diplomacy* was published, he took me to task in parliament for what I had written. In typical PW style, he tried to ridicule me, citing passages of the book dealing with the SSC. His point was that, "How can you take this author seriously if this is the kind of crap he produces?" So if I had been this important figure, you'd figure PW would have known of me, and I would have been in and out of the corridors of power, which I've never been.' A 1983 *Politikon* article by Geldenhuys and Hennie Kotzé about decisionmaking in the State Security Council brought further government enmity. He recalls being called out by the State Security Council secretary: 'He gave us a dressing down! He was furious. And after this article, I'd written an op-ed for the *Sunday Times*, and he was waving that at us, having highlighted the offensive passages. Again, if I had been this influential advisor/architect, why would this guy do this?'[68]

One can postulate that Geldenhuys, and other academics who made similar assertions about their limited access and influence, are lying about their roles in the equation. It would behoove those still working in South Africa to understate their ties to the old government. The similarity of findings among academics and decision-makers, however, suggests that outside experts truly did not have meaningful impact on high-level foreign policymaking before 1990. No academic claimed anything beyond incidental contact with decision-makers, or significant 'back channel' ties to the working levels. More significantly, none of the decision-makers themselves gave much credence to the role of academics as a key influence. Certain articles may have been glanced at in passing or excerpted by an assistant, but not to any lasting effect.

Why was this impact so limited? Several interviewees cited the fast pace of government and South Africa's war footing from the 1970s. As Barnard explains, 'In intelligence, you don't have the luxury of a long, peaceful period. You have to make decisions on the run. I always explained to people that, "Do you think Napoleon had time for consultations at the Battle of Austerlitz?" It doesn't work that way.'[69] Decisionmaking in all departments was ad hoc, influenced on a daily basis by events that in many cases were beyond the South African Government's control. When policy is reactive rather than proactive, considered academic inputs by their nature have only so much scope for impact. This seems to have been the overarching reason for academia's light footprint before 1990.

Experts' Newfound Influence During the Transition

South Africa's transition to majority rule, sparked by FW de Klerk's 2 February 1990 speech announcing the unbanning of the ANC and release of Nelson Mandela, upset a host of long-extant dynamics in the country, and the relationship between government and academia was no exception. Academics between 1990 and 1994 had unprecedented influence on and access to the ANC and government in shaping the foreign policy of a democratic South Africa. This period introduced into the mix a host of new academic actors, individuals and institutions, while others departed the scene.

The Roots of ANC-Academic Foreign Policy Interaction

Interaction between the ANC in exile and South African foreign policy academics was minimal until the 1980s. The nature of the ANC's international outreach until that time—largely focused on isolating the apartheid government and simply surviving—did not necessitate a deep interaction with academics on topics like South Africa's post-apartheid foreign policy; there would be time for that later. The ANC had, however, a small but highly competent group of foreign affairs experts like Thabo Mbeki and Pallo Jordan, as well as academics like Davies. In addition, ANC Department of International Affairs (DIA) and Department of Information officials were clearly aware of academic outputs from South Africa, incorporating them into their own analytical products. One 1984 document, ascribed to the Research Unit of the Department of Information and Publicity, called 'Apartheid Distabilisation [sic]: Pretoria's Regional Strategy' cited Geldenhuys in its analysis of South African regional policy.[70] The author's review of other internal analytical documents on such topics as US and Soviet foreign policies further displayed a sophisticated understanding of international affairs.

Emerging contact between white South Africans and ANC officials during the 1980s—such as the secret talks between Willie Esterhuyse and ANC leaders that helped kick off the negotiations toward majority rule—created the space for increased interaction between South African foreign policy academics and ANC officials, at conferences in Europe and throughout the region. Vale remembers attending seminars in the mid-1980s in Mozambique and Zimbabwe where he was able to discuss external issues, like the future of the sub-region, with ANC officials like Mbeki and Mac Maharaj.[71] These contacts led to more in-depth talks by 1988 in Lusaka, where Vale and ANC DIA officials like Mbeki, Yusuf Saloojee, and Josiah Jele discussed the need for an ANC-aligned think tank to help inform its thinking on foreign affairs.[72]

Attention to academic outputs did not come solely from the ANC in exile, as Sara Pienaar of SAIIA recounts:

About 1986, after Gorbachev came to office, the USSR started getting a lot of attention, and I did a lot of media work. And one day, we got a handwritten envelope with a funny, cramped sort of writing from Pollsmoor jail. And it said, 'Dear Dr. Pienaar, I have listened to you and Dr. John Barratt with interest in your broadcasts, and I found this very illuminating. As you may know, I'm a political prisoner and my means are very small, but would it be possible for you to send me your publications? Signed NR Mandela.' Of course, John said we've got to be careful this isn't the government trying to mess us around. We took the letter to George Bizos; he was digging in his garden one Saturday morning, and he said it was real. So we started sending Mandela for everything we produced, and we got a letter from him later thanking us. I think he was looking for some understanding of whether the USSR would keep supporting the ANC.[73]

Shaping a New Foreign Policy ...

The ANC's February 1990 unbanning and the subsequent return of its Lusaka-based leadership touched off a heady four-year period during which time academics had a significant ability to weigh in on South Africa's future foreign policy. There was a quick realization by the ANC leadership that while the Freedom Charter and subsequent ANC documents contained some general foreign policy guidelines, such as solidarity with liberation movements, South Africa's reemergence into the international community meant the soon-to-be government had to take policy positions on a host of issues, necessitating inputs from outside experts.[74] By early 1991, the ANC's DIA commenced a series of meetings between their officials and prominent South African academics on the tenets of a post-transition foreign policy.[75] The core group of ANC officials and academics was a small one. From the ANC side, Mbeki was intimately involved; remembers Vale, even though 'Thabo didn't come to all of the meetings, his spirit was always there.'[76] Participants recalled other key players as Aziz Pahad; DIA spokesman Stanley Mabizela; DIA members Saloojee, Frene Ginwala, and Mavivi Myakayaka-Manzini; and a handful of other more junior officials who came and went as needed.[77]

Vale, who founded the Center for Southern African Studies (CSAS) at the University of Western Cape (UWC) in 1990, was tasked by Mbeki to lead the academic group.[78] CSAS colleague Rob Davies accompanied him; Anthoni van Nieuwkerk and Gary van Staden of SAIIA; John Daniel, recently returned from exile and at University of Durban-Westville; Vincent Maphai of UWC; and Maxi Schoeman of RAU.[79] With the exception of Maphai, the makeup of the academic component was largely white, although then-junior non-white academics like Vasu Gounden, Sipho Maseko, and Hussein Solomon also were involved in some discussions.[80] Most of these participants were ideologically on the same page, largely espousing an 'idealist' rather than a 'realist' or 'liberal' foreign policy outlook. However, the latter group, of whom Barratt could be considered the most prominent member, was afforded opportunities to weigh in on policy at public seminars and closed meetings.[81]

These discussions had several aims. They addressed prosaic issues, such as how to get training for ANC diplomats that would help them integrate into a new DFA and how to establish the previously mentioned ANC think tank.[82] This emerged in 1995 as the Foundation (later Institute) for Global Dialogue. However, the primary aim of the discussions was to devise a paper stating the tenets of ANC foreign policy.[83] Vale took the lead in drafting this document, which after consultations with fellow academics and civil society groups, emerged in October 1993 as 'Foreign Policy in a New Democratic South Africa: A Discussion Paper.'[84] This document stated, among its seven principles, that the ANC would emphasize human rights as a hallmark of South Africa's post-transition foreign policy and that it would prioritize southern Africa and the broader continent in its outreach.[85]

This discussion document provided the framework for the December 1993 article in American journal *Foreign Affairs* entitled 'South Africa's Future Foreign Policy,' credited to Nelson Mandela.[86] After the ANC signed off on the idea, the article was primarily drafted by Vale, who claims it on his CV. 'The intellectual structure of the piece is my own. The opening paragraphs were written by Gary van Staden, the, "I was in jail but the world was changing," etc. The piece on trade was written by Rob Davies, and the piece on finance by Alan Hirsch.'[87] Vale sent the piece back to the ANC's Shell House headquarters via Kader Asmal; it came back with certain edits and deletions ('one was about support for Aung San Suu Kyi'), but Vale doubts Mandela himself ever read the piece beforehand.[88]

Academic interviewees who were a part of this process remember these years as some of the most exciting and heady of their careers. As Vale recalls, 'Few people get the opportunity to straddle two sides and have these interactions.'[89] Another academic, sociologist Roger Southall, remembers, 'For the first time I felt as a political scientist that people apart from other political scientists wanted to talk to me.'[90] Academics, so long neglected by government, now were involved in policymaking, with their inputs given serious consideration and incorporated into policy documents. Workshops and discussions during the day would bleed into informal discussions at night at participants' houses.[91] Such networking opportunities were unprecedented and gave hope to many of the academic participants that they would be included in the new government.

... and Reshaping the Defense Establishment

Concurrent with discussions on a new foreign policy were similar discussions involving academics on reform of South Africa's post-transition defense apparatus, particularly on how to rein in the military and be less threatening toward the region. According to Laurie Nathan, a leading 'progressive' voice on defense matters, the ANC shortly after its unbanning realized at a conference in Lusaka with representatives of the defense establishment that it had few experts on defense. 'Every time someone from the ANC camp made a proposal, someone like [longtime *Cape Times* military correspondent] Willem [Steenkamp] would say, patronizingly, "Nice idea but you don't know what you're talking about." That pissed off the ANC people, but I started thinking about it. I liked the concept of non-offensive defense, whereby you could defend yourself but not attack your neighbors. Nice idea, but could it be possible?'[92]

This realization sparked the ANC's 1991 establishment of the Military Research Group (MRG), which combined representatives of academia, Umkhonto we Sizwe (MK), and civil society to debate future defense policy. First meeting at Shell House in November 1991, the MRG met approximately 30 times during the next four years.[93] The group had a core membership of about a dozen; Nathan, Jacklyn Cock of the University of the Witwatersrand, and Gavin Cawthra were the leading academic figures, while Rocky Williams and Calvin Kahn headed up the MK contingent.[94] The group wrote reports, organized conferences, and liaised with representatives of the SADF to conceptualize concrete proposals to take into constitutional negotiations.[95] While Cawthra acknowledged that many MRG proposals were watered down during the negotiations, they provided the underpinnings for much of what emerged with regard to defense policy.[96]

Another task of the MRG was to build ties to the SADF establishment in the run-up to the transition. Prominent defense analysts Steenkamp and Heitman—who served as SADF reservists and had strong ties within the force—were utilized to this aim. Steenkamp remembers him and Heitman initiating the first, highly secretive, contact between MK and SADF officials after being approached by the MRG in 1991. 'Then it moved like something out of a movie. The MRG was in Johannesburg; [Chief of Defense Force Staff Pierre] Steyn was in Pretoria, so a safe house was organized in Sandton. Steyn would slip away in secrecy to meet with them, and that's where the talking started. [SADF chief] Kat Liebenberg had no knowledge of it; I doubt de Klerk did either.'[97] Such contact was key to building up trust between MK and SADF components in the run-up to the transition.

While the broadly anti-militarist MRG emerged as the dominant actor on defense policy during the transition, it was not the only player. Another attendee of the 1990 Lusaka conference, former artillery Lieutenant Colonel Jakkie Cilliers—who resigned from the SADF in 1988 for political reasons—took a more nuanced view than that of the MRG, pushing sweeping change within the SADF but maintaining that a professional military under strong civilian control still had a place in South Africa.[98] Launched in 1990, Cilliers' Institute for Defense Policy (IDP) was at first distrusted by both sides of the divide, with the SADF and MK each viewing it as a proxy for the other.[99] Cilliers admits that it at first was difficult to position the Institute along the existing ideological spectrum: 'People could not understand our motivation,' he notes.[100] However, a combination of tireless work and his ability to establish a close friendship with MK head Chris Hani helped build IDP's credibility with the ANC. In addition, a SADF harassment operation against him also helped: 'MK found out about this within Military Intelligence, and that established my credibility within MK.'[101] Given the prohibition on formal contact between SADF and MK during the early 1990s, Cilliers notes that IDP played a valuable role in exposing the two sides to one another through its seminars and lectures, and he also authored a military code of conduct in 1992 which (although never formally adopted) sought to lay down markers for conduct by both sides during the transition.[102]

A Time of Unprecedented Academic Impact

Overall, the period from 1990 to 1994 was one of unprecedented access by academics to the key formulators of foreign and defense policy (taking into account that while not yet in government, the ANC was the 'government-in-waiting'). Academics drafted key policy documents and established the frameworks that would bracket South African policy after the transition. While the ANC may have provided the normative 'skeleton' for such policies, academics were invaluable for putting analytical 'meat' on the bones. The exercise, notes Aziz Pahad, 'was useful, marrying academic inputs with practitioner inputs. I think we produced some bloody interesting discussion documents at that time.'[103] Experts with views in keeping with those of the ANC's leadership played a dominant role, but, in line with the democratic ethos of the United Democratic Front, all viewpoints were represented. The question, however, was whether a 'government-in-waiting' would have the same openness to debate and engagement after it formally took power.

1994 and After: Back to Earth

Given the experience of the previous four years, many foreign policy academics had high hopes that they would continue to have access and influence under a democratic, ANC-led government that emphasized openness in the policymaking arena.[104] The ANC in its 1994 foreign policy discussion document, as well as DFA in its 1996 Green Paper on foreign affairs, referenced the need to interact with universities and academic institutions. A profusion of new actors and a revitalization of existing ones, fueled by the newfound interest of Western donors, spurred optimism that academic expertise on foreign and defense policy issues would be vastly improved and increasingly valuable to government. Ideas like the creation of a foreign policy advisory council, which would have formalized interaction with government, were revived.[105] Several academics even harbored ambitions of being included in the new foreign policy apparatus. This, however, this did not come to fruition.

By mid-1994, it was clear to many of the participants in foreign policy discussions that they would not be joining the new government. Several participants in the transitional talks had at least notions that they would be asked to take government positions. As John Daniel remembers, 'I thought a job like a DDG [Deputy Director-General] position was a strong possibility, even a probability. There had been a lot of speculation in the press; the *Mail & Guardian* had done a piece on whites who were going to make it big, and I was part of that.'[106] Several interviewees said Vale thought he would receive a top post, possibly the Director-Generalship of the department, but Mandela elected to retain holdover Rusty Evans. Observers have differing viewpoints about why Vale was not offered this or any other significant job; a combination of his race, predilection to argue, immodesty, and inability to build a trusting relationship with the ANC leadership all were cited. As Pahad points out, 'Anybody who says publicly, "I wrote that Mandela speech," will run into difficulty ... How many people wrote how many speeches?'[107] Vale himself cites Mbeki's desire to maintain a firm grip on foreign policy now that he was deputy president.[108] Whatever the case may have been, there was no movement of leading foreign affairs thinkers into government during this period, nor would there be through 2008.[‡]

Institutional Players, New and Old

The period from about 1992 to 1996 saw the emergence of several institutions with competencies in foreign affairs, while old ones were forced to 'adapt or die,' in the words of PW Botha. In this new, crowded landscape, organizations were forced to fight one another for expertise, government contracts, and access to decision-makers—not to mention donor funds pouring in from around the world. Universities tended to be the losers, with the balance of power among expert entities shifting from increasingly cash-strapped universities to private, donor-funded think tanks. Many of the strategic studies' centers established at universities during the 1970s and 1980s had folded by the early 1990s;

only ISSUP carried on into the new century, although it remained a small, shoestring organization. Even Vale's CSAS, which shared the outlook of the new government, folded by the late 1990s, having lost co-director Rob Davies to parliament.[109]

The two most established players also had a fight to survive. South Africa's oldest independent foreign affairs research organization, SAIIA, entered the new democratic era on the verge of collapse. 'I took over in 1993 at a terrifying time,' remembers former SAIIA National Director Sara Pienaar, who succeeded Barratt. 'Our corporate funding had dried up; they were already seeing the future laid elsewhere.'[110] With a budget of only a few hundred thousand rand, Pienaar was forced to halve the staff just to keep the organization solvent. Greg Mills, who Pienaar hired as director of research and succeeded her as national director in 1996, remembers his new role as, 'essentially director of nothing,' given the staff cuts.[111] SAIIA also had to redefine its role, having long served more as a facilitator of public dialogue than a conductor of serious research. As longtime SAIIA fellow Tim Hughes notes, 'SAIIA used to call itself South Africa's window on the world; now the door's open. So what role do you play?'[112] The other established think tank player, the Africa Institute, also had to redefine itself in this new era, particularly given that its quasi-governmental status meant that it had to get into, and stay in, the new government's good graces, given that its parliamentary disbursement covered almost all of its budget.[113] AISA saw the departure of several senior researchers after 1994, while limited government funding—only R3.2 million in 1999, covering just 17 total staff—did not enable it to compete with better-funded competitors.[114]

SAIIA and AISA had the additional challenges of competition from a host of new institutional actors. One of the key new players was Cilliers' IDP, which was renamed the Institute for Security Studies (ISS) in 1996 and through the 1990s broadened its focus from domestic security reform to also examine continental security issues.[115] Another new player on the security front was the Durban-based African Center for Constructive Resolution of Disputes (ACCORD), founded in 1992 by Vasu Gounden with an initial focus on conflict mediation and peacemaking among domestic actors in the run-up to the 1994 national election.[116] After its work on peacemaking and conflict mediation in KwaZulu-Natal before the 1994 election helped defuse tensions there, the South African Government in 1995 tasked ACCORD with assisting its efforts to bring peace to Burundi. ACCORD established a robust civic education program there, boosting the capacity of rebel groups to engage in negotiations, and has become regarded as one of South Africa's most effective non-governmental players in the African peacekeeping and peacemaking arena.[117]

Several other new or re-branded entities also had foreign affairs competencies. Johannesburg's Center for Policy Studies, although mostly focused on domestic issues, began focusing on Africa in the mid-1990s, particularly after former Rhodes scholar Chris Landsberg joined it in 1997; he became director in 2002 and subsequently emerged as one of the leading foreign policy scholars in the country.[118] The Center for Conflict Resolution (CCR), headed by Laurie Nathan from 1992 to 2003, was another body that was originally oriented internally but moved its focus outward to play a role in continental peace building, particularly in Lesotho and Burundi.[119] Cape Town's Institute for Justice and Reconciliation emerged in the mid-1990s as a leader on post-conflict military integration and transitional justice topics, active in places like Liberia, Burundi, and Rwanda.[120]

The most influential new player, however, was the previously mentioned Foundation for Global Dialogue, established in 1994 with a 5 million Deutschemark (approximately R3 million at the time) grant from the German Government through the Friedrich Ebert Stiftung.[121] 'During a 1992 state visit, Helmut Kohl told Mandela he might want to think about an in-house policy think tank,' recalls Anthoni van Nieuwkerk, who left SAIIA shortly thereafter to work with the ANC's international desk on setting up the new organization.[122] The expectation was that this new think tank would provide a 'progressive' alternative to existing structures. Current Executive Director Siphamandla Zondi, reflecting on the attitudes of the time, notes, 'SAIIA was seen as having Jan Smuts' heritage, seen as closer to the DP [Democratic Party] and the British liberal tradition. ISS was conservative, Afrikaner. CPS [the Center for Policy Studies] was Ford Foundation.'[123]

Upon its 1995 establishment, Yale-educated Garth le Pere was brought on board as the Foundation's executive director, a post he would hold until 2009. Renamed the Institute for Global Dialogue (IGD) in 1999, the IGD's goal was to undertake research that was pertinent to government priorities. Normalizing relations with post-Abacha Nigeria was one early focus, for example. 'That was a priority for Mbeki, so we did quite a lot of work around that relationship,' van Nieuwkerk remembers. 'We took a group there, brought a group here, talked about transitions, and so on.'[124] While seeking to establish itself as *primus inter pares* among experts, particularly in regard to government access, le Pere and IGD's board (which had early members as disparate as Barratt and Stanley Mogoba of the PAC) sought to maintain its analytic independence from the ANC.[125] Aziz Pahad emphasizes that the party and government wanted IGD to have this independence: 'We said we didn't want it to be a party hack structure; we wanted critical thinking [...] We would have regular meetings with them, to discuss programs and see if we can direct their work in directions that they needed, not to influence their analysis. In government, we sometimes don't have time to think, so we wanted them to be an independent think tank.'[126]

Donors and Independence

Newfound interest by donors, particularly governments and private entities from Western Europe and the United States, was a key driver behind this explosion of think tanks. Global interest in South Africa after the transition was a huge boon to SAIIA, and whereas Barratt would never accept foreign government money, Pienaar jettisoned this stance, actively seeking donor sponsorship of research projects and conferences.[127] SAIIA's ability to host high-profile functions in its dedicated spaces, Jan Smuts House on the campus of the University of the Witwatersrand, further boosted its exposure.[128] By 2010, under Mills and his successor (in 2005) Elizabeth Sidiropoulos, the Institute was able to build its endowment to R18 million and reduce its dependence on corporate funding to just 4 percent of its budget.[129] Similarly, ISS, with its Pretoria offices easily accessible to the diplomatic corps, also became a donor darling, with funding by Western European governments allowing it to expand its continental presence to Nairobi, Dakar, and Addis Ababa by 2009.

Funding from foreign donors—and in the case of SAIIA, big business—raised some questions from the ANC government about the influence of such funding on the entities in question and created problems for entities trying to influence government. Despite SAIIA's drastically changed budgetary profile, Pahad recalls that 'Greg [Mills] was looked at as someone who represented business interests, because of where SAIIA comes from.'[130] Other organizations elicited similar reactions; as one academic notes, 'If you ask about ISS, they say it belongs to Sweden and Norway. If you ask about CCR, they're also with Norway, Sweden, and Denmark.'[131] Mills describes the paradox that goes along with seeking foreign funds: 'You had to have a profile, you had to write about issues, and that made the government far more suspicious. You had a terrific tautology. To be effective in your role, you had to have profile. That gained you the money, but undercut your relations with government.'[132]

Competition for resources also affected inter-organizational relationships among think tanks, hindering collaborative work. As CCR Executive Director Adekaye Adebajo, a Nigerian, notes, 'I've seen—being an outsider myself—that it's quite an antagonistic and backbiting environment, NGO [non-governmental organization] one, and they're competing for the same resources, even though it's not a zero sum game.'[133] This competitive atmosphere was noticed in the DFA and, according to Pahad, limited the DFA's desire to work with them. 'We used to try to bring these think tanks together whenever there was a crisis, but the competition between them was too much.'[134] Only IGD remained 'pure' in this sense, surviving mostly off of its endowment and research contracts with government, at least through to 2008. According to le Pere, about 40 percent of its research output during the Mandela years and 30 percent during the Mbeki years was private, commissioned research by government.[135] This privileged position, in turn, raised questions with other academics about the degree of IGD's independence from the government; as with the allegations about foreign funders, they wonder whether they could be sufficiently critical of government when government so frequently commissioned its work.

Early Continuity, 1994–6 ...

If anything, engagement between government and academia on foreign policymaking was more robust than ever during the immediate post-transition period, given the need to turn the loose outlines of policy into actual strategies. The period between 1994 and 1999 saw the drafting of White Papers on Intelligence (1995), Defense (1996), and International Peace Missions (1999), as well as the 1996 Green Paper discussion document (never turned into a White Paper) on foreign policy—all but the intelligence document elicited significant comment and scrutiny from the academic community.[136] Conferences consisting of government representatives and experts were called to debate not only the content of draft documents, but also broader conceptual questions, debating such concepts as 'national interest' and 'security'—if not always successfully.[137]

Academic influence also expanded into new realms of the broader foreign affairs spectrum. Trade policy, never previously a topic of interaction, opened up to academic inputs, with the under-capacitated Department of Trade and Industry seeking experts during negotiations with the European Union on a Trade, Development, and Cooperation Agreement signed in 1999.[138] Even the constitution was subject to expert inputs, with Annette Seegers called upon to act as primary drafter of Chapter 11, which dealt with defense matters.[139] The Foundation for Global Dialogue, in its first paper, resuscitated Olivier and Geldenhuys' idea of a foreign policy advisory council that would act as a leading think tank.[140] (The advisory council idea made no headway during the Mbeki years, although an interim structure was set up in 2010.)

The reasons for such continuity during the immediate post-transition years can be ascribed to a combination of the glaring need for expertise within government and interpersonal ties established during the transition period between academics and certain new officials. As Nathan refers to it, this period was 'a moment of upheaval, where policymakers are not confident their staff can meet the demands.'[141] The Departments of Defense and Foreign Affairs were undergoing a rapid, unsettling integration process that often left behind old staff unwilling to take on drastic rewrites of their *raisons d'etre* and new staff—from the ANC and homeland governments—largely unable to formulate new ones. This lack of capability opened doors for outside inputs; as le Pere opines, 'I think in many ways, we brought a sharp analytical edge that might have been missing in DFA.'[142]

The personal ties built up during the transition also played a key role. Two deputy ministers, Aziz Pahad at DFA and Ronnie Kasrils at the Department of Defense, were key interlocutors for foreign policy academic experts, as was Water Affairs (and later Education) Minister Kader Asmal in his guise as chair (from 1995) of parliament's National Conventional Arms Control Committee.[143] Kasrils in particular consulted across the ideological spectrum. He developed a close relationship with Nathan, whom he asked to rework the first draft of the Defense White Paper and with whom he would continue to work during his tenure as intelligence minister (2004–8), but also 'old order' analysts like Heitman and Steenkamp, who wrote a chapter of the 1996 Defense Review.[144] Steenkamp recalls that: 'I did a lot of work for Kasrils, mainly deciphering the generals' bullshit. I'd read documents for him and say, "Ok, Ronnie, the landmine is in paragraph 37." He'd say, "Fine, draft me a reply." I had a lot of fun with that. Me, some chickenshit reserve force officer, writing, "Dear General, I'm afraid I can't go along with paragraph 37."'[145]

... *Limited by End of Mandela Presidency*
Interviewees and observers note that the nature of interaction between academia and government began to change around 1996. Between then and the end of Mandela's administration, the days of conferences and exhaustive consultation with a broad range of academic actors on policy came to an end.[146] Interaction moved from the formal realm to the informal, from public to private. Interviewees cited several reasons for this shift, the most popular being that this

was a natural reaction to increasingly well-defined policy priorities. Shelton, reflecting on the 'endless talk shops' of the time, agrees that a move away from widespread consultation was probably necessary. 'The objectives were clear, so stop the debate. We don't need to debate it again and again.'[147] The process of formal interaction was immensely time-consuming—the White Paper on International Peace Missions took 18 months, for example—and something for which government principals with tight schedules did not have the time.[148] 'I think academics complain that we cut the process short and ignored them afterward,' says Aziz Pahad. 'Well, I think there's an element of that, but we never anticipated the pressures of governance.'[149]

There are more skeptical views of the issue. One is that the ANC government did not really care about the public inputs of academics in the first place; in the words of Roger Southall, the exercises of the previous five years were 'a marketing exercise to get people on board.'[150] Another view is that the new environment was an ANC reaction to growing criticism from outside experts on South Africa's policies, particularly where they viewed discrepancies between its actions and its stated commitments to human rights. Le Pere remembers the issue of South African arms sales to governments that violated human rights as a contentious issue with government. 'Here, we said, you have to decide, because the normative was rubbing up against the pragmatic, and you cannot have your cake and eat it,' he recalls. 'We didn't make ourselves very popular at that point.'[151] In all likelihood, a combination of these factors most likely played a role, with the outcome being that government–academic interactions during Mbeki's tenure would look very different than under Mandela.

The Process of Engaging Government

While Mandela's presidency was about foreign policy formulation, Mbeki's time in office was about implementation, turning his vision into reality. With academics having developed and ratified this vision through the previous decade, their roles receded into the background, at least in terms of public view. Outside experts, however, continued to engage with government throughout Mbeki's presidency, particularly at the working levels.

Limited Direct Academic Interaction with the Presidency ...

Nelson Mandela personally had little engagement with academics on foreign policy issues. John Daniel remembers one meeting Mandela held with 22 political science professors and heads of department in 1995, although national reconciliation, not foreign affairs, was the topic of discussion.[152] Mbeki, however, was a different character. He had dealt personally with people like Daniel and Vale from his time in Lusaka, was aware of their writings, and—even if he could not always be there—was an active participant in discussions on foreign policy during the transition and after. Le Pere remembers a conference of academics and government officials he convened on Nigeria in 1999 at Mbeki's behest. 'On the second day, talking about the strategic relationship between the two countries, Mbeki came for an entire afternoon. We were about to start the conference in the afternoon, when [Mbeki political advisor] Titus Mafolo came in and said the president would be coming! And he didn't want to sit at the high table; he said, "I'm just going to participate." The session was supposed to conclude at 5; he was still going at 7.'[153]

Mbeki could also be a very challenging, even hostile, interlocutor. Van Nieuwkerk recalls an incident around 1998 at an IGD meeting where he gave an unsatisfactory answer to a Mbeki question. 'He could kill you with his stare, Thabo. He didn't smoke it, but he had his pipe. And he looked at me for three minutes, somebody told me after, without saying a word. Now if I do that to you now, you'll probably leave. It's a power thing. He finished me.'[154] Mbeki soon walked out of the meeting, effectively ending it, and shutting down debate on the issue. Upon reflection, van Nieuwkerk recalls that his answer, related to the Great Lakes region, probably was inadequate, but 'he's got a whole intelligence service that tells him every morning what's going on. Academics are a bit slow on these issues.'[155]

As president, Mbeki had, from all accounts, little personal interaction with outside experts. Chris Landsberg, an academic alleged to have close ties to the president, said, 'I'll go as far as saying

that I didn't meet him once alone during his presidency [. . .] For all
of the rumors and ideas about how close I was to him, the whiskey
drinking stuff, guess what, he's too careful a man to do that.'[156] Le
Pere and Kenyan academic Shadrack Gutto, of UNISA, are two
others viewed as having close ties to the president, but both
downplayed their direct access. Rather, all note that their interaction
tended to be with the president's intermediaries, particularly Aziz
Pahad and Presidency policy coordinator Joel Netshitenzhe.[157]

. . . but Some Ministerial Engagement

According to interviewees within government and academia,
interaction between ministers and academics also was limited.
Defense Minister Mosiuoa Lekota had little meaningful interaction
with academics; Nathan recalls him asking for papers, only
forgetting that Nathan had already submitted them.[158] His deputy,
Mluleki George, was outright dismissive of academic inputs: 'We
didn't use much of the think tanks or experts, because sometimes
they analyze, and in Defense you don't need analysis, especially long
term. You need to know what is happening now.'[159] At the
Department of Intelligence, outside of Nathan's long-standing
relationship with Kasrils, no other academic mentioned interacting
with him or his predecessors, Lindiwe Sisulu (2001–4) or Joe
Nhlanhla (1999–2001). There were exceptions, however. Sydney
Mufamadi, Mbeki's local government minister who also served as his
point man on Congo and, later, Zimbabwe, was cited by many as a
minister who sought out briefings from outside experts.[160] Le Pere
adds that IGD was contracted by the Treasury at Minister Trevor
Manuel's behest to prepare him for chairmanship of the G20; IGD
produced more than a dozen private briefing papers for him.[161]

Few academics have fond memories of Foreign Affairs Minister
(1999–2009) Nkosazana Dlamini-Zuma, widely describing her as
overtly anti-intellectual and frequently taking umbrage at think tank
inputs (even those from IGD) as being presumptuous.[162] Fortunately
for academics, her deputy, Aziz Pahad, proved her polar opposite
when dealing with outside experts. Academics from all sides of the
ideological divide described Pahad as their primary interlocutor in

government, someone who actively sought out academic inputs on a host of issues. As le Pere recalls, Pahad 'took seriously this whole business of good ideas and good debates, policy relevant research.'[163] He was the primary interlocutor for IGD throughout le Pere's tenure as IGD head. His interactions, however, were across the board. 'Aziz would come to us to ask us to write a paper about Morocco or Zimbabwe,' notes Tim Hughes of SAIIA, who also recalls SAIIA being asked by Pahad for a continental threat assessment on September 12, 2001.[164] UNISA professor Rok Ajulu remembers Pahad reaching out to him about his opinions on Zimbabwe and other issues.[165] Hughes and others also recall Pahad's co-deputy Sue van der Merwe as another figure that listened to informed outsiders.[166]

Working Level Engagement is More Robust

Academics had differing levels of interaction with working-level (director-general and below) interlocutors in the Departments of Defense, Intelligence, Trade and Industry, and Foreign Affairs, with interaction with the latter clearly the most robust. The Presidency under Mbeki also would reach out to scholars on foreign policy. Landsberg cites the international affairs sections government's 10- and 15-year reviews as examples of this outreach, while Hughes notes that SAIIA was called upon to participate in a scenarios exercise with the Presidency toward the end of the Mbeki administration. Several academics said they were contacted by arms of the intelligence services—the external South African Secret Service, internal National Intelligence Agency, and coordinating National Intelligence Coordinating Committee—during the 2000s, such as after the September 11, 2001 World Trade Center terrorist attacks.[167] Seegers, for example, says SASS called her and others together as part of a 2004 panel on a ten-year review of defense policy.[168] However, several noted that outreach from intelligence frequently focused on domestic issues, such as xenophobia and the potential for terrorist attacks in South Africa.

During Mbeki's tenure, Trade and Industry Minister Alec Erwin increasingly called upon outside experts for policy briefs and conference presentations.[169] Despite this, elements of the department have shown themselves hostile to opinions that do not square with government policy, particularly those that adhere to free trade principles. Several interviewees cited Peter Draper of SAIIA—who started Trade and Industry's first in-house research department before leaving government in 2003—as an especially unpopular figure among the department's senior management for his free trade orientation. Even IGD was frustrated in its attempts to influence trade policy.[170]

The DFA, however, showed itself more open than its counterparts in its dealings with outside experts during the Mbeki administration, if not always in a consistent fashion.[171] Most academic interviewees opined that the DFA's openness to academic inputs from the director-general level on down increased during the Mbeki administration. Directors-General Jackie Selebi (1998–9), Sipho Pityana (1999–2002), and Ayanda Ntsaluba (2002–11) all actively sought outside experts on a host of topics, while senior officials like Kingsley Mamabolo and Welile Nhlapo also earned high marks for accessibility and desire to hear external opinions.[172] This openness by principals clearly filtered down to mid- and lower-level officials. Training was well developed, with academics from a range of institutions lecturing at the DFA's Diplomatic Academy, an institution that works with the University of Pretoria.

Levels of interaction, formal and informal, tended to be most robust on specialized issues where the departmental knowledge base was weak. East Asia is a good example. Garth Shelton, a preeminent Asia scholar, says he was consistently included in discussions on Asia—particularly China–South Africa relations—throughout Mbeki's administration. As he notes, 'In 2000, South Africa was preparing for the Forum on China Africa Cooperation. The meeting was going to be held in Beijing, and DFA assembled 5 or 6 academics around a table with the DFA China staff. And we had a whole day session on what is Africa's response to a 20-page document China had provided on China-Africa relations.'[173] The DFA took all of the academics' inputs seriously, as many (if not all) were included in the final document. Since that time, Shelton notes that he—as well as other China scholars, like Martyn Davies, head of the Center for

Chinese Studies during the Mbeki presidency—were frequently called upon, formally and informally, by the DFA.[174]

Africa is another topic that generates frequent interaction between government and outside players, particularly in dealing with continental conflict zones. ACCORD and ISS were key players on this front. According to the late Henri Boshoff of ISS, 'We are at this stage so integrated with the West Africa desk that there's a standing arrangement that we meet.'[175] Sudan was a particularly robust area of engagement. Representatives of nearly all of the large think tanks and several universities were included in internal departmental discussions on Sudan; several have hosted seminars on the topic.[176] The DFA partnered with UNISA to provide capacity assistance to south Sudan and tapped Shadrack Gutto, then of Wits, to lead a delegation to south Sudan in 2004, based on the Kenyan's relationships with Sudanese intellectuals.[177] On Somalia, UNISA professor Iqbal Jhazbhay—an expert on the region and member of the ANC's Religious Affairs Committee—was often engaged.

Informal relationships between diplomats and academics—originating from old friendships, students reaching back to professors, or even from an official seeing an op-ed written by a scholar—emerged from the increasingly closed environment of the late 1990s as the dominant form of interaction in the early Mbeki administration. The DFA's Policy Research and Analysis Unit (PRAU), however, from its 2003 founding under diplomat and ANC intelligence official Mo Shaik, sought to formalize and regularize interactions with academia. 'I remember Mo saying at the time, "This unit is about thinking out of the box,"' recalls SAIIA's Elizabeth Sidiropoulos. 'It's about thinking about alternative policy solutions; we can't work in a box.'[178] PRAU held, among other things, bi-annual one-day conferences on key topics, ranging from South Africa's role in Africa to Pretoria's positions on the UN Security Council.[179] Participants spoke highly of these, noting that they encompassed a broad range of academic opinions and have sparked some thought-provoking exchanges, particularly between think tanks with differing views. PRAU also called on academics for specific briefing papers on their areas of expertise, as well as using them to brief outgoing ambassadors.[180] Despite this, observers and even members question PRAU's impact on the policy environment. Shaik left after only a year, and the unit floundered, lacking both seasoned staff (which cycled in and out before having enough time to build expertise) and a clear direction. Its work, according to one academic observer, was 'not deep. If it was a student paper, it would get 60–70 percent.'[181] It suffered a further blow when it was moved from the Ministry to the Diplomatic Training Academy shortly after Shaik's departure, where it lacked direct contact with the minister. Mavivi Myakayaka-Manzini, who headed PRAU from 2007–10, said that through her tenure 'there was huge debate raging about where PRAU should actually be, and what exactly its role should be [. . .] under training, it was very difficult for PRAU to operate and do the work it should do. Also the capacity it was given was not sufficient for it to be an effective tool for policymaking within government.'[182]

Mixed Contact with Other Entities

The Presidency and departments were not the only parts of government with which academics dealt. Unlike the pre-1994 period—when MPs had no meaningful interaction with academics— interaction between parliament and outside experts after the transition was regularized, both in formal and informal capacities.[183] The former includes briefings to the PCFA and the broader parliament on pertinent issues (like Africa Institute briefings on the Pan-African parliament in 2002) as well as organizing study trips.[184] In 2003, for example, the Institute for Justice and Reconciliation organized a visit by members of the PCFA to southern Sudan, allowing them to meet a range of Sudanese actors and better acquaint them with the situation. The PCFA also has, on occasion, sought to convene foreign policy academics from Western Cape universities, although such interaction has been haphazard.[185] Outside of government, the ANC National Executive Committee Subcommittee on International Affairs also met with academics; former head Myakayaka-Manzini says the ANC would meet with experts on foreign policy issues at least annually.[186]

Zimbabwe: A Door Opened, then Shut

Pretoria's reaction to the political and economic collapse of Zimbabwe from 2000 was the most hotly and widely debated South African foreign policy issue of the Mbeki administration, with academia being no exception. Most institutions were highly critical of South Africa's 'quiet diplomacy' policy on the grounds that it was ineffective in forcing Mugabe to respect the rule of law. SAIIA was especially active on Zimbabwe, criticizing the government but also seeking to bring ZANU-PF and the MDC together; it was able to host then-Finance Minister Simba Makoni and MDC leader Morgan Tsvangirai at a public conference in November 2001.[187] While far less critical than SAIIA, IGD also pushed for results from South African efforts in Zimbabwe, a stance that grew firmer over time. Only Chris Landsberg emerged as a strong proponent of the South African approach; his book, *The Quiet Diplomacy of Liberation*, reinforced the viewpoint that, as with South Africa's liberation, only by maintaining dialogue and resisting calls for drastic action can change be affected.

Despite broad criticism from academia, the government during Mbeki's first term actively sought inputs from scholars on Zimbabwe. In what appears to have been an unprecedented exercise, four leading scholars—Landsberg, van Nieuwkerk, le Pere, and Moeletsi Mbeki, who was affiliated with SAIIA—were invited to a closed round-table on February 5, 2002 convened by Intelligence Minister Lindiwe Sisulu to discuss options dealing with Zimbabwe. 'There must have been 40 people—all of the relevant parastatals, Eskom which was providing electricity credits, Transnet providing use of our rolling stock, the deputy governor of the Reserve Bank, the heads of SASS and NIA,' remembers le Pere, who noted that Aziz Pahad and the military service chiefs were also in attendance.[188] Lasting more than three hours, the meeting was 'a powerful discussion,' and one that reached agreement on a set of five carrots and five sticks that should be considered in dealing with Harare.[189] The academic participants had to hand over their notes when they departed.

Coming just three days before the president's State of the Nation speech, le Pere said he expected to see the session's outcome reflected in the speech. He was wrong; Mbeki made minimal and non-committal reference to Zimbabwe in the speech.[190] 'We were told later that he dismissed the document,' le Pere remembers.[191] Such lack of consideration of differing viewpoints—academic and otherwise—on Zimbabwe would throughout the rest of Mbeki's time in office be the norm, even those from seemingly 'insider' academics. Ajulu traveled to Zimbabwe in 2002 as part of an Africa Institute delegation, which afterward produced a scenarios report and a critique of quiet diplomacy; it is unclear whether this reached Mbeki, but it clearly had no effect on his policy direction.[192] Nevertheless, the government maintained informal ties to Zimbabwe experts. Several—including le Pere, Ajulu, and Landsberg—remember dealing informally with Pahad throughout Mbeki's first term. However, le Pere remembers him becoming increasingly defensive about the government's stance. 'What's the alternative?' Pahad would often demand.[193] Ajulu remembers that he would counter that while of course diplomacy must by its nature be quiet, it also had to produce results. 'But we found that kind of constructive criticism was not really welcomed.'[194] As late as early 2004, Pahad met with academics 'to clear the air' on Zimbabwe, although this meeting turned out to be a simple recitation of the government's line, declaring that the government saw no alternative to its current path.[195] Engagement on the issue, probably due largely to fatigue on the part of scholars seeing little chance of influencing the government line, was minimized thereafter.

Zimbabwe was not the only issue where academic engagement was shunned. The NEPAD initiative was another significant example of the government not seeking out academic inputs in advance.[196] Hughes remembers convening the first conference on the NEPAD plan in November 2001, the day after the project was unveiled; there was no outreach from government on the idea in advance or invitation to academics to make submissions.[197] Pretoria's 2007 decision to reject a vote on Myanmar (Burma) in the UN Security Council was another example. It is worth noting that these issues were the exception rather than the rule, at least quantitatively. At the same time, they show that once Mbeki made up his mind on an issue, it was not likely to be raised again.

Whose Voice Mattered, and Why?

As is seen by those included in the Zimbabwe conversations, not all academics and think tanks were created equal. Representatives of SAIIA in particular feel that they were left out of policy debates on Zimbabwe and other sensitive topics. 'There was an unspoken rule that SAIIA shouldn't be included on certain fora,' said one academic affiliated with SAIIA. 'Latin America? Talk to them! They have someone who speaks Spanish. Zuma goes to Colombia as deputy president, and you have to talk to us about what it means to have a bilateral with Colombia; what are we going to talk about beside coffee and cocaine and crime?'[198] However, on issues like the Middle East, Iran, or Zimbabwe, where SAIIA was definitively at odds with the government position—and unafraid to publicly say so—they would not be consulted. That said, this relationship improved by the end of the Mbeki administration, in large part due to a concerted effort by Sidiropoulos to reshape perceptions of SAIIA and position it as a resource for the government rather than as a critic.[199]

It is clear that certain academics and institutes had 'inside tracks' to the top levels of government, usually through close relationships with Pahad. Cunningham Ngcukana, Mbeki's NEPAD advisor, said he and others in the Presidency would deal frequently with le Pere and Landsberg; others have raised Ajulu and Gounden as other preferred interlocutors.[200] Landsberg and le Pere do not deny that they had 'insider' status in dealing with government, but both were quick to note that their access should not be overstated. As previously noted, their direct contact with Mbeki was limited, and Landsberg adds, 'Did I have Aziz's number? Yes I did. If I used it twice a year, it was a lot.'[201] Similarly, le Pere notes that while he concedes IGD was considered 'first among equals' among think tanks, 'We had to earn it' with consistently solid work.[202]

Why these academics and their institutes had preferred status is a matter of much—often heated—debate within the academic community, with 'outsiders' and 'insiders' having sharply differing views on the matter. Many in the former category ascribe much 'insider' access to the fact that these academics preached to the proverbial choir, tailoring their analyses to fit the government line. 'Some academics get subcontracted on specific issues,' noted one relative outsider, 'but they exercise self-censorship. To get the contracts, they can't be critical.'[203] Such a charge was frequently leveled toward IGD, which benefited from government tenders for conferences and analytic production throughout the Mbeki adminis-tration. Even Landsberg notes that the popular paradigm during the Mbeki years was that 'the more you engage, the more of a lackey you become.' Despite this comment, he rubbishes this view. 'The more I engaged government the more I learned that if you are there merely to engage on the assumption they want you to give uncritical advice, that's the quickest way to fall out of favor,' he notes.[204] He speaks almost in awe of the level of intellectual capacity within the top levels of government, whether looking at social, economic, or foreign policy. 'These guys kept throwing challenges at you.'

The 'insider' view, in contrast, is that the complaints of those not actively consulted have an air of sour grapes about them. As Landsberg opines, think tanks and academics 'often wished to engage on the basis where they should simply be allowed to dish out advice and criticism without government taking offense.'[205] In his view, it is perfectly normal that the key decision-makers in government would not seek out academics and organizations that slated its decision-making consist-ently in the press. He also is of the opinion that think tanks and academics have been overly thin-skinned when their inputs have not had an impact on policy, particularly given that the government is under no obligation to operationalize those inputs. Several policymakers cited this perceived arrogance, of demanding a seat at the table, as an irritant.

In discussing the topic with those from all sides of the analytic spectrum, a few key determinants came to the fore regarding whether one was consulted:

— *Trust.* As Landsberg noted in 2000, 'If you want to be close, you are going to have to learn to respect secrecy. Your first inclination should not be to try and divulge this information in public; I think there's a tendency to want to do that.'[206] There was a perception, true or not, that several leading 'outsider' scholars had a propensity to leak what should be private interactions to the media. Nathan adds that this trust must also extend to a principal's senior staff, many of which tend not to like outsiders having privileged access.[207]

— *Humility.* Several interviewees cited one's ability to keep one's ego in check as imperative to maintaining a close relationship. Several cited Vale's openness about citing the Mandela *'Foreign Affairs'* article as an example of what not to do; Vale consequently has had almost no interaction with government since the mid-1990s. Several interviewees acknowledged drafting speeches and policy statements that were accepted by principals with barely a revision, but they were only able to maintain this access by keeping quiet about it.

— *Location.* A seemingly prosaic issue, but several experts, particularly those in Cape Town, cited geography as a determinant of whether one is actively consulted. As Karen Smith of Stellenbosch notes, 'It's a cost factor. They invite us, often getting the invitations for something in two days. "We'd love you to come, but we're not paying for your flight."'[208]

— *Personal/party relationships.* Personal ties clearly play a role in determining one's level of informal access. Ajulu, for example, remembers having many open and frank conversations with Pahad on South Africa's role on the continent, but 'it was different for me because I've been friends with Aziz for 30 years, so we can talk very freely.'[209] Nathan adds that, 'A big part is idiosyncratic; it's connecting with a comrade.'[210] That said, personal ties probably should not be overstated as a determinant of access; neither le Pere nor Landsberg professed to close friendships with ANC principals.

— *Race.* Many academics, white and black, cited race as a factor that would dictate whether one was included as an insider, particularly in light of Mbeki's call for the rise of a black intelligentsia.[211] As Adebajo claims, 'The fact that so many think tanks are not transformed racially, it's a problem for government to take them seriously. You have to take those issues seriously to understand this. It's not a deracialized space, but rather one that promotes privileged whites.'[212] While it is impossible to quantify the role of race as a determinant, the fact that all of the most prominent 'insider' academics—le Pere, Landsberg, Ajulu, Gounden, Gutto, and others—were not white suggests that race was a factor in determining whether one had influence.

Conclusion: Limited, but Not Non-Existent, Influence

The information above provides worthwhile insight into the access that academia had to the Mbeki administration, but measuring real impact is far more difficult. As le Pere and Vickers pointed out in a 2004 article, 'Under the present government, there is ample room for making inputs but whether these are taken into account is another matter.'[213] Interviewees from government had a difficult time justifying the latter point; while most were complimentary of academic inputs, none could point to an issue where academics had a 'game-changing' effect on policy. Of course, in well-capacitated governments, it is rare that any outsider can contribute insights so unique as to be paradigm shifting. As Olivier notes, an academic adds value 'through osmosis,' adding to the policy debate slowly through written products, training, and first-hand interactions.[214] An academic could have a significant impact on a decision-maker's thinking, but it could come years after the fact, making measuring such an impact next to impossible.

That said, the role of academics from 1990 onward, and especially during Mbeki's administration, should not be understated. First, it was evident through a body of interviews that academic inputs were widely sought and used. While there were 'red lines' where outside influence, academic or otherwise, would not have impact on government—such as on Zimbabwe and trade policy—on many others academics played essential roles, drafting speeches and policy documents for mid- and high-level officials. On non-controversial topics, knowledgeable academics put scholarly meat on the skeleton of government policy.[215] Temporally, the comparison is stark.

Academic institutions and think tanks before 1990 had nowhere near the access that they did thereafter. It is access that continues to this very day, if not always regularly.

Reflecting on his own career as an outside advisor to government, longtime UNISA strategic studies professor Deon Fourie in a 2009 article suggested that he (in the guise of Machiavelli) 'was wrong to believe that an unbiased scientific teacher was wanted. In the game of bureaucratic politics one had to help build careers, not give the right answers.' He advises future Machiavellis to 'choose their princes more carefully,' warning against careerists who would view contrary advice as 'a threat to the prince's own self-image.'[216] This raises the ultimate question: was Thabo Mbeki a prince who would lay his policies bare to outside assessment and critique? The answer is an unsatisfying yes and no. Yes, in the sense that his government was generally open to accepting and seeking out academic inputs on foreign policy; no, in that certain issues (like Zimbabwe) were off limits for discussion. Mbeki could have done better on this front; likewise, his policy goals might have been more successful. Yet, when Mbeki is held up against his pre-1994 predecessors, who generally shunned academic inputs on foreign policy, he and his administration come out looking like paragons of openness.

CHAPTER 6

BUSINESS

During the past two decades, globalization has brought foreign policy into the private sector's crosshairs, with firms pushing their governments to pursue policies that would allow businesses to expand outward or protect their interests at home from outside incursions. South African businesses—which have expanded their global presences significantly since 1994—are no exception. Thanks to the transition to majority rule, today South African companies account for the largest proportion of capital investment in Africa, where they were long marginalized. Less clear, however, is the degree to which they have sought to play a role in South African foreign policymaking—has the business community sought to lobby government to seek free trade pacts, visa waivers, inclusion in trade missions, and other concessions that would help it do business abroad? This chapter will examine this question to determine whether South African business has had success as a foreign policy actor, before and since 1994.

The Origins of the South African Business Community

Corporate South Africa dates to the 1871 discovery of diamonds in Kimberley, which for the first time opened up what had been a rural, agrarian society to an influx of European and American capital. The consolidation of mining claims by aspiring magnates like Barney

Barnato and Cecil Rhodes created the first sizable conglomerates in the country; the two merged their holdings into the De Beers Corporation in 1888. The 1886 discovery of gold on the Witwatersrand—and the subsequent need for more foreign capital to exploit the deposits—hastened the growth of the mining industry. This move also spawned the birth of what would become South Africa's largest conglomerate, Anglo-American, by (among others) Ernest Oppenheimer in 1917.[1] While mining was the primary engine for economic growth, it also spawned a host of secondary industries—such as in engineering, financial services, and manufacturing—and new firms developed to meet the needs of an increasingly wealthy and urbanizing population. Not all of this growth was purely from the private sector; parastatals like the Electricity Supply Commission (ESCOM, today Eskom), founded in 1923, also emerged as powerful corporate entities, as did the Industrial Development Corporation, which was established in 1940 to drive South Africa's wartime industrial growth.[2]

With the expansion of the private sector came the foundation of business groupings designed to represent their interests in dealing with government. Mining led the way, with the Chamber of Mines founded in 1887, followed by the Association of Chambers of Commerce and Industry in 1892, and the Federated Chambers of Industry in 1917.[3] Agriculture also had a representative body, the South African Agricultural Union, founded in 1904. These associations represented the interests of their memberships in lobbying government for policies (mostly in the domestic realm) that would benefit their members, but they rarely worked toward common goals. In the 1920s, for example, mining interests clashed with those of manufacturing and agriculture over protectionism, with the latter broadly opposed to free trade principles. Smuts, then prime minister, tended to side with mining interests, given their vast contribution to government revenues, while Hertzog tended to be more sympathetic towards the rural agricultural interests that constituted his political base.[4]

Overall, the main focus of South African business before 1948 (and particularly before World War II) was internal, seeking to exploit South African resources while developing the burgeoning domestic market. There was some expansion into southern Africa beginning in the 1920s, with companies like South African Breweries and Anglo-American setting up operations in Northern and Southern Rhodesia. The main external focus, however, was on the export of minerals and agricultural products to markets in Europe (particularly Great Britain) and the United States.

The Post-1948 Expansion of South African Capital

The end of World War II ushered in a new era for South African firms, one that would no longer be limited to south of the Limpopo. Encouraged by blandishments from the Industrial Development Corporation, South African firms started to look at investment opportunities further afield.[5] Export growth to industrialized economies continued apace, while by the 1960s, South African firms like Anglo-American began to seek out capital investments across the world. There was also a focus on opportunities in Africa, with groups like the Federated Chambers of Industry and the South African Foreign Trade Organization actively helping private sector businesses identify opportunities on the continent.[6] African decolonization from the late 1950s proved only a minor hindrance to business expansion, in part due to government support for business expansion. Although some newly-independent states—notably Zambia—sought to isolate South Africa, they largely failed.

South African firms also, unsurprisingly, remained active in neighbors still governed by white governments, colonial or otherwise. South Africa's already extensive investment in Rhodesia increased after UDI in 1965, outstripping British outlays and leading some pundits to claim this capital infusion helped convert Rhodesia 'from a British colony to a South African dependency.'[7] Colonial Mozambique and Angola attracted South African investment, particularly through South African construction involvement in large infrastructure projects like the Cabora Bassa hydroelectric scheme, although it dropped off significantly after they were granted independence in 1975.[8]

South African penetration also took place outside the immediate sub-region. South African firms were rumored to operate in Kenya from the early 1960s, and in 1968 South African cigarette manufacturer Rothmans was even allowed to start a subsidiary there.[9] *Francophonie* proved particularly attractive, and several Francophone countries, notably Zaire, had no qualms about doing business with South African firms.[10] Construction giant Murray & Roberts reported in 1976, for example, that they were 'doing a fair amount of work in what used to be called French Africa.'[11] As international pressure mounted on South Africa into the 1980s, its business ties with the continent actually expanded. Between 1984 and 1988, South African trade with the rest of the continent grew from an estimated $650 million to more than $1.5 billion, increasing the continent's share of total trade from 6.5 to 10 percent.[12] Former Deputy Foreign Minister (1986–9) Kobus Meiring recalled traveling extensively—and secretly—on the continent to help South African firms make inroads, and by 1990 South African firms 'were quietly doing business with almost every country on the continent.'[13]

The Roots of Government's Fraught Relationship with Business
Government–business relations before 1994 were characterized by alternating periods of cooperation and contention, undergirded throughout by deep-seated NP suspicions of the largely English-speaking business community. Most capital—particularly in the mining sector—was in the hands of English speakers; in 1948, Afrikaners owned 25 percent of the manufacturing sector, 6 percent of industry writ large, and just 1 percent of the mining sector.[14] This started to change after 1948, with government preferences for Afrikaner firms and the pooling of Afrikaner capital allowing for the establishment of several Afrikaner-owned companies that would emerge as some of the country's largest, including media firm Nasionale Pers, insurance giants Santam and Sanlam, and the KWV wine cooperative.[15] Anton Rupert's tobacco-driven conglomerate Rembrandt, incorporated in 1948, would emerge as another giant of the South African business world, and one with an international footprint. Nevertheless, these firms were relative latecomers with nowhere near the economic footprints of mining companies.

Meanwhile, English big business found great difficulty in lobbying the hostile and suspicious government. Premier Milling CEO Tony Bloom, for example, once famously remarked, 'English speaking business has about as much effect on government policy as a Ping-Pong ball bouncing off a stone wall,' a perception with which Anglophone businessmen widely agreed.[16]

From the government side, intelligence chief Niel Barnard admits that there was certain skepticism about the loyalty of English business, particularly mining giant Anglo-American, which had a dual presence in South Africa and Great Britain. 'Bear in mind that Anglo and De Beers [in London] were whispering in the ear of their people here,' says Barnard in recounting reasons for government, and Afrikaner, mistrust of Anglo. 'Remember we have the expression in Afrikaans of a *soutpiel* [literally 'salt penis'], which the English speaking people detest. One foot in London, one foot in South Africa [. . .] Many of them were never true South Africans; they always had a backup.'[17]

Nevertheless, by the 1970s, divisions between English and Afrikaans business started to break down, with an increasing number of Afrikaner businessmen expressing disenchantment with what they viewed as an excessive involvement of government in the economy.[18] Both sections increasingly came to regard apartheid as, in the words of Anglo-American Executive Gavin Relly, 'an ethnic, quasi-socialist system pursued by an Afrikaner oligarchy not imbued with free enterprise principles.'[19] Furthermore, the increasing difficulty in doing business around the world, including in traditional Western markets, had a deleterious effect on English and Afrikaans business and led businesses of all stripes to push for domestic reforms. Government leaders, however, until the late 1980s were of the mind that business had no role in defining government policy and should remain uninvolved.[20] Attempts to weigh in on policies—be they foreign or domestic, either by English- or Afrikaans-speaking businessmen—were viewed as not only unwelcome, but unpatriotic.[21]

Limited Foreign Policy Interest or Engagement

Business was keen to push for domestic reforms that would allow them to expand their footprints on the continent and around the world, but in general it did not push for direct changes to Pretoria's foreign policy, or significant government help in doing business abroad. That is not to say they did not work together, as there were periods characterized by a close working relationship, the strongest of which occurred during Vorster's *détente* exercise on the continent in the 1970s. Pretoria facilitated business investment in states that limited criticism of South Africa's internal policies, finding many receptive audiences on the continent.[22] To encourage business expansion, the South African Government put up investment guarantees and took other steps to encourage businessmen to look abroad. Pretoria, for example, made a $6.3 million investment pledge that financed tourism magnate Sol Kerzner's development of tourism facilities on Madagascar's island of Nosy Be.[23] It also provided loan guarantees to fund the building of a Sun International hotel in Comoros in the late 1980s.[24] Despite South African prohibitions on holding multiple passports, the DFA allowed businessmen with the rights to European passports to use them in their travels on the continent, where a South African passport could prove a liability.[25] DFA officials also frequently met with representatives of South African firms moving onto the continent.[26] Longtime diplomat Jeremy Shearer, for example, says the DFA worked closely with Kerzner on his Nosy Be project, providing, among other things, advice on dealing with Malagasy officialdom and occasionally un-ruffling the feathers of Malagasy officials offended by the abrasive South African businessman.[27]

In Influencing Government, the South Africa Foundation is Powerless ...

The South Africa Foundation, founded in 1959, was the leading business group of the pre-1994 period focused on promoting South African business abroad, and its up-and-down relations with government epitomize the often-fraught ties between the two sides. The Foundation was established by 25 leading businessmen to 'formulate and express a coordinated view on macro-economic and other national issues and to promote the interests and further growth of South Africa's private sector' as well as to present 'a true picture of

South Africa to the world.'[28] From its establishment, the Foundation proved a useful public relations tool for the South African Government, as well as an unofficial liaison to Western capitals where it established offices (the first being London in 1961).[29] Not bound by red tape or diplomatic protocol, the Foundation was able to open doors inaccessible to South African diplomats, even in relatively friendly capitals, and take a higher public profile than government representatives.[30] In addition, the character of its membership—overwhelmingly English-speaking and anti-NP—was useful in projecting a positive image of South Africa; as longtime diplomat and, later, head of the South Africa Foundation Neil van Heerden notes, 'They could explain externally that not everyone in South Africa supported apartheid.'[31]

This makeup, however, also contributed to the government's decision to keep it at arm's length. Its English character, big business orientation, and largely anti-government politics did it no favors in winning support among NP politicians.[32] The fact that it was self-financing, and thereby independent of government control, also did it no favors with Pretoria.[33] Diplomats remember personal relations with Foundation representatives being excellent, but the institutional ones as quite weak, due to mutual suspicion. Shearer remembers that 'When I was in DC, I had a friendly relationship with the rep of the SA Foundation, John Chettle. But it was limited to being friends; it did not enter the official field at all. The Foundation saw government as being a pariah, and didn't want to be tarred in the same way [...] We were helpful as people, but not as an office.'[34] Van Heerden echoes similar views: 'We exchanged thoughts and contacts, though they were completely separate.'[35]

... as are Magnates

South Africa's two most prominent businessmen in the pre-1994 period—Anglo-American Chairman (1957–82) Harry Oppenheimer and Rembrandt Group Founder and CEO Anton Rupert—endured significant difficulties throughout their careers in pushing the South African Government to make policy reforms that would help business. Most of these reforms, however, were in the domestic realm, and both men largely avoided the foreign policy agenda.

Inheriting the chairmanship of Anglo upon father Ernest's death in 1957, Harry Oppenheimer stepped into the driver's seat of a firm whose dominant position within the South African economy cannot be overstated. In 1985, for example, Anglo alone accounted for 56 percent of the entire value of the Johannesburg Stock Exchange.[36] Despite this economic dominance, Oppenheimer—a United Party MP from 1948 to 1958, a major funder of the Progressive Party, and an outspoken critic of apartheid—had virtually no relationship with the government.[37] Neil van Heerden remembers introducing Oppenheimer to PW Botha at the 1979 Carlton conference: 'We had a lunch break, and we had a central table for PW and we quietly tried to steer people to his table. I saw Harry Oppenheimer there, who I knew personally, and I said "Harry, I'd like you to sit with PW," and he said, "Oh, but I don't know him!" The head of Anglo had never met PW!'[38] Oppenheimer admitted in 1982 that he had to rely on Afrikaner business colleagues to communicate with Vorster, as he similarly had no relationship with him.[39]

Anglo and government did on occasion pursue common interests. Pretoria found Oppenheimer and other Anglo executives to be useful conduits to regional leaders of countries where Anglo had investments or potential interests, like Zambia's Kenneth Kaunda, Zimbabwe's Robert Mugabe, and Mozambique's Samora Machel.[40] Gavin Relly, Oppenheimer's successor as chairman, even organized the 1975 Victoria Falls conference between Vorster and Kaunda while serving as head of Anglo's Zambia operations.[41] Oppenheimer and Anglo also remained staunch opponents of Western sanctions through the 1980s—leading to speculation that the firm used its financial clout to bully the Progressive Party into taking the same stance.[42] In all, however, these relations never grew beyond the realm of opportunism; neither Anglo nor Oppenheimer was able to influence Pretoria's foreign policy.

A self-made Afrikaner (and one-time Broederbond member) from the Cape who turned a garage operation manufacturing cigarettes into a global, multi-billion dollar conglomerate, Anton Rupert would seem far better positioned than Oppenheimer to influence Pretoria. Despite this, the two men shared several similarities, a trait that blunted Rupert's sway. Like Oppenheimer, Rupert sought to develop an international business portfolio that would eventually stretch from Canada to Europe to Fiji, and in seeking to expand it straddled the fine line between loyalty to his country and criticism of its governing party's policies.[43] Also like Oppenheimer, Rupert from the very start of his business career in the 1940s was unafraid to criticize apartheid, urging reforms on economic grounds. Rupert—who famously stated about the black community in 1966, 'If they do not eat, we do not sleep'—was adamant that the welfare of white and non-white South Africans was inextricably tied together, claiming that if blacks were not allowed to share South Africa's wealth, they would be driven toward communism.[44] He urged Verwoerd, for example, to allow black landownership in Soweto after the Sharpeville riots as a means to promote stability and stop the flow of foreign capital from the country, and through the 1980s urged reforms that would give non-whites a more significant stake in the economy—and make it easier for businesses to employ them.[45] These interventions opened him up to attack from NP leaders and questions about his patriotism, which tended to be more vitriolic than those on Oppenheimer given he was an Afrikaner.[46]

While his criticisms scuttled any chance Rupert may have had of influencing foreign policy, there is no indication that he tried especially hard to do so. Rupert, in fact, remained a booster of South Africa abroad and a strong opponent of sanctions and disinvestment. He praised the government when he saw it making steps toward reform, saying in 1985, 'Some of my compatriots take pleasure in only revealing our horrors and none of our achievements [. . .] We are doing our best.'[47] He also backed Botha's CONSAS plan, investing heavily in neighboring states like Lesotho.[48] Despite his criticisms, Rupert—both through personal connections and by dint of his wealth—also had excellent access to South Africa's post-1948 premiers; he was particularly close to Strijdom, although his perceived 'liberal' reputation led Verwoerd to view him with suspicion.[49] Pik Botha also considered him a confidante. Describing him as a 'great friend,' Botha recalls, 'I would go out to Rupert's wine farm and discuss things with him in confidence. After PW condemned me for my black president speech in parliament [in 1986], I phoned Rupert and we had lunch, just the two of us, and I explained I was considering resigning and forming my own party. And he said, "Don't go. Stay, work from inside.'"[50]

Business and PW Botha: Thwarted Foreign Policy Impact

PW Botha's 1978 ascension to the premiership was greeted with much enthusiasm by big business, with the hope that he would prove more receptive to their interests than any post-1948 prime minister. With the exception of outreach on the continent, business relations with his predecessor, John Vorster, were particularly cool. Although Vorster and his cabinet had no qualms about accepting donations from firms or using businessmen like Louis Luyt as fronts for Information Department schemes, Vorster took the line that 'the business of business is business' and that the private sector should stay out of government affairs.[51]

Botha, in contrast, had shown himself open to taking inputs from the business community during his 1966–78 stint as defense minister. In 1972, he established the Defense Advisory Council to draw in outside advice on policy issues, including heads of leading mining firm Gencor and conglomerate Barlows (later Barlow Rand).[52] Botha cultivated these ties throughout his tenure, and the Defense White Paper of 1977 explicitly included the private sector as a key actor in the state's 'Total Strategy.'[53] After Botha ascended to the premiership, his successor, Magnus Malan, expanded the council to include representatives of nearly all top firms, including Anglo-American, Sanlam, Old Mutual, and South African Breweries.[54] The council had benefits for both sides. Business leaders, for example, were able to get concessions from the SADF on service requirements to ensure a sufficient supply of white manpower.[55] The government, in contrast, was able to bring on board an array of skeptical and occasionally outright hostile actors from big business—particularly English big business—and co-opt them into a mutually beneficial partnership.[56]

Early on, Botha looked as if he would live up to this promise and indicated he was for the first time willing to incorporate the private sector more broadly into the government's foreign policy strategy.[57] The high point came at the November 1979 Carlton conference in Johannesburg, where Botha convened 300 business leaders—including non-white businessmen like Sam Motsuenyane and JN Reddy—to emphasize the need for government and the private sector to work more closely.[58] To this end, Botha requested that business be an active participant in promoting economic development in southern Africa under the guise of the prime minister's CONSAS idea, which would ultimately bind the region—the homelands and the independent states of the region—together under South African economic leadership.[59] Following on the conference, the government created two public–private sector enterprises, the Development Bank of Southern Africa and the Small Business Development Corporation, aimed at facilitating this partnership in the region.[60] The business community was impressed with Botha's initiative, with large and even medium-sized businesses anxious to take advantage of potential export and investment markets.[61] Even Oppenheimer commented that the CONSAS concept 'attracts us all, and businessmen will want to help.'[62] Outside the region, business also saw value in working closely with government to fight the battle against sanctions and keep export markets open.[63]

By mid-decade, however, Botha's refusal to initiate domestic reforms in the face of growing economic isolation led the business community to pull away from government.[64] The relationship bottomed out after the August 1985 'Rubicon' speech, where high expectations for reforms were dashed by Botha's combative remarks, sparking a sharp decline in the rand and an increasingly precarious economic position for the country at large. The English-language financial press, notably the *Financial Mail*, quickly turned on Botha, calling for his resignation, claiming Botha had 'dashed their [business] hopes and eroded their wealth.'[65] Corporate leaders grew increasingly dissatisfied with Botha's failure to grasp free market principles.[66] The disenchantment was mutual, with Botha also infuriated by business outreach to the exiled ANC, which he described as 'showing signs of weakness to the enemies of South Africa.'[67] Botha, according to former cabinet colleagues, also harbored an inherent distrust of the *geldmag* (money power) of English big business and paid little heed to its overtures. As former Finance Minister Barend du Plessis bluntly states, 'I would listen to big business, but PW would denigrate me for that.'[68]

No Discernable Pre-1994 Business Impact

Was business ever able to have an impact on foreign policy before 1994? Although Munger claimed in 1965 that business 'may from time to time contribute significantly to the shaping of South African foreign policy,' there is no indication that it actually did so.[69] Concerns by businessmen and farmers about the economic consequences of severing Commonwealth ties had no impact on Verwoerd's decision to do so, for example, while business concerns about Botha's regional destabilization strategy—unpopular with business on the grounds that it upset relations with regional trading partners, angered Western capitals, and in certain instances even damaged South African-owned capital assets in neighboring states— similarly had no effect.[70] According to former Deputy Foreign Minister (1991–4) Renier Schoeman, business inputs had no effect on regional security considerations, noting, 'If collateral damage was done to business [in a raid], don't think there was a general sitting thinking, "Oh, we just built a nice new supermarket in Swaziland, we can't go bomb everybody." Who's going to say that? No one around that table. It's a very wussy sort of thing.'[71]

It is worth noting that during this period, business made almost no effort to weigh in on policy and seek changes in foreign policy (beyond those domestic changes that turned external opinion). From the business standpoint on foreign affairs, outside of a period of engagement during the 1960s and 1970s, firms generally had little time for government, which was a burden rather than a boon for companies seeking to do business abroad. According to former Trade and Industry Minister Dawie de Villiers, 'The big companies in South Africa looked after themselves. They would call when they needed something serious [. . .] but Anglo or General Mining would look after themselves.'[72] The only government assistance he recalled was in the sanctions-busting realm, but this was limited to 'those who couldn't look after themselves, like fruit exporters.'[73] From the business side, executives noted they had little to no interaction with the commercial or economic sections of embassies abroad, finding their involvement generally of little value. Overall, the strained relationship between business and government ensured that this community had no real impact on the foreign policymaking process.

Business and Foreign Policy, 1994–2008: Frustrated Ambitions

South Africa's return to the community of democracies opened the world's doors to its products and investment (and vice versa), giving South African business real incentive to weigh in on its government's foreign policy, particularly toward the booming African market. The theoretically more open policy environment should also have allowed firms to make their policy preferences known and have them considered. Ultimately, neither hypothesis would prove true.

Post-1994 Outward Business Expansion

The dominant paradigm of South African business since 1994 in relation to the outside world has been its rapid expansion on the African continent. Unshackled by sanctions and negative perceptions, South African businesses between 1994 and 2008 significantly increased their presence worldwide and on the continent, in terms of both exports and foreign direct investment. Totaling just R75 billion in 1994, South African exports surged to more than R643 billion by 2008, proving a massive boon to companies oriented externally.[74] Although exports to Africa accounted for about only 15 percent of South African exports in 2008, trade with the rest of Africa showed the biggest growth in that period, jumping a whopping 328 percent between 1994 and 2003.[75] Importantly for South African firms, while exports to the industrialized world were heavily skewed toward primary commodities, exports to the continent tended toward profitable value-added manufactured products.

Beyond exports, the period from 1994 to 2008 also saw increasing South African corporate expansion around the world, such as the

2002 acquisition of Miller in the United States by South African Breweries. As with exports, however, Africa registered the most significant regional increase, driven by South African firms realizing that the domestic market was too small and saturated to offer many growth opportunities. Although turbulent, huge swathes of the continent's nearly 1 billion people were ignored by Western investors, giving South African firms an opportunity to cash in; as one South African businessman noted, 'Africa is a huge market; it may be turbulent sometimes, but it eats and uses toiletries every day.'[76]

To this end, capital investment in African countries by South African firms saw a huge jump after the transition, increasing from R3.7 billion in 1994 to an estimated R80 billion by 2006.[77] By 2008, almost all of the top 100 firms on the Johannesburg Stock Exchange had an African presence, up from only a handful in 1994.[78] Michael Spicer—a longtime Anglo-American executive (and deputy director of SAIIA in the 1980s) who took over as South Africa Foundation (later Business Leadership South Africa) head in 2005— echoes this point, noting that all 80 of the association's members have an African presence, whereas only about ten would have had one in 1994.[79] These firms have come to dominate the African market, with 19 of the continent's 20 largest companies (and 62 of the top 100) being South African as of 2006.[80] This expansion has focused on a host of sectors, including standbys like mining and brewing as well as telecommunications, financial services, and retail.[81]

Notably, this South African investment was continent-wide rather than focused just on its neighbors in the Southern African Development Community (SADC). Nigeria, with its massive population and oil wealth, became a significant destination for South African capital, while Anglophone countries in east and west Africa also proved promising (although France's hold on its former colonies has proved difficult to pry loose).[82] That is not to say, however, that South African firms abandoned southern Africa; its private-sector investment in SADC dwarfs that of any other country and its firms are omnipresent in most regional markets.[83] Also of note is that South African investment was not just from the private sector. By 2008, South Africa's Transnet ran Cameroon's railroad and had rehabilitated those of Nigeria; Eskom managed power plants in Mali, Tanzania, and Zambia; and Airports Company South Africa managed the airports of seven African countries.[84] The continent's economy had truly become 'South African-ized.'

Government Facilitation Efforts a Mixed Bag

From the start the ANC government was enthusiastic about South African business expansion in Africa, with DFA Director-General Jackie Selebi saying in 1995 that such growth would create employment opportunities in South Africa while benefitting the continent.[85] Following the example of de Klerk—the first South African leader to include South African businesspeople on state visits— both Mandela and Mbeki were active in facilitating opportunities for South African firms abroad and including them in travels. These inclusions proved valuable in Africa, with Sudan and Congo-Kinshasa providing two instances where Mbeki's inclusion of businesspeople on a visit resulted in investment deals.[86] Although Pretoria did not underwrite private-sector operations on the continent as it did in the 1970s, the post-1994 government took several steps to encourage South African business to invest in Africa.[87] The government vastly expanded its African diplomatic presence from 1994 to 2008, covering nearly the whole continent by the end of Mbeki's term, and commercial/economic sections in embassies were increased to help South African firms. Foreign exchange regulations also were loosened to facilitate African investment, particularly in SADC.[88]

Not all of Pretoria's interventions were met with enthusiasm by South African firms. Several African governments and host-country businesses expressed bemusement about the 'un-African' ways in which South African firms conducted themselves, while there was also dissatisfaction in several countries about South African business practices, brought to light in 2003 allegations by workers in a Shoprite store in Zambia that they were mistreated by South African managers.[89] To address these concerns, the government and the ANC from the early 2000s sought to institute a code of conduct for businesses operating on the continent. While DFA discussions of a code did not make it past the planning phase, the ANC at its 2007

Polokwane conference called in a resolution for a legally-binding code that would mandate firms hold themselves to high ethical standards when operating in Africa, especially with regard to labor regulation.[90]

The push for a code of conduct and better business behavior was undergirded by Pretoria's desire that business foster positive perceptions of South Africa. 'Business plays a very important role,' says former ANC International Relations Head Mavivi Myakayaka-Manzini. 'Say for instance, when a South African firm is going to open a business in Nigeria, it must be informed by our foreign policy. That's why we had to discuss their behavior on the continent so it's in line with our foreign policy, which is to create equal relations, promote development, and ensure it's not a dominating relationship.'[91] If business got out of line, however, it could theoretically damage South Africa's ambitions for political leadership on the continent.[92]

The push for a code never reached critical mass during the Mbeki administration, being hindered by logistical difficulties—how could the South African Government force a firm to abide by stricter regulations than those of the host country? Even Aziz Pahad acknowledges this, noting that while it was important for business to play a constructive role in African economies, 'A legislative charter cannot work. You can't impose BEE [Black Economic Empowerment] on a company operating in another country. They live by local rules.'[93] Still, calls for it rankled some in the business community, who took them as a sign of continued mistrust and a lack of appreciation. 'Companies complain that government is way too quick to believe when African governments complain South African firms are behaving badly,' a prominent business consultant notes. 'I talk to Shoprite often, and there's always some random NGO who says Shoprite is ripping off workers in some country, and government here believes the NGO.'[94]

Even beyond the code of conduct issue, businesses have found government attempts to assist them lacking, particularly from a capability standpoint. 'We're nowhere near a team mentality between business and government, so what that meant was in Africa, business paddled its own canoe,' Spicer notes. 'It didn't feel there was mileage in getting with political authorities, because they'd ask whether we were coming to exploit the local populations and so on. And a lot of the big firms had better networks than government.'[95] Multinationals found Pretoria's diplomatic expansion in Africa to be of little use to them, seldom using embassies' commercial and economic sections.[96] Academic and businessman Vincent Maphai—who has held senior executive positions at SABMiller and BHP Billiton—says while he has always sought out South African embassies in Africa, 'It was more out of politeness, saying, "I'll be there, here's what I'm doing." For me, it's nice if my ambassador is there to launch a project, but I've never said, "Here's what we want to do, can you help us?"'[97] Other complaints by business included a lack of coordination between the DFA and Department of Trade and Industry in helping South African firms and a lack of government support for South African firms lobbying for large-scale African infrastructure projects funded by international financial institutions like the World Bank.[98]

The difficulties of retailer Shoprite Checkers—which by 2008 had more than 100 stores in 15 African countries and was the biggest private employer in Africa—in dealing with the government on its investments in Angola provide a telling example of Pretoria's lack of responsiveness to the business community. For example, although Shoprite Checkers and many other South African firms view Angola as prime territory for investment, Angolan bureaucratic intransigence has erected significant hurdles to doing business there. 'We're doing business there of about R500 million, and one of the things that hampers our business is that it takes you something like three weeks to get a single entry visa,' fumes CEO Whitey Basson, who also cited customs barriers, onerous disease controls, and excessive paperwork as problems.[99] Basson notes that he has approached the South African Government for help on this, but to little avail. 'Have we had any success? I'd emphatically say no,' he says.[100]

The Mechanics of Government–Business Interaction

The 1994 political transition did not catch white business unaware or unprepared; leading South African businessmen and corporations—notably Anglo-American—had been laying the groundwork for relations with the ANC since 1985.[101] Business continued its full court press after 1990—Anglo hosted the ANC's first meeting on South African soil in 1990 at the Vergelegen wine estate, for instance, and corporates showed few qualms about footing the bill for ANC activities during the transition period.[102] This cultivation of the ANC produced meaningful and early payoffs. After iterating that nationalizing mines, banks, and industry was ANC policy upon Nelson Mandela's 1990 release from prison, the party dropped its socialist rhetoric, with Mandela emphasizing his government's support of free-market principles.[103] Nevertheless, the business community—both individual firms and associations—had to adapt to new players, a sometimes-rocky process that, under Mbeki, was marred by an underlying sense of mistrust.

Key Institutional Players, New and Old

Business groupings, new and old, played a dominant role in the interactions between government and business after 1994. The South Africa Foundation—rechristened Business Leadership South Africa (BLSA) in 2005—remained the leading organization of big business and foreign investors in South Africa, with its 80 members representing the country's largest firms. Many key institutional actors predating 1994—like the South African Chamber of Business, South African Foreign Trade Organization, and South African Chamber of Commerce and Industry—continued to operate, while a significant new player emerged in 2004 with the creation of Business Unity South Africa (BUSA). A merger of the Black Business Council and predominantly white Business South Africa, BUSA emerged as one of the country's first racially mixed business organizations. Several interviewees expressed the opinion that BUSA, with more black businesses represented, was the grouping closest to government during the Mbeki administration, particularly in relation to BLSA. As Maphai claims, 'BLSA is seen as the past.'[104] Mbeki would meet with BUSA representations regularly, and BUSA would select businesses to travel along with the president on state visits.[105]

The focus of these groups, however, was overwhelmingly on domestic issues, particularly how the business community could address the country's development needs. Similarly, the fora through which government interacted with the private sector, like the National Economic Development and Labor Council and Big Business Working Group, paid little attention to foreign policy matters when meeting with government.[106] There were some exceptions. The NEPAD Business Forum, founded in 2002, included more than 200 South African firms and associations with an eye on supporting Mbeki's NEPAD initiative and promoting the continent as an investment destination. It did not, however, seek to lobby the South African Government on policy.[107] Also, The South African Chamber of Business and a handful of other groups also paid attention to South African trade policy, although the business community was by no means unanimous on the issue.[108] 'The business community is very divided,' on trade issues, trade policy expert Peter Draper notes. 'I don't see an organized constituency in that respect.'[109]

Solid Relations with Mandela ...

Businessmen of all races and backgrounds have largely fond remembrances of President Mandela and his openness to the business community. As van Heerden recalls, 'I had very good contacts with Mr. Mandela, and he was very accessible and helpful. He helped me a lot in Africa and arranged for me to do some things. He was very accessible, even on a cell phone.'[110] Mandela met regularly with an agglomeration of about 15 top (primarily white and English) business leaders, known as the Brenthurst Group, and he also had good relations with the Afrikaans-speaking business community, consulting figures like Anton Rupert on decisions that would have an impact on the business community, such as before the 1998 appointment of Tito Mboweni as Reserve Bank Governor (although he did not always take such advice, appointing Mboweni despite business reservations).[111] Nonetheless, as befitting Mandela's generally inward focus, his interaction with business tended to be on domestic concerns.

... and Touchy Ones with Mbeki

Mbeki's interactions with the business community were more regular and structured than those of Mandela, although participants have less favorable perceptions of their robustness and impact. Mbeki had three working groups—on agriculture, big business, and black business—in which he would participate, usually about biennially, and he also sat on three business-focused councils, related to information technology, international investment, and international marketing.[112] Broadly, the participants in these groups could be split into white South African business, black South African business, and non-South African business, each of which had considerably different experiences with the president.

The overwhelming view of white businessmen is that Mbeki did not like or trust them. 'Mbeki had a love hate relationship with business,' recalls Spicer, referring specifically to largely white-owned major corporations. 'Pragmatically, he understood globalization and that they needed to engage with it. We have to talk to business, but can we trust them? They were the handmaidens of apartheid.'[113] Neil van Heerden has a similar perspective: 'We understood that Mbeki was so overwhelmingly sensitive that white business would still call the shots that he did not want to be anywhere near us or associate with us.'[114] In describing this mistrust, van Heerden recalled an anecdote of a meeting between Mbeki and the Foundation during Mbeki's tenure as deputy president:

The most acute example [of his mistrust] is that shortly after he became deputy president, he let us know that it would be ok to have a dinner with him and cigars. We jumped at this, and decided before the dinner that we should take something along. The idea came up that in most big South African corporations, there's spare capacity of senior people who are still young enough to be active. After the dinner, we kicked back, and the head of the Foundation, Conrad Strauss of Standard Bank made this proposal to Mbeki, for corporations to second people at their cost in fields of expertise that you need. We thought this was a nice idea. Well, Mbeki didn't so much as respond with

one breath, and afterward people close to him said he viewed
this as the absolute insult, why were we so stupid. That was the
end of a productive relationship.[115]

Outside of regular meetings, Mbeki's contact with white big business
was limited. 'I never got to see Mbeki [while he was president]; I was
scheduled to see him twice but never got to see him,' recalls van
Heerden, who (like others) noted that his appointments with Mbeki
were shunted off to Presidency Minister Essop Pahad.[116] As for the
meetings that did occur, Johann Rupert—Anton's son and successor
as Rembrandt head—described them as 'orchestrated PowerPoint
exchanges [. . .] not a frank dialogue.'[117]

Mbeki also viewed business critiques of government economic
policies, no matter how well intentioned, and suggestions on
improving them with suspicion and contempt. The business
community's first organized attempt came in 1996 with its Growth
for All document, which lobbied for more decisive economic reforms
in the face of declining investor confidence and a weakening rand. As
academic Antoinette Handley describes it, Growth for All 'broke all
the rules' in the nascent interaction between government and
business, with the document using blunt language to criticize
government economic policy.[118] Spicer's view is that the government
viewed Growth for All through the lens of 'Who are these people to
tell us what to do?' on economic policy, believing business could have
handled the process more adroitly.[119] For Mbeki more specifically,
Spicer believes that the broadly neoliberal prescriptions of Growth
for All mirrored many aspects of Mbeki's not-yet-unveiled
Growth, Employment, and Redistribution program, ultimately
making it more difficult to sell to the unions and other actors on the
left of the economic spectrum. However, he notes that business did
not know about Growth, Employment, and Redistribution, or vice
versa, 'which indicates that the relationship wasn't that close.'[120]

Mbeki's mistrust in part stemmed from a perception that white
businessmen were trying to undermine the economy internationally.
One must remember, says Maphai, that 'the major firms—Anglo,
SAB, Sappi, quite a few—the first thing they did after 1994 was

move their listings to London or New York. It left a bad taste with everybody.'[121] At one 2002 meeting of the black business working group, he went so far as to say that white businessmen were 'badmouthing the economy [and] spreading negative sentiment about the South African economy abroad and elsewhere.'[122] He also erupted in 2004 after Anglo CEO Tony Traher said that while South African political risk was declining, it had not yet disappeared. In an online letter, Mbeki defended his government's record for enacting the most business-friendly policies in South African history and attacked Traher for suggesting that the government of a democratic South Africa presented more risk than its apartheid-era predecessor.[123]

The perception of white business is that leading black businessmen like Saki Macozoma, Reuel Khoza, Patrice Motsepe, and others had far better and more intimate access to the president than white businessmen did. This appears to have been the case, given close political and personal relationships between them; Khoza says Mbeki sought to surround himself with black businessmen 'who could think,' and in their interactions he enjoyed 'debating issues and challenging issues.'[124] However, those close to Mbeki deny that only black business had an influence. Essop Pahad cites Khoza and Macozoma as business leaders to whom Mbeki would listen, but also cited Spicer as being influential.[125] A common denominator for both black and white business, however, is that their discussions were focused heavily on the domestic realm, with issues like black economic empowerment taking priority.

While domestic business was largely out of the policy loop, foreign businesspeople with a presence in South Africa had excellent access to Mbeki and, in the view of those around the president, held sway with him, particularly in the area of how to draw foreign investment to South Africa. 'When he had his international investment council; Bill Rhodes [of Citigroup] was on it, Niall Fitzgerald [of Reuters], the guy from Commerzbank [Martin Kohlhausen], Tony O'Reilly [of Independent Media], [the heads of] Tata, Mittal. He listened very closely to them,' Essop Pahad remembers. 'We'd have a meeting all together on Saturdays, and on

Sundays he'd have one-on-ones, with Frank [Chikane] and Mojanku [Gumbi] sitting in.'[126] Smuts Ngonyama recounted a similar list of influential foreign businessmen, adding Ghanaian mining magnate Lazarus Zim to the list.[127] In the eyes of political analyst Steven Friedman, Mbeki's mistrust of white big business accounted for his willingness to listen to outsiders: 'Foreign business at least had the virtue of not being involved in the old order like white SA business.'[128]

Zimbabwe Inefficacy Displays Business's Limited Influence
Zimbabwe was the most significant foreign policy issue on which the business community sought to influence government during the Mbeki administration, and its inefficacy exemplifies their lack of clout with Pretoria. Although difficult to quantify given the ring fencing of operations there by South African investors, the collapse of the Zimbabwean economy from 1999 to 2008 had a deleterious effect on firms investing there.[129] Although some companies were able to scrape up bargain-basement assets, most firms operating in Zimbabwe saw profits plunge and a handful—particularly private agricultural holdings by South African investors—were seized by the Zimbabwean Government or its proxies.[130] Parastatals dealing in Zimbabwe faced an even more difficult situation, with Eskom and Sasol—the Zimbabwean Government's main suppliers of electricity and oil, respectively—being owed several hundred million rand by their Zimbabwean counterparts by 2004.[131] Although the Zimbabwean electricity authority was ultimately able to clear its debts, its long-term indebtedness led Reuel Khoza, then chairman of Eskom—heretofore a defender of Pretoria's Zimbabwe policy—to declare in 2003 that South Africa should show Zimbabwe a 'red card' if it continued to default on its payments.[132]

Business did try to raise the issue in its interactions with Mbeki and senior DFA officials, but its attempts resulted in no tangible results.[133] Neil van Heerden in his role as executive director of the South Africa Foundation on one occasion attempted to raise the issue in a meeting with Mbeki, but was given an unsatisfactory 90-minute response with no opportunity for rejoinder.[134] Van Heerden remembers being shut down in other attempts to raise the issue:

I had requests from business leaders to meet with government urgently about Zimbabwe to talk about what was happening there, and we made absolute zero progress. The guy I talked to there was Aziz, but it didn't work at all. Imagine taking four or five guys across to Pretoria, and sitting with them eyeball to eyeball and telling them about their concerns. I'd get calls from them weeks later and nothing would happen. Aziz would promise you the sky, but do nothing. Absolutely nothing.[135]

Criticism of Mugabe by the business community did not only come from white business leaders. Sam Motsuenyane, who led South Africa's 2002 election observation mission to Zimbabwe, notes that he raised his concerns with Pretoria after those flawed elections, but to little avail.[136] Khoza, continuing his football metaphor, also remembers raising Zimbabwe in his interactions with Mbeki and other senior officials. '[Mbeki] used to say if someone would misbehave, they would get the yellow card or the red card. So we would debate that, and say on the balance of what you debated, Mugabe is driving the economy into the ground, he's exterminating whole villages like in Matabeleland. That deserves a red card.'[137] Khoza recalls Saki Macozoma as another leading black businessman who would air his criticisms of Mugabe. These critiques, however, had no impact on Pretoria's approach toward its northern neighbor.

Conclusion: Never a Player, Past or Present

The conclusion of this chapter is clear—business was not, before or after 1994, able to influence government's foreign policy. Looking at the 1994–2008 period, Aziz Pahad bluntly states, 'Business overall was not a driver of foreign policy. Too early. It will in later years.'[138] South African business did take advantage of Pretoria's diplomatic efforts beyond its borders, particularly in Africa, but it did not actively tried to lobby on policy. Unlike many other actors examined in this study, however, the blame for the business community's ineffectiveness cannot be ascribed to a lack of access to government—particularly under the Mbeki administration, various business groupings had regular access to the president and other senior leaders. Even if the quality of the interactions was lacking, they still were able to raise external issues. Yet, beyond Zimbabwe, they chose not to do so. A combination of three factors appears behind this inability to have an influence on foreign policy, before and after 1994:

- *Disinterest:* South African business has always focused first on maximizing profits, preferring to ignore the government policy-making sphere than trying to influence it, especially with regard to external affairs. Speaking specifically about the post-1994 business community, van Heerden opined, 'Very few business leaders [...] really take an interest in directly political questions and fewer still [are] interested or involved in foreign affairs questions.'[139] Business has only sought to interject itself into political conversations when the government was making policies detrimental to its profit-ability, such as its pre-1994 push for apartheid reforms and post-1994 efforts to influence economic policy. Foreign policy was very much a secondary concern in both instances; as Spicer notes, 'Business hasn't drawn up a foreign policy agenda; the domestic agenda is far more important.'[140]

- *Disunity:* Another disincentive to make foreign policy inputs is that there is no 'business community' that can make them. As noted earlier, firms in export industries (like manufacturing) have different priorities than, say, mining firms seeking lower trade barriers. Even on Zimbabwe, firms benefiting from the inflow of human capital into South Africa would have had a very different perspective on the issue than a firm victimized by expropriation or a collapsed Zimbabwean market. Hence, the business community has not spoken with one voice on foreign affairs.

- *Disinclination:* Lastly, business appears to have avoided the foreign policy realm for the simple reason that avoiding criticism of the government beyond what is absolutely necessary is a generally sound principle for the bottom line. As historian Hermann Giliomee observed, 'There are ways government can punish you, so business prefers to keep its head below the parapet. Business can be harmed by changes in the regulatory environment, so silence is safe.'[141] If business was to expend its political capital in attacking the government or demanding reforms, or both, it was in the domestic realm where it mattered. Forcing the government's hand on foreign policy concerns was not worth the risk or the effort.

CHAPTER 7

PARLIAMENT

The role of international legislatures in foreign policymaking must be viewed in the larger context of their influence on public policy writ large. Academic Philip Norton identifies three types of legislatures in regard to the policy process—policymakers, policy influencers, and those with little or no impact—with a combination of laws and political culture accounting for the differentiation.[1] In the foreign policy realm, while legislatures in most democratic countries have specific competencies for influencing foreign policy debates, they often do not assert these powers or use them to challenge the executive on its foreign policy priorities.[2] As Christopher Hill notes, 'Given the number of occasions when even the parliaments with relevant powers do not assert themselves to halt treaties or to interrogate the foreign and defense budgets, it is clear that it will take an unusual combination of circumstances for the executive to have its agreement with another state overturned by parliament at home.'[3] In general, legislatures 'confirm, rather than initiate, foreign policy,' although the United States Senate—which has the additional power to confirm ambassadors and senior officials—is an exception.[4]

There are many reasons for a lack of legislative involvement. First, legislators' chief concern is what gets them elected and retained in office, and foreign policy—outside of times of war or other crises—is seldom a vote getter. Second, legislators rarely have competencies in foreign affairs and often lack interest in the topic, outside of participation in trips abroad during recess sessions. Third, as noted with the issue of academic engagement, temporal and human factors cannot be ignored. A certain speaker of parliament may be very taken by foreign policy concerns and elevate them in the legislature, but there are no guarantees that his or her successor will share the same priorities. Similarly, 'hot' foreign policy issues, like a war, can drive foreign policy to the front burner of legislative agendas, while they would fall back in peacetime. The implications of this general lack of engagement by legislatures are the topic of debate. Joseph Frankel echoes a realist perspective when he refers to parliaments as 'large, clumsy bodies' whose 'participation upsets diplomacy.'[5] The liberal counterpoint, voiced in post-World War II Great Britain, is that a strong parliament engaged on foreign policy matters could counter unchecked executive power, particularly over such decisions as going to war.[6]

All of these issues will be considered when assessing the role of South Africa's parliament in the foreign policy process. This chapter will tease out questions of public engagement, expertise, and personal interests to see whether parliament has ever had the power and inclination to be a foreign policy player. The role of portfolio committees (post-1994) and party study groups (past and present) also will be examined in detail.

Foreign Affairs Legislative Powers Before 1994

To understand how parliament since Union in 1910 has played a role in the foreign policy process, one must first examine the legal basis for legislative involvement in the field. The powers of parliament to weigh in on foreign policy before 1994 stem from four documents: the South Africa Act of 1909, the act of the British parliament that established Union; the 1926 Balfour Declaration, which afforded the dominions limited powers to control their foreign relations; and the constitutions of 1961 and 1983. Although none of the four documents dealt extensively with parliament's foreign policy role, they did spell out the basics of legislative–executive interaction on the topic.

Pre-Republican Confusion

Neither the South Africa Act nor the Balfour Declaration offered much guidance about the role of parliament in foreign policymaking. The former document says nothing specific about South Africa's foreign relations, given that the Union's dominion status meant it had no independent foreign policy. Command of military forces in South Africa was granted to the British King, through his governor-general, taking parliament out of that equation.[7] The Senate had the power to 'appoint committees to investigate specific matters,' although it does not appear to have ever done so with regard to external affairs.[8] The Balfour Declaration theoretically granted dominions power to conduct their own foreign relations, although the vagaries of its wording left the degree of this independence from London in question.[9] While the declaration did not specifically mention parliamentary responsibilities, it raised the question of whether the South African people's elected representatives could repudiate Great Britain's foreign policy. In terms of parliamentary responsibility, the only practical change it spurred was the adding of a separate external affairs budget vote following the 1926 creation of that department.

Nevertheless, South African premiers did call on parliament to affirm the two major issues of the pre-1948 period, namely entry into the World Wars. Louis Botha won overwhelming support in 1914 for South African entry, although by 1939 entry into the Second World War was a far more hotly contested issue. Prime Minister Hertzog had long advocated South African neutrality in the event of war, but he also stated that parliament would decide on the course of action.[10] This would be no party line exercise—although the United Party controlled 111 of the legislature's 150 seats, Party membership was divided on the issue. During the September 3, 1939 special parliamentary session that debated whether to enter the war, supporters of entering the conflict argued—as did Botha 25 years earlier—that South Africa's membership in the Commonwealth compelled it to enter the war, refuting Hertzog's argument that Balfour allowed states to choose their own course of action.[11] Smuts' motion to enter the war carried the day by a tight margin of

80 to 67, splitting the Party and elevating Smuts to the premiership. Ultimately, however, neither vote appears to have had any legal basis; rather, they were held for political reasons. The question of parliament's pre-republican legal status with regard to foreign policy was never adequately resolved.

Parliament and Foreign Affairs Under the 1961 and 1983 Constitutions

Neither South Africa's 1961 republican constitution nor its 1983 tri-cameral constitution gave parliament any additional responsibilities in the foreign affairs realm; rather, both cemented executive primacy on foreign policy. Both documents affirmed that the state president was vested with the rights to appoint diplomats, enter into international treaties, and declare war or make peace.* Parliament was given the final say on budgetary decisions and, theoretically, could have voted down defense and foreign affairs budgets, although this never occurred.[12] MPs also had the right to ask questions for the record of ministers, including on issues of foreign affairs. The 1983 constitution additionally allowed for the creation of joint standing committees across the three houses that would 'consider' bills related to 'general affairs' affecting all three racial groupings, one of which was foreign affairs.[13] Committees had about 25 members; opposition members were included in proportion to the various parties' representation, although the chair was always from the NP.[14] Committees had the power to draft legislation and amend legislation submitted from the executive before it could be put to a vote, as well as query their respective ministers on any topics they saw fit, particularly before budget votes.

Although limited, South Africa's parliament until 1994 had, in theory, some power to hold the executive accountable for foreign policy decisions. In reality, it did not do so. Deon Geldenhuys notes that up to 1948, parliament did not display 'the slightest interest' in the activities of the then Department of External Affairs.[15] Debates in parliament after 1948 were slightly more robust but, largely driven by the increasingly ineffective opposition, made little dent on government policy. Foreign policy through the 1970s was not a front burner issue. As long-time MP Japie Basson remembers, 'Debates in parliament during the 1960s and 1970s were over flags and anthems and race and farming, not so much foreign policy.'[16] Longtime opposition leader Colin Eglin echoes this point, noting 'in general, there were debates on foreign policy, but not the dominant debates— they were on internal politics and the emergence of the ANC.'[17] From the mid-1970s, the executive largely kept members of parliament in the dark on Pretoria's diplomatic initiatives and military incursions, and MPs gave little scrutiny to the foreign affairs and defense budgets, even after the 'Muldergate' Information scandal.[18]

After 1983, the committees dealing with foreign policy generally did not challenge the executive; much like their counterpart committees dealing with domestic issues, they simply rubber-stamped government policy.[19†] Committees would query their ministers, often at length—longtime committee stalwart Boy Geldenhuys remembers the foreign affairs committee would spend up to five days before the DFA budget vote questioning the minister on various aspects of foreign policy—but they never offered more than token amendments to budgets.[20] Secrecy around specifics of the defense budget kept that debate particularly vague. The committees, which met infrequently, also suffered from the fact that Departments of Foreign Affairs and Defense were not departments that generated much legislation. As Pik Botha recalls, 'In my years, Foreign Affairs only passed one law, and that was on diplomatic immunities and privileges. Foreign Affairs was not a law maker.'[21]

Another strike against the committees' effectiveness was the fact that the executive treated the committee's potential oversight roles— as well as that of the larger parliament—with little respect. Obfuscation and even outright lying characterized ministerial interactions with parliament, and specifically the committees. During Vorster's *détente* efforts of the 1970s, Foreign Minister Hilgard Muller (1964–77) was careful to avoid revealing the states and leaders with which Pretoria was quietly dealing; when questioned by opposition members, he shut down debate by saying such 'delicate matters' ought not be publicly discussed.[22] The foreign or defense ministers would similarly shut down questions on issues that involved external defense engagement, such as cross-border operations or arms sales, on the grounds that they endangered national security.[23] After the Angola invasion, both Defense Minister PW Botha and Foreign Minister Muller flatly denied that South African troops were inside Angola, not even taking the supposedly trustworthy NP caucus into confidence.[24] So, while the committees theoretically gave parliament power to weigh in on foreign policy, in reality they did not do so and were effectively ignored by the executive.

The Role of the National Party Foreign Affairs Study Group
Most power in parliament to influence policy debate lay within the NP study groups pertaining to specific departments. These groups, of which there were about two dozen in the early 1980s, would meet approximately monthly during the parliamentary session (about five or six times per year) to discuss the issues up for debate; ministers and senior civil servants would often be called upon to brief them.[25] Foreign affairs and defense both had study groups, with the former being one of the most popular, growing to nearly 70 members by the late 1980s.[26] The group's popularity stemmed from the opportunities for foreign travel, the issue's supposedly 'high profile' nature, and the possibility of membership opening the doors to a diplomatic posting (as it did for several members).[27] Its popularity, however, was not a reflection of its influence. Former members remember that outside of meeting with foreign visitors and occasionally traveling abroad, the group was little more than a talk shop with no influence on policy.[28] The foreign minister would occasionally brief the group, but neither Muller nor Botha were responsive to questions, briefing only on what they were working on at the time and frequently emphasizing the sensitivity of the issues discussed.[29]

Several Reasons for Pre-1994 Parliament's Lack of Influence

In addition to a legal framework that largely excluded it from policymaking, parliament's impotence also was the result of an acquiescent ruling party caucus with little inclination to challenge its leadership on foreign affairs; the ineffectiveness of the parliamentary opposition; and the fact that most MPs showed little interest in foreign policy debates.

National Party Caucus Discipline

NP parliamentary dominance between 1948 and 1994 is difficult to overstate. After scraping into power with 52 percent of the seats in the 1948 election, the NP from 1953 to 1989 never held fewer than 60 percent of seats in the lower House of Assembly, winning a high of 81 percent in the 1977 election. This overweening control meant that only a major breach of discipline within the NP caucus would have fostered serious questioning of government policy, foreign or otherwise, in parliament. That was not to be the case; the NP caucus would prove exceptionally disciplined in its parliamentary votes until 1994, for institutional- and career-related reasons.[30] Although caucus members represented individual constituencies and had to be mindful of opinion back home, the NP was characterized by a strong element of public conformism.[31] 'When I entered parliament in 1987, we were told by the chief whips, "You are new here, you should listen," and that was the way of controlling MPs,' former MP and NP spokesman Johan Steenkamp notes. 'The whips told us, "If you stand up in caucus, you destroy your political career."'[32] Rather, MPs took policy direction from the prime minister/president, cabinet, and the Party's provincial congresses.[33]

Caucus discipline on foreign policy also was a result of general agreement on the issues. Within the Party, former minister and NP foreign affairs study group chairman Dawie de Villiers remembers, 'Foreign affairs was never a contested issue. It didn't figure high on the radar screen,' in comparison to domestic issues.[34] Foreign policy after 1948 was occasionally of interest as a constitutional issue; according to Basson, there was a divide in the NP caucus over continued membership in the Commonwealth, with Malan's Cape backers in favor and Strijdom's Transvaalers against.[35] After Verwoerd decided—without consulting parliament or his cabinet—to withdraw in 1961, however, there was no other issue that engaged the caucus.[36] Interviewees also cited trust in government principals, notably Pik Botha, as a reason for a lack of caucus debate on the topic. 'There was a perception that Pik knew what was best, and there wasn't much need to question him,' Steenkamp remembers.[37] It was understood among group members, and the broader NP caucus, that the prime minister and the foreign minister made foreign policy.[38]

Opposition Ineffectiveness

Given NP dominance, the political opposition—first the United Party, later the Progressives and Conservatives—could do little to affect foreign policy, even if they occasionally did use it to attack the government to score political points. The United Party was particularly active in this regard, playing to the Party membership's generally pro-British attitudes by attacking the government on such issues as its refusal to back Great Britain during the 1956 Suez Canal crisis and its moves toward withdrawal from the Commonwealth.[39] Nevertheless, party leader (1956–77) De Villiers Graaff was careful to emphasize that his loyalty was to South Africa first, justifying his arguments on the latter issue on the grounds that Commonwealth withdrawal would leave South Africa without allies.[40] The other notable issue on which Graaff attacked the government was what he described as its insufficiently supportive stance toward Rhodesia in the immediate post-UDI period.[41] 'The people of South Africa will never forgive the prime minister if he sits idly by while civilized government and stability are destroyed in Rhodesia as they have been in so many African states,' Graaff stated in parliament in early 1966.[42] For the most part, however, these attacks were political and focused on isolated instances rather than the broader foreign policy thrust; Graaff himself later noted that he could not remember significant differences over foreign affairs outside of Rhodesia.[43]

The United Party's 1977 split and the subsequent rise of the Progressive Federal Party—which became the leading opposition party after that year's general elections—as well as PW Botha's 1978 assumption of the premiership changed the nature of government– opposition relations in parliament. Opposition MPs, led by

Progressive Federal Party leader Colin Eglin, immediately became more vocal on the foreign policy front, attacking the government over the Information scandal, angering the tempestuous prime minister.[44] In retaliation, Pik Botha in April 1979 accused Eglin in parliament of having leaked confidential information about the possibility of a settlement in Southwest Africa to the American ambassador, sparking a controversy that forced him out as Party leader.[45] Thereafter, the opposition's foreign policy focus cooled for the rest of the 1980s, while its resistance to international sanctions put it on the same page as the ruling party.[46]

General Disinterest and Discomfort

A final reason for parliament's lack of power with regard to foreign policy stemmed from MPs' own inexperience and lack of interest in the topic. In his memoirs, former Information Service head Piet Meiring recalls that upon visiting parliament in the early 1960s he was 'amazed how disinterested the legislators on either side of the House were in South Africa's rating abroad' and noted how they wanted to avoid foreign affairs discussions altogether.[47] This disinterest clearly displayed itself on parliament's foreign trips, which were more boondoggles than efforts to learn about conditions abroad. Longtime diplomat Donald Sole noted in his autobiography that MPs—particularly those from the NP—on official trips abroad were remarkably ignorant of the pertinent issues; he recounted one incident where an NP parliamentarian visiting Germany thanked his hosts by delivering a speech 'which could be described as, and certainly was regarded by his hosts as, neo-Nazi.'[48]

Renier Schoeman acknowledges that domestic issues took primacy in parliamentary debate, but he attributes the lack of involvement in foreign affairs more to discomfort with the topic than disinterest. 'In foreign affairs, people often didn't have a view. The average sort of guy, what the hell would he know about moving from bilateralism to multilateralism, for example? It's a specialty sort of area of government, and people didn't have experience in that regard.'[49] While parliament had talented professionals from many fields, few had a background in foreign affairs beyond Pik Botha and Denis Worrall, who had been a diplomat and academic, respectively.

Parliament and Foreign Policy After 1994:
New Tools, Same Results

South Africa's transition brought with it expectations that parliament would be a more transparent and representative body that could check untrammeled executive power. By most accounts it did not live up to this hope, and in several ways—particularly with regard to a dominant ruling party caucus driving through executive-approved legislation—strongly resembled its predecessor. Parliament, as before 1994, does not have extensive formal powers to influence foreign policy. Foreign policy discussions are far more transparent and frequently more robust than before 1994, but they seem to have had little impact on the ultimate policy outcomes.

Parliament's Post-1994 Foreign Policy Responsibilities and Powers

With regard to foreign relations, South Africa's 1996 constitution does not differ greatly from its 1961 and 1983 predecessors. As before, the executive is vested with the responsibility to appoint diplomats with no obligation to consult parliament beforehand.[50] The president and cabinet are further empowered to negotiate and sign international agreements, again with no need to consult parliament.[51] The president also has the power to deploy the Defense Force internally or externally, although he (or she) is bound to 'promptly' inform parliament of any such deployment.[52] One difference is that both the National Assembly and National Council of Provinces must ratify agreements before they can take effect and can reject them, although no rejection occurred between 1994 and 2008.[53]

The new constitution entrenched the role of portfolio committees in the legislative process, the responsibilities of which are similar to those of the pre-1994 parliament. Committees, including those dealing with foreign policy, have powers to monitor and investigate their respective departments and consider their budgets, as well as introduce and amend legislation.[54] They also have the power to summon any person to appear before them to give evidence and provide documentation as needed. The key difference between pre- and post-1994 committees is in their transparency. Unlike previously, nearly all meetings—barring those dealing with intelligence matters—are open to the public; committees have the right to close meetings if sensitive issues are to be discussed, but rarely do so.

With regard to foreign relations, several committees—notably Defense and Trade and Industry—dealt with various aspects of international affairs between 1994 and 2008, but only the Portfolio Committee on Foreign Affairs (PCFA) focused exclusively on the topic and as such will be the main focus of study here. Like other committees, the PCFA is tasked with oversight of its respective department and the broader conduct of South African foreign affairs, to include consideration of draft legislation and international treaties.[55] As before 1994, however, foreign affairs is a topic on which parliament generally does not have to pass much legislation, and only a handful of bills were considered during the Mandela and Mbeki administrations.

An Activist Portfolio Committee on Foreign Affairs Under Mandela

Members of the PCFA in 1994 were determined to take advantage of the newfound openness in the South African foreign policy debate to be heard on key issues. The committee, under the chairmanship (1994–7) of academic and ANC activist Raymond Suttner, engaged civil society, academia, and the broader public to discuss the key issues of the day.[56] The committee also established direct lines of contact with the DFA in an effort to make sure the department—the leadership of which was still dominated by holdovers of the previous government—followed the new government's policy priorities. The executive was, at least publicly, acquiescent to this greater oversight, with Foreign Minister (1994–9) Alfred Nzo telling parliament in 1994 that he hoped to consult closely with it to 'conduct South Africa's international relations in a transparent manner.'[57]

The Mandela-era committee—which included such ANC heavy-weights as Ebrahim Ebrahim, Fatima Hajaig, Charles Nqakula, Danny Jordaan, and Jackie Selebi—early on sought to interject itself into the policy debate and was unafraid to criticize executive branch government policy. Suttner, its indefatigable chairman, was particularly outspoken in championing the 'idealist' foreign policy principles generated by the ANC during the 1990–4 transition. Suttner attacked DFA and the executive for such stances as support for foreign arms sales; a heavy focus on building trade and economic relations; and overemphasis on building relations with the West rather than with other African countries.[58] Suttner also urged South African recognition of Western Sahara and—while ultimately supportive of recognizing Beijing—advocated careful study of whether South Africa should switch its China recognition or hew to a more nuanced 'two Chinas' stance.[59] Regarding the policymaking process, Suttner during this time criticized the committee's status as a purely ratifying body and called for a reassessment of whether the committee could be brought into decisionmaking during the conceptualization stage.[60]

The committee's forcefulness, however, did not translate into policy impact. Suttner claims that the committee was never briefed in advance on any key policy decisions and in general played no meaningful role 'except to be told what was being done.'[61] The DFA paid little heed to the committee's inputs. For example, despite a 1996 PCFA decision to support a total ban on anti-personnel landmines at a UN conference on the issue, the DFA ignored the position in favor of one defending the use of 'smart mines' (although it subsequently supported a total ban).[62] The Presidency similarly ignored the committee on key issues. Although Suttner says Mandela sought his inputs and advice on the China debate—and later offered him the ambassadorship to Beijing—Mandela's November 1996 announcement that South Africa would switch recognition caught the committee by surprise.[63] The PCFA, and broader parliament, was also kept in the dark about the 1995 Nigeria crisis.[64] Suttner remembers that the PCFA tried to hold a special hearing to discuss Nigeria shortly after the Ken Saro-Wiwa assassination but 'we were shot down by [senior DFA official] Abdul Minty.'[65] Parliament similarly was not consulted prior to the 1998 Lesotho invasion.[66]

Structural shortcomings were a key hindrance on the PCFA's ability to exert influence. First, and foremost, the executive had no formal obligation to seek PCFA endorsement of its decisions in advance.[67] Similarly, there was no systematized interaction between the department and the PCFA; briefings by the minister and other senior officials were ad hoc.[68] Another problem was the mismatch between the skills base of the committee and the workload with which they had to deal. While the PCFA had many leading thinkers on foreign policy, their obligations to other committees spread their talents thinly, and they lacked adequate research staff.[69] This was particularly damaging during the first post-transition parliament, when South Africa's global reengagement meant the ratification of numerous treaties and conventions—23 of them in 1997 alone—without parliament being able to give them close scrutiny.[70]

Such formal shortcomings could have been partly addressed through the development of close and collaborative relationships between principals on both sides, but this was not to be. The PCFA's often-confrontational tactics with the DFA resulted in an acrimonious relationship developing between Suttner and Director-General Rusty Evans, a holdover from the previous government.[71] Similarly, while Suttner describes cordial ties with President Mandela, he believes Nzo, Pahad, and Mbeki—who from 1994 played the dominant role in foreign policy formulation—viewed him as an irritant.[72] 'There were personal issues in relation to me,' notes Suttner in regard to these poor relations, which probably stemmed from a combination of personality mismatches and the likelihood that these principals—who had worked together for years in exile—probably did not welcome Suttner's interjection into the policy process.[73]

Suttner's experience during this time was greatly dispiriting. In 1995, he wrote that the 'traditional culture of secrecy' around foreign affairs made it nearly impossible to influence the policy process, and the following year he asserted that the 'new portfolio committee has been working to monitor what the Department of Foreign Affairs does as well as help with the process of foreign policymaking. So far it has not been very successful with either of those two tasks.'[74] He further lamented that it was 'not clear that the Presidency relates on a regular and coordinated basis with other foreign policy structures when it makes interventions on foreign policy questions' and that 'the process of decisionmaking on foreign affairs has not changed substantially since the ANC came to power.'[75] Looking back more than a decade later, Suttner is blunt in stating that he 'never influenced foreign policy' during his time as committee chair.[76] In 1997, Suttner was redeployed from parliament to serve as ambassador to Sweden, replaced by Ebrahim Ebrahim. Little changed in the operation of the committee; as Pahad noted the following year, 'There is still not a system whereby major foreign policy issues are taken to parliament, even to give information only.'[77]

In discussing this period, Pahad himself was complimentary of Suttner, calling him one of the better minds on foreign affairs but adding that he was 'not a practitioner.'[78] Pahad asserts that the PCFA's problems stemmed from the fact that Suttner was more concerned with taking on the structures of the old DFA rather than the content of policies, taking a confrontational line that was unproductive. Furthermore, Pahad found Suttner's insistence that all meetings be open to the press and public problematic: 'You can only give them generalized briefings; you can't take them into confidence with the media there, on things like what our mediators were doing.'[79]

Parliament in the Mbeki Era

One cannot discuss the PCFA during Thabo Mbeki's presidency without first understanding the change in the nature of the legislative–executive relationship that took place after he took office. The legislature, particularly from 1994 to 1997, was a body remembered by participants and observers as one of open debate and discussion, even within the ANC parliamentary caucus. As former ANC MP Andrew Feinstein argues, 'During the Mandela years the caucus room had resonated with sharp debate and discussion, passionate argument and profound polemic, the discourse that characterized the ANC and the internal resistance movement, a broad church all of whose congregants felt able to speak their mind and argue their view.'[80] Looking at that same caucus just over a year after Mbeki's assumption of power, Feinstein altered his assessment, calling the caucus 'a more disciplined, choreographed and constrained party, a party fearful of its leader, conscious of his power to make or break careers, conscious of his demand for loyalty, for conformity of thinking.'[81] ANC stalwart Ben Turok elaborated on this point, noting that under Mbeki, 'there was a certain discouragement of participation and asking difficult questions [. . .] it was laying down the line and setting the tone.'[82]

The ANC caucus' role became one of affirming, not debating, ANC policy; as one of Mbeki's key acolytes, longtime Reserve Bank Governor Tito Mboweni, said, 'Parliament thinks it can make policy on behalf of people. This is not so. [Parliament's] role is to implement ANC policy.'[83] Policy direction was decided at the ANC's party conferences every five years, while the ANC's NEC and National Working Committee—both chaired by Mbeki—clarified issues as necessary (more on this in Chapter 8). Decisions were then passed down to cabinet and, ultimately, the ANC caucus itself. '[ANC Headquarters] Luthuli House reaches out to parliament via the chairpersons and whips,' says longtime ANC MP Albertina Luthuli in describing the policymaking environment. 'The ruling party in parliament has to take its cue from the party itself. Policy is shaped there, and it has to come down to direct us,' she notes, although Luthuli acknowledged the caucus would debate its policy directives and could sometimes tweak them.[84]

The place to discuss and critique these positions was, as before 1994, in individual study groups that hammered out party positions in advance of formal committee meetings.[85] 'The study group is actually the structure that really deals with issues as they come from Luthuli House and the direction of the party,' Luthuli says. 'It eventually has to come up with a position, which you then take to the portfolio committee.'[86] Study group members included those who sat on the formal committee, but other caucus members could sit in as well, usually meeting after plenary on Tuesdays or Wednesdays. Study group would frequently call upon outsiders to brief them. 'If I'm not clear on something, I could request someone from the embassy or DFA to unlock something for us,' recalls PCFA and study group member Mtikeni Sibande, who said the group would frequently call upon Aziz Pahad to explain elements of policy.[87]

Once the ANC caucus reached a consensus on a policy direction, there was no ground for an independent position. As Luthuli notes, 'I've watched what happens in the older democracies, your country [the United States], the UK, where you get members of the same party disagreeing in the broader chamber. We don't function that way [...] yet.'[88] As with the NP, ANC party discipline under Mbeki was ironclad. South Africa's post-1994 proportional representation system is a significant driver of this discipline; the Party list system placed extensive power in the hands of Mbeki and his acolytes, meaning they could drop sitting MPs from the next electoral list or 'redeploy' them during their terms to a less influential (and less remunerated) position.[89] For MPs with few other career prospects, this was a daunting threat and was effective in keeping them in line.[90] In all, this resulted in a situation where, according to Mbeki's biographer, Mark Gevisser, 'Loyalists were promoted, often without the necessary skills, while free-thinkers were iced out, and began hemorrhaging from the institution.'[91]

Some Progress by the Portfolio Committee on Foreign Affairs ...
The function of the PCFA during Mbeki's administration was in many ways a microcosm of that of parliament in the same period. On the surface, both entities had an air of functionality; debates took place, ministers were questioned, questions were raised. The PCFA made strides in its operations under Mbeki. An analysis of Parliamentary Monitoring Group records, for example, shows that the PCFA met far more frequently during Mbeki's tenure than under Mandela; the committee met 32 times in 2003 and neared 30 on other occasions, while 15–20 was more the norm during Mandela's years. Research capacity, bolstered by more budgetary resources, led to an improvement in the quality of PCFA reports and reduced its reliance on the DFA for information and analysis, notes Tim Hughes of the SAIIA, a longtime observer of parliament.[92]

Ties between the PCFA and DFA also improved during the Mbeki administration. The departure of Suttner in 1997 and, more importantly, Evans in 1998 saw a renewed effort by department principals to develop ties to PCFA members. Although Minister Dlamini-Zuma only briefed the PCFA six times during her tenure, Directors-General Sipho Pityana (1999–2002) and Ayanda Ntsaluba (2002–11) often met with the committee. Deputy Ministers Pahad and, in particular, Sue van der Merwe also were frequent interlocutors with MPs.[93] PCFA chair Job Sithole (2004–8) praised the openness of the relationship, calling it 'over and above the normal constitutional dispensation.'[94] The committee also expanded its reach to draw more frequently on academics, civil society representatives, and foreign diplomats.[95] Hughes remembers former PCFA chair Ebrahim Ebrahim (1997–2002) as 'probably the most open chair and most open MP I ever encountered. He was open to inputs, suggestions, and even joined the SAIIA committee on an *ex-oficio* basis and would come to meetings.'[96] Hughes also recalls Sithole as receptive to outside representations: 'He took his role very seriously, took his committee very seriously, his budgetary and programmatic responsibilities seriously. He'd meet with us at the beginning of each year and say what the committee was interested in that year.'[97]

Last, the committee during both the Mbeki and Mandela years was marked by generally good relations between the ANC and opposition representatives, who populated the committee in a rough reflection of the parties' popular support. PCFA members from both sides of the aisle described inter-party relations as very solid in the post-1994 period. ANC MPs cited longtime foreign policy mavens Colin Eglin of the Democratic Alliance, Boy Geldenhuys of the New National Party, and Ben Skosana of the Inkatha Freedom Party as knowledgeable and respected members of the committee.[98] Debate between the opposition and ruling party on foreign affairs tended to be limited, with general agreement between the two sides over most issues.[99] Geldenhuys and Skosana agreed that because of this consensus on the overall thrust of South African foreign policy, relations with ANC members were smooth; besides Zimbabwe, there was little to fight about.

... but No Real Increase in Power

Such increased interactions—as well as the committee's frequent trips abroad—enhanced the quality of the debate within the PCFA, but at the end of the day, cross-party debate was the culmination rather than the beginning of the committee's influence on policy. Parliamentarians from both sides frequently complained through Mbeki's tenure that they had almost no impact on the foreign policy debate.[100] Although Sithole says that his relationships with key Presidency foreign policy figures allowed the committee to 'be taken into confidence on certain things and briefed and know when major pronouncements were coming,' the opinion of the committee was not asked in advance.[101] If legislators had an effect on foreign policy, it was through their participation in the ANC's international affairs structures.[102] Pallo Jordan, who chaired the PCFA from 2002–4, says, 'In terms of relative weight of the debate, NEC discussion would carry more weight than, say, the PCFA. We were in the fortunate position that I was part of the NEC, NWC, and chairing the PCFA, so there was that direct connection.'[103]

There are several examples of parliament's reactive, not proactive, nature in policy debates. One of the hallmarks of Mbeki's foreign policy agenda, NEPAD, was launched on October 31, 2001 without any discussion of it occurring in parliament; as an astonished Hughes notes, 'Parliament didn't have a voice on the singular blueprint for Africa's recovery.'[104] Pretoria's 2007 UN Security Council vote to keep Burma (Myanmar) off the agenda is another example. 'The decision on Burma was taken at the UN; I don't remember being privy to that. I don't remember being briefed on that, unless it was done in my absence,' longtime ANC committee member Mewa Ramgobin notes.[105] Albertina Luthuli also does not remember the committee being queried in advance on this vote.[106]

Capacity of MPs on the committee, particularly during the Mbeki years, was another widely cited problem. Many of the foreign affairs mavens of the Mandela-era PCFA either left parliament or were promoted, leaving what many observers describe as a relatively weak bench on foreign policy issues. Examining the committee member-ship, Pahad opines, 'People were not properly chosen; if you go through the membership, you realize that people were learning on their feet [. . .] in many ways, they were as uninformed as the general public. That's why you saw little coming out of parliament.'[107] He argues that the ANC study group on foreign affairs was similarly weak and 'made no real input into policy thinking.'

Probably in large part owing to these capacity shortcomings, the PCFA tended to take a 'DFA knows best' mentality, much as before 1994. 'To a large extent, DFA would answer our questions if we had them,' Luthuli notes. She adds, however, that if the DFA was not able to win over the committee, the PCFA response was generally to move on: 'Sometimes, they will be able to convince you of their positions, but sometimes not. We just move forward, telling the department we don't see things that way.'[108] In that same vein, neither the DFA budget nor treaties put forward for ratification received much scrutiny from the committee.[109] Hajaig cited the latter issue as one that deserves additional scrutiny in the post-Mbeki period: 'Now it gets signed and comes to us to be ratified whether we like it or not. And there were some that we had major problems with; we had to sign it and make a note that there are these issues that we want to discuss. That's not really sensible, but we're working at it, that parliament must have a say beforehand and not afterward.'[110] Throughout the Mbeki era, ANC MPs saw their roles as enforcers, rather than influencers, of the government's foreign policy. 'There was never a situation where we directly as a committee of parliament influenced directly the formulation of foreign policy,' says Sithole, 'but once those decisions were made, we were tasked with ensuring those pronouncements were carried out by DFA.'[111]

In reflecting on the period, committee members express little discomfort with the fact that they did not challenge government foreign policy orthodoxy.[112] While acknowledging that parliament has a role to play in the international arena, even Sithole said it should only get involved 'on a limited basis.'[113] Fatima Hajaig, who briefly co-chaired the committee, also acknowledged this acquiescent attitude toward the executive: 'We allowed things to happen in a particular way. For instance, foreign policy was made by the president, DFA would implement it, and we would know about it secondhand. And we'd sort of accept that.'[114] Discussion of pressing issues tended to be cursory. 'It would be far-fetched to say the PCFA goes into an intensive discussion over these issues. We do it in passing, to the extent we can,' says Ramgobin. 'Many times it's a *fait accompli.*'[115]

Parliament and Zimbabwe

One issue where the committee and the ANC parliamentary caucus more broadly displayed its failure to question and critique government was on Zimbabwe. The opposition, and particularly Democratic Alliance leader (1999–2008) Tony Leon, made the issue a chief priority from the start, sensing that this was a rare example of a foreign policy issue that could win them votes, especially among white voters.[116] Despite this, critiques did not come just from the opposition; there were early hopes that ANC MPs would assert their independence on Zimbabwe, particularly in early 2000 when Pallo Jordan tabled a resolution criticizing Zimbabwean President Robert Mugabe and asserting that elections later that year could not be free and fair.[117] Jordan says that he took a critical stance precisely to give parliament an independent voice, one that could be used to take a multi-pronged approach to dealing with the Zimbabwean Government: 'Government as government, DFA, can say one thing, but there has to be a way to articulate the real values of the ANC. That can be given to parliamentarians, and if there are complaints, you can explain it away that these are MPs, not part of government.'[118]

The ANC caucus and its members on the PCFA never lived up to these expectations. Despite what Sithole describes as deep disagreement within the ANC caucus on the issue ('There was never an agreement or understanding on this within the ANC. There wasn't even a 70 percent consensus.'), ANC MPs never publicly criticized government policy toward Zimbabwe.[119] Parliament sent observers to four Zimbabwean elections during Mbeki's presidency (2000, 2002, 2005, and 2008) but always endorsed their conduct (despite the protests of opposition members of the delegations). Sithole says he would visit Zimbabwe to liaise with its parliament's then-Speaker Emmerson Mnangagwa, and try to influence him, but such visits had no discernable impacts.[120] Somewhat amazingly, Parliamentary Monitoring Group records show the PCFA specifically met on Zimbabwe—a pressing foreign policy crisis on South Africa's borders—just six times between 1999 and 2008, a number dwarfed by its meetings on the Middle East.

Conclusion: An Impotent Foreign Policy Body

Parliament, in both its pre- and post-1994 conceptions, had almost no impact on the South African Government's foreign policy. The reasons for this lack of effect were remarkably similar—a constitutional dispensation that consolidated power over foreign policy in the executive; rigid ruling party discipline; a broad consensus on foreign affairs among both ruling party and opposition MPs; and a general disinterest in the topic among parliamentarians, who knew and understood that foreign affairs issues were not vote-getters at election time. This general disinterest post-1994 is noted in research by Jo-Ansie van Wyk showing that of the 2,910 questions tabled in parliament in 1997, only 58 were related to foreign policy, and these were asked by just 13 MPs.[121] A small, core group of MPs—notably ANC MPs Jordan, Ebrahim, Hajaig, and Ramgobin, alongside Eglin, Geldenhuys, and Skosana from the opposition—dominated discussion of foreign policy, more out of personal interest than any political necessity. Ultimately, this general willingness, past and present, to accept executive control of the foreign policy process has undermined the body's ability to influence foreign policy, or even test the limits of its potential power.

CHAPTER 8

RULING PARTIES

Preceding chapters have covered distinct 'outsiders' to the decision-making process with generally limited abilities to influence policy. Ruling parties, however, occupy unique ground. They are decidedly not outsiders, as the political decision-makers in government generally come from their ranks. In the South African context, however, the apartheid-era NP and the post-transition ANC have existed as entities technically separate from the government, with independently functioning structures. Party policies were intended to inform those of government, although there has been no legal mandate for elected officials to follow party orthodoxy lockstep. Of course, as Thabo Mbeki learned when he was ousted as ANC leader in 2007, being perceived as ignoring party policy could have disastrous political consequences.

This chapter will examine the degree to which the NP and ANC—as distinct entities apart from government—influenced South Africa's foreign policy debate while they were ruling parties, as entities separate from government. It also will examine whether party structures had the capability of and interest in making independent inputs on foreign policy, how such inputs were made, and whether the debate was broad-based within the Party. The chapter also will devote significant attention to the ANC's governance and foreign policy structures while it was in a liberation struggle before 1994 to better understand how they influenced its practices as a political party thereafter.

The National Party's Nonexistent Foreign Policy Influence

The NP from 1948 to 1994 had, as a distinct entity, almost no influence on South Africa's foreign policy and no real means to weigh in on such discussions. As shown earlier, debate on foreign policy outside government came from NP-affiliated entities like the Broederbond, or by NP MPs, and even there it was limited. The NP's biggest limitation as a policy actor was its federal nature. The Party's four provincial organs were autonomous with regard to organizational matters, each with its own constitution, and they were constantly in competition with one another (particularly the Cape and Transvaal) over policies and patronage.[1] Provincial structures held annual meetings, but at a national level the Party only met through rare federal congresses (only two held between 1941 and 1984) or on the federal council, which consisted of representatives of the provincial structures.[2] The council was a forum for raising contentious issues, but it had no real power over the provinces. Former Natal administrator and NP national information officer Con Botha recalls that the federal council 'could make no binding decisions; it could recommend [policies] but these only became official policy once the four provinces had ratified them.'[3]

At a provincial level, the Party generally assigned a member of its information team to handle foreign policy issues and write briefs if necessary.[4] Foreign affairs was a low priority, however, and, as in parliament, they largely deferred to the prime minister and foreign minister on these issues: 'Foreign policy was never under pressure' within the party,' says former Minister Dawie de Villiers.[5] Provincial and federal meetings were more concerned with political horse-trading and domestic policy than with international issues. That said, political jockeying could have an effect on the personalities involved in foreign policymaking; Niel Barnard, for example, acknowledges that his appointment was in large part due to PW Botha owing the Free State NP for backing his successful 1978 run for the Party leadership.[6]

ANC Decisionmaking Structures in Exile: Precursor or Outlier?

Before understanding how the ANC weighed in on government foreign policy after 1994, one must first examine the movement's decisionmaking traditions dating back to its founding in 1912. These processes were fine-tuned during the movement's three decades in exile, a period that still has relevance for the modern-day Party. Of particular importance were the ANC's conduct of international diplomacy and its formulation of foreign policy in exile, particularly the structures involved in making and implementing those decisions; its ability and willingness to make those decisions in a broad-based, 'democratic' fashion; and the interpersonal and intra-structural dynamics that shaped those decisions.

The Elite Nature of African National Congress Exile Decisionmaking

Oliver Tambo's 1960 flight into exile meant that he had to constitute a movement outside the country essentially from scratch, ensuring the broadest possible participation while being cognizant of security concerns and possible infiltration. Keeping cadres, particularly those outside of the movement's home base, informed and involved would prove difficult for the next 30 years, and especially early on. The movement tried to keep its external membership unified through periodic holding of consultative conferences. The first of these was held in August 1962 in Dar es Salaam, and another broader meeting—including the domestic underground and representatives of the affiliated SACP—was held in Lobatse, in the then Bechuanaland protectorate, that October.[7]

The movement met twice more in 1965 in Tanzania, but many elements of the Party—particularly from its Umkhonto we Sizwe (MK) armed wing—were dissatisfied with the leadership over what they viewed as a lack of communication, incompetence, and a

propensity toward luxurious living while they struggled.[8] This
growing dissent led to a week-long conference held in April 1969 at
Morogoro, Tanzania, attended by 70 ANC and allied organization
members, in an effort to mollify concerns and better coordinate the
armed struggle.[9] Tambo addressed the complaints head on, admitting
that leadership of the external mission was 'not organizationally
geared to undertake the urgent task of undertaking people's war' and
announcing the immediate dissolution of the NEC.[10] The conference
also decided that non-black South Africans could join the ANC
(if not yet the NEC); shrunk the NEC from 23 members to a more
manageable nine; affirmed Oliver Tambo as the movement's president
(he had previously been acting); and replaced Duma Nokwe with
Alfred Nzo as the ANC's secretary general.[11] It would, however,
prove the last consultative conference until a meeting at Kabwe,
Zambia, in 1985, the last before the ANC's unbanning.

Given the infrequency of broad-based decisionmaking conferences, day-to-day decisions were taken by a small leadership cadre at
Party headquarters—especially the NEC—with little regular
external consultation. 'It wasn't a very democratic system [...] and
it would be a mistake to think that the ANC consulted up and down
the way we do now,' notes Ben Turok, then editor of the ANC's
Sechaba magazine and based in London.[12] Internal democracy was
undermined by a need to keep its communications covert—
particularly given the security threats faced by South African
Government forces—and a Soviet influence in the movement that
emphasized secrecy.[13] The lack of secure communications meant
movement cadres outside Lusaka had little opportunity to influence
decisions. 'Most of those day-to-day, month-to-month type of
decisions would have been made by ANC officials, without a great
deal of participation of the members,' recalls ANC stalwart Pallo
Jordan, who asserts that Tambo, Secretary-General Alfred Nzo, and
Treasurer-General (from 1976) Thomas Nkobi were dominant
figures.[14] Aziz Pahad seconds this point: 'Policies came from Lusaka,
and we had to implement them where we were.'[15]

While the undemocratic nature of ANC decision-making rankled
many party cadres, Tambo's painstaking commitment to consultative

leadership and outreach to members worldwide helped him hold the movement together. NEC members recall Tambo as staying above the fray when chairing the committee, facilitating free-flowing discussion and ensuring that all members agreed on a decision before implementing it.[16] Jordan, a NEC member since 1985, recalls that Tambo would usually allow the member with primary responsibility for the issue at hand to chair the pertinent NEC meeting:

> He intervened as was necessary; he never wanted to dominate discussion. He would usually allow a lot of debate. What endeared lots of people was that even if it were known that OR [Tambo] disagreed with a viewpoint, he would encourage the person with that viewpoint to air it so it could be discussed. And then, usually at the end, he would intervene, drawing the threads together. At the end of the meeting, unless it was a very exceptionally divisive issue, everyone came out thinking that their viewpoints were weighed and included in the consensus. Everyone felt ownership in the decision.[17]

Tambo also made efforts to consult with other cadres whenever possible, either at headquarters or on trips abroad, meetings that helped party leaders keep abreast of international dynamics. 'The decision center was Lusaka, but there was room to influence in centers where there was a flow of information,' recalls future DFA Director-General Sipho Pityana, then a young exile in London. 'Tambo was passing through London every now and then, as was Thabo [Mbeki] and [Johnny] Makatini. Invariably, there would be sessions and discussions around a range of issues.'[18] Turok also remembers London as a key meeting point for the ANC's Lusaka-based leadership and its cadres based elsewhere in the world, adding that he would meet privately with Tambo whenever he would visit.[19]

African National Congress Foreign Policy Goals and Objectives

As noted in Chapter 2, the ANC's international engagement dates to shortly after its foundation, although they would prove inconsistent until the movement was forced into exile. From 1960 onward, the goals of the ANC's international outreach included raising awareness of the human rights abuses committed by Pretoria and the unjust nature of the apartheid system; raising funds to allow the movement to operate and to facilitate the armed struggle; increasing Pretoria's international isolation; and establishing the ANC as the 'sole legitimate representative' of South Africa's liberation struggle.[20] These goals would prove challenging for the first two decades in exile; in reality, the movement through the mid-1970s was focused on survival above all else.[21] By the late 1970s, however—especially after the 1976 Soweto riots—ANC efforts started to pay off, with the movement able to generate mass support for the anti-apartheid struggle and increased Western public pressure for the release of Nelson Mandela.[22] This pressure, in conjunction with the broader international anti-apartheid movement and allies like the United Democratic Front back home, was essential to pushing previously skeptical Western governments to pressure Pretoria to make reforms.

While the ANC's foreign policy in exile was undergirded by a commitment to solidarity with other oppressed people, it never lost sight of its overarching goal—the toppling of Pretoria's apartheid government. 'What it always boiled down to in the end was what was going to help our movement [...] Any debate would always end there,' Jordan notes.[23] While these decisions generally were not contentious within the ANC, there was debate over tactics. Jordan says: 'For example, at the height of the Vietnam War, what was our stance on participating in the protests worldwide against the war? The decision was that we would have to support the struggle against the war in Vietnam, because the Vietnamese were waging a liberation struggle,' even though such a stance would not endear the ANC to skeptical Western governments supporting the war.[24] Essop Pahad recalls other debates about how to best align the ANC with black leaders in the United States; although many in the movement supported the more radical views of Malcolm X and the Black Power movement, the dominant view was that overt support for a more strident movement would undermine the ANC's standing among most Americans, thereby undermining its chances of building broader support.[25] The 1968 Soviet invasion of Czechoslovakia was another issue that sparked debate among ANC and SACP cadres.[26]

Even closer to home—given the ANC's significant presence in Great Britain—was the question of how to treat the increasingly active Irish Republican Army (IRA) in the late 1960s. 'In Britain, 1969, you had the beginnings of the civil rights movement in Northern Ireland, and in the 1970s the IRA reviving,' Jordan says. 'Now, where does that put you? Here, the oldest anti-colonial struggle against the oldest colonial power; what do you do?'[27] The ultimate conclusion was to support principles of equal rights and attack British authorities for violations of civil liberties like detention without trial—'They were doing exactly what Vorster was doing,' Jordan says.[28] However, the need to maintain good ties with the British government meant that the ANC would not openly support IRA attacks—even though the IRA assisted the ANC with reconnaissance for the 1980 Sasolburg attack, according to Kader Asmal, then head of the Irish Anti-Apartheid Movement.[29] Fortunately for the ANC, its good relations with official Sinn Fein allowed them to escape pressure; they 'understood our position and never pressed us.'[30]

Day-to-Day Foreign Policy Decision-Making and Implementation

While building international support was a tenet of the ANC's efforts to topple the apartheid government, it was not an issue to which the Party leadership devoted extensive time and energy. 'On a day to day basis, you didn't have to make many radical decisions in those days,' Jordan notes.[31] NEC meetings—irregular through the mid-1980s—generally did not focus on international outreach, although certain events, such as the 1984 signing of the Nkomati Accord, would raise issues such as regional outreach for discussion.[32] Conferences similarly did not prioritize external affairs; Morogoro and Kabwe, for example, focused on organizational issues that would make the ANC better able to wage the armed struggle in South Africa. Despite this, they were not ignored altogether. Several conference resolutions at Morogoro referenced other international anti-colonial struggles and thanked the OAU for its support, while outgoing Secretary-General Duma Nokwe presented a paper on international affairs.[33] Similarly, resolutions related to building international solidarity were introduced at Kabwe.[34]

One outcome of Morogoro—the creation of formal departments within the organization—would come to play a significant role in the conduct of the movement's international efforts. Before Morogoro, writes Jordan, the ANC had less-formal 'desks' to which specific people were assigned, but without supporting infrastructure.[35] Now tasks would be carried out more formally, and the new DIA would from 1969 spearhead the ANC's international efforts.[36] The DIA, which was attached to the president's office, operated as the pseudo 'foreign ministry' of the ANC, managing its missions worldwide and coordinating outreach to the UN and governments.[37] It would, however, take time to get up to speed; although established on paper at Morogoro, it lacked funding and organization under its first head, Nokwe, from 1969 to his death in 1978. Only after Josiah Jele replaced him that year would the DIA's operations become more structured.[38] Jele would stay in that job until 1983, when he was replaced by the ANC's representative at the UN in New York, Johnny Makatini, who in turn was succeeded by Thabo Mbeki after Makatini's death in 1988.

By the time of the ANC's 1990 unbanning, DIA in Lusaka coordinated the operations of the ANC's 43 missions worldwide (more than the South African Government had at the time), but it remained relatively small. 'We must not pretend it was exceptionally strong,' notes Aziz Pahad, who would serve as the DIA's deputy head from 1990.[39] A January 1989 report on the state of the organization following Makatini's death described the department as having nine members (organized into six geographical desks and a research desk) who would meet bi-weekly to plan and discuss reports.[40] The DIA's working-level officials acted much like desk officers in a foreign affairs department, managing the flow of paper and dealing with administrative matters; one 1988 document, for example, details DIA efforts to mollify Zambian officials upset by drunken ANC cadres shooting Zambian citizens.[41]

The DIA was not the only ANC entity dealing with external affairs. The MK, by dint of its operations throughout southern Africa, was an important actor whose leadership took a significant interest in the

ANC's external orientation, specifically with regard to how those foreign ties affected its ability to wage the armed struggle.[42] Another, even more important, group was the movement's Department of Information and Publicity (DIP), also founded at Morogoro. Although primarily aimed at propagandizing for the ANC within South Africa, the DIP had a strong international component, producing press statements, fact sheets, memoranda, and newsletters aimed at winning support around the world.[43] Much of this effort was aimed at the West, where early support was weak.[44] One of its leaders (1985–9), Thabo Mbeki, would play a major role in the conduct of these relations.

Thabo Mbeki and the Pragmatism of the African National Congress' Foreign Policy Agenda

Thabo Mbeki was only 42 years old when he was named head of the DIP, but he had significant international experience. After going into exile in 1962, he had spent eight years studying and working for the ANC in Great Britain; had undergone training in the Soviet Union; and served as an ANC representative in Botswana, Swaziland, and Nigeria.[45] Close to Tambo from his time in London and an NEC member since 1975, Mbeki was given the influential position as political secretary in the Office of the President in 1978. Mbeki's first major coup was his successful 1978 advocacy—at the urging of Makatini and with the support of Tambo—for the ANC to cooperate with an American documentary about the ANC, which helped dispel views that it was a 'terrorist' organization.[46]

As head of the DIP, Mbeki emerged as the dominant figure in directing the ANC's international outreach, expanding the movement's outreach to the West and rolling back its culture of secrecy. Whereas the ANC's diplomacy through the late 1970s was heavily Africa-centric, specifically in seeking to counter South African outreach on the continent, Mbeki throughout the 1980s focused significant attention on winning support for the ANC and the broader anti-apartheid movement in the West, particularly the United States and Great Britain.[47] 'It was clear that we needed to work with the Americans and British, because they were the powers in the world,' remembers Essop Pahad, who was working for the

ANC and SACP in London during the 1980s.[48] Mbeki also recognized the need to expand the ANC's base beyond black Americans, organized labor, American Democratic Party, and British Labour Party. According to Pahad, 'Mbeki said to me once that he had come to London, and the CIA Station Chief saw him and said, "Listen Thabo, you're going to America. When you go, don't only meet your friends,"' urging him to reach out to Republican leaders, particularly moderates. 'Interestingly enough, Thabo struck up a good relationship with [conservative Georgia Republican] Newt Gingrich. Very interesting [. . .] of all people. I used to say, "What? Good grief!" He'd say, "Listen you, how do you think we're going to make a breakthrough if we don't develop good personal relations with people like Gingrich?"'[49] This lobbying would prove key to the 1986 passage of sanctions in Congress and the subsequent congressional override of Republican President Ronald Reagan's veto.[50]

Mbeki's pragmatic courtship of the West was not universally popular within the movement, particularly among cadres associated with the MK and SACP, but he had a core group of allies that helped him overcome internal opposition. Nzo, Makatini, and Aziz Pahad shared and supported his pragmatic tendencies, although no ally was more important than his friend and mentor Oliver Tambo.[51] The ANC president fully bought into Mbeki's efforts to expand the movement's support base, himself meeting with Western officials (like US Secretary of State George Shultz) and business leaders to state the ANC's case.[52] The two men had a symbiotic relationship. Tambo's protection allowed Mbeki to ignore his critics in the movement, while Mbeki proved a useful lightning rod for absorbing attacks that might otherwise be made against Tambo.[53] Tambo's trust in and affection for his protégé helped ensure Mbeki's emergence as the movement's de facto 'foreign minister' by the late 1980s.

The African National Congress and Foreign Policymaking After 1994

Before delving into the ANC's post-transition foreign policymaking, one must first explain the executive structures by which the ANC has governed itself and made its policy decisions since it last updated its party constitution in 1991:

- The ANC's *National Conference*—held every five years, last in December 2012—is the 'supreme ruling and controlling body' of the ANC, according to its constitution.[54] The conference adopts resolutions that set the policy program of the Party until the next conference. Conference also elects the Party's leadership, including the 'top six' of president, deputy president, secretary-general, deputy secretary-general, treasurer, and national chairperson. The ANC president is tasked with acting as the Party's spokesman and leads only under the supervision of the NEC.[55]
- The conference also elects the ANC's National Executive Committee, whose membership consists of the 'top six' and 80 elected members (60 until 2007). The NEC is tasked with leading the ANC between conferences interpreting the (often vague) conference resolutions as it sees fit.[56] The full NEC, normally helmed by the national chairperson, is supposed to meet as often as every three months. Nearly all ANC cabinet ministers were represented on the NEC during the Mandela and Mbeki administrations.[57]
- The NEC subsequently elects a *National Working Committee* from its ranks, which deals with the day-to-day operations of the ANC. It includes about a quarter of the NEC's members; there is no set number. Although the ANC constitution does not specify how often it must meet, members say it met about bi-weekly during the Mandela and Mbeki presidencies.[58]
- Members of the NEC are divided into *NEC subcommittees* that broadly mirror government departments and deal with those issues.[59] These subcommittees—which have no prescribed meeting schedule—generally include appropriate ministers, deputies, parliamentary committee chairs, and other ANC officials with expertise and interest in the appropriate issue. Subcommittees can also include non-NEC members.
- Lastly, the ANC has *departments* within its Luthuli House headquarters in Johannesburg to manage the function of the

NEC subcommittees and intervene on substantive issues where appropriate. By the end of the Mbeki administration, full- and part-time ANC officials numbered about 500.[60]

Foreign Policy of Limited Interest within Party

Foreign affairs from the ANC's unbanning to the end of Mbeki's Party presidency in 2007 was, in general, a low priority for all levels of the Party. At the top, ANC conferences from 1991 to 2007 devoted little time to foreign policy, passing mostly vague and innocuous resolutions on external matters that largely mirrored government policy.[61] In the NEC and National Working Committee, foreign policy issues were also lightly covered except in the case of significant global events, like the September 11, 2001 terrorist attacks or the 2003 US invasion of Iraq; domestic issues like service delivery took up far more time.[62] Discussion of foreign affairs was even less robust at the branch and provincial levels of the ANC. Although conference resolutions since 1991 called for building greater grassroots capacity to discuss and debate foreign policy, this never came to pass. There was little sub-national party debate on foreign affairs under Mandela and Mbeki, with only two provincial structures—Limpopo and KwaZulu-Natal—establishing (seemingly perfunctory) international relations committees as prescribed by conference resolution.[63]

With little interest and attention paid by the top and bottom sections of the Party, day-to-day responsibility for ANC debate and discussion of foreign policy fell to two linked entities: the ANC's Department of International Relations (successor to the DIA) and its NEC subcommittee for International Relations.

The Ups and Downs of the Department of International Relations

After the ANC was unbanned in 1990, the DIA emerged as a chief actor in the debate over South Africa's post-transition foreign policy. DIA head Mbeki, Aziz Pahad (by then his deputy), and other leading figures participated in discussions with the DFA and academics (see Chapter 5) on both the broader principles of a democratic South Africa's foreign policy and the more mundane matters of staffing and departmental transformation. Several of its members participated in the Transitional Executive Council Subcommittee on International Affairs, which set the stage for the integration of ANC, PAC, and homeland foreign affairs entities into the DFA.[64] The 1994 transition, however, left the DIA—like other ANC entities—severely short of capacity, turning it into what Aziz Pahad describes as a 'paper structure,' given that most of its officials (like Pahad himself) were absorbed into the DFA or deployed elsewhere in the Party and government.[65] Longtime ANC representative in Canada Yusuf Saloojee succeeded Mbeki as DIA head in 1994, but Saloojee ran more or less a one-man operation until he left in 1997.

Recognizing this weakness, the 1997 ANC National Conference called for the department to be re-launched as the Department of International Relations.[66] The department was tasked with monitoring international developments; making policy recommendations to the NEC and conference; and managing relations with foreign political parties with which the ANC was aligned, according to Mavivi Myakayaka-Manzini, who succeeded Saloojee and stayed in that position until 2007 (when she was succeeded by current Deputy Foreign Minister Ebrahim Ebrahim).[67] Myakayaka-Manzini also chaired the NEC Subcommittee on International Relations and would represent it at meetings of the National Working Committee when the need arose. However, most observers and participants agreed that the department did not play a meaningful role in party foreign policy debates, acting more as a secretariat for the NEC subcommittee. The department was also too small—only four full-time officials, at most—to develop its independence and internal infrastructure.[68]

The NEC Subcommittee for International Relations: A More Influential Body

While the department dealt with the administration of managing the Party's foreign affairs and debates on policy, the NEC subcommittee for International Relations acted as the debating chamber where its members would determine which issues merited further discussion in the broader NEC. 'We would normally prepare documents for discussion for the broader NEC, and that's where the serious debate would take place,' subcommittee member Pallo Jordan recalls.[69] The subcommittee, according to Myakayaka-Manzini, generally consisted of between 15 and 20 members and would meet as often as once a month, and sometimes more.[70] Its composition changed but generally included the foreign minister (either Nzo or Dlamini-Zuma), Deputy Minister Aziz Pahad, the minister of trade and industry, the chair of Parliament's PCFA, and other ANC members in government foreign policy jobs.[71]

Some interviewees questioned whether the subcommittee played a meaningful role in driving government foreign policy; former PCFA chair Raymond Suttner, for example, went so far as to say 'it had no influence at all' on the foreign policy debate during the Mandela administration.[72] Most participants, however, disagreed with this characterization, describing the subcommittee as a vibrant center for debate during both Mandela and Mbeki's Party presidencies. While most issues were not contentious, some—like the decision to recognize China—provoked robust debate within the senior Party ranks. Former Defense Minister (1999–2008) and ANC national chairperson (1997–2007) Mosiuoa Lekota cited relations with Angola as a hotly debated issue in the subcommittee, with participants seeking to balance the Party's desire for negotiated solutions to conflicts with its hopes to maintain good ties with the MPLA, its ally during the struggle.[73] The government's stance toward Western Sahara was another that sparked vigorous discussion, according to longtime PCFA and subcommittee member Fatima Hajaig:

Under President Mandela, I remember he called a meeting at Tuynhuys to discuss Western Sahara. We said they have been our allies for a long time, and what Morocco is doing is not correct. Morocco was being very adamant that Western Sahara belonged to them, and they would take it where they wanted to. We had good relations with Morocco, but Madiba said, 'No, the people of Western Sahara have suffered enough. The OAU has recognized it as an independent state, so we should as well.' But some people said we have very good relations with

Morocco, so Madiba said, 'Ok, let's put it on hold for a while and discuss it.' So we held on, didn't make a declaration that we were recognizing Western Sahara.[74]

Moving into Mbeki's Party presidency, Zimbabwe emerged as another contentious issue, with ANC leaders split over how to criticize Mugabe's abuses of human rights while maintaining dialogue with the ZANU-PF government. Jordan, a critical ANC voice toward Zimbabwe, describes 'heated debate, and interesting debate' about Zimbabwe in the subcommittee after the 2002 elections there, noting that a majority of subcommittee members wanted President Mbeki to support Mugabe at the forthcoming Commonwealth Summit; 'Go there, Mr. President, and say "Right on, Bob!"' was the prevailing sentiment, he notes.[75] Lekota, another critic of Pretoria's Zimbabwe policy, says that Zimbabwe 'caused a lot of unease amongst us' within the Party and was probably the most debated foreign policy issue of the Mbeki presidency.[76] He further notes that ANC members who had been in exile, like Mbeki, tended to be 'more accommodating' toward Mugabe and ZANU-PF, whereas those inside South Africa during the struggle were much more critical, particularly given Mugabe's massacres of ANC-aligned Zimbabwe African People's Union sympathizers during the Matabeleland massacres of the early 1980s.[77]

Debates within the subcommittee were generally bounded by broadly accepted Party principles, particularly with regard to solidarity with other liberation movements and oppressed peoples worldwide. 'If you look at our relationship with Cuba,' says subcommittee member and PCFA chair Job Sithole, 'you can argue whether we should be doing more or less. But you'll never win an argument saying cut the ties with Cuba.'[78] Discussion was about tactics more than underlying philosophy. On Palestine, for example, Essop Pahad recalls that 'some wanted more militant statements— Ronnie [Kasrils] felt very strongly about things like sanctions. We'd debate that and ask him, "Why are you calling for sanctions when the PLO isn't?" There would be those kind of discussions. There was never in my time any kind of fundamental difference of opinion in how one understands something.'[79] Sithole seconds this point: 'When the ANC says it will support the Palestinian struggle, we may differ how we do it. We may debate that difference. But the policy position remains.'[80]

Participants in NEC subcommittee discussions recall that while they were open to all viewpoints, once a decision was reached, members were expected to adhere to it without question. 'Once the majority had taken a decision, it becomes the decision of the ANC. You can't say it's anymore contentious,' notes Myakayaka-Manzini.[81] Job Sithole makes a similar point, noting, 'You have freedom of speech in the ANC to say anything under the sun, but once the position is arrived at, there's an expectation that your argument, as good as it was, the conference has spoken on the matter. People tend to shelf their own personal views.'[82] Revealing dissenting opinions outside the organization, particularly in the press, was strongly frowned upon; as long-time PCFA member Mewa Ramgobin notes, 'disciplined' members 'share disagreements in the portals of the ANC itself [. . .] not through the media.'[83]

Mbeki: Still Dominant, but a Dictator?

Thabo Mbeki's 1997–2007 presidency of the ANC has been widely characterized as a period during which power was consolidated and tightly controlled by his office, with the consensus-based approach of the NEC disregarded or, at best, given lip service. Gumede, among others, argues that this 'presidentialization' of the ANC under Mbeki undermined the NEC and weakened the Party, as both a bureaucratic entity and a democratic body.[84] On the whole, the evidence to this effect is compelling. Mbeki strengthened the Party president's office at Luthuli House and took control of the ANC's appointment structure that placed ANC cadres in government positions, taking that responsibility from branches and provincial structures.[85] This tight control rankled many cadres and helped spark the uprising that led to his ouster as party leader at the 2007 Polokwane conference in favor of Jacob Zuma. That said, Mbeki's tighter grip on the Party did not happen in a vacuum; his leadership was affirmed at the 1997

Mafikeng and 2002 Stellenbosch conferences, with no significant objections raised about his consolidation of power.

Mbeki's grip on the Party and longstanding interest in foreign affairs would lead one to expect that he ran the ANC's foreign policy discussions in a similarly tight-fisted fashion. However, participants in the Party's foreign policy debates say this was not the case. Members of the NEC describe him as generally taking a back seat in foreign policy discussions and not dictating to other committee members. Much like Tambo, Mbeki—who normally did not chair NEC meetings, deferring to Lekota as national chairman—would absorb all views and then speak last. According to Essop Pahad, 'There was this view that Mbeki imposed a view, but by and large he just stepped back. He spoke out just once up front about his position on Zimbabwe, when he was coming under attack for it.'[86] Myakayaka-Manzini echoes this view, claiming that because of the collective nature of ANC decision-making, no decision could be attributed solely to Mbeki: 'If that was the case, our foreign policy would have changed by now. And it hasn't changed.'[87]

Pahad and Myakayaka-Manzini's views must be viewed with somewhat skeptical eyes, given that both were considered allies of Mbeki. However, Pallo Jordan—one of the Party's independent voices on foreign policy and, in some ways, a long-time rival of Mbeki's—also says Mbeki was open to debate and discussion during his tenure. He recalls one incident in 2002 when a woman was sentenced to death by stoning in northern Nigeria for adultery:

Mbeki was like, 'Well, it's Nigeria, be careful, ethnic problems, etc. And these characters who wanted to stone this woman were justified under sharia law, so we have to be mindful of that.' But we insisted; we said, 'BS, man, you can't come here with laws elaborated in the seventh century and use it for pretext for doing barbaric things. We cannot possibly condone an African state stoning a woman,' and he had to shift. I'm sure he felt the same way deep down, but he was balancing the political issues. But he said, 'Fine, fine chaps, you're absolutely right.'[88]

Hence, while Mbeki as Party president dominated the ANC and stamped his imprint on the Party, his reputation as an 'autocrat' on foreign policy issues appears overblown.

Conclusion: African National Congress has been an Influential, Independent Foreign Policy Role Player Since 1994

There is no comparison between the NP and ruling party ANC's abilities to influence foreign policy, with the ANC's post-1994 structures having far more input than those of the moribund NP. Renier Schoeman, who has a unique perspective from serving as deputy foreign minister under FW de Klerk and later as an ANC member, says, 'On the foreign affairs structure in the ANC, there's a lot of engagement. I think the policy is closer to the party as an organization. The inputs are far more significant than under the NP.'[89] This greater influence of the Party can be chalked up to several factors, including the ANC's well-developed foreign policy apparatus developed in exile, its better organized party structures, and its national rather than provincial character, which allowed its top national leadership to meet on a regular basis.

Differentiating the role of the Party from that of government in making foreign policy is difficult in the post-transition dispensation. ANC foreign policy structures included nearly all of the relevant government foreign policymakers, providing them with a forum for debate that otherwise would not exist. 'The NEC members are there, the minister is there, and we can engage on the issues,' notes Sithole in describing subcommittee meetings.[90] The proverbial 'hats' were rearranged as well. The ANC in this context eliminated rank and title in its proceedings, allowing participants to weigh in on the issues as equals (rather similar, in fact, to the Broederbond in this context). Mluleki George, deputy minister of defense under Mbeki and a member of the subcommittee, remembers, 'The conversations would flow smoothly, because they were conversations of comrades. Your position in government does not matter in organizational matters— you're all the same.'[91] This cross-fertilization made it difficult at times to tell whether policy positions originated with 'government' or 'party.'

Nevertheless, while party structures did weigh in on foreign policy debates, the question also arises about to what degree they were 'democratic' in being representative of the broader ANC. While participants took pains to emphasize that Mbeki did not run an autocracy on foreign policy debate, the subcommittee in particular can still be described as an oligarchy where, in the words of Jeffrey Herbst, 'decisions are debated and decided within an extremely limited circle.'[92] That said, even if an oligarchy, it appears to have been an oligarchy by consent; there were no impediments to broader participation beyond members' disinterest. Foreign policy was a minor component of conferences since 1991, while generating little interest at the branch and provincial levels. Furthermore, most (but not all) members of the NEC Subcommittee for International Relations were elected at ANC elective conferences as the leading representatives of the Party, another boost to the subcommittee's democratic credentials. While the Party's Department of International Relations was strapped for funds and lacked capacity, there is no indication that this was because of a concerted effort by ANC leaders to limit its influence; all Party departments suffered from the same shortages. In the end, the ANC's inputs on foreign policy may not have encapsulated the views of all of the Party's members, but they did result from a democratic process and influenced the country's external relations.

CHAPTER 9

GOVERNMENT DEPARTMENTS

A government is not an individual. It is not just the president and his entourage, nor even just the and Congress. It is a vast conglomerate of loosely allied organizations, each with a substantial life of its own. Government leaders sit formally on top of this conglomerate. But governments perceive problems through organizational sensors. Governments define alternatives and estimate consequences as their component organizations process information; governments act as these organizations enact routines.[1]

—Graham Allison, in *Essence of Decision, Explaining the Cuban Missile Crisis* (1971)

With this chapter, the focus moves to the realm of the government actors responsible for implementing, and sometimes making, South African foreign policy. While South African premiers and presidents have always been the final decision-makers on foreign policy (to be examined in the next chapter), they have at times delegated this role to the principals (primarily but not always ministers) in government departments with foreign affairs responsibilities. The DFA and Department of Defense have historically been the two most prominent ones, and their roles will be examined at length here. Other departments—like Trade and Industry, Treasury, Information, and civilian intelligence agencies—also will be looked at where appropriate. The goal of this chapter is to determine to what extent the principals of these government departments have acted as 'policy influencers' or 'policymakers' rather than just 'policy implementers' in the external realm, as well as to examine how interdepartmental relations—positive and negative—have influenced the decision-making process.

The Influence of Government Departments Before 1994

From the 1920s until 1994, two government departments—the Departments of Foreign Affairs and Defense—tended to alternate dominance of the foreign policy domain. The DFA (known as the Department of External Affairs until 1961) was founded in 1927 as a result of the previous year's Balfour Declaration granting dominions greater self-government and providing for independent diplomatic services.[2] Defense, which was split off from the Interior Department by the Defense Act of 1912, played a secondary role in foreign policymaking for its first five decades, poorly funded and undermanned with the exception of buildups during the World Wars.[3]

Post-1948: Early Foreign Affairs Dominance ...

The post-1948 NP government viewed both the military and the diplomatic corps as inherently 'English' institutions that would have to be (and were) 'Afrikanerized' in the 1950s and 1960s. The DFA, however, was able to maintain its primacy in the foreign policy arena in large part due to the cabinet machinations of Foreign Minister (1955–63) Eric Louw, the first man to hold the portfolio independent from the prime minister. Louw was South Africa's most experienced diplomat at the time, having from the mid-1920s served as a trade representative and ambassador in Washington and several European capitals. His brusque personality and dogged defense of South African (and more specifically Afrikaner) self-determination made him few friends— particularly among British officials—but put him in good stead within the NP.[4]

Louw was named minister of economic affairs when the NP took power in 1948 and emerged as the Party's leading foreign affairs spokesman, frequently representing the country abroad (even though Malan retained the foreign affairs portfolio).[5] Louw exercised significant sway over the policymaking process: he was instrumental in distancing South Africa from the orbit of Great Britain and the Commonwealth, successfully lobbying for South African neutrality during the Suez Crisis of 1956, while also advocating closer technical cooperation with (and assistance to) Africa's emerging independent states.[6] A skilled political infighter in cabinet, Louw—before and after becoming foreign minister—ensured his primacy on foreign policy matters would remain unchallenged.

Defense Minister (1948–59) FC Erasmus was a target of Louw, at least in part over political disagreements stemming from Erasmus's efforts to reach out to English voters.[7] As economic affairs minister (until 1956), Louw and Finance Minister Nicholaas Havenga starved the Department of Defense of funds; its spending in 1949 (£11.5 million) was actually higher than in 1960 (£11 million), with Louw arguing Western allies should supply equipment for foreign missions.[8] After becoming foreign minister, Louw also asserted himself on external defense policy at the expense of Erasmus.[9] For example, Louw, not Erasmus, represented South Africa at the 1955 Simon's Town conference that provided the Royal Navy with continued access to that strategic naval base.[10] He also masterminded a 1957 change to defense policy that determined the South African military 'should concentrate more on internal security and less upon the preparation of a task force for use outside South Africa,' further clipping its wings externally.[11] Even through the early 1960s, the DFA was able to thwart defense efforts to boost its influence, notably scotching military leaders' efforts to arm Katangese rebels during the Congolese civil war in the early 1960s.[12] The Defense Department's foreign policymaking clout was limited to the point that Munger wrote in 1965 that 'the influence of the South African military upon the formation of South African foreign policy is quite minimal.'[13]

... *Yields to Contested Terrain by 1960s*

The DFA's dominance began to weaken in the early 1960s. Growing international isolation after the Sharpeville massacre and withdrawal from the Commonwealth minimized the importance of increasingly besieged diplomats, who could do little through traditional means to improve South Africa's standing abroad. The move toward armed struggle by the ANC and PAC in the early 1960s, combined with the march toward the independence of African states, mooted diplomatic 'partnership' efforts in Africa while making security a far greater concern. Personality also played a role. While Malan and Strijdom were happy to let Louw dominate in the foreign policy realm, Verwoerd had a keen interest in international affairs and less interest in Louw's counsel.[14] By 1961, Verwoerd had begun to freeze out the 'undiplomatic diplomat,' generally ignoring Louw until poor health forced his retirement in 1963.[15]

Louw's successor was former Pretoria mayor and ambassador to London Hilgard Muller, a Rhodes scholar and Latin professor at the University of Pretoria who was the polar opposite of Louw personality-wise.[16] The qualities that made Muller a respected diplomat, however, worked against him in the top job; as Don Sole asserted in his memoirs, 'His natural diffidence and disinclination to push himself forward were qualities which constitute a distinct handicap for any foreign minister.'[17] Muller, who stayed in the job until 1977, had little interest in policymaking, preferring, in Sole's words, to implement policy 'in a fashion least calculated to give offense.'[18] Longtime diplomat Albert van Niekerk agrees, saying, 'He made no policy within DFA. The issues of the world steered policy, not Muller. He didn't like confrontation.'[19] Verwoerd generally bypassed Muller in seeking advice, as did his successor, John Vorster, opening the door for several aggressive and ambitious cabinet colleagues to fill the void.[20]

The Information/Department of Internal Affairs Clash

The first serious challenge to the DFA's primacy came from the Department of Information in the early 1970s. South Africa's Information Bureau was set up during World War II, and in 1948 was made a sub-department of External Affairs, with the mandate to disseminate information about South Africa abroad, massage its image, and combat criticisms of apartheid policies.[21] Verwoerd turned the Department of Information into an independent department in the mid-1960s, and its energetic (and often confrontational) posture in improving South Africa's image abroad quickly clashed with the staid, 'stick-in-the-mud' efforts of the DFA.[22] Relations deteriorated after Connie Mulder—the Transvaal NP leader with his eye on the premiership—took over as Minister of Information in 1968. From 1973 to 1978, Mulder and his equally ambitious Information secretary, Eschel Rhoodie, embarked on a series of well-funded secret projects abroad, including financing lobbying efforts, funding British and American political campaigns, and attempting to buy American newspapers (most notably the *Washington Star*) to propagandize for South Africa.[23] Money for the project—about $100 million total—came from the defense budget at Vorster's behest.

The DFA was told little about the special projects. Muller knew about some of the covert operations, but he could do nothing to stop the more politically powerful Mulder. Blowback was noticeable in Washington, where Ambassador (1971–4) Frikkie Botha was kept out of the loop on his embassy Information staff's secret efforts. 'Mulder had set his mind to pay a visit on [then-Vice President] Jerry Ford. So without bringing me into the picture, this was all done very quietly, *sub rosa*,' notes Botha, who knew Ford well from an earlier posting in Washington. 'I saw [Ford] at Blair House after Mulder had seen him, and he said "Oh, you're back." I said I hadn't been anywhere, and he said, "When your Secretary [Minister Mulder] was here, they told me you were away."'[24] On another occasion, an American senator told Botha, '"I was told by your Information man that I mustn't pay much attention to you because you're anti-South African Government and were responsible for his father being incarcerated during World War II." I was just a lowly soldier in North Africa; I couldn't have been involved in that.'[25] Muller and Vorster ignored Botha's complaints about this interference, and he was ultimately recalled from Washington in 1974.

The Rise of the Bureau of State Security ...

The DFA's primacy also faced a challenge from South Africa's new civilian intelligence organ. The country had no national intelligence service before 1961, instead relying on British intelligence for its limited needs.[26] A State Security Committee, modeled on the British Joint Intelligence Committee, was set up in the early 1960s as a coordinating body, but it had no collection or operational arm.[27] In 1963 then-Justice Minister Vorster created a new civilian agency, Republican Intelligence (RI), headed by his close confidante (and cellmate during his World War II detention) Security Branch head Hendrik van den Bergh, although it lacked external capacity.[28] To correct this, Vorster in 1968 transformed RI into a 'central intelligence organization' with the capability of operating externally.[29] This new entity, the Bureau of State Security (BOSS), also was headed by van den Bergh and was intended to be the country's preeminent intelligence outfit.[30] From its first budget—which slashed the intelligence budgets for Military Intelligence and Security Branch—it was clear that BOSS would be treated as *primus inter pares* in the South African intelligence field.

From 1968 to 1978, van den Bergh—who carried the title of special advisor on state security in the Prime Minister's Office—was the most influential foreign policy actor in South Africa beside Vorster. While allegations that van den Bergh was the 'power behind the throne' are probably overblown, he was clearly the prime minister's closest advisor, as well as primary 'fixer' and crisis manager, in the foreign arena.[31] Van den Bergh was Vorster's main emissary to Africa, for example, quietly travelling the continent to build support for Vorster's *détente* efforts, notably organizing the 1975 Victoria Falls conference between Vorster and Zambian President Kenneth Kaunda.[32] Van den Bergh would also prove of great assistance to Vorster on Rhodesia, acting as an emissary to Salisbury, who could deliver tough messages to the Smith government, and also working domestically—particularly within the Broederbond—to sell Vorster's realist stance to conservative Afrikaner audiences.[33] Although he generally had friendly relations with the DFA (which he probably regarded as a passive player), he was a leading backer of the Department of Information's efforts in the 1970s.[34]

... and Defense, Under Botha

Meanwhile, the foreign policy influence of the Department of Defense rapidly increased from the early 1960s. With African states becoming independent and South Africa more isolated, defense budgets started to climb rapidly, topping £100 million by 1964.[35] The real rise in the influence and funding of defense, however, did not come until the 1966 appointment of Cape NP leader PW Botha as defense minister. Although he was a professional politician with no military background, Botha took quickly to defense issues, familiarizing himself with military theory and imposing his ideas of professional management on the department.[36] By the mid-1970s, Botha had transformed the Department of Defense into a major power, winning massive budgetary increases. When he assumed the premiership in 1978, the defense budget was nearly 5 times greater than in 1973, accounting for nearly 20 percent of government spending and about 5 percent of GDP.[37]

South Africa's 1975 invasion of Angola in an effort to install a friendly government there before its November independence from Portugal marked the emergence of the Department of Defense's primacy in making critical foreign policy decisions. Fearing potential Soviet intervention and blowback from African states that South Africa was trying to woo, the DFA favored a 'hands-off' approach toward the soon-to-be independent states of Angola and Mozambique.[38] The DFA, however, was sidelined early on, with the Department of Defense and BOSS jockeying for primacy: Botha, seeing an opportunity to install a friendly government on Namibia's border, pushed for invasion while van den Bergh preferred clandestine support for UNITA to outright invasion, believing that US Central Intelligence Agency assistance would be forthcoming.[39] Botha ultimately won the fight, and from August 1975 SADF troops secretly moved into Angola to support UNITA efforts.

Meanwhile, the DFA was kept out of the loop on proceedings almost entirely, not even learning of the venture until later that

August, after it received a formal protest note from Portugal (then still the colonial power) about the invasion.[40] Pik Botha remembers warning Vorster that the United States would not support the invasion, but he was ignored, with Vorster heeding van den Bergh's ultimately erroneous guidance that the Americans would intervene.[41] The DFA did successfully press for withdrawal of SADF forces in 1976, but the DFA's cautions against cross-border operations would be ignored for the rest of the Vorster administration. Then foreign minister, Pik recalls being overruled by PW Botha when he pushed back on the next major Angolan intervention, the Cassinga attacks of 1978:

I was sitting in cabinet, and said I opposed it. PW Botha and about a half of the ministers supported it, but about half sided with me. I said that the UN Security Council would not understand that we accepted [Resolution] 435 but were now doing an attack like this. It was a heated discussion. Normally, cabinet meetings did not last beyond the midday lunch break. This one did; we met again in the afternoon. PW then said to Vorster, 'If it will help you, if the attack is successful you can claim the credit, but if it fails, I will accept responsibility.' Vorster got very annoyed, saying to PW, 'I am the Prime Minister, not you. Whether it fails or succeeds, I accept the responsibility.' And Vorster gave permission for the attack to continue. Fortunately, while it did meet condemnation, it was not too acrimonious. But it indicates to you we did not always agree.[42]

The 1977 discovery and publication by the *Rand Daily Mail* of the Department of Information's secret projects (which included domestic components like the establishment of the *Citizen* newspaper) ultimately led to Vorster's resignation the following year. While Mulder was long the favorite to succeed Vorster, his involvement in the scandal—widely dubbed 'Muldergate'—killed his chances, allowing Cape leader PW Botha (helped by support from Free State Party structures and from Pik Botha, who threw his support to PW after his run for the premiership stalled) to succeed Vorster as Party leader and, in October 1978, prime minister. Botha's ascendancy meant a housecleaning in the top ranks of the foreign affairs apparatus and a strengthening of the Department of Defense's role. Information disappeared altogether as an independent department, folded into the DFA (briefly known thereafter as the Department of Foreign Affairs and Information). Van den Bergh, discredited by his involvement in 'Muldergate' and long a bitter enemy of Botha, resigned the day Botha took office and his service was soon renamed and revamped.

The Department of Foreign Affairs'
Decline Continues Under Botha

PW Botha's ascendancy into the top job only accelerated the military's influence in the policymaking realm. The SADF, for example, was granted the power to undertake cross-border raids and conduct operations up to 150 km inside Angola without seeking ministerial or cabinet approval if it deemed the threat serious to South African security.[43] In addition, Defense Minister (1980–91) Magnus Malan served as Botha's 'right-hand man' within the cabinet. Previously appointed army chief of staff, army chief, and chief of the Defense Force during the 1970s by Botha, Malan was a strident anti-communist and a skilled bureaucratic manager whose strategic and administrative outlooks were very similar to that of the prime minister.[44] Spending remained high through the 1980s, accounting on average for about 4 percent of GDP and 13 percent of the overall budget.[45]

Meanwhile, the DFA and its flamboyant *verligte* minister, Roelof 'Pik' Botha, saw its role diminished under PW Botha. The former MP and diplomat was only 46 in 1977, when he was appointed to succeed Muller. Vorster had backed his rise, taking an almost paternalistic interest in Botha's career, possibly viewing him as a potential successor given his support among young Afrikaners and English speakers more broadly.[46] Despite his support for PW Botha's candidacy, Pik was by no means a confidante of the new prime minister, nor much liked by him. 'Pik and he had a roller coaster relationship,' longtime DFA official and ambassador to Washington Herbert Beukes notes. 'After a visit to PW, Pik would come over with a big smile and give us the thumbs up and say "PW's on our side." Then three days later, it would change just like that.'[47] The prime minister throughout his 11-year tenure continually deferred to his military and intelligence leadership over his foreign minister in foreign policy matters, often not bothering to consult Pik beforehand.

Yet, despite all of this, Pik survived for 17 years, which can be chalked up to his usefulness abroad, exceptional political skills, and resonance with white voters. 'Pik had networks; he could speak to Kissinger or [US Secretary of State James] Baker or [West German Foreign Minister Hans-Dietrich] Genscher. He was effective in that sense,' academic and diplomat Gerrit Olivier notes.[48] While his colleagues in parliament and cabinet may have been cool toward him between election cycles, Botha says, 'When it came to elections, I was expected to hold meetings from Cape Town to Messina, and from Komatipoort to Upington, from Springbok to Pofadder.'[49] Louis Nel, Botha's deputy from 1984–6, describes Pik's oratory skill in stumping for Muller, his charisma-challenged predecessor, before the 1977 national election:

Muller always invited someone to make the political speech [. . .] and in 1977, he invites young Pik Botha, just back from the UN. So Pik goes to Beaufort West to address this packed house, and Pik talks about being ambassador to the UN. And he goes on about Muller being in New York, and spending a day listening to attacks on South Africa in the General Assembly. The next morning, Muller had to address these attacks, and they're sitting in our offices working on the reply late into the night. Dr. Muller, he said, stood up and walked to the window, looked at the millions of lights in New York, and he turned to Pik and said, 'I wonder if it rained in Beaufort West?' The audience got to their collective feet to give a spontaneous standing ovation. To do that in two minutes is not possible for any politician, but Pik did it with that story.[50]

Pik did play a leading role in addressing several of South Africa's key foreign policy challenges of the 1980s: the independence of Zimbabwe, negotiation of the 1984 Nkomati Accord with Mozambique, and the 1990 independence of Namibia.[51] However, PW Botha's clear favoritism of Defense over the DFA ensured that foreign affairs played a secondary role in most key foreign policy decisions dealing with regional destabilization. Although the issue of what Pik knew remains in question, it is clear that he was not told everything about SADF support for RENAMO even after the Nkomati Accords were signed in 1984.[52] The DFA was rarely apprised of cross-border raids in advance (like the 1982 attack on Maseru), and was usually told as they were underway.[53] 'As a department, DFA's influence was limited, if not zero [...] especially on major issues, it was zilch,' Olivier bluntly assesses.[54]

The coordinated May 1986 SADF attacks on Harare, Lusaka, and Gaborone during the visit of the Commonwealth Eminent Persons Group epitomized this lack of communication and demonstrated the military's ability to dictate Pretoria's foreign policy.[55] Pik recalls being informed of those raids after the fact:

Take that thing in Gaborone. I think I may have been acting Minister of Defense at that. I was in the north when the SSC [State Security Council] was meeting here. And a General Staedler was sent by PW to the north, to a game farm where I was, to inform me—not ask me—that this thing was planned. I warned him that this thing might have very serious consequences, but he said to me, 'Mr. Minister, it is too late. All of the operations are already going. That's why I was sent here, because the president wants to inform you so that your department can inform the world outside.' I played no role in getting that decision off the ground.[56]

According to Denis Worrall, at the time ambassador to London, Director-General Neil van Heerden also had no advance notice of the raid: 'He got a phone call from [SADF chief] Jannie Geldenhuys at 3 am to come to the operations HQ. He didn't even know where it was. So he got there, and they told him right now, our planes are over Botswana.'[57] Tellingly, the raid came only a few days after an agreement was reached that the Department of Defense would give the DFA 24 hours' advance notice for any raids.[58]

Pik's treatment by the military epitomized the generally condescending relationship toward the DFA by the Department of Defense. While some senior and working-level DFA officials were able to develop solid ties with their Defense Force colleagues, most felt that they were not respected by the military. 'The Defense Force regarded DFA as ineffective and as wimps, not able to stand up to them,' veteran diplomat Dave Steward notes. 'My personal relationship with the military and Military Intelligence was reasonably sound, just as it remained for many years with Malan. But that's not to say they weren't pulling the wool over my eyes.'[59] Pik Botha claims this disregard for the DFA started at the top with PW Botha; recounting efforts to stop the Defense Force from distributing a piece of propaganda, Pik recalls PW telling him, 'Your boys are weaklings.'[60] Both Military and National Intelligence suspected that the DFA (and Pik in particular) leaked information, which they used as a justification for not discussing operations with the department in advance.[61] Defense leadership also had no compunction about lying to Pik outright, as Steward recalls:

> On 24 May 1985, I woke up and we were confronted with the crisis of this Special Forces guy Wynand du Plessis, who was caught by the Angolans near an oil platform in Cabinda. Rae Killen, then Director-General, came to me, and I said we must do a few things. One is to stop the Defense Force from communicating to the press until we know what's going on. We went to see [SADF Chief] Constandt Viljoen, and Viljoen said they had a recce group dropped from a submarine to surveille a SWAPO base near the complex. I asked him, 'General is that the truth.' And at least he had the good grace to smile when he said '80 percent.' Later that day, Malan had a briefing for cabinet, and he went on about the SWAPO base and the submarine, and I grabbed Pik and said,

'They're lying to you.' He didn't believe me [...] 'Never.'
I think he liked to be one of the *manne*, taken into confidence,
but they were playing him like a trout. That was the
relationship. Not only was Malan lying to him, but he was
enjoying lying to him.[62]

Barnard and the National Intelligence Service:
Stalking the Middle Ground

It was clear from PW Botha's first cabinet briefing on national
security, which was provided by a SADF general, that South Africa's
civilian intelligence structure would have a difficult time asserting
itself under the new prime minister.[63] Although many in the
military wanted BOSS dismantled altogether, Botha did not take this
route and instead renamed it the Department of National Security
(DONS) in August 1978, although not before transferring most of
its responsibilities to Military Intelligence.[64] Its budget was slashed
from R35 million in 1978 to under R30 million the following
year, with the remainder probably absorbed by the defense budget.[65]
A 1980 conference in Simon's Town between DONS, Military
Intelligence, the Security Police, and DFA also formalized a division
of labor between the departments, with DONS instructed to focus on
analyzing global and regional political developments, as well as
developments related to banned entities like the ANC.[66]

PW Botha's 1979 appointment of University of Free State
professor Lucas Daniel 'Niel' Barnard, just 30 years old and with no
background in intelligence, also was widely viewed at the time as a
sign that Botha intended the DONS to be a second-tier bureaucratic
player. Barnard, who had recently returned from studying nuclear
strategy at Georgetown University in Washington DC, was an
unknown figure in South Africa. Even Barnard was caught by
surprise: 'When I returned from Georgetown in October 1979, I was
informed to see Prime Minister PW Botha at the Union Buildings.
No one told me before the time what it was all about, and it was, to
put it mildly, something I didn't expect. PW told me that he'd like
to appoint me as [intelligence] chief, and I'd have 48 hours to decide.

I'd never met him previously.'[67] Barnard accepted and became head of the renamed National Intelligence Service (NIS) the next year.

Barnard acknowledges that his appointment was a result of political trade-offs and compromises. Given Botha's longstanding rivalry with van den Bergh but likely opposition if he tried to scrap the entire civilian intelligence outfit, 'He clearly decided to try to downgrade the old BOSS from a fully functional intelligence service to a service responsible for analyzing intelligence [. . .] Against that background, the move was made to get some academic they can trust, who has no operational experience, and let us try by that way, by stealth, to gradually deny the old bureau operational capacity and develop an analytical capacity.'[68] Barnard fit that bill, and was additionally helped by the political horse-trading that got Botha elected as Party leader: 'I think it was payback time for [provincial leader Alwyn] Schlebusch for delivering the Free State.'[69] Deputy Defense and Intelligence Minister Kobie Coetsee, another Free Stater, also was widely viewed as a patron—although it is unclear to what degree this patronage was motivated by both men viewing Barnard as a potential political rival.[70]

Barnard emerged early on as a pragmatist with regard to South Africa's external relations. Just after the conclusion of the Lancaster House Agreement that led to Zimbabwe's independence, Barnard implored Botha that South Africa should 'not move like Ian Smith'; the government should use its strength to reach a settlement on its own terms.[71] Barnard claims that the NIS from 1984 officially took the line in its (still classified) annual reports that a negotiated settlement was the only solution for South Africa's problems, while the NIS from the early 1980s began reaching out to the ANC through proxies like Willie Esterhuyse of Stellenbosch University.[72] This culminated with Barnard's dozens of meetings with Nelson Mandela in prison between 1988 and 1990. His outlook led him to clash with counterparts at Military Intelligence throughout the decade, both because of organizational rivalries but also increasingly divergent worldviews:

In the 1980s, two schools of thought developed in our
intelligence community. On the one hand, driven by MI
[Military Intelligence]—strongly supported by PW, having
been their minister—there was the view that the Communists
are fighting against us in Mozambique and Zimbabwe and
Zambia, and the only way to try to counter that was to fight the
enemy further abroad, in an extended defensive capacity. You
have to understand the mindset; they were threatening our
existence, arming proxy forces, and it was true the Communists
were arming them with AKs and tanks. So let's create the
capacity with RENAMO and UNITA and so on. One can argue
about that. From the NIS perspective, we didn't deny the
existence of enemy forces on our borders, but our argument was
that the main problem we were facing was internal, not
external, and until you address the internal problems, you
won't make progress.[73]

Given PW Botha's clear affinity for the military, Barnard's influence
on him is still much debated, but appears to have been significant. 'I
think PW trusted Barnard, but I don't think he was as close [...] as
the military guys,' says Cabinet Secretary and Presidency Director-
General (1984–92) Jannie Roux.[74] Barnard may have met with
Botha weekly, but so did the head of Military Intelligence, adds
former Military Intelligence Chief Tienie Groenewald.[75] Military
Intelligence was also able to conduct operations without having to
consult with the State Security Council (SSC) in advance.[76] However,
Barnard's excellent access to Botha and decade-long tenure indicates
that the picture is much more nuanced. As Barnard notes, 'If you see
the president every second day, and you give him some bullshit, after
the tenth day, he'll say, "You're wasting my time." But if you
convince him after some time that you know what's going on and
give him good advice, that's what happened in our situation.'[77] He
adds, 'We had a wonderful personal understanding. He would
invariably discuss even cabinet reshuffles with me, and I would
always give him my opinion.'

The Role of the State Security Council: How Much did it Matter?
From 1978 to the end of the Botha administration in 1989, the
SSC was the South African Government's most prominent—and
infamous—foreign policy decision-making group. Established as a
statutory body in 1972 by an act of parliament, the SSC was composed
of about a dozen top government officials (the number varied) to
advise the prime minister on security matters.[78] Under Vorster, however,
the SSC lacked a functioning secretariat and met only sporadically; the
prime minister preferred to discuss security issues with the whole
cabinet or with just close advisors like van den Bergh.[79] PW Botha—
convinced a more structured body was needed after the 1975 Angola
incursion—upon becoming prime minister in 1978 immediately moved
to strengthen the SSC.[80] The committee, for example, would meet on
the Monday before bi-weekly Wednesday cabinet meetings, where it
would set much of the agenda.[81] Botha also provided for the SSC to
have a robust full-time secretariat staffed by members of the SADF,
civilian intelligence services (who generally accounted for most of the
staff), and the DFA, chaired by a senior military officer, which
fluctuated between 50 and 80 through the 1980s.[82]

The power of the SSC is a matter of debate, even to this day. Pik
Botha was adamant in stating, 'Remember one thing about our SSC: it
had no executive power. None. The SSC, like other committees, could
only make recommendations, not decisions [...] An impression has
been created that the SSC ruled the country. That is not correct.'[83]
However, Pik represents a distinct minority view. 'Any crucial decision
in the 1980s here was taken by the SSC, and PW rammed it through
the cabinet,' claims Barnard, a key SSC participant.[84] Presidency
Director-General Jannie Roux, who was the main note taker for SSC
meetings, seconds this point, noting that 'the role of the SSC is
overstated in a sense in that it didn't control everything, but if you're
talking security issues, which were its responsibility according to the
law, it did.'[85]

Technically, the broader cabinet was tasked with ratifying SSC
decisions and recommendations; in reality, this was not the case, as
cabinet only rarely pushed back against the SSC.[86] Deputy Trade and
Industry Minister (1984–8) Kent Durr cited one rare instance where

he and his department were able to thwart a defense proposal in the SSC that would have altered South African funding of the Southern African Customs Union:

> [Defense Minister Magnus Malan] said, 'Why the hell should we be paying hundreds of millions of rand to people hosting our enemies under the terms of SACU?' But we got the information, and we discovered that they were buying back everything from us with the money we were giving them. And they were buying high value-added items from us with that money. I also realized through prayer that this was something that would hit at innocent people and would be in our long-term detriment. So I had an argument with the military on this, and I refused to do it. The SSC called me in—who was this intransigent deputy minister telling them what to do? And I told them exactly what they should do, and I told them I would resign if they did it. They listened to me and backed off.[87]

Ultimately, PW Botha dominated the SSC. Minister of Law and Order Adriaan Vlok noted in 2006 that Botha strongly emphasized the 'need to know' principle, asking pertinent ministers to stay behind after SSC or cabinet meetings to discuss ongoing operations.[88] 'If they wanted to discuss something that was really sensitive, it wasn't done in the SSC. I never heard anything in the SSC that was terribly exceptional,' Steward says. De Klerk, a sometime member of the SSC during the 1980s, noted in his memoirs that South Africa's nuclear program was never discussed in the SSC.[89] 'The reality was that the real stuff didn't happen in the SSC; it really happened in the coterie around PW,' noted Dave Steward, who cited Malan, Barnard, and lower-level officials like Private Secretary Ters Ehlers as part of that inner circle.[90] DFA official Piet Viljoen, who served as SSC secretary for a period, describes Botha's dominance of the body:

> PW Botha met with his securocrats and made all important policy decisions before the SSC meetings, which just rubber-stamped whatever he had decided. PW Botha allowed the

meetings to ramble on and discuss the issues, but when he had enough, he would simply state his decision. I had a seat at a separate desk to the left of the president, and on occasion he would lean over and say, 'I think they have now talked enough,' and then state the decision.[91]

FW de Klerk: Flipping the Script

FW de Klerk, upon becoming president in August 1989, had a very different view of the policymaking role of the security establishment. De Klerk in his memoirs described being misled by his top military commanders on various operations they continued to run after he took office, noting that he was forced to bring his top commanders in line.[92] He showed no compunction about doing so, firing Malan as defense minister in 1991 and dismissing 16 senior officers in one day in December 1992 for continued involvement in covert activities. De Klerk also slashed defense spending every year he was in office, bringing it from more than 4 percent of GDP to just 2.4 percent (and 6.5 percent of the budget) by 1994.[93] De Klerk as president immediately reasserted the power of cabinet over the SSC, which he had viewed with suspicion for several years.[94] Although he could not disband the SSC immediately, due to its statutory nature, it was made into an 'advisory' council under a broader new cabinet Committee on Security Management, meeting less frequently, and he empowered the cabinet to challenge its recommendations.[95] He also slashed the sizes of the SSC secretariat and Office of the State President, bringing the latter from more than 500 to about 90 members by 1994.[96]

De Klerk's relations with the NIS, which he moved into his office shortly after taking power, were mixed. De Klerk speaks fondly of Barnard in his memoirs, noting that he moved him from the NIS to be director-general of constitutional development to take advantage of his negotiating skills.[97] The former intelligence chief is less glowing in his assessment of de Klerk, however, characterizing him as distrustful of the NIS and contending that de Klerk was far more cautious than Botha in using the service operationally.[98] The DFA, in contrast, saw its standing improve measurably under de Klerk. Although the two men were not close personally, Pik Botha emerged as de Klerk's key foreign policy advisor from 1989, pushing the new president to make bold domestic political steps to ameliorate Western pressure and convincing de Klerk to travel extensively through Europe, North America, and Africa during his tenure to demonstrate Pretoria's good will and to build support for his domestic negotiation efforts.[99]

The Post-1994 Bureaucratic Realignment

Nelson Mandela's 1994–9 administration was a time of great upheaval within Pretoria's foreign policy establishment, mirroring what was going on in government more broadly. The key government foreign policy actors—the Departments of Foreign Affairs, Defense, Intelligence, and a newly important Department of Trade and Industry (DTI)—were forced to reassess their *raisons d'etre* in the immediate post-transition period, unveiling discussion documents and undertaking review processes to determine their future priorities. These departments also struggled with racial integration, at both the working and leadership levels, a situation that resulted in intradepartmental tensions and a loss of skills as older civil servants retired. A tight fiscal environment for all foreign policy-related departments added to the difficulties of the period.

The Department of Foreign Affairs is Back on Top Under Mandela, but Plagued by Problems

South Africa's post-1994 demilitarization and international acceptance brought with it expectations that the DFA would emerge as the leading foreign policy actor in South Africa. During the Mandela years, however, the DFA faced several daunting challenges. Like other departments, the DFA had to address issues of transformation, and in its case the department had to bring more than 500 former homeland and ANC diplomats into its nearly 2,000-strong (largely white) bureaucracy.[100] This process, not considered 'complete' until 2004, would take up much of the DFA leadership's time and energy during the Mandela years. Furthermore, the department had to deal with stagnant funding in the face of an expanded global footprint. The DFA's budget was almost flat between 1994 and 1999, but at the same the department had to significantly expand its global presence, with South Africa having established relations with more than 160 countries by 1997.[101]

Weak leadership was another major hindrance to foreign affairs. As the public face of South African diplomacy, Foreign Minister (1994–9) Alfred Nzo—a surprise appointment—was criticized by cabinet colleague Kader Asmal as having 'no experience of international diplomacy and no taste for the rigors of travel, the nuances of international relations or the importance of guiding the new South Africa through a complex, globalized, modern world.'[102] This inexperience, and Nzo's low-key personality, had negative ramifications for the department, allowing other ministers to move in on the DFA's traditional turf, such Trade and Industry Minister Alec Erwin taking over responsibility for the first free trade negotiations with the European Union.[103] Nzo also had trouble asserting his leadership within the department, particularly in bringing to heel Director-General (1992–8) Rusty Evans, who hewed to a more 'realist' perspective than that of the ANC, advocating that South Africa should conceptualize its national interest around issues of security and financial benefit rather than issues of human rights or sympathy for the ANC's struggle-era allies.[104]

Nelson Mandela's highly personalized conduct of foreign policy did not help matters. Mandela was known to not inform Nzo and other ministers about the outcomes of calls with foreign leaders, for example, and often made pronouncements—like announcing the 'one China' policy in 1996 and defending Zimbabwean military involvement in Congo-Kinshasa in 1999—without consulting the department beforehand.[105] He appointed old friends as ambassadors and on many occasions worked through them directly, rather than through the department in Pretoria.[106] The department was even cut out of state visits. Tom Wheeler remembers, 'I was chief director for human rights at one state, and [Iranian President] Rafsanjani got in to see Mandela without DFA being asked for a briefing. They had a one on one with no one present, and after that Mandela said, "Why do we vote against the Iranians? Now we must abstain."'[107]

Despite Nzo's torpor, the DFA began to assert itself after the 1998 appointment of Jackie Selebi, previously South Africa's ambassador to the UN in Geneva, as director-general. The tenacious Selebi embarked on a strategic planning process that elucidated the department's key goals and objectives alongside a plan to achieve them.[108] Selebi, ideologically aligned with then-Deputy President Mbeki, emphasized South Africa's commitment to an 'African Renaissance' as well as to tying its foreign policy to domestic priorities.[109] Selebi also was an able bureaucratic infighter who pushed back against attempts to impede on the DFA's turf; for example, he successfully fought South African Secret Service attempts to increase their overseas presence on the grounds that the money could be better spent otherwise.[110]

Moves Toward Greater Coordination (and Control) Under Mbeki

Thabo Mbeki's 1999 ascension to the national presidency brought greater coordination among departments on policy, with Mbeki and his expanded Presidency acting as the final decisionmaker. Although relations between government departments on foreign policy during the Mandela years generally were not competitive, they lacked harmonization. South Africa's 1998 intervention in Lesotho— whereby the DFA was kept out of the loop by the Presidency and Department of Defense—epitomized this, as did lack of communication over the China recognition issue. This poor communication can in large part be pinned on the lack of a coordinating mechanism. Mandela's newly expanded cabinet did not prioritize foreign policy issues, and given the disestablishment of the SSC by de Klerk, there were no mechanisms by which the departments dealing with those topics could meet. The small size of Mandela's office—only 27 people at its peak—further limited its ability to play a coordinating role among departments.

Mbeki took several steps to remedy the situation. First and foremost, he expanded the Presidency, growing it to 337 by 2004, a level not seen since PW's Botha's administration.[111] It would serve as the ultimate judge of interdepartmental conflicts, allowing

Mbeki to weigh in where he saw fit.[112] Mbeki in October 1999 also implemented a cabinet cluster system that created five (later seven) cabinet committees of ministers dealing with similar issues to ensure better interdepartmental coordination.[113] Foreign affairs was most broadly covered by the committee on International Relations, Peace, and Security (IRPS), which included the president, 15 ministers (notably foreign affairs, defense, intelligence, and trade and industry, although also less important ministries like Sport, Environmental Affairs, and Energy), and their deputies.[114] However, the Committees on Economics and on Justice, Crime Prevention, and Security also played a role in appropriate foreign affairs issues.

According to participants, the clusters were where most of the serious debate took place on policy formulation, foreign and domestic. 'In [the full] cabinet, there were discussions, but more in committee than cabinet process; committee clusters would bring decisions to the full cabinet,' former Minister Pallo Jordan notes.[115] The IRPS cluster was particularly important, given the government's prioritization of domestic delivery issues. Aziz Pahad, a cluster participant as deputy minister of foreign affairs, notes, 'You must appreciate that international relations was not high on the agenda of cabinet. It normally went through the cluster system.'[116] Participants say the IRPS structure was particularly useful in bringing on board inputs from departments often ignored in the foreign policy process, as Sydney Mufamadi—minister of safety and security under Mandela and provincial and local government under Mbeki—describes:

There could be something in Mozambique where another ministry gets involved; say there's an issue related to water, then the Ministry of Water Affairs would be kept posted. I was Minister of Safety and Security for five years. Sometimes through Intelligence or Foreign Affairs, we'd hear about the proliferation of weapons in Mozambique, some of which end up here [...] At DPLG [the Department of Provincial and Local Government], we had disaster management as a responsibility, and of course the Defense Force went to Mozambique and played a role. But we actually led the SA response to the disaster in

Mozambique. We had to. DFA had in that sense to pilot us into that situation. So a matter can arise from anywhere. The Minister of Health could come to cabinet and talk about malaria in SADC, and it's particularly acute in Swaziland and Mozambique, so my colleagues and I recommend A, B, C, and D. So things can be initiated by the Presidency or other ministries.[117]

Mbeki also pushed for better coordination at a sub-ministerial level with the 2000 creation of the Policy Coordination and Advisory Services (PCAS) unit within the Presidency. The PCAS replaced the Presidency's existing Coordination and Implementation Unit, which had been established in 1997 but lacked the staff and resources to manage the coordination process.[118] Described by Tim Hughes as the 'engine room' of policy integration, PCAS served as the bridge between the Presidency and departments, monitoring departmental performance while keeping Presidency principals apprised of developments.[119] PCAS was subdivided into five chief directorates that mirrored those of the cabinet committees and brought together working-level staff—from director-general on down—to discuss policy formulation, with all ministries required to submit draft bills and proposals to it for scrutiny.[120] The IRPS and (to a lesser extent) economic chief directorates covered a host of issues related to foreign affairs, including trade, international investment, marketing, and peace and security issues.

These moves stamped Mbeki's imprint on the formulation of South Africa's foreign policy. As Aziz Pahad bluntly states, 'All major issues were driven from the Presidency. DFA of course put in inputs, but the process was driven from the Presidency.'[121] Valuing accurate intelligence and good analysis, Mbeki in 2001 also created a Presidential Support Unit within the Presidency to advise on foreign affairs, specifically performing an intelligence gathering and analysis function. It was a small unit, only five members, but was made up of trusted senior officials (like veteran diplomat Welile Nhlapo), many of whom had intelligence backgrounds.[122] The Presidential Support Unit was a trusted source of information for the president; according to former PCFA Chair Raymond Suttner, it was especially valuable in advising on African issues.[123] Mbeki also set up a National Security Council to consider foreign and domestic issues, with potential security threats to South Africa, although it met only sporadically.

The Department of Foreign Affair's Role Under Mbeki

The DFA inherited by Mbeki was in far better shape bureaucratically than five years before, but the department's influence on the president would prove mixed during his presidency. Mbeki's choice as foreign minister—Mandela's brusque minister of health, Nkosazana Dlamini-Zuma—came as a surprise, given Dlamini-Zuma's lack of diplomatic experience. 'She didn't originally want the job,' a veteran diplomat notes. 'She was asked by Mbeki to do it, but she had not lobbied for it or prepared herself. She has said this in so many words; she was completely taken aback. She had no background in diplomacy.'[124] According to a veteran journalist, she left the meeting with Mbeki where he named her foreign minister in tears, upset that she had been thrown into a portfolio where she had no competency.[125] Many, and perhaps Dlamini-Zuma herself, viewed her appointment as an effort by Mbeki to, in essence, retain the Foreign Ministry for himself. She was widely thought—by interviewees and other analysts—to have played a secondary role in policy formulation, instead acting as the department's formal representative in cabinet and South Africa's primary representative to the world.[126]

That said, the DFA was not bereft of senior officials with policy impact. Veteran diplomat Welile Nhlapo was widely regarded as the government's point man and leading expert on central Africa, for example, while Abdul Minty was the go-to official on proliferation matters. '[Minty] would brief the minister or president directly' on nuclear issues, Aziz Pahad says.[127] The leading policy figure in the DFA, however, was Mbeki's longtime friend and confidante Aziz Pahad. 'Nkosazana was the minister and implementer, and Mbeki's defender, but Aziz ran policy,' states one insider, a view echoed by many observers.[128] Described as the 'strategic brain' of the DFA, Pahad was particularly influential on issues related to the Middle East, and Mbeki frequently deployed him to crisis spots like Palestine, Iraq, and Zimbabwe.[129] The affable Pahad also played a valuable internal role in the department, smoothing feathers ruffled by the tempestuous minister.

Despite the Presidency's extensive interest in foreign policy issues, it did grant the DFA a great deal of independence in its day-to-day conduct, especially on less 'hot-button' issues. 'On things like conferences and mundane issues, we played a key role,' says DFA Director-General (1999–2002) Sipho Pityana. 'Then you'd isolate the more difficult issues for higher levels.'[130] The Presidency notably did not participate in the development of the Kimberley Process, one of South Africa's foreign policy 'success' stories of the Mbeki era, letting the DFA and the Department of Minerals and Energy dominate.[131] The Presidency also deferred to the DTI and DFA on trade policy, lacking the technical expertise to take the lead.[132]

Also, outside of the Presidency, DFA was the recognized leader on foreign policy among departments. Although Aziz Pahad admits to some squabbles over turf, 'We had to come to grips quickly with the notion that foreign policy is not the sole mandate of DFA. Our role is to coordinate; we don't have experts on everything.'[133] The only significant area in which the DFA clashed with another department was over trade with the DTI. While the DTI generally played the lead role on trade policy and in negotiations, trade specialist Mills Soko notes, 'There was a debate at some point about whether DTI should focus more on industrial and competition policy, hiving off trade policy to DFA. DFA under Dlamini-Zuma had a strong interest in trade and commercial diplomacy.'[134] The two departments clashed over the overarching goal of trade talks, with the DTI favoring 'hard lines' that sought to maximize benefit to South Africa while the DFA focused on the broader, geo-strategic interests, including maintaining good relations with developing world partners.[135] The DTI generally won these battles.

Meanwhile, Defense is a Bit Player

While the DFA and DTI saw their profiles rise as foreign policy actors after 1994, no department saw more of a decline in external influence than previously dominant Department of Defense, hampered by resource constraints, and uncertain mandate, and poor leadership throughout the Mandela and Mbeki presidencies. The new South African National Defense Force—an amalgamation of the SADF, homeland, and liberation movement armed forces—came into existence on April 27, 1994, and from the start was starved of resources.[136] De Klerk-era cuts to military spending continued after 1994, dropping its expenditure to 1.6 percent of GDP by 1997, where spending would hover through the Mbeki presidency.[137] Although the SANDF—at the behest of politically powerful Defense Minister Joe Modise—in 1999 acquired modern fighter aircraft, corvettes, and submarines in a controversial multi-billion rand deal, spending on 'big-ticket' acquisitions was not matched by necessary expenditures on pay, maintenance, and spares necessary for the force's operability.

Mandate was another problem. The 1996 constitution stated that the military would have strong civilian control (including oversight by parliament) as well as a 'primarily defensive orientation and posture,' but it said little else about the role of the armed forces, particularly as an external actor.[138] White papers on defense (1996) and peace missions (1998), as well as the 1998 defense review, sought to flesh out the SANDF's future role, and they identified humanitarian, peacekeeping, and 'flag-flying' operations as 'secondary' functions of the SANDF related to the foreign affairs sphere.[139] However, these documents—particularly the defense review—were not informed by a clear vision of South Africa's national interest and future foreign policy priorities; as defense analyst Len le Roux notes, 'The military expected that politicians would provide this guidance, but this did not happen.'[140] The Treasury was also not sufficiently consulted to determine what sorts of expenditures would be realistic for a future force.

Mbeki upon taking office did little to address these problems, but at the same time came to rely on the increasingly overstretched SANDF as a major tool in implementing his foreign policy priorities. With only a handful of troops deployed as peacekeepers before 1999, Mbeki drastically increased the SANDF's external footprint, and by 2006 it had more than 3,000 troops deployed to continental hotspots like Congo-Kinshasa, Burundi, and Sudan to participate in peace support missions. These deployments would prove a significant strain on the defense budget and the military itself, given that high rates of HIV and poor fitness forced the SANDF to scramble to find enough fit troops to send on these missions. Although Pretoria did wave off some requests for assistance—like Liberia in 2003—due to lack of resources, Mbeki largely ignored capacity shortfalls when committing South African troops.[141] Although a National Office for the Coordination of Peace Missions was established in the DFA in the late 1990s to consider and manage these deployments, Mbeki largely bypassed it, according to late ISS military analyst and former SANDF officer Henri Boshoff. 'It was never used [Mbeki] didn't listen to [Defense Minister Mosiuoa] Lekota or anyone else. He would make a decision and make the military do it.'[142] Military claims of overstretch were generally dismissed.

Several observers cited the ineffectiveness of Defense Minister (1999–2008) Mosiuoa 'Terror' Lekota as a major reason the Department of Defense was not able to push back. As one cabinet colleague notes, 'Terror also did not understand the role of the military as an instrument of foreign policy' and was unable to think strategically about South Africa's role on the African continent and push for the necessary capacity.[143] Lekota entered the cabinet without having any background in military issues, but as the cabinet colleague notes, Mbeki 'in appointing his first cabinet, there are so many markers that are called in at that point. Terror was chair of the ANC, so you had to give him a prominent role.'[144] The ANC chairmanship on its own was a full-time job, and many observers described Lekota as an 'absentee minister' during his tenure, putting Party business ahead of his cabinet job. 'Lekota never understood the military and never tried,' says one military analyst. 'Some guys I know said Lekota never read documents; he'd be given drafts of things like "Vision 2020" and just sign them.'[145]

Conversely, Lekota and his deputy (2004–8) Mluleki George throw much of the blame for the Department of Defense's lack of resources back on the cabinet, particularly Finance Minister Trevor Manuel, a longtime opponent of increased military spending.[146] 'I must be honest—he was never helpful,' George notes. 'He has a bad understanding of defense. In those days, people would say there's no war, so we don't need to spend money on defense. To me that's a stupid argument [...] that chap is stupid with the military.'[147] Lekota says that while Mbeki was sympathetic to the need for greater military spending, 'Given that there was no external threat, defense budgeting was not a priority, particularly in comparison to internal concerns [Mbeki] could not ride roughshod over cabinet priorities.'[148] Not everyone agrees with Lekota. As Kader Asmal claims in his memoirs, 'The national budget was largely a set of Mbeki's decisions, which is a painful thing to say in view of my friendship with Trevor Manuel.'[149]*

No Sub-National Influence on Foreign Policy

Government influence on foreign policy both before and after 1994 came at a national level, with almost no input from provinces or municipalities. Unlike its predecessor documents, South Africa's 1996 constitution gives provincial and local governments the power to pursue agreements related to trade, investment, and other linkages, and it also provides that the National Council of Provinces—parliament's upper house, established to represent provincial views—ratify international agreements, giving these sub-national entities some theoretical power.[150] Some provinces (particularly Gauteng, Mpumalanga, and Western Cape) and cities have been active in pursuing external linkages, particularly in seeking out investment opportunities, but these efforts have not sought to influence foreign policy more broadly.[151] Also, despite its theoretical power, the National Council of Provinces lacked any distinct provincial identity and ANC dominance meant it simply acted as a 'rubber stamp' for the ruling party during the Mbeki administration, much like the National Assembly.[152]

Conclusion: The Ebb and Flow of Departmental Influence

The influence of South Africa's various government departments in foreign policy formulation, as this chapter has shown, has been in constant flux since the earliest days of the Union. There are a couple of obvious reasons for this. One is that the needs of the country, determined by the executive, are clearly linked to departmental influence. Information and intelligence dominated in a period where Pretoria sought to quietly improve its not-yet irreparably damaged reputation abroad. Defense grew in stature when the focus shifted from solicitude to outright defiance. The DFA reasserted itself in the transition and immediate post-transition period, when reengagement with the world was the priority. And under Botha and Mbeki, both of whom inserted themselves personally into the foreign policy process and sought to retain a close hold on it, the Presidency (and SSC under Botha) played strong coordinating roles. These dominant departments also have been characterized by significant funding advantages over their rivals; clearly the adage 'he who has the gold, makes the rules' applies.

Another clear conclusion is that departments as entities are less important than the people who lead them. From Louw to van den Bergh to Magnus Malan to Aziz Pahad, the relationships between the executive and leading departmental principals (not always the minister, as Pahad's case shows) has been perhaps the clearest marker of departmental influence. All of these close relationships translated into their departments having clear primacy in the foreign policy process. Leaders like Malan, de Klerk, and Mandela lacked particular departmental advisors, and tellingly, their tenures were times of interdepartmental competition. An ability to protect one's bureaucratic turf against potential rivals is another determinant of departmental influence, particularly in periods of competition. Louw's turf protection under Malan and Strijdom; Mulder and Rhoodie's sidelining of the DFA under Vorster; and Dlamini-Zuma's assertion of the DFA's turf under Mbeki all fit this bill. This did not just happen at the ministerial level. The ability of working-level defense officials to run roughshod over the DFA in the SSC and Jackie Selebi's aggressive defense of the DFA turf under Mandela also serve as fitting examples.

CHAPTER 10

THE PRIME MINISTER
AND PRESIDENT

To conclude, this chapter examines the foreign policy role of South Africa's prime ministers (until 1984) and presidents, who have had significant constitutional power in the foreign policy sphere. The 1961 constitution vested the state president with the power to declare war and make peace; enter into international treaties; accredit diplomats; and command the military, although in reality these powers were given to the prime minister due to the presidency's ceremonial nature.[1] The 1983 constitution, which eliminated the office of prime minister and gave the Presidency real teeth, included almost identical language about the powers of the president, though it diminished cabinet oversight of the decisionmaking process.[2] As noted in Chapter 7, the 1996 constitution provides for greater oversight from parliament, at least on paper, but gives the executive similar foreign policy powers, including the 'negotiating and signing of all international agreements.'[3]

Less clear, however, is how each of these leaders used that power. For example, to what extent did these leaders dominate the decision-making process versus delegating on issues of foreign policy? Did they care about foreign policy? Did they rely on any particular advisors on foreign affairs? Are there commonalities, or notable differences, that can be discerned? To answer these questions, this chapter will examine the foreign policy engagement of each prime minister/president since Smuts, specifically their interests in the topic; their respective worldviews; their experiences in the international arena, through travel or policymaking; and their individual decisionmaking styles—closed versus consultative, micromanaging versus delegating, and discouraging or encouraging of debate. A study of each leader will help determine the degree to which personal characteristics of South African leaders—particularly their interest in and openness to consultation—have had an effect on whether foreign policy has been open to outside inputs.

Smuts and Hertzog

South Africa's two premiers between 1919 and 1948, Jan Smuts and JBM Hertzog, brought drastically different styles to the decision-making process in foreign policy. After being seconded to London to help in planning the war effort, Smuts emerged after the First World War as South Africa's preeminent internationalist, participating in the drafting of the Treaty of Versailles and helping lay the groundwork for the League of Nations.[4] Upon returning to South Africa in 1919 and assuming the premiership after the death of Louis Botha (whose poor health and general disinterest kept him from playing much of an international role during his 1910–19 administration), Smuts retained a keen interest in foreign affairs. He advocated close cooperation with the Empire, kept a watchful eye on developments at the League of Nations and, closer to home, unsuccessfully advocated Rhodesia to be absorbed by South Africa in 1923.[5]

While Smuts' involvement in foreign affairs gave him significant status abroad, it did not play as well at home, leading to accusations that he was more interested in global affairs than those in South Africa, a contributing factor to his ouster as prime minister in 1924. His interest in foreign affairs never waned over the next 15 years—as leader of the opposition until 1933, then Hertzog's deputy—raising external issues in speeches on the *platteland* and warning of the coming storm in Europe.[6] The outbreak of war brought Smuts back to the premiership, and during this second stint he cemented his status as South Africa's most internationally recognized figure, both with his service on Churchill's war cabinet and in his subsequent work in the founding of the UN.[7] His status waned at home in the post-war years, however, and in 1948 his pro-Commonwealth United Party lost to the surging republican Nationalists, with Smuts even losing his Standerton seat. Once again, accusations of preferring the global stage to the smaller one at home factored into the electoral outcome.

Smuts was an autocratic decision-maker; as one unsympathetic biographer described him, 'Smuts rules his ministers with a rod of iron. They were mentally dragooned. There was no disputing his will.'[8] Both friends and foes describe him as brusque in his dealings with others, showing 'all too obvious lack of interest in people and their problems beyond the immediate difficulty on which that had come to consult him as clients.'[9] These proclivities appeared to worsen after World War II; as Smuts' *aide-de-camp* in London, Don Sole, notes, 'In his handling of South Africa's post-war problems, Smuts had a belief in his own omniscience and declined to consider advice from his own officials or indeed from any other source that ran contrary to his own ideas.'[10]

Smuts' imperiousness carried over to the foreign policy arena. In a 1944 letter, Sole wrote that there existed 'no foreign policy except what's in General Smuts' head.'[11] This self-reliance dated back to the last war, when Smuts appeared not to take into account any input from South Africa during the drafting of Versailles or his inputs on the League of Nations, showing his preference for executive decision-making in concert with his fellow heads of state rather than politicians back home.[12] Smuts generally ignored the Department of External Affairs (DEA) as prime minister, paying little heed to the permanent secretaries running the department or to his ambassadors, many of whom were political rivals sent abroad for convenience.[13] He had no real advisors on foreign policy; even his right-hand man and deputy, Jan Hofmeyr, was not known to have been consulted on external issues.[14]

Smuts' interest in and conduct of foreign policy contrasted sharply with that of Hertzog, prime minister from 1924–39, who according to one contemporary account 'neither claims nor desires to be a world statesman.'[15] Foreign policy was a minor focus for Hertzog, whose attention was on empowering Afrikaners in the economic and political realms at home.[16] Although not enthusiastic about South Africa's membership in the Commonwealth, the issue was not a priority for him and he generally accepted those ties, at least until the outbreak of war in 1939.[17] Perhaps given this relative disinterest, Hertzog showed greater willingness to consult on foreign policy among a trusted group of advisors. 'He listened to [External Affairs Secretary HD] Bodenstein,' recalls Don Sole, while others cite Smuts, Defense Minister Oswald Pirow, Finance Minister Nicholaas Havenga, and roving diplomat Eric Louw as others with whom Hertzog consulted.[18] Hertzog, unlike Smuts, had a soft spot for the DEA. Sole recalls Hertzog's last day in office after losing the September 1939 parliamentary vote on entering the war. Hertzog came to the department to say goodbye to the staff, and ended up spending nearly 30 minutes with Sole, the junior member of the department. 'One of the things he said to me, which I've never forgotten and lived throughout my career, was that "you people in Foreign Affairs are in a different position from those in other bureaucracies, because you represent the nation. The nation is the whites, blacks, Indians, and coloureds, don't you forget that."'[19]

DF Malan

NP leader DF Malan assumed the premiership from Jan Smuts in 1948, determined not to make the mistake as being seen prioritizing international issues ahead of domestic ones.[20] Despite retaining the position of foreign minister—possibly to frustrate Eric Louw, South Africa's leading diplomat but a man with whom Malan had a contentious relationship—Malan did not show any great interest in foreign affairs. Although committed to the idea of a South African republic, he took no steps during his premiership that would have isolated South Africa and hoped it could remain part of the Commonwealth.[21] Although Malan was the first foreign leader to visit independent Israel, he did not travel abroad as frequently as Smuts.[22] He was open to inputs from ministers like Havenga, and—

to the surprise of many diplomats in that very 'English'
department—from the DEA. At first, Sole recalls, 'He was very
suspicious, but what changed him was Mrs. Malan, who told him,
"These people have grown up in the British Mandarin tradition. They
serve the country, not the government, and you can trust them."'[23]
Malan became particularly close to Foreign Secretary DD Forsyth,
who was key to convincing Malan to enter the Korean conflict
alongside UN forces in 1950.[24]

Nevertheless, Malan did on occasion make unilateral foreign
policy pronouncements, but they were rarely well-informed ones.
Malan had a particular interest in Africa, and was the driving force
(without input of DEA officials or cabinet members) behind the
'African Charter' that aimed to keep the continent Christian, anti-
communist, and non-militarized, an idea that got little traction at
home or abroad.[25] He also strongly (but unsuccessfully) advocated
absorbing the High Commission territories on South Africa's
borders, against the advice of the DEA.[26] Despite this interest in
Africa, he displayed little knowledge of its politics or geography; in a
1955 conversation with Malan, Munger found that the former prime
minister 'made it only too clear that he believed Ghana was east of
Nigeria.'[27]

JG Strijdom

A small-town lawyer from the rural northern Transvaal, Johannes
'Hans' Strijdom was the least worldly South African leader, having
practically no foreign exposure through his cabinet responsibilities
(he had been minister of lands) or travel before becoming premier in
1954.[28] As Don Sole recalls, 'Strijdom had little interest in foreign
affairs and saw his task in South Africa as maintaining the identity of
the white man.'[29] He adds, 'I was overseas for most of Strijdom's
tenure. When Eric Louw decided to reduce representation at the UN
and I came back, he took me in to have a chat with Strijdom. He
wasn't the least bit interested.'[30] The only issue with a foreign policy
connection in which Strijdom showed any interest was with regard to
South Africa becoming a republic, although he did not press the issue

during his premiership, leaving it to his trusted successor, Hendrik Verwoerd. Strijdom was the first prime minister to delegate the foreign affairs portfolio, and he was content to let Eric Louw, a close ally, dominate that sphere. Strijdom, a leading proponent of *baaskap* with little respect for black South Africans, did not even bat an eye at Louw's attempts to build nascent relations with independent black-ruled states, a clear display of his disconnectedness.[31]

Hendrik Verwoerd

In 1937, future business titan Anton Rupert applied for a job at Johannesburg's new Afrikaans newspaper, *Die Transvaler*, and was interviewed by its editor, Dutch-born former psychology professor HF Verwoerd. Rupert ultimately declined the job due to a conflict with his studies, but also because he did not relish working for Verwoerd, whom he described as 'restless, rather autocratic and opinionated.'[32] Rupert's judgment of the man, with whom he would clash in later years, would prove remarkably accurate.

A mild surprise as successor to Strijdom, Verwoerd during his 1958–66 premiership dominated his cabinet, party, and the state like no other leader, before or since. He was unapologetically authoritarian and 'overruled ministers on departmental matters and in general created the impression that he alone was making all the decisions.'[33] He often understood his ministers' portfolios better than they did and treated them like 'schoolboys' in cabinet.[34] In the same vein, he often introduced legislation without seeking ministerial or parliamentary inputs.[35] A workaholic who would put in 16- to 18-hour days, Verwoerd had an almost superhuman certainty in his decision-making, with even his wife acknowledging that he would not make concessions once he had made a decision, which he tended to do quickly.[36] Thereafter, Verwoerd would tolerate opposition from neither supporter nor critic.[37] If his logic did not prevail over his opponents, he would simply talk them into the ground, sometimes speaking for hours to the point where his confused audiences would go along with his reasoning, no matter how abstruse.[38]

Although Verwoerd is best remembered for his conceptualization of separate development and work to codify apartheid, he was keenly engaged on foreign policy, particularly after the 1960 Sharpeville massacre began focusing global attention on South Africa. He took great interest in Namibia matters, endorsing the DFA's ultimately successful 1961–6 legal battle in the International Court of Justice regarding the legality of South Africa's occupation.[39] Future Foreign Minister Pik Botha, then a lawyer on the case, recalls, 'Because of the importance of this case, we had direct access to Verwoerd. He wanted weekly roundups of what was going on to keep track of the case.'[40] Botha's recollection hints at Verwoerd's predilection for micro-management, poring over diplomatic reports and seeing fit to involve himself in matters dealt with by junior diplomats. Longtime diplomat Tom Wheeler recalls, 'I as a junior officer in 1961 would put up a memo on something like the Red Cross, and it would come back a while later with marginal notes by Verwoerd on it. That's the extent to which he was involved.'[41]

Verwoerd's conduct of foreign policy was a microcosm of his overarching decision-making style, famously taking the decision to withdraw South Africa from the Commonwealth without consulting either cabinet or parliament.[42] This authoritarianism led Munger to famously state in 1965, 'If one were to list the most important people making foreign policy, the names might well run: 1. Dr. Verwoerd 2. Dr. Verwoerd 3. Dr. Verwoerd 4. Foreign Minister Muller 5. The cabinet and 6. Secretary GP Jooste, Brand Fourie, Donald Sole, and one or two other professionals.'[43] Verwoerd lacked senior foreign policy advisors, freezing out Eric Louw as foreign minister and largely ignoring his successor, Muller. While Jooste, Sole, and Africa envoy Albie Burger generally had good access to Verwoerd, even they were ignored if they did not agree with the prime minister. 'Verwoerd just didn't listen if he didn't agree,' Sole says.[44]

Verwoerd's stance toward external affairs throughout most of his tenure was exemplified by his 'block of granite' position, refusing to be cowed by Western criticism or to be flexible in South Africa's application of apartheid, once even banning his MPs from attending diplomatic mixed-race functions. By the end of his tenure (and life), however, Verwoerd began to show a greater appreciation for the nuances of foreign relations. He took a cool stance, for example, toward Rhodesia's November 1965 Unilateral Declaration of Independence, placing pragmatism above any racial solidarity with Rhodesia's whites.[45] Verwoerd also held talks in 1966 with Lesotho's new prime minister, Leabua Jonathan, and appeared to be moving toward normalizing relations with that newly-independent neighbor. In fact, on the morning of September 6, 1966, Verwoerd told his caucus he would be making an important foreign policy announcement in his speech in parliament that afternoon.[46] However, parliamentary messenger Dimitris Tsafendas stabbed Verwoerd to death before he could make that speech; as Verwoerd was not one to use notes, no one will ever know what he would have announced that day.[47]

John Vorster

John Vorster, Verwoerd's minister of justice and successor, was in terms of personality and vision drastically different to his predecessor: plain-spoken, deliberate, and while intelligent, by no means intellectual.[48] Whereas Verwoerd had an overarching vision for the country, Vorster was reactive, a counter-puncher not wedded to any particular ideology. Perhaps as a result of his legal background, Vorster seldom took snap decisions, considering all permutations before making choices.[49] Whereas Verwoerd was a micromanager, Vorster saw his role as more of a 'chairman of the board,' making decisions when necessary but generally allowing his ministers to run their own portfolios, seeking consensus wherever possible.[50] While Vorster's style of governance may have been politically wise and allowed capable ministers to thrive, however, it lacked an effective coordinating mechanism and was not undergirded by an overarching strategy. Hence, ministers operated their departments like independent fiefdoms rather than interconnected entities, and Vorster's administration was characterized by the most significant interdepartmental competition over foreign policy ever seen in South Africa.[51]

Although Vorster had no foreign policy experience before becoming prime minister, he developed an interest in and strategic understanding of the pertinent issues, evidenced by his attempts at *détente* with the continent and his taking a hard line toward Rhodesia, which he thought would help ameliorate Western pressure on South Africa.[52] In making his foreign policy choices, Vorster relied on the advice of a small group of advisors, both inside and outside government, toward whom he showed unshaking loyalty.[53] BOSS Chief Hendrik van den Bergh was first among equals in providing advice, although the DFA Director-General Brand Fourie and Information Secretary Eschel Rhoodie were also trusted.[54] Late in his administration, Foreign Minister Pik Botha moved into this inner circle. 'He treated me like a younger little brother. I could discuss anything with him [. . .] He gave me complete freedom to undertake negotiations on Rhodesia,' Botha recalls.[55]

Vorster's management shortcomings prevented the country from developing a coordinated, overarching foreign policy and would come to have deleterious consequences for his administration. As noted in the previous chapter, the DFA was caught flat-footed by Vorster's choice—after much deliberation—to intervene in Angola in 1975, a decision driven largely by Defense Minister PW Botha that ultimately derailed Vorster's *détente* efforts.[56] Similarly, Vorster kept the DFA and other departments in the dark about Information's secret projects, the discovery of which was largely responsible for bringing his premiership to an end in 1978.[57] It also effectively ended the career of Information Minister Connie Mulder, long the favorite to succeed Vorster, who lost out to the minister from whose departmental funds Information's monies originated, the Defense Department's PW Botha.

PW Botha

PW Botha's 1978 assumption of the premiership was the culmination of a political life that had begun in 1936, when 20-year-old Botha gave up his legal studies in Bloemfontein to work for the NP in Cape Town. As an organizer and, from 1948, an MP, he gained a reputation for possessing a fiery temper and for being willing to do the dirty work necessary to achieve his political aims. Longtime opposition leader Colin Eglin recalls Botha attending United Party meetings in the early 1950s 'to ask questions, to make interjections, to harass the speakers and generally to disrupt the proceedings—on occasions not without the use of brute force.'[58] He entered Verwoerd's cabinet in 1958 as deputy minister of internal affairs and Vorster made him defense minister in 1966. As noted, his tenure was marked by a significant increase in the Defense Department's resources and influence, but he was continually frustrated by the Vorster cabinet's disorganization and internecine battles.

Botha showed from the start of his administration that it would be a far more disciplined one than that of his predecessor, with decision-making codified and all ministers singing off the same hymn sheet, a style described by one academic as more 'forceful managing director' than 'chairman of the board.'[59] Botha ensured the cabinet was given a proper secretariat (which for the first time would take detailed notes and provide proper agendas for meetings) and that the SSC's capacity was bolstered.[60] By the time he left office in 1989, the Office of the State President would have more than 500 employees that served a coordinating and implementing role. These structures combined to ensure that all departments worked toward a common goal, with Botha able to monitor progress along the way.

The creation of structures was not, however, the only means by which Botha maintained control over his government and cabinet—he also used intimidation. Botha's aloofness from his cabinet and the NP caucus resembled that of Verwoerd, but whereas Verwoerd's intellect awed his ministers into silence, Botha's ministers simply feared him. 'If he went to cabinet determined to get approval for something, he would get it,' recalls Dawie de Villiers.[61] Interviewees had countless stories of Botha's thuggish and belittling behavior toward his ministers, even those considered among his confidantes. FW de Klerk in his memoirs said Botha in cabinet meetings 'sat at the head of the elongated oval cabinet table and presided over proceedings sometimes like a benevolent father and sometimes like a great bird of prey [...] His style did not encourage free and open

debate. Ministers who were imprudent enough to embark on courses
that did not please him were very quickly, and often quite brutally,
cut down to size.'[62] Given the paucity of free and open debate,
cabinet and SSC meetings tended to be peremptory, with decisions
made by Botha directly or offline with the counsel of a few key
advisors. Describing the proceedings, longtime Cabinet Secretary
Jannie Roux recalls that, 'PW would listen to two or three ministers
and say, "Ok, enough discussion, here's the decision."'[63]

That said, while many of his ministers lived in fear, they also had
a great respect for Botha's loyalty and consistency. 'He could be
nasty [...] boy, there were times when he was nasty,' Magnus
Malan, Botha's defense minister and close confidante, recalls in his
memoirs. However, 'If he gave you the green light you could
depend on him—not like other politicians. He's a man's man, he's a
hell of a good friend to have, but he's a nasty enemy.'[64] Many noted
that one had to learn how to approach Botha, particularly after
he became even more erratically temperamental after a stroke
around 1982.[65] As Military Intelligence Chief Tienie Groenewald
notes, 'You had to learn to know him. If he was in a bad mood,
you did what you had to do and got out. If he was in a good mood,
you could sometimes spend a lot of profitable time with him. He
took a lot of advice; people don't realize that [...] He'd listen when
you spoke sense.'[66]

While Botha may have appeared to make hasty decisions in formal
structures, they were backed by extensive research, consultation, and
contemplation. Once remarking, 'Remember what King Solomon
said: "The more advisors you have the more wise decisions you will
make,"' Botha appointed commissions of inquiry on a host of issues,
seeking out the best minds in the country to sit on them.[67] While
impatient, Botha was not unapproachable; as Don Sole describes in
his memoirs, Botha was always 'ready to listen as long as he was
satisfied that I was not wasting his time.'[68] While it happened rarely,
ministers and government officials could stand up to him and change
his mind, although Pik Botha notes that in making arguments,
'Everything needed to be supported.'[69]

Botha relied on a small inner circle of trusted advisors, although he was not as close to any of them as Vorster was with van den Bergh. Press Secretary Jack Viviers, Private Secretary Ters Ehlers, and Cabinet Secretary Roux all were cited as being part of this inner circle, with Malan, Barnard, and Constitutional Development Minister Chris Heunis considered the most influential cabinet-level figures.[70] However, Roux—who was frequently described as Botha's 'gate-keeper' in contemporary accounts—contends that their influence should not be overstated. 'I always said, the guy who is going to be the power behind PW's throne has yet to be born; PW was the power behind his own throne [. . .] he was his own man.'[71] Roux paints a picture of Botha as an isolated figure, personally and professionally. 'PW didn't leave friends; he didn't care about it. I predicted he would die a lonely man, and he died a lonely man. He had some friends, but they weren't strong-minded people who could change his mind on important things.'[72]

The characteristics of Botha's decision-making—process orientation, trust in the security apparatus, reliance on a few advisors, and even his short temper—all were reflected in his conduct of South Africa's foreign policy. Botha's 12 years as defense minister certainly gave him experience in the world of foreign policy, but he was not widely traveled (not leaving the region during his premiership, save for a 1984 trip to Europe), and according to most observers he lacked a sophisticated worldview. In the view of US Assistant Secretary of State for Africa (1981–8) Chester Crocker, Botha was deeply suspicious of American 'constructive engagement' efforts in southern Africa given his 'very African penchant for believing that distant foreigners were the source of his problems and could become his *deus ex machina*.'[73] Botha's perceptions of the outside world were also very much shaped by his proclivity for not being seen as succumbing to pressure, either internally or externally. Botha's handling of the 1985 'Rubicon' speech—in which he scotched Western expectations of a reformist speech, severely damaging the country's economy in the process—reflected this defiance.[74]

Botha had no time or patience for the niceties of diplomacy, and his proclivity for taking the advice of his security apparatus over his diplomats is well covered. As with domestic challenges, Botha's temper could boil over when foreign envoys delivered messages he did not like. Barnard recalls the visit of Klaus Kinkel, then West German intelligence chief and later foreign minister, in the early 1980s after Bonn's ambassador to the UN had been attacking South Africa:

> I told Kinkel that PW is going to go after him about his ambassador. I said, 'Don't argue with him; I know him.' So they're having coffee and tea, and typically, PW asks him, 'That ambassador of yours in New York, what the hell is he up to?' And Kinkel, against all good advice, tried to make a stand. I even tried after the first interaction to sort it out, but Kinkel insisted, and PW got into him. And I can recall the German lady trying to translate, her mouth stopped, and I said, 'You see, Kinkel, she's stopped translating because she's never seen something like this.'[75]

A second stroke in 1989 finally led Botha's long-cowed cabinet to take him on, forcing him out as Party leader and, soon thereafter, as president. The world was changing—Namibia was moving toward independence, the Soviet Union was collapsing, and Botha was even holding talks with Mandela. Most of his cabinet colleagues, however, doubt he would have had the courage to take the final steps of unbanning the ANC and freeing Mandela. He was of a different, bygone era. Barnard says 'Remember one thing when talking about PW [...] it was like taking Truman or Eisenhower to the late 1980s. PW started his career in 1948 in parliament. In 1948, Truman was still president. Always take that into account.'[76] Instead, that responsibility would fall to his successor, Education Minister FW de Klerk.

FW de Klerk

The tendency of the NP caucus to elect prime ministers with drastically different personalities, biases, and preferences from their predecessors continued with the elevation of FW de Klerk. Despite having a 'conservative' reputation, de Klerk, a lawyer by training, was more of a consensus seeker than Botha and was respected within cabinet for his intellect.[77] His brother, respected journalist Willem de Klerk, described him in a biography as 'a team man who consults others, takes them into his confidence, honestly shares information with his colleagues, and has a knack for making people feel important and at ease.'[78] Even-tempered and phlegmatic, de Klerk had no propensity for Botha-esque temper tantrums, which was welcomed by ministers who had walked on eggshells for years.[79] Contrasting de Klerk's style with that of his predecessor, Dawie de Villiers says, 'FW on the other hand was a good lawyer, good listener [. . .] he could be very argumentative, and if he had a point he wouldn't let it go. But as a lawyer, he'd say, can we work it this way. He has strong views, but was an open and considerate man.'[80]

De Klerk quickly changed the style of decision-making at the top. The full cabinet became the forum for debate and discussion; as de Klerk notes in his autobiography, 'there was no place for inner circles and no bypassing the cabinet. All important decisions were taken by the cabinet, which was given full access to all the facts that could influence its decisions.'[81] 'FW didn't really have a kitchen cabinet,' says diplomat Dave Steward, de Klerk's close advisor and cabinet secretary from 1992.[82] Cabinet participants note that the change was quite drastic. 'FW would let the debates continue. In PW's time, we never had cabinet meetings longer than 9 am to 1 pm. With FW we sat until 7 or 8 at night,' recalls Roux, who remained cabinet secretary until 1992.[83] Compared to Botha, says Finance Minister Barend du Plessis—who unsuccessfully challenged de Klerk for the Party leadership—'FW was much more democratic, encouraging of open discussion and free exchange of ideas. He was a very good chairman, highly intelligent, and he could really summarize a thing well [. . .] if you had something to say to PW, he regarded it as an interruption, whereas FW welcomed it.'[84] Pik Botha, citing de Klerk's legal training as an influence, noted that he was 'very objective, listening, giving everyone a chance, then giving a resume of what was a fair reflection of the mood.'[85]

De Klerk took a personal interest in foreign policy: 'FW took foreign affairs, particularly repairing SA's image abroad, very seriously,' Steward says.[86] However, the demanding nature of his job, given the negotiations process, and his emphasis on letting ministers control their portfolios meant he left a relatively small personal footprint on foreign policymaking. As Steward notes, 'Cabinet took decisions, and ministers were responsible for their portfolios. Pik took decisions on foreign affairs, so to a large extent, FW would rely on Pik's advice. He would do so critically and not accept everything, but there was no doubt Pik was foreign minister [...] Pik was thrilled about this; after all these years he could do his job!'[87]

Nelson Mandela

Few leaders assume their country's top job while already a statesman of international renown; Nelson Mandela was a notable exception. In the four years between his 1990 release and his 1994 election, Mandela had scoured the globe to build support for the negotiation process and raise money for the ANC, establishing himself as a global celebrity. Including his travels around Africa in the early 1960s, he was easily the most traveled leader in South Africa's history. However, despite his international renown and although he maintained a robust travel schedule throughout his presidency, Mandela could not be described as a 'foreign policy' president, focusing most of his time and attention on issues of national reconciliation, state stability, and service delivery. 'There were only two foreign policy issues on which Mandela took a hands on approach—on others he had a watching brief—they were Lockerbie and East Timor,' his deputy foreign minister, Aziz Pahad, says.[88]

Although Mandela lacked a consistent interest in the foreign policy realm, he could be a forceful, unpredictable, and decidedly unilateral actor when his interest was piqued. Neither Mandela's public expressions of outrage over Nigerian dictator Sani Abacha's killing of Ken Saro-Wiwa in 1995 nor his 1996 announcement that South Africa would recognize China over Taiwan were coordinated with the DFA or cabinet in advance.[89] Pahad said both decisions surprised him. 'I don't think he consulted us in Foreign Affairs,' notes Pahad about Mandela's Nigeria stance, which he knew would not be popular on the continent. 'He took that decision. We then had to pick up the pieces, because we knew there would be no oil sanctions in place, that many African countries would see that position as either mad or not in their interests, or that of the continent.'[90] These and other examples—like announcing South Africa would continue to sell arms to Rwanda on the day the DFA was to announce its cessation, or his premature announcement of Zaire peace talks in 1997—led to criticisms that Mandela's personal statements made foreign policy.[91]

In conducting his foreign relations, Mandela relied on a small coterie of trusted officials and ministers to act as his personal envoys. His use of director-general in the Presidency, Jakes Gerwel, to convince Libyan leader Muammar Gadhafi to extradite the Libyan suspects in the 1986 Lockerbie bombing was perhaps the best-known example, although there are many others.[92] Mandela dispatched Sydney Mufamadi, then minister of safety and security to Mozambique in 1994 and Lesotho in 1998 to defuse tensions in those countries.[93] Mangosuthu Buthelezi, in cabinet as minister of home affairs, recalls Mandela using him as a go-between with Zimbabwean President—and Buthelezi's former schoolmate—Robert Mugabe on Lesotho and other issues, given that the interpersonal relations between the presidents were, in Buthelezi's understated words, 'a bit sour.'[94]

In managing his cabinet and government writ large, Mandela's personal authority loomed large. However, Mandela was generally too focused on 'big picture' issues, like national reconciliation, to weigh in on fine policy points, while his office was too small to effectively play a policy-crafting or coordinating role.[95] While deeply respected by his cabinet, he rarely presided over its bi-weekly meetings and seldom inserted himself into detailed discussions when he did.[96] Hence, in terms of the mechanics and detail of policymaking, both foreign and domestic, Mandela delegated most of this responsibility to his deputy president, Thabo Mbeki, who acted as a 'virtual prime minister' from the very beginning of his presidency.[97] Mbeki's domination of policy was particularly noticeable in the foreign affairs realm, where he (and Aziz Pahad, his most trusted advisor) took the reins in crafting the tenets of South African foreign policy. Mandela could still make waves with his statements and actions, but these were only distractions to Mbeki's construction of a comprehensive foreign policy.

Thabo Mbeki

South Africa's second post-transition president has been the subject of extensive media treatment, but yet Thabo Mbeki remains a divisive and mysterious figure. His critics have savaged him as a bully and an autocrat who surrounded himself with yes-people and refused to listen to divergent viewpoints. They attack him for intellectual arrogance, for refusing to acknowledge that his preconceptions may have been wrong, notably with his refusal to accept the link between HIV and AIDS. His closest advisors (and even some of his political rivals), however, paint a different, more nuanced, picture: of an exceptional listener who encouraged debate—albeit within set parameters; of a world-class intellect who was able to skillfully bring about subordinates to his worldview; of a workaholic whose intensive research convinced (and sometimes intimidated) ministers and Party principals to support his stances. All of these qualities, they note, were magnified in the foreign policy arena, where his experience and expertise were unsurpassed. Of course, neither damnation nor hagiography accurately portray Mbeki (or any leader); this section will attempt to unravel Mbeki's decision-making style in the foreign policy arena.

Mbeki as the Key Foreign Policy Driver
One topic that needs no debate is Mbeki's clear and unflinching interest in international relations, one that—as noted previously—dates back to his days as an ANC representative and principal in its DIA. During the transition period, he dominated ANC proceedings that discussed South Africa's post-transition foreign policy—even when he was not physically present, Party participants recognized his

authority.[98] As deputy president, he retained his primacy in the foreign affairs arena. Tom Wheeler recalls Mbeki's office making a decision on a disarmament issue in the mid-1990s: 'We asked if perhaps the president should weigh in on this, and she said, "No, that's irrelevant." That indicates the relationship; Mandela was the iconic figurehead, not the decisionmaker.'[99]

Mbeki was the first South African leader to bring a distinct and overarching ideology to South African foreign policy, one that emphasized solidarity with the continent and broader 'global South' in an effort to bring about prosperity and equality with the developed world. Taking advantage of the global attention focused on South Africa, Mbeki used his platform to advocate the developing world (and Africa in particular) having a greater say in global economic governance.[100] His formulation of the NEPAD exemplified this commitment, as well as his preference for establishing structures that would address and correct the continent's underdevelopment.[101] That said, Mbeki's unquestioning alignment of South Africa with the rest of the continent and developing world, as well as his refusal to criticize human rights abuses and misgovernance in those countries, led to criticisms that such commitment was detrimental to South Africa's interests, particularly given that its economic relations straddled north and south.[102]

In the eyes of most observers, Mbeki set the frameworks for foreign policy discussions, with subsequent debate taking place within those clearly defined boundaries. As academic Maxi Schoeman described the process, 'Mbeki takes the lead, sets the guidelines and indicates what he wants and where he wants to take the country (and the continent).'[103] Debate tended to be about modalities, not the decision itself.[104] As another academic who had dealt with him first-hand describes him as follows: 'Mbeki is a difficult chap to engage academically. First and foremost, you must agree with him, and if you don't, there's no discussion.'[105] Mbeki also saw little need to bring others along while formulating his grander ideas; with NEPAD, for example, even his closest advisors were not informed of it before the project's 2001 launch.[106]

Mbeki's personal stamp on policy formulation, foreign and domestic, was clear, and rivaled only maybe by Smuts and Verwoerd. He would stay up late into the evening researching and drafting speeches and other documents, like his weekly ANC letters. 'Long before us, President Mbeki perfected these bloody computers,' Aziz Pahad says. 'You can see the speeches he wrote himself, and those his speechwriters wrote. I told people, "You can give him a draft, and the next morning it will be a totally different document."'[107] This personal touch also applied to his research, as—according to biographer Mark Gevisser—Mbeki did not trust others to filter his information, preferring to seek it out from the source and come to his own conclusions.[108] 'Mbeki, if he wants to know something he gets on the Internet. He just reads it,' Pallo Jordan notes. 'You give him a report and walk away; he'll call you back to discuss if he wants to.'[109]

Dictator or Debater?

Mbeki's personal stamp on policy (foreign and domestic) sparked widespread allegations that he behaved as a 'dictator' or a 'Stalinist,' shutting down debate that might undermine his positions. 'There was a tighter system under Mbeki [. . .] a shutting down, a closing off of discussion, an insider/outsider perspective,' claims veteran ANC MP Ben Turok.[110] Other accounts indicate that many in the ANC parliamentary caucus were cowed into silence during debate because they feared Mbeki's backlash.[111] His 'closed-off' personality did not help matters; he lacked the warmth and bonhomie of Mandela in his interpersonal dealings. Whereas many interviewees describe Mbeki as jovial and open during his time in exile, they note that he became increasingly distant—and at times hostile—after returning to South Africa, particularly after becoming deputy president. 'Mbeki is a very strange guy. Rather self-contained, self-sufficient. He didn't need other people all that much,' says one parliamentarian.[112]

Although he lacked the temper of a PW Botha, Mbeki could be similarly brusque and impatient with colleagues or subordinates who were not living up to his expectations, something that did not help bolster his popularity with them.[113] As an intelligence official told Gevisser, 'He wants to engage with you as an equal, and if you're useless, he'll tell you. He's not going to protect you or soften things for you,' a sentiment echoed by several interviewees.[114] 'He doesn't suffer fools gladly,' Pallo Jordan notes. 'If you come to him and what you are saying is self-evident BS, he'd brush you off. And the person who wouldn't be listened to would think, "He's not even going to weigh what I have to say, how dictatorial." But I don't think he was dictatorial.'[115] Jordan adds, 'Where he differs from Tambo is that he's not as patient with people who are fools. He may not say it, but he would make it clear. Tambo was much more accommodating.'[116]

Mbeki's supporters claim many criticisms originated from subordinates bitter about their inability to persuade the better-prepared (and sometimes rude) Mbeki to adopt a policy position. As Sydney Mufamadi notes, 'If you say, "Mr. President, my department wants to do this," and the president says, "Motivate me," and the minister can't do that, [Mbeki] disagrees. So you go back to your department, and you say the suggestion was shot down by the president!'[117] Woe betide a minister or advisor less prepared than the president. As Aziz Pahad notes, 'You had to be very prepared if you go into a debate with him. In *legkotla* [cabinet retreats], we'd be very happy not to go first, because for the first three presentations, he would pick them apart [. . .] If you wanted to influence, you had to make sure you came in with new information, not things he already knew.'[118] Mosiuoa Lekota echoes Pahad's points: 'It was always extremely difficult to find better-researched views on positions on issues. I think [the reason] a lot of people who became hostile to him, especially his peers, is that he always found much more evidence, and they didn't do as much research work as him. And they lost. In due course, they said he was a dictator. He was not a dictator. He did better research than them and did more thorough work.'[119]

Mbeki also, according to participants, was open to discussion in cabinet and small groups, synthesizing and critiquing the conversation rather than dominating it. 'Mbeki followed the OR [Tambo] tradition,' Aziz Pahad says. 'He never intervened until the end' of cabinet meetings.[120] His goal, according to Gevisser, was to let debate occur rather than dictating a position, then summarizing the submissions of each participant to ensure that each felt included in the final decision. 'Before he takes a decision, Mbeki synthesizes thoroughly,' says former ANC Spokesman Smuts Ngonyama. 'He puts it back to you. He'll say, "People are saying ABCD, others are saying this," and he'll ask the question, "Chief, did you consider ABCD? I agree with you on A and C, but did you consider these other things." It makes you think. You can't come to Mbeki with an issue that has not been thought out thoroughly.'[121] That said, he would on occasion ask what Calland describes as an 'arrow-like question that invariably goes to the heart of the matter,' to both ministers and civil servants.[122]

The Role of Mbeki's 'Kitchen Cabinet' on Foreign Policy

From his time as deputy president, Mbeki relied on a small group of advisors on international issues who were given varying responsibilities in the formulation and conduct of foreign policy. A handful of senior DFA officials—most notably Aziz Pahad, but also Jackie Selebi and UN Ambassador Dumisani Khumalo—were part of this inner circle, assisting in the formulation process but also acting as links to the DFA, ensuring that policies were carried out. Other advisors in the Presidency included his legal advisor Mojanku Gumbi, who was a key envoy to the Inter-Congolese Dialogue; PCAS and communications Head Joel Netshitenzhe; economic advisor and Head of the NEPAD Secretariat Wiseman Nkuhlu; Presidency Director-General Frank Chikane; and Provincial and Local Government Minister Sydney Mufamadi.[123] Minister in the Presidency Essop Pahad—perhaps Mbeki's closest personal friend—also was a key advisor, serving as a 'gatekeeper' and 'fixer,' although he was not much involved in foreign policy.[124]

The question, however, is whether these advisors had much influence on Mbeki's decision-making. Many in the ANC alleged that Mbeki had surrounded himself with 'yes men' as advisors since the late 1970s, while others questioned the quality of the brainpower around Mbeki. As one leading ANC official notes, 'You can't see them being equals to him [. . .] If you're looking for a number two, I don't think there was one.'[125] Another claimed that people like the Pahad brothers and Mufamadi were incapable of standing up to

Mbeki and that Mbeki 'needs a devil's advocate, not a praise singer.'[126] Former ANC MP Andrew Feinstein—no fan of Mbeki's—asserts in his book that, 'On the whole, Mbeki's advisors are intellectually inferior to him and do not challenge his views vigorously. Like all national leaders, he lives in an artificial world, insulated from daily reality.'[127] One academic familiar with both Mandela and Mbeki compares the latter's openness to counsel with that of his predecessor, questioning whether Mbeki ever had the depth of friendship to receive tough advice:

> Thabo is very complex. He's only had two friends, Essop and Aziz [...] Thabo's character was that he overwhelmed the relationships around him. And because of that, he didn't have the kind of advisors who would tell him things honestly, which was very different from Mandela. You could go in and talk to him. He gave you space, and I saw that personally. He would never make a final decision without coming to Walter [Sisulu]. You'd come home and see them on the stoop, and you knew it was an important decision. It was interesting to see them interact. Walter would tell Mandela if he shouldn't do something. I don't think Thabo had that relationship with anyone.[128]

Those around Mbeki, however, discount the criticism that they were weak and could not disagree with the president. 'Mbeki loves debating issues. Not publicly. He likes testing ideas,' Aziz Pahad says.[129] While most acknowledge that they could not change Mbeki's mind on the broad thrust of policies, they could influence him on how to implement them. 'You saw tactical shifts in China and Zimbabwe, on the day-to-day approach,' Aziz Pahad notes. 'On Zimbabwe, when they came for that loan of $2 billion, he set up a committee and listened to advice on how you could not give that loan without conditions or guarantees.'[130]

Mbeki's Persuasive Style in Evidence on Zimbabwe
Mbeki's questioning stance was particularly noticeable in debates on Zimbabwe, where rather than stifling debate he used it to win

support for his stance toward Mugabe. 'He clearly wanted a solution in Zimbabwe; he was unhappy with how Mugabe was doing things,' DFA Director-General (1999–2002) Sipho Pityana says. 'On the other hand, he felt somewhat constrained' by potentially negative African opinion (as with Nigeria in 1995) and a need to keep SADC united, particularly in light of Zimbabwean, Angolan, and Namibian intervention in the Congo.[131] Pityana adds, 'When we came to power, we were haunted by the Rwandan genocide. There was a very strong fear of a repeat of that. That's why South Africa had to operate within SADC.'[132] Hence, while many in cabinet and government viewed Zimbabwe as a singular issue, Mbeki viewed it as a piece of a much larger puzzle in which peace and security in the Great Lakes was paramount.

Mbeki's intense study of Zimbabwe made it difficult for his cabinet and other foreign policy actors to trump his arguments. 'It's very difficult to argue against Zimbabwe because he is very, very sharp,' Essop Pahad notes. 'He says, "OK, this is the land issue, this is what happened under British colonial rule, this is how the land was redistributed, these are the whites who bought the land, this is what happened under Smith, here's the land that was taken—you can't argue you don't need land reform."'[133] Mbeki also was highly cognizant of the interplay within the Zimbabwean government and the ruling ZANU-PF, arguing that forcing out Mugabe could play into the hands of hardliners. Ngonyama recalls that Mbeki would manage debate within the ANC NEC to win support for his stance toward Zimbabwe:

On Zimbabwe, one or two people would actually say we're a bit slow on this and so on. We're slow in intervening, or we're soft. And he would ask the question, 'What is it comrades are suggesting we do in Zimbabwe?' Then we'd start scratching our heads. Nobody would stand up. One or two people would stand up and say quiet diplomacy is ok, but we must make sure the Zimbabwean government doesn't abuse our position and we don't strengthen Mugabe. Mbeki would genuinely ask the question of what we need to do now to prevent that from happening. So we'd resolve that the position of the ANC was that we should respect the sovereignty of Zimbabwe and help Zimbabweans solve their own problems. That wasn't coming from Mbeki; that was from the NEC.[134]

Conclusion: Leaders Have Significant Foreign Policy Sway, Should They Seek It

As this chapter has shown, South African leaders have been of wildly different stripes with regard to how they make foreign policy, making generalities difficult. On the surface, one is tempted to archetype them; the domineering Smuts, Verwoerd, and Mbeki; the generally disengaged Malan, Strijdom, and Mandela. But that is too simple. As shown, Mbeki fostered debate (even if he dominated it) among his advisors on the modalities of South African foreign policy. Also, while both were seen to have had other priorities, both Malan (evidenced by his African Charter) and Mandela (on Nigeria and China, for example) took a close personal interest in particular external issues. That said, a few overarching conclusions about prime minister/president influence on foreign policy are clear:

- *Interested leaders have a greater say over foreign policy.* Unsurprisingly, South African leaders with significant personal interests in foreign policy (Verwoerd and Mbeki, in particular) have played a far more dominant role in making foreign policy than those who have not. The head of government with the least personal interest, Strijdom, was by a long shot the leader who most directly delegated foreign policy.
- *Robust bureaucratic structures equal strong executive control of foreign policy.* On a more formalized level, the creation and building of bureaucratic structures (like the SSC under Botha and PCAS under Mbeki) correlate with strong control of the national leader over foreign policy. Such structures have less to do with the formulation of policy than its implementation; they ensure that all departments are on the same page and are working toward the same goals.

– *Advisors' influence is strongly correlated to leaders' interest.* The importance of 'kitchen cabinet' advisors and decision-making delegates (like foreign ministers) is amplified in situations where leaders have little interest in foreign affairs or (like Mandela, with Mbeki) competing priorities for their time.

Mbeki's Role in South African Foreign Policy

What does this say about Thabo Mbeki's role in South Africa's foreign policy debate and what this meant for its democratic nature? Judging by the three criteria above, Mbeki clearly dominated South African foreign policy and was not particularly receptive to inputs from foreign policy actors outside of government, particularly when these visions clashed with his own view of the world. However, the accounts of those closest to him do not paint the picture of a dictator in the foreign policy arena, particularly with regard to his inner circle of advisors. Mbeki could be a domineering figure when he did not find his interlocutors' research up to his standards, but he was not a bully in the same vein as Verwoerd or Botha. Furthermore, the changes in South Africa's post-1994 dispensation meant Mbeki could not dominate foreign policy to the same degree as his predecessors. As noted in previous chapters, Mbeki had to contend with more active and involved outside actors like the press and academia; parliamentary oversight (if spotty) from the PCFA; and a far larger government foreign policy apparatus than any of his predecessors. Unlike, say, Verwoerd, Mbeki's foreign policy could not escape press notice, academic analysis, or business consternation, and Mbeki certainly did not have the time to peruse the memos of junior officials, given the expansion of South Africa's government foreign policy apparatus. Overall, Mbeki may not have come across as the most 'democratic' leader with regard to foreign policy, especially given his predilection to dismiss inputs he found insufficiently supported—or markedly contrary to his worldview—but he, and the system he inherited, nonetheless allowed them to be heard.

CHAPTER 11

CONCLUSION—ROOM, BUT NOT WILLINGNESS, FOR ENGAGEMENT

The preceding chapters have broken down how all of the various South African actors with an interest the country's foreign policy have, from the time of Smuts through the administration of Mbeki, been able to influence the executive's decisions. A few takeaways:

– *Public opinion* has never mattered in foreign policy formulation, and it will not matter unless citizens take external issues into account at the ballot box. Otherwise, there is no reason for the government of the day—ANC or otherwise—to take stock of what the largely disengaged public has to say. As polls have shown, South Africans of all races have too many domestic concerns to give foreign policy much consideration, with even the collapse of neighboring Zimbabwe not proving enough to interest anything but an elite segment of society. There is, however, hope of seeing a more engaged populace. Programs like Model United Nations, sponsored by SAIIA since 1992, have gotten students interested in foreign relations, many of whom, according to Elizabeth Sidiropoulos, have gone onto careers in the DFA.[1] Greater emphasis on history and geography in schools would serve a similar purpose, although South Africa will first have to tackle its problems of basic literacy.

- *Pressure groups* have shown themselves able to mobilize on foreign policy issues intermittently throughout South African history, from labor's refusal to offload Italian ships in the 1930s to the well-organized, multi-stakeholder effort in 2008 that stopped arms from being shipped to Zimbabwe. Poor communications between organizations, limited resources, and general lack of focus on external issues, however, have made such interventions the exception rather than the rule. Many of these factors are now changing. The widespread use of the Internet and mobile telephones in South Africa has made it easier than ever to establish an organization and communicate with like-minded groups and potential followers on a tiny budget. The capability, therefore, is there; the question will be whether these groups seek to interject themselves more forcefully into government's foreign policy debates.

- Although certain prominent media figures—like Alf Ries, for example—have been moderately influential in the foreign policy field, the influence of the *press* as a whole has generally been negligible on foreign affairs, and if anything will likely decrease in the future. The 'loyal' Afrikaans press from the 1940s through the early 1980s derived some influence from its standing as an official organ of the NP, although foreign affairs generally were not its gambit. Since that time, press–government relations have become increasingly strained, and the lack of a 'party organ' news source since 1994 has driven greater ANC suspicion of and antipathy toward the media, as evidenced by periodic attempts to muzzle it. Additional factors limiting the media's influence are the limited readership of the print press, its lack of influence on voters, and—for foreign relations in particular—its declining coverage of external issues.

- *Academia* focused on foreign affairs has seen perhaps the greatest leap in influence of any external actor since 1994. Despite analyses portraying some foreign policy academics as key government advisors before 1994, research in Chapter 5 indicates that academics were rarely consulted, either in a personal capacity or systematically. Beginning in the transition period, however, academics were brought into discussions with the government and ANC on the development of a future South African foreign policy. After 1994, individual academics, universities, and think tanks—all of which have broadened and deepened their coverage of international relations—have been brought in for consultations by government departments. While their inputs have not always been welcomed or acceded to, academics have proved valuable to working-level officials covering technical issues or little-studied countries. South Africa's need for sophisticated analysis of global trends and specific issues almost certainly will increase, particularly in light of its growing prominence in the developing world, meaning demand for these inputs will likely increase at the working level. At higher levels, however, relations with government are likely to ebb and flow, depending on the interpersonal relations between decision-makers and experts, as well as executive receptivity to their inputs.

- The *business* community has significant ability to sway decision-makers, notably through its ability to make political donations, but has never done so effectively. Since 1994, businesses—especially those focused on expansion on the continent—have not been able to work together in a united fashion toward common goals, such as expanding regional and continental markets. Organizations like BUSA and BLSA, which should be discussion forums for these debates, have done little to conceptualize a 'business foreign policy' or better lobby the executive on issues like reducing visa restrictions. Overall, the business community in general has significant untapped potential to influence South Africa's foreign policy debate; whether it will do so is in its own hands.

- *Parliament* has never, neither before nor after 1994, meaningfully interjected itself into the foreign policy debate. Opposition MPs like Colin Eglin, Boy Geldenhuys, and Ben Skosana have made valuable contributions by asking tough questions, but the majority of Party caucuses have largely left foreign affairs to the executive. A large part of this has been because of willing acquiescence—neither the NP nor ANC leadership was or is fond of promoting backbenchers that ask difficult questions. This assent is not always willing; Raymond Suttner's removal as PCFA chair appears linked to his independent-mindedness and willingness to question the executive on its foreign policy priorities. Could parliament in the future play a more activist role? It certainly has the power to do so through its approval of treaty ratification, an area that Ben Skosana notes is a PCFA priority for greater engagement in the Zuma administration.[2] However, South Africa's party list electoral system gives little incentive for independent action by ruling party legislators.

– No *ruling party* in South African history has shown itself, as an entity, to be a player in foreign policy formulation. The ANC in exile had an active foreign policy arm through its DIA, but its expertise was subsumed by the DFA after 1994. Today, the ANC's Department of International Relations is nothing but a shell, and as an entity does not play a role in foreign policy formulation for many of the same reasons that ANC MPs in parliament do not. The NEC Subcommittee for International Relations showed itself during the Mbeki period to be an occasionally robust debating chamber for issues, but its relevance and influence depends on the makeup of its members (and the party president). These, of course, are both 'elite' entities; party members at the ground level have shown little interest in or impact upon foreign policy.

– It is necessary to deconstruct the question of *government departments'* influence on foreign policy. As bureaucratic entities, departments like the DFA (renamed Department of International Relations and Cooperation in 2009), Defense, DTI, and Intelligence have generally served as implementers rather than formulators of policy at the broader level, although interdepartmental competition serves to hash out the finer points of policy direction. However, department principals—ministers, deputy ministers, directors-general, special advisors, and other top officials—have since the time of Smuts and Hertzog served as leading advisors to the head of government/head of state. That said, their influences have ebbed and flowed over time based on their personal relationships with the national leader and the leader's departmental affinities. Such competition seems likely to continue—given that the appointment of principals will always have political overtones and implications, ministerial influences are likely to fluctuate depending on the relationships and preferences of the president.

– Last, it is clear that the personality, interest, and decision-making style of the *national leader* are the key factors that determine whether outside voices are heard in the foreign policy arena. South African law has since 1910 given the executive extensive sway in making foreign policy, and some leaders—notably Smuts, Verwoerd, and Mbeki—have taken advantage of this to put their personal imprint on their external policies. That said, even under the more consultative and delegating heads of government (like Strijdom and Vorster, for example), foreign policymaking has been the preserve of a select few individuals, trusted ministers and advisors around the leader. Barring unforeseen changes to South Africa's constitution that would require more formalized consultation in policymaking, this pattern looks set to continue.

Now, one must return to the original question of this study—is post-1994 South African foreign policy 'democratic?' Is it subject to the approval of South Africa's populace? Do interested actors have the opportunity to weigh in on its direction and focus? Has this changed over time, particularly from the pre- to post-transition periods? Does this translate into impact? Or does the foreign policymaking process remain, in the words of an author writing during Vorster's era, 'a secretive, almost cabalistic business?'[3] These questions shall be broken down individually.

Does the Broader South African Populace have the Opportunity to Weigh in on Foreign Policy?

By and large, the answer here is yes. Part of the answer lies in the fact that South African voters—the white populace before 1994 and all citizens thereafter—have been able to vote freely for their representatives at national elections using whatever criteria they have seen fit. There have been a host of external issues over the past 70 years on which voters could have influenced foreign policy at the ballot box, such as the choice to fight alongside the Allies in World War II, Commonwealth departure, Rhodesia policy, regional destabilization, post-transition external orientation, and Zimbabwe. However, this has not happened. Voters have never in South African history made foreign policy a deciding, or even marginal, factor in contesting a national election. Given that lack of public interest, it is unsurprising that the government of the day believes it has a mandate to pursue whatever foreign policies it wishes.

One might counter that citizens lack a voice between elections to affect foreign policy (or domestic policy for that matter). There is an element of truth here; South Africa's system does not allow for parliamentary by-elections, for example, which could serve to capture protest votes over unpopular policies. In addition, while every South African belongs to a parliamentary constituency with a specific representative, few South Africans know who their representatives are, and Afrobarometer polling shows that South Africans are far less likely to interact with their elected representatives than citizens of other African countries.[4] Hence, MPs could do a better job of responding to their constituents, although given the limited powers of parliament, whether this would subsequently have an influence on foreign policy is doubtful.

Do Interested Actors have the Opportunity to Weigh in on Foreign Policy's Direction and Focus? Has this Changed over Time?

This question must be examined from pre- and post-1994 perspectives. Under the old dispensation, outside actors (including parliament) had almost no ability to make formal representations to government on foreign policy. Whatever interaction there was came through informal connections between the head of government and his ministers with leading businessmen, journalists, academics, or church leaders. Those inside the political *laager*, like MPs and

Afrikaans newspapermen, had more of an inside track, but they could only push so far before being shut down.

If there has been one drastic change in the foreign policy environment post-1994, it is the significant improvement in the amount of formal dialogue between the government and outside actors in making policy. The Green Paper/White Paper process demands that draft bills be circulated for comment from the general public and interested organizations. Business has formalized, regular interaction with government through BUSA, BLSA, and other groups. Labor is represented within the tripartite alliance. Church leaders had regular access to Mandela and Mbeki. Academics, particularly in the foreign policy arena, have had far more access to decisionmakers than they did before 1994. Only perhaps the press has seen a diminution of its access, although journalists still do have their networks into government, sometimes at a very high level. Lastly, parliament, through the establishment of the portfolio committee system, has been given a greater formal voice in the policy process. All of this access translates into an ability to make representations on foreign policy issues and challenge the executive.

Does this Access Translate into Influence?

Has the quantity of access post-1994 translated into greater quality of access? Namely, have outside inputs clearly influenced policy outcomes in the external arena? The answer here appears for the most part to be no. Countless interviewees complained that their interactions with government on foreign policy—especially with President Mbeki and his closest advisors—tended to be formalistic 'box-checking' exercises that resulted in no policy shifts, particularly toward Zimbabwe. Even COSATU, a member of the tripartite alliance, showed no ability to move Pretoria on Zimbabwe policy, or on issues like Swaziland or China where they had a vested interest.

Government decision-makers have countered that these outside representations approached the issues too simplistically, ignoring complicating factors that governments have to deal with. That may be true, but with one notable exception, the same 'cabalistic' decision-making process described earlier characterized the 1994–2008 period. Both Nelson Mandela and Thabo Mbeki made most of their foreign policy decisions—in shaping the direction of policy and dealing with day-to-day situations—in a personalized fashion, using a few trusted advisors to discuss policy implications and implement the decisions. Outside voices provided food for thought—especially academics, who could bring a wealth of expertise, particularly on more obscure issues—but an analysis of the policymaking process during this time suggests their inputs had only a marginal impact on the policy process. Ultimately, as the constitution dictates, the president was the leading foreign policy actor, and President Mbeki in particular took this to heart.

Final Words: Patient, Heal Thyself

To conclude, we must examine the 'notable exception' mentioned above, which was the 2008 government decision—under intense pressure from civil society—to stop an arms shipment from China to Zimbabwe coming through the port of Durban. As discussed in Chapter 4, an organized coalition of civil society groups (including COSATU), given significant coverage by the press, was able to raise public awareness of this shipment to the extent that the National Conventional Arms Control Committee was forced to back down and send the supply ship elsewhere. This was a striking reversal in the government's non-interference policy toward its northern neighbor, and a clear signal that a well-organized challenge to Pretoria's foreign policy could force the government to change course on an issue.

Hence, the question: Why has this not happened more, particularly in relation to Zimbabwe, the dominant foreign policy issue of the 2000s? Some of the reasons have been addressed, particularly the general lack of public engagement on foreign policy issues, but the 2008 situation shows that widespread public interest need not be the only prerequisite for action. One particular observation springs to mind as to why this does not happen more in South Africa, namely the abysmal level of communication among interested actors.

One of the more surprising findings in researching this study was to learn how little foreign policy actors in South Africa communicate with one another, both 'outside their boxes' and 'within their boxes.' For the former, even though business and COSATU generally have had the same interests in Zimbabwe and have wanted to see the same reforms, they generally have not talked to one another. The churches do their thing, academics do something else, and so on, even though they all have similar views on particular issues. Part of this is understandable—social networks tend to be insular, so CEOs and union bosses would not necessarily run in the same circles. South Africa's segregated history and social geography also account for this. Even more striking, however, is how little little communication there is within these each of the individual boxes. Business groupings rarely communicate with one another, nor do think tanks. Even religious groups have limited interactions across sectarian lines.

The message here is simple. Until South Africans with common interests start talking with one another and better coordinating their activities, they will have little ability to influence the South African Government on foreign policy. As the 2008 incident showed, organized pressure can bring about a change in government course, but history has shown that South African leaders are not likely to go out of their way to take such inputs on board. Limited public input and debate is in the interest of governments when it comes to foreign policy, since it allows them to move more quickly and efficiently. Foreign policy presidents with a vision for South Africa's external orientation, like Mbeki, also generally do not appreciate extensive public comment that would be a 'fly in the ointment' for such visions.

South African law codifies the 'closed' nature of the country's foreign policymaking process, and that law is unlikely to change any time soon. Yet South African democratic institutions give actors an opportunity to make their voices heard. Until outside actors learn to do so in a concerted, consistent, and organized way, South Africa's foreign policy will remain an elite preserve.

APPENDIX

LIST OF INTERVIEWS

Please note that not all interviewees are cited in the text; some interviews were cut from the final text, and other interviewees are quoted on background. All dates are 2010 and were conducted in person unless otherwise noted.

Adekeye Adebajo	March 3
Rok Ajulu	July 21
Derek Auret	June 7
Niel Barnard	July 14
Japie Basson	June 15
Whitey Basson	June 30
Chris Bennett	September 9
Herbert Beukes	June 16
Simon Boshielo	January 25
Henri Boshoff	January 25
Con Botha	June 9
JSF 'Frikkie' Botha	May 19
Pik Botha	February 1
Mangosuthu Buthelezi	August 3
Jakkie Cilliers	July 22, 2011 (Skype)
Scarlett Cornelissen	June 29
John Daniel	July 28

Dawie de Villiers	November 1
Ebbe Dommisse	June 3
Peter Draper	October 14
Barend du Plessis	May 22
Jan du Plessis	July 21
Kent Durr	June 11
Colin Eglin	March 23, 2011
Peter Fabricius	January 26
Jannie Ferreira	February 23
Andre Fourie	August 16
Deon Fourie	May 25
Dianna Games	October 11
Boy Geldenhuys	September 6
Deon Geldenhuys	January 29
Jannie Geldenhuys	May 28
Mluleki George	October 21
Rex Gibson	March 11, 2011
Hermann Giliomee	February 24
Vasu Gounden	August 2
Tienie Groenewald	May 28
Shadrack Gutto	May 27
Fatima Hajaig	September 21
Helmoed Heitman	May 5
Mike Hough	July 21
Tim Hughes	February 3; July 7
Pallo Jordan	June 25; April 7, 2011 (Email)
J.J. Joubert	February 18
Reuel Khoza	October 25 (Phone)
Chris Landsberg	July 23
Mosiuoa Lekota	March 25, 2011
Garth le Pere	May 25
Albertina Luthuli	November 1
Rob Mackay	March 3
Willie Madisha	September 1
Mondli Makhanya	October 11
Vincent Maphai	June 1, 2011
Bongani Masuku	May 25
Chris Matlhako	July 23

Richard Menatsi	February 17
Greg Mills	May 24
Sam Motsuenyane	May 29
Sydney Mufamadi	October 15
Mavivi Myakayaka-Manzini	November 19 (Phone)
Laurie Nathan	August 16
Theo Neethling	July 18
Louis Nel	October 11
Philip Nel	September 8
Smuts Ngonyama	March 2
Cunningham Ngcukana	May 24
Gerrit Olivier	January 20
Ken Owen	June 30
Aziz Pahad	January 28
Essop Pahad	May 27
Father Peter John Pearson	May 4
Sara Pienaar	March 2
Sipho Pityana	May 25
Mzukisi Qobo	January 29
Hopewell Radebe	May 27
Mewa Ramgobin	November 10
Jannie Roux	May 28
Renier Schoeman	November 2
Annette Seegers	February 23
Gerald Shaw	July 7
Jeremy Shearer	July 21
Garth Shelton	January 26
Mtikeni Sibande	September 1
Elizabeth Sidiropoulos	May 26
Job Sithole	May 24
Ben Skosana	September 21
Karen Smith	September 23
Mills Soko	March 1
Don Sole	May 5
Hussein Solomon	October 12
Roger Southall	January 25
Michael Spicer	October 11
Yolanda Spies	January 25

Johan Steenkamp	May 18
Willem Steenkamp	May 18
Dave Steward	June 4, 7
Raymond Suttner	June 2 (Email)
Mathata Tsedu	May 31, 2011
Ben Turok	September 30
Baby Tyawa	March 3, 2011 (Email)
Harvey Tyson	March 11, 2011
Peter Vale	September 8
Janis van der Westhuizen	June 29
Theuns van der Westhuizen	May 14
Hennie van Deventer	May 21
Neil van Heerden	June 24
Albert van Niekerk	July 5
Anthoni van Nieuwkerk	January 26
Denis Venter	May 28
Ton Vosloo	June 9
Tom Wheeler	January 29
Denis Worrall	January 18, 2011
Siphamandla Zondi	May 27

NOTES

Chapter 1   Understanding South African Foreign Policymaking

1. Breuning, M., 2007, *Foreign Policy Analysis: A Comparative Introduction*, Palgrave Macmillan, New York, p. 5.
2. Banjo, A., 2009, 'A Review of Parliament-Foreign Policy Nexus in South Africa and Namibia', *Canadian Journal of Politics and Law*, Vol. 2, No. 3, p. 61.
3. Frankel, J., 1963, *The Making of Foreign Policy: An Analysis of Decision Making*, Oxford University Press, Oxford, p. 2.
4. Johnson, A., 2001, 'Democracy and Human Rights in the Principles and Practice of South African Foreign Policy', in *South Africa's Foreign Policy: Dilemmas of a New Democracy*, edited by Broderick, J.; Burford, G.; and Freer, G., Palgrave Press, New York, p. 15.
5. See Barber, J., 2004, *Mandela's World: The International Dimension of South Africa's Political Revolution 1990–99*, Ohio University Press, Athens, pp. 88– 91 and the ANC's 'Foreign Policy Perspective in a Democratic South Africa', December 1994.
6. Huntington, S., 1996, *The Clash of Civilizations and the Remaking of the World Order*, Free Press, London.
7. Diamond, L.; Linz, J.; and Lipset, S., 1988, *Democracy in Developing Countries, Volume One: Comparing Experiences with Democracy*, Lynne Rienner, Boulder, p. XVI.
8. Holsti, O., 1992, 'Public Opinion and Foreign Policy: Challenges to the Almond-Lippmann Consensus', *International Studies Quarterly*, Vol. 36, No. 4, p. 440.

9. Gumede, W., 2005, *Thabo Mbeki and the Battle for the Soul of the ANC*, Zebra Press, Cape Town, p. 60 and p. 135.

10. Snyder, R.; Bruck, H.; Sapin, B, Hudson, V.; Chollet, D.; and Goldgeier, J., 2003, *Foreign Policy Decision-making*, Macmillan Press, New York, p. 52.

11. Breuning, *Foreign Policy Analysis*, p. 5.

12. For a discussion of this topic, see Schoeman, M., 2000, 'South Africa as an Emerging Middle Power', *African Security Review*, Vol. 9, No. 3, as well as Schoeman, M. and Alden, C., 2003, 'The Hegemon That Wasn't: South Africa's Policy Toward Zimbabwe', *Strategic Review for Southern Africa*, Vol. 23.

13. Calland, R., 2004, *Anatomy of South Africa: Who Holds the Power?* Zebra Press, Cape Town, p. 15.

 * While researching and writing this piece during 2009–11, I was serving as a diplomat accredited to the US Consulate in Cape Town; I previously served (2004–6) at the US Embassy in Pretoria. The views expressed in this book are those of the author and do not necessarily reflect those of the US Department of State or the US Government.

Chapter 2   A Brief History of South African Foreign Policy

1. Vandenbosch, A., 1970, *South Africa and the World: The Foreign Policy of Apartheid*, University of Kentucky Press, Lexington, p. 58.

2. Spence, J., 1965, *Republic Under Pressure: A Study of South African Foreign Policy*, Oxford University Press, Oxford, pp. 8–9.

3. Stevens, R., 1970, 'South Africa and Independent Black Africa', *Africa Today*, Vol. 17, No. 3, p. 32.

4. Barber, J. and Barratt, J., 1990, *South Africa's Foreign Policy: The Search for Status and Security 1945–1988*, Cambridge University Press, Cambridge, p. 1.

5. Ibid., p. 56.

6. Henshaw, P., 1996, 'Britain, South Africa, and the Sterling Area: Gold Production, Capital Investment, and Agricultural Markets 1931–1961', *The Historical Journal*, Vol. 39, No. 1, p. 223.

7. Southall, R., 1999, 'South Africa In Africa: Foreign Policy Making During the Apartheid Era', Institute for Global Dialogue Occasional Paper 20, p. 7.

8. Geldenhuys, D., 1994, 'The Head of Government and South Africa's Foreign Relations', in *Leadership in the Apartheid State: From Malan to de Klerk*, edited by Schrire, R., Oxford University Press, Oxford, pp. 252–3.

9. Barber and Barratt, *South Africa's Foreign Policy*, p. 38.

10. Stultz, N., 1969, 'The Politics of Security: South Africa Under Verwoerd, 1961–66', *The Journal of Modern African Studies*, Vol. 7, No. 1, p. 9.

11. Barber, J., 2004, *Mandela's World: The International Dimension of South Africa's Political Revolution 1990–99*, Ohio University Press, Athens, p. 59.

12. Jaster, R.; Mbeki, M.; Nkosi, M., and Clough, M., 1992, *Changing Fortunes: War, Diplomacy, and Economics in Southern Africa*, Ford Foundation, New York, p. 9.
13. Massie, R., 1997, *Loosing the Bonds: The United States and South Africa in the Apartheid Years*, Doubleday, New York, p. 76.
14. Pelzer, A. (editor), 1966, *Verwoerd Speaks: Speeches 1948–1966*, APB Publishers, Johannesburg, pLVI.
15. Davidson, B., 1974, 'South Africa and Portugal', *A Journal of Opinion*, Vol. 4, No. 2, p. 10.
16. Hepple, A., 1967, *Verwoerd*, Penguin, Johannesburg, pp. 194–5.
17. De St. Jorre, J., 1977, 'South Africa: Up Against the World', *Foreign Policy*, No. 28, p. 58.
18. Dalcanton, C., 1976, 'Vorster and the Politics of Confidence, 1966–1974', *African Affairs*, Vol. 75, No. 299, p. 172.
19. Barber and Barratt, *South Africa's Foreign Policy*, p. 215.
20. Davies, R. and O'Meara, D., 1985, 'Total Strategy in Southern Africa: An Analysis of South African Regional Policy Since 1978', *Journal of Southern African Studies*, Vol. 11, No. 2, p. 185.
21. Bowman, L., 1971, *South Africa's Outward Strategy: A Foreign Policy Dilemma for the United States*, Ohio University Center for International Studies, Athens, p. 8.
22. Barber and Barratt, *South Africa's Foreign Policy*, p. 146.
23. Nyangone, E., 2008, 'South Africa's Relations with Gabon and the Ivory Coast: 1969–1994', unpublished doctoral dissertation, University of Stellenbosch, p. 88.
24. Sanders, J., 2006, *Apartheid's Friends: The Rise and Fall of South Africa's Secret Service*, John Murray Press, London, p. 102.
25. Cobbett, W. 1989, 'Apartheid's Army and the Arms Embargo', in *War and Society: The Militarization of South Africa*, edited by Cock, J. and Nathan, L., David Phillip Press, Cape Town, p. 226.
26. Fig, D., 1984, 'Theorizing South Africa's Foreign Policy: The Case of Latin America', unpublished doctoral dissertation, University of Cape Town, p. 20.
27. Dadoo, Y., 1997, 'Relations with the Middle East and Arab World', in *Change and South African Foreign Relations*, edited by Carlsnaes, W. and Muller, M., International Thomson Publishing, Johannesburg, p. 176.
28. Polakow-Suransky, S., 2010, *The Unspoken Alliance: Israel's Secret Relationship with Apartheid South Africa,* Pantheon Books, New York, p. 6.
29. Pfister, R., 2005, *Apartheid South Africa and African States: From Pariah to Middle Power, 1961–1994*, Tauris Academic Studies, London, p. 49.
30. Hanlon, J., 1986, *Beggar Your Neighbors: Apartheid Power in Southern Africa*, James Currey Ltd, London, p. 15.
31. Conchiglia, A., 2007, 'South Africa and its Lusophone Neighbors: Angola and Mozambique', in *South Africa in Africa: The Post-Apartheid Era*, edited by Adebajo, A.; Adedeji, A.; and Landsberg, C., UKZN Press, Scottsville, p. 237.

32. Davies, R., 1989, 'The SADF's Covert War Against Mozambique', in *War and Society: The Militarization of South Africa*, edited by Cock, J. and Nathan, L., David Phillip Press, Cape Town, p. 105.
33. Purkitt, H. and Burgess, S., 2005, *South Africa's Weapons of Mass Destruction*, Indiana University Press, Bloomington, pp. 148–9.
34. Mills, G., 2000, *The Wired Model: South Africa, Foreign Policy and Globalization*, Tafelberg, Cape Town, p. 238.
35. O'Meara, D., 1996, *Forty Lost Years*, Ravan Press, Randberg, p. 354.
36. Schrire, R. and Silke, D., 1997, 'Foreign Policy: The Domestic Context', in *Change and South African Foreign Relations*, edited by Carlsnaes, W. and Muller, M., International Thomson Publishing, Johannesburg, p. 6.
37. Danaher, K., 1984, *In Whose Interest: A Guide to US-South Africa Relations*, Institute for Policy Studies, Washington DC, p. 7.
38. Rall, M., 2003, *Peaceable Warrior: The Life and Times of Sol Plaatje*, Sol Plaatje Educational Trust, Kimberley, p. 138.
39. Meli, F., 1989, *South Africa Belongs to Us: A History of the ANC*, Indiana University Press, Bloomington, p. 49.
40. Ellis, S. and Sechaba, T., 1992, *Comrades Against Apartheid: The ANC and the South African Communist Party in Exile*, Indiana University Press, Bloomington, pp. 75–6.
41. Somerville, K., 1984, 'The USSR and Southern Africa since 1976', *The Journal of Modern African Studies*, Vol. 22, No. 1, p. 99.
42. Pfister, R., 2003, 'Gateway to International Victory: The Diplomacy of the African National Congress in Africa, 1960–1994', *Journal of Modern African Studies*, Vol. 41, No. 1, p. 53.
43. Thomas, S., 1995, *The Diplomacy of Liberation: The Foreign Relations of the ANC Since 1960*, Tauris Publishing, London, p. 26.
44. Pfister, 'Gateway', pp. 51–3.
45. Macmillan, H., 2009, 'The African National Congress of South Africa in Zambia: The Culture of Exile and the Changing Relationship with Home, 1964–1990', *Journal of Southern African Studies*, Vol. 35, No. 2, p. 317.
46. Barrell, H., 1992, 'The Turn to the Masses: The African National Congress' Strategic Review of 1978–79', *Journal of Southern African Studies*, Vol. 18, No. 1, p. 70.
47. Shubin, V., 2008, *The 'Hot' Cold War: The USSR in Southern Africa*, Pluto Press, London, p. 241.
48. Thomas, *Diplomacy*, p. 124.
49. Gevisser, M., 2007, *Thabo Mbeki: The Dream Deferred*, Jonathan Ball, Johannesburg, p. 374.
50. Callinicos, L., 2004, *Oliver Tambo: Beyond the Engeli Mountains*, David Phillip Press, Cape Town, p. 482.
51. Thomas, *Diplomacy*, p. 153.

52. Shubin, V., 1996, 'The Soviet Union/Russian Federation's Relations with South Africa, with Special Reference to the Period since 1980', *African Affairs*, Vol. 95, No. 378, p. 15.

53. Lodge, T., 1987, 'State of Exile: The African National Congress of South Africa, 1976–86', *Third World Quarterly*, Vol. 9, No. 1, p. 13.

54. Pfister, 'Gateway', p. 59.

55. Lyman, P., 2002, *Partner to History: The U.S. Role in South Africa's Transition to Democracy*, US Institute of Peace, Washington DC, p. 53.

56. Evans, G., 1996, *South Africa in Remission: The Foreign Policy of an Altered State*, *The Journal of Modern African Studies*, Vol. 34, No. 2, p. 253.

57. Shubin, V., 1995, *Flinging the Doors Open: Foreign Policy of the New South Africa*, Centre for Southern African Studies, University of the Western Cape, p. 2.

58. Landsberg, C., 2004, *The Quiet Diplomacy of Liberation: International Politics and South Africa's Transition*, Jacana, Johannesburg, p. 88.

59. Ibid., p. 98.

60. Pfister, 'Gateway', p. 65.

61. Landsberg, *Quiet Diplomacy*, p. 106.

62. Sampson, A., 2000, *Mandela: The Authorized Biography*, Random House, New York, p. 413.

63. Mbeki, T., 1994, 'South Africa's International Relations: Today and Tomorrow', in *From Pariah to Participant: South Africa's Evolving Foreign Relations, 1990–1994*, edited by Mills, G., South African Institute of International Affairs, Johannesburg, p. 204.

64. Paruk F., 2008, 'The Transitional Executive Council (TEC) As Transitional Institution to Manage and Prevent Conflict in South Africa (1994)', unpublished MA thesis, UNISA, p. 134.

65. Geldenhuys, D., 1992, 'The Foreign Policy of Transition in South Africa', *Foreign Policy Issues in a Democratic South Africa*, edited by Venter, A., Papers from a Conference of Professors World Peace Academy, Johannesburg, p. 43.

66. Nzo, A., 1999, 'Foreign Minister's Budget Vote Address', March 4, 1999, *South African Journal of International Affairs*, Vol. 6, No. 2, p. 223.

67. Bischoff, P. and Southall, R., 1998, 'Early Foreign Policy of Democratic South Africa', in *African Foreign Policies*, edited by Stephen Wright, Westview Press, Boulder, p. 156.

68. Taylor, I., 2001, *Stuck In Middle GEAR: South Africa's Post-Apartheid Foreign Relations*, Praeger Press, London, pp. 162–3.

69. 'Foreign Policy Perspective in a Democratic South Africa', ANC, December 1994.

70. Quoted in Landsberg, C., 2005, 'In Search of Global Influence, Order and Development: South Africa's Foreign Policy a Decade After Political Apartheid', *Policy: Issues and Actors*, Vol. 18, No. 3, p. 10.

71. Landsberg, 'In Search of Global Influence', p. 16.

72. Geldenhuys, D., 2006, 'South Africa's Role as International Norm Entrepreneur', in *In Full Flight: South African Foreign Policy After Apartheid*, edited by Carlsnaes, W. and Nel, P., Institute for Global Dialogue, Midrand, p. 99.

73. Landsberg, *Quiet Diplomacy*, pp. 176–8.

74. Alden, C. and le Pere, G., 2003, 'South Africa's Post-Apartheid Foreign Policy—From Reconciliation to Revival?', Adelphi Paper 362, Oxford University Press, Oxford, p. 22.

75. Quoted in Van Nieuwkerk, A., 2006, 'South Africa's Post-Apartheid Foreign Policy Decision-making on African Crises', unpublished doctoral dissertation, University of the Witwatersrand, p. 144.

76. Quoted in Gumede, *Thabo Mbeki*, p. 178.

77. Alves, P.; Kalaba, M.; Wilcox, O.; Fundira, T.; and Williams, B., 2006, 'Deepening Integration in SADC: South Africa—SADC's Economic Engine', Friedrich Ebert Stiftung, Johannesburg, p. 73. Available at: http://library.fes. de/pdf-files/bueros/botswana/04926.pdf (accessed March 11, 2014).

78. Alden, C. and Soko, M., 2005, 'South Africa's Economic Relations with Africa: Hegemony and its Discontents', *Journal of Modern African Studies*, Vol. 43, No. 3, p. 374.

79. Ahwireng-Obeng, F. and McGowan, P., 2001, 'Partner or Hegemon: South Africa in Africa', in *South Africa's Foreign Policy: Dilemmas of a New Democracy*, edited by Broderick, J.; Burford, G.; and Freer, G., Palgrave Press, New York, p. 73.

80. Mlambo, A., 2000, 'Partner or Hegemon? South Africa and its Neighbors', *South African Yearbook of International Affairs 2000/01*, South African Institute of International Affairs, Johannesburg, p. 69.

81. Quoted in Gumede, *Thabo Mbeki*, pp. 198–9.

82. Raymond Suttner, 'South African Foreign Policy and the Promotion of Human Rights', *South African Yearbook of International Affairs 1997*, South African Institute of International Affairs, Johannesburg, p. 300.

83. Alden and le Pere, 'South Africa's Post-Apartheid Foreign Policy', p. 24.

84. Muller, M., 1999, 'South African Diplomacy and Security Complex Theory', *Round Table*, No. 352, p. 592.

85. Benjamin, L., 2001, 'South Africa and the Middle East: Anatomy of an Emerging Relationship', in *South Africa's Foreign Policy: Dilemmas of a New Democracy*, edited by Broderick, J.; Burford, G.; and Freer, G., Palgrave Press, New York, p. 159.

86. Bischoff and Southall, 'Early Foreign Policy', p. 165.

87. Alden, C., 2001, 'Solving South Africa's Chinese Puzzle: Democratic Foreign Policymaking and the Two Chinas Issue', in *South Africa's Foreign Policy: Dilemmas of a New Democracy*, edited by Broderick, J.; Burford, G.; and Freer, G., Palgrave Press, New York, p. 132.

88. Landsberg, C. and Monyae, D., 2006, 'South Africa's Foreign Policy: Carving a Global Niche', *South African Journal of International Relations*, Vol. 13, No. 2, p. 142.

89. Quoted in Mills, *The Wired Model*, p. 300.

90. Hughes, T., 2004, *Composers, Conductors and Players: Harmony and Discord in South African Foreign Policymaking*, Konrad Adenauer Stiftung, Johannesburg, p. 79.

91. Vale, P. and Maseko, S., 1998, 'South Africa and the African Renaissance', *International Affairs*, Vol. 74, No. 2, p. 285.

92. Ajulu, R., 2001, 'Thabo Mbeki's African Renaissance in a Globalizing World Economy: The Struggle for the Soul of the Continent', *Review of African Political Economy*, Vol. 28, No. 87, p. 34.

93. Quoted in Feinstein, A., 2007, *After the Party: A Personal and Political Journey Inside the ANC*, Andrew Jonathan Ball, Johannesburg, p. 88.

94. Landsberg, C., 2007, 'South Africa and the Making of the AU and NEPAD: Mbeki's "Progressive African Agenda"', in *South Africa in Africa: The Post-Apartheid Era*, edited by Adebajo, A.; Adedeji, A.; and Landsberg, C., UKZN Press, Scottsville, p. 202.

95. Taylor, I., 2006, 'Contradictions in South African Foreign Policy and NEPAD', in *In Full Flight: South African Foreign Policy After Apartheid*, edited by Carlsnaes, W. and Nel, P., Institute for Global Dialogue, Midrand, p. 171.

96. Landsberg, 'South Africa and the Making of the AU', p. 202.

97. See the 1996 Defense White Paper and 1998 Defense Review.

98. Solomon, H., 2002, 'The Poverty of Pretoria's Preventative Diplomacy in the Great Lakes Region', *South African Yearbook of International Affairs 2002/03*, South African Institute of International Affairs, Johannesburg, p. 141.

99. Maroleng, C., 2005, 'Cote d'Ivoire: Perils and Prospects', *South African Yearbook of International Affairs 2005*, South African Institute of International Affairs, Johannesburg, p. 33.

100. Landsberg, *Quiet Diplomacy*, p. 163.

101. Jordaan, E., 2008, 'Barking at the Big Dogs: South Africa's Policy Towards the Middle East', *Round Table*, Vol. 97, No. 397, p. 555.

102. Roberts, R., 2007, *Fit to Govern: The Native Intelligence of Thabo Mbeki*, STE Publishers, Johannesburg, p. 168.

103. Van Nieuwkerk, A., 2007, 'A Critique of South Africa's Role on the UN Security Council', *South African Journal of International Affairs*, Vol. 14, No. 1, p. 71.

104. *The Economist*, 2008, 'The See-No-Evil Foreign Policy', November 15.

105. *The Financial Gazette (Harare)*, 2009, 'GDP Drops Sharply', April 17.

106. Hank, S., 2010, 'RIP Zimbabwe Dollar', Cato Institute, Washington DC, May 3.

107. Hughes, *Composers*, p. 113.

108. McKinley, D., 2004, 'South African Foreign Policy Towards Zimbabwe Under Mbeki', *Review of African Political Economy*, Vol. 31, No. 100, p. 359.

109. Schoeman, M. and Alden, C., 2003, 'The Hegemon That Wasn't: South Africa's Policy Toward Zimbabwe', *Strategic Review for Southern Africa*, Vol. 23, p. 17.

110. Honey, P., 2007, 'African Migrants: Fewer than was Thought', *Financial Mail*, February 16.

111. Hughes, *Composers*, p. 138.

112. Gumede, p. 294.

113. Quoted in Barber, 2004, pp. 190–1.

114. Quoted in Prys, M., 2007, 'Regions, Power and Hegemony: South Africa's Role in Southern Africa', Paper presented at the Sixth Pan-European International Relations Conference, Turin, September 12–15, p. 10.

115. Hughes, *Composers*, p. 117.

116. Landsberg, *Quiet Diplomacy*, p. 174.

117. Schoeman and Alden, 'The Hegemon that Wasn't', p. 5.

118. Dlamini, K., 2002, 'Is Quiet Diplomacy an Effective Conflict Resolution Strategy?', *South African Yearbook of International Affairs 2002/2003*, South African Institute of International Affairs, Johannesburg, p. 176.

119. Van Nieuwkerk, 'South Africa's Post-Apartheid Foreign Policy Decision-marking', pp. 188–9.

120. Gumede, *Thabo Mbeki*, p. 187.

121. Gevisser, *Mbeki*, p. 440.

122. Quoted in Roberts, *Fit to Govern*, pp. 177–8.

123. Alden, C. and le Pere, G., 2010, 'Strategic Posture Review: South Africa', *World Politics Review*, p. 28.

124. Mbeki, M., 2002, 'Towards a More Productive South African Foreign Policy', *South African Yearbook of International Affairs 2002/03*, South African Institute of International Affairs, Johannesburg, p. 18.

Chapter 3   Public Opinion and Pressure Groups

1. Spence, *Republic Under*, pp. 100–1.

2. Pienaar, S., 1997, 'Relations with Central and Eastern Europe', in *Change and South African Foreign Relations*, edited by Carlsnaes, W. and Muller, M., International Thomson Publishing, Johannesburg, pp. 10–11.

3. Ibid.

4. Interview with Japie Basson, June 15, 2010.

5. Hepple, *Verwoerd*, pp. 200–1.

6. Good, R., 1973, *UDI: The International Politics of the Rhodesian Rebellion*, Faber and Faber, London, p. 130.

7. Interview with Renier Schoeman, November 2, 2010.

8. Interview with Derek Auret, June 7, 2010.

9. Interview with Boy Geldenhuys, September 6, 2010.

10. Munger, E., 1965, *Notes on the Formation of South African Foreign Policy*, The Castle Press, Cape Town, p. 48.
11. Du Pisani, A., 1988, 'What do We Think? A Survey of White Opinion on Foreign Policy Issues No. 4', South African Institute of International Affairs.
12. Interview with Dave Steward, June 4, 2010.
13. Interview with Henri Boshoff, January 25, 2010.
14. Stiff, P., 2002, *The Silent War: South African Recce Operations 1969–1994*, Galago, Germiston, p. 119.
15. Interview with Dawie de Villiers, November 1, 2010.
16. Shelton, G., 1986, 'Theoretical Perspectives on South African Foreign Policy Making', *Politikon*, Vol. 13, No. 1, p. 12.
17. Adams, J., 1984, *The Unnatural Alliance*, Quartet Books, London, p. 23.
18. Ibid., p. 9.
19. O'Meara, *Forty Lost Years*, p. 46.
20. Adam, H. and Giliomee, H., 1979, *Ethnic Power Mobilized: Can South Africa Change?*, Yale University Press, New Haven, p. 250.
21. Serfontein, H., 1979, *Brotherhood of Power: An Expose of the Secret Afrikaner Broederbond*, Rex Collings Limited, London, p. 84.
22. Wilkins, I. and Strydom, H., 1980, *The Super Afrikaners*, Jonathan Ball, Johannesburg, p. 10.
23. Munger, E., 1967, *Afrikaner and African Nationalism*, Oxford University Press, Oxford, p. 65.
24. Viljoen, G., 1979, 'An Afrikaner Looks Ahead,' in *The Afrikaners*, edited by Munger, E., Tafelberg, Cape Town, p. 168.
25. Interview with Hermann Giliomee, February 24, 2010.
26. Interview with Barend du Plessis, May 22, 2010.
27. Welsh, D., 2009, *The Rise and Fall of Apartheid*, Jonathan Ball, Johannesburg, p. 199.
28. Interview with Hennie van Deventer, May 21, 2010.
29. Interview with Hennie van Deventer, May 21, 2010.
30. O'Meara, D., 1977, 'The Afrikaner Broederbond 1927–1948: Class Vanguard of Afrikaner Nationalism', *Journal of Southern African Studies*, Vol. 3, No. 2, p. 168.
31. Moodie, T., 1975, *The Rise of Afrikanerdom: Power, Apartheid, and the Afrikaner Civil Religion*, University of California Press, Berkeley, p. 111.
32. Wilkins and Strydom, *The Super Afrikaners*, p. 192.
33. Serfontein, *Brotherhood*, pp. 156–8.
34. Nel, P., 1990, *A Soviet Embassy in Pretoria?*, Tafelberg, Cape Town, p. 96.
35. Munger, *Notes,* p. 82.
36. Interview with Johan Steenkamp, May 18, 2010.
37. Geldenhuys, D., 1984, *The Diplomacy of Isolation: South African Foreign Policy Making*, St. Martin's Press, London, p. 31.
38. Wilkins and Strydom, *The Super Afrikaners*, p. 185.
39. Munger, *Notes*, p. 45.

40. Interview with Boy Geldenhuys, September 6, 2010.

41. Nel, *A Soviet Embassy in Pretoria?*, p. 96.

42. Geldenhuys, *Diplomacy*, p. 165.

43. Pienaar, *South Africa and International Relations*, p. 88.

44. Ilsley, L., 1940, 'The War Policy of South Africa', *The American Political Science Review*, Vol. 34, No. 6, p. 1185.

45. See 'Adopted Resolutions on Foreign Policy', ANC 48th National Conference, July 1991 and 'Commission Reports and Draft Resolutions: International Relations', ANC National Policy Conference, June 2007.

46. Selebi, J., 1999, 'South African Foreign Policy: Setting New Goals and Strategies', *South African Journal of International Affairs*, Vol. 6, No. 2, p. 207.

47. Black, D., 1995, 'Comparative Experiences for a New South Africa', in 'Parliaments and Foreign Policy: The International and South African Experience', conference report, Center for Southern African Studies, p. 76.

48. Lodge, T., 1999, 'Policy Processes within the ANC and Tripartite Alliance', *Politikon*, Vol. 26, No. 1, p. 5.

49. Olivier, G., 2006, 'Ideology in South African Foreign Policy', *Politeia*, Vol. 25, No. 2, p. 181.

50. Le Pere, G.; Pressend, M.; Ruiters, M.; and Zondi, S., 2008, 'South Africa's Participation in the System of Global Governance: A Review Prepared for the Presidency's Fifteen Year Review', Institute for Global Dialogue, unpublished, p. 17.

51. Le Pere, G. and Vickers, B., 2004, 'Civil Society and Foreign Policy', in *Democratizing Foreign Policy? Lessons from South Africa*, edited by Nel, P. and Van der Westhuizen, J., Lexington Books, Lanham, p. 75.

52. Nel, P., 1999, 'The Foreign Policy Beliefs of South Africans: A First Cut', *Journal of Contemporary African Studies*, Vol. 17, No. 1, p. 124.

53. Ibid.

54. Interview with Ben Skosana, September 21, 2010.

55. Interview with Job Sithole, May 24, 2010.

56. Interview with Essop Pahad, May 27, 2010.

57. Interview with Fatima Hajaig, September 21, 2010.

58. Interview with Job Sithole, May 24, 2010.

59. Interview with Scarlett Cornellissen, June 29, 2010.

60. Interview with Job Sithole, May 24, 2010.

61. Interview with Henri Boshoff, January 25, 2010.

62. Interview with Baby Tyawa (email), March 14, 2011.

63. Interview with Sydney Mufamadi, October 15, 2010.

64. Interview with Anthoni van Nieuwkerk, February 26, 2010.

65. Interview with Aziz Pahad, January 28, 2011.

66. Venter, D., 2001, 'South African Foreign Policy Decision-Making in the African Context', in *African Foreign Policies, Power and Process*, edited by Khadiagala, G. and Lyons, T., Lynne Rienner, Boulder, p. 161.

67. Alden and le Pere, 'South Africa's Post-Apartheid Foreign Policy', p. 18.

68. Naidoo, K., 2004, 'South African Civil Society and the Making of South African Foreign Policy,' in *Apartheid Past, Renaissance Future: South Africa's Foreign Policy 1994–2004*, edited by Sidiropoulos, E., South African Institute of International Affairs, Johannesburg, p. 186.

69. Nel, P.; Taylor, I.; and van der Westhuizen, J., 2000, 'Multilateralism in South Africa's Foreign Policy: The Search for a Critical Rationale', *Global Governance;* Vol. 6, No. 1, p. 53.

70. Landsberg, C., 2010, *The Diplomacy of Transformation: South African Foreign Policy and Statecraft*, Macmillan, Johannesburg, p. 150.

71. Clarke, D., 2010, *Africa: Crude Continent, The Struggle for Africa's Oil Prize*, Profile Books, London, p. 210.

72. Interview with Father Richard Menatsi, February 17, 2010.

73. Gumede, *Thabo Mbeki*, p. 288.

74. Hughes, *Composers*, p. 138.

75. Interview with Father Richard Menatsi, February 17, 2010.

76. Interview with Father Richard Menatsi, February 17, 2010.

77. Interview with Aziz Pahad, January 28, 2011.

78. Gumede, *Thabo Mbeki*, p. 135.

79. Interview with Simon Boshielo, January 25, 2010.

80. Peete F. and Bateman B., 2006, 'I Love the ANC, Says COSATU's Madisha', Independent Online, September 6.

81. Interview with Chris Matlhako, July 23, 2010.

82. Raymond Suttner, 'A Brief Review of South African Foreign Policy Since 1994', *Umrabulo*, Issue 1, Fall 1996.

83. James Barber, *Mandela's World: The International Dimension of South Africa's Political Revolution 1990–99*, Ohio University Press, 2004, pp. 88–91.

84. Sidiropoulos, E. and Hughes, T., 2004, 'The Challenge of South Africa's Africa Policy', in *Apartheid Past, Renaissance Future: South Africa's Foreign Policy 1994–2004*, edited by Sidiropoulos, E., South African Institute of International Affairs, Johannesburg, p. 63.

85. Ngubentombi, N., 2003, 'South Africa's Foreign Policy Towards Swaziland and Zimbabwe', *South African Yearbook of International Affairs 2003/04*, South African Institute of International Affairs, Johannesburg, p. 151.

86. SAPA, 2006, 'COSATU Thanks Members for Swazi Blockade', April 13.

87. Hughes, *Composers*, p. 138.

88. Phimister, I. and Raftopoulos, B., 2004, 'Mugabe, Mbeki & the Politics of Anti-Imperialism', *Review of African Political Economy*, Vol. 31, No. 101, p. 399.

89. Hughes, *Composers*, p. 29.

90. Interview with Chris Matlhako, July 23, 2010.

91. Interview with Simon Boshielo, January 25, 2010.

92. Interview with Bongani Masuku, May 25, 2010.

93. Interview with Willie Madisha, September 1, 2010.

94. Interview with Willie Madisha, September 1, 2010.

95. Interview with Bongani Masuku, May 25, 2010.

96. Interview with Simon Boshielo, January 25, 2010.
97. Interview with Simon Boshielo, January 25, 2010.
98. Interview with Cunningham Ngcukana, May 24, 2010.
99. Interview with Aziz Pahad, January 28, 2011.
100. Interview with Sydney Mufamadi, October 15, 2010.
101. Interview with Pallo Jordan, June 25, 2010.
102. Alden, 'Solving South Africa's Chinese Puzzle', p. 126.
103. Interview with Sydney Mufamadi, October 15, 2010.
104. Interview with Bongani Masuku, May 25, 2010.
105. Interview with Pallo Jordan, June 25, 2010.
106. Dugger, C., 2008, 'Zimbabwe Arms Shipped by China Spark an Uproar', *New York Times*, April 19.
107. Fritz, N., 2009, 'People Power: How Civil Society Blocked an Arms Shipment for Zimbabwe', SAIIA Occasional Paper 36, pp. 4–5.
108. BBC News, 2008, 'Zimbabwe Arms Ship Quits South Africa', April 19.
109. Fritz, 'People Power', p. 8.
110. Masiza, Z., 1999, 'Silent Citizenry: Public Participation and Foreign Policy-making', Center for Policy Studies, Policy Brief No. 15.
111. Munger, *Notes*, p. 51.
112. Stultz, 'The Politics of Security', p. 14.
113. Wallace, W., 1971, *Foreign Policy and the Political Process*, Macmillan Press, New York, p. 44.
114. Habib, A., 2005, 'State-Civil Society Relations in Post-Apartheid South Africa', *Social Research*, Vol. 72, No. 3, p. 683.
115. Interview with Sydney Mufamadi, October 15, 2010.
116. Interview with Father Peter John Pearson, May 4, 2010.
117. Interview with Bongani Masuku, May 25, 2010.
118. Interview with Bongani Masuku, May 25, 2010.
119. Interview with Bongani Masuku, May 25, 2010.
120. Interview with Willie Madisha, September 1, 2010.
* Boshoff's comments came three years before the March 2013 deaths of 13 South African soldiers at the hands of rebel forces in the Central African Republic.

Chapter 4   The Press

1. Frankel, *The Making of Foreign Policy*, p. 72.
2. Parsons, W., 1995, *Public Policy: An Introduction to the Theory and Practice of Policy Analysis*, Edward Elgar, London, p. 107.
3. Hill, C., 2003, *The Changing Politics of Foreign Policy*, Palgrave Macmillan, New York, p. 277.
4. Ibid., p. 276.
5. www.southafrica.info/about/media/news.htm (accessed March 11, 2014).

6. Potter, E., 1975, *The Press as Opposition: The Political Role of South African Newspapers*, Rowman and Littlefield, Totowa, p. 38.
7. Pogrund, B., 2000, *War of Words: Memoirs of a South African Journalist*, Seven Stories Press, New York p. 29.
8. Horwitz, R., 2001, *Communication and Democratic Reform in South Africa*, Cambridge University Press, Cambridge, p. 37.
9. Potter, *Press*, p. 67.
10. Mervis, J., 1989, *The Fourth Estate: A Newspaper Story*, Jonathan Ball, Johannesburg, p. 15.
11. Pogrund, *War of Words*, p. 26.
12. Potter, *Press*, p. 50.
13. Mervis, *The Fourth Estate*, p. 122.
14. Massie, *Loosing the Bonds*, p. 10.
15. Hepple, *Verwoerd*, p. 52.
16. Potter, *Press*, p. 73.
17. Welsh, *The Rise and Fall of Apartheid,* pp. 173–4.
18. Dommisse, E., 1979, 'The Changing Role of the Afrikaans Press', in *The Afrikaners*, edited by Munger, E., Tafelberg, Cape Town, p. 100.
19. Pollak, R., 1981, *Up Against Apartheid: The Role and Plight of the Press in South Africa*, Southern Illinois University Press, Carbondale, p. 12.
20. O'Meara, *Forty Lost Years*, p. 106.
21. Adam and Giliomee, *Ethnic Power Mobilized*, p. 205.
22. Ibid., p. 233.
23. Adam, H. and Uys, S., 1988, 'Eight New Realities in Southern Africa', in *South Africa in Transition: To What?*, edited by Kitchen, H., Center for Strategic and International Studies, Washington DC, p. 122.
24. Interview with Ton Vosloo, June 9, 2010.
25. Pollak, *Up Against Apartheid*, p. 13.
26. Interview with Ebbe Dommisse, June 3, 2010.
27. Potter, *Press*, p. 135.
28. Ibid., p. 148.
29. Botha, J., 1967, *Verwoerd is Dead*, Books of Africa, Johannesburg, p. 121.
30. Potter, *Press*, p. 135.
31. Barron, C., 2006, 'Alf Ries: Propagandist for the National Party', *Sunday Times*, November 5.
32. Interview with Peter Fabricius, January 26, 2010.
33. Interview with Hennie van Deventer, May 21, 2010.
34. Interview with Ton Vosloo, June 9, 2010.
35. Interview with Ebbe Dommisse, June 3, 2010.
36. Interview with Theuns van der Westhuizen, May 14, 2010.
37. Interview with Ton Vosloo, June 9, 2010.
38. Interview with Theuns van der Westhuizen, May 14, 2010.
39. Interview with Ton Vosloo, June 9, 2010.

40. Jackson, G., 1993, *Breaking Story: The South African Press*, Westview Press, Boulder, p. 40.
41. Pogrund, *War of Words*, p. 90.
42. Email from Harvey Tyson, February 28, 2011.
43. Horwitz, *Communication*, p. 46.
44. Shaw, G., 2007, *Believe in Miracles: A Reporter's Story*, Ampersand Press, Cape Town, p. 62.
45. Shaw, G., 1999, *The Cape Times: An Informal History*, David Philip Publishers, Cape Town, p. 265.
46. Ibid., p. 292.
47. Interview with Rex Gibson, March 11, 2011.
48. Jackson, *Breaking Story*, p. 111.
49. Potter, *Press*, p. 122.
50. Interview with Ken Owen, June 30, 2010.
51. Interview with Ebbe Dommisse, June 3, 2010.
52. Interview with Willem Steenkamp, May 14, 2010.
53. Interview with Rex Gibson, March 11, 2011.
54. Shaw, *Cape Times*, p. 267.
55. Interview with Willem Steenkamp, May 14, 2010.
56. Interview with Peter Fabricius, January 26, 2010.
57. Interview with Theuns van der Westhuizen, May 14, 2010.
58. Interview with Niel Barnard, July 14, 2010.
59. Interview with Niel Barnard, July 14, 2010.
60. Interview with Hennie van Deventer, May 21, 2010.
61. Interview with Ton Vosloo, June 9 2010.
62. Interview with Ebbe Dommisse, June 3, 2010.
63. Interview with Rex Gibson, March 11, 2011.
64. Pogrund, *War of Words*, p. 47.
65. Interview with Harvey Tyson, March 11, 2011.
66. Good, *UDI*, p. 129.
67. Interview with Ebbe Dommisse, June 3, 2010.
68. Interview with Pik Botha, February 1, 2010.
69. Papenfus, T., 2010, *Pik Botha and His Times*, Litera Publications, Pretoria, p. 190.
70. Interview with Peter Fabricius, January 26, 2010.
71. Interview with Ton Vosloo, June 9, 2010.
72. Interview with Peter Fabricius, January 26, 2010.
73. Interview with Ken Owen, June 30, 2010.
74. Interview with Hennie van Deventer, May 21, 2010.
75. Interview with Hennie van Deventer, May 21, 2010.
76. Interview with Ken Owen, June 30, 2010.
77. Interview with Hennie van Deventer, May 21, 2010.
78. Interview with Ken Owen, June 30, 2010.
79. Interview with Ken Owen, June 30, 2010.

80. Owen, K., 1988, 'A Fundamental Shift in South African Politics?', in *South Africa in Transition: To What?*, edited by Kitchen, H., Center for Strategic and International Studies, Washington DC, p. 27.
81. Interview with Hennie van Deventer, May 21, 2010.
82. Interview with Mondli Makhanya, October 11, 2010.
83. Interview with Ton Vosloo, June 9, 2010.
84. Interview with Hopewell Radebe, May 27, 2010.
85. Interview with Mondli Makhanya, October 11, 2010.
86. Barkan, J., 2005, 'Emerging Legislature or Rubber Stamp? The South African National Assembly After Ten Years of Democracy', CSSR Working Paper No. 134, University of Cape Town Centre for Social Science Research, p. 18.
87. Interview with Ton Vosloo, June 9, 2010.
88. Interview with Mathatha Tsedu, May 31, 2011.
89. Interview with Mathatha Tsedu, May 31, 2011.
90. Interview with Mathatha Tsedu, May 31, 2011.
91. Interview with Mathatha Tsedu, May 31, 2011.
92. Interview with Mondli Makhanya, October 11, 2010.
93. Calland, *Anatomy*, p. 194.
94. Interview with Jan-Jan Joubert, February 25, 2010.
95. Interview with Mathatha Tsedu, May 31, 2011.
96. Interview with Mathatha Tsedu, May 31, 2011.
97. Potter, *Press*, p. 84.
98. Interview with Mondli Makhanya, October 11, 2010.
99. Author's private archive.
100. Calland, *Anatomy*, p. 194.
101. Interview with Ton Vosloo, June 9, 2010.
102. Author's private archive.
103. Interview with Mondli Makhanya, October 11, 2010.
104. Interview with Mondli Makhanya, October 11, 2010.
105. Interview with Peter Fabricius, January 26, 2010.
106. Interview with Mondli Makhanya, October 11, 2010.
107. Author's private archive.
108. Interview with Mondli Makhanya, October 11, 2010.
109. Interview with Aziz Pahad, January 28, 2011.
110. Interview with Mondli Makhanya, October 11, 2010.
111. Interview with Ton Vosloo, June 9, 2010.
112. Interview with Mathatha Tsedu, May 31, 2011.
113. Interview with Peter Fabricius, January 26, 2010.
114. Interview with Peter Fabricius, January 26, 2010.
115. Interview with Jannie Ferreira, February 23, 2010.
116. Interview with Mathatha Tsedu, May 31, 2011.
* While aimed at Afrikaans-speaking audiences, *Die Burger* was actually first published in Dutch. Its first Afrikaans-language articles did not appear until 1916, and it was not fully in Afrikaans until 1921.

† In referring to the 'English' press, we refer to the white English press, not black newspapers or magazines written in English. The black print press—English or vernacular—was almost completely ignored by the NP government, on both foreign and domestic issues.

Chapter 5   Academia

1. Munger, *Notes*, p. 34.
2. Geldenhuys, *Diplomacy*, p. 169.
3. Interview with Deon Fourie, May 25, 2010.
4. Munger, *Notes*, p. 39.
5. Ibid., p. 53.
6. Interview with Denis Venter, May 28, 2010.
7. South African Institute of International Affairs, 'History of SAIIA', www.saiia.org.za.
8. Pfister, *Apartheid South Africa*, p. 21.
9. Vale, P., 2003, *Security and Politics in South Africa: The Regional Dimension*, UCT Press, Cape Town, p. 68.
10. Sara Pienaar, 1997, 'Relations with Central and Eastern Europe', in *Change and South African Foreign Relations*, edited by Carlsnaes, W. and Muller, M., International Thomson Publishing, p. 130.
11. Leysens, A. and Fourie, P., 1997, 'Relations with Latin America', in *Change and South African Foreign Relations*, edited by Carlsnaes, W. and Muller, M., International Thomson Publishing, Johannesburg, p. 156.
12. Geldenhuys, *Diplomacy*, p. 169.
13. Leonard, R., 1983, *South Africa at War*, Lawrence Hill, Westport, p. 177.
14. Interview with Philip Nel, October 8, 2010.
15. Interview with Niel Barnard, July 14, 2010.
16. Interview with Philip Nel, October 8, 2010.
17. Interview with Mike Hough, July 21, 2010.
18. Interview with Louis Nel, October 11, 2010.
19. Munger, *Notes*, p. 52.
20. Interview with Don Sole, May 5, 2010.
21. Interview with Philip Nel, October 8, 2010.
22. Interview with Niel Barnard, July 14, 2010.
23. Interview with Philip Nel, October 8, 2010.
24. Interview with Sara Pienaar, March 2, 2010.
25. Fourie, D., 2009, 'What Happened to Machiavelli's Advice to the Prince? Experience in Teaching Strategic Studies', unpublished, p. 1.
26. Geldenhuys, J., 2009, *At the Front: A General's Account of the Border War*, Jonathan Ball, Johannesburg, p. 87.

27. Seegers, A., 1996, *The Military in the Making of Modern South Africa*, Tauris Publishing, London, p. 133.
28. O'Brien, K., 2010, *The South African Intelligence Services: From Apartheid to Democracy, 1948–2005*, Routledge, Milton Park, p. 50.
29. Polakow-Suransky, *The Unspoken Alliance*, p. 130.
30. Kenkel, K., 2005, 'Whispering to the Prince: Academic Experts and National Security Policy Formulation in Brazil, South Africa and Canada', unpublished doctoral dissertation, University of Geneva, p. 146.
31. Fourie, 'Machiavelli', p. 2.
32. Alden, C., 1996, *Apartheid's Last Stand: The Rise and Fall of the South African Security State*, Macmillan Press, London, p. 44.
33. Fourie, 'Machiavelli', p. 3.
34. Interview with Deon Fourie, May 25, 2010.
35. Interview with Tienie Groenewald, May 28, 2010.
36. Interview with Deon Fourie, May 25, 2010.
37. Griffiths, R., 1991, 'The South African Military: The Dilemmas of Expanded Influence in Decision-making', *Journal of Asian and African Studies*, Vol. 26, No. 1, p. 79.
38. Fourie, 'Machiavelli', p. 3.
39. Gossman, A., 2010, 'The South African Military and Counterinsurgency: An Overview', in *South Africa and Contemporary Counterinsurgency: Roots, Practices, and Prospects*, edited by Deane-Peter Baker and Evert Jordan, UCT Press, Cape Town, p. 90.
40. Interview with Deon Fourie, May 25, 2010.
41. Interview with Chris Bennett, September 9, 2010.
42. Interview with Helmoed Heitman, May 4, 2010.
43. Interview with Jannie Geldenhuys, May 28, 2010.
44. Interview with Mike Hough, July 21, 2010.
45. Interview with Mike Hough, July 21, 2010.
46. Munger, *Notes*, p. 52.
47. Interview with Sara Pienaar, March 2, 2010.
48. Geldenhuys, *Diplomacy*, p. 170.
49. Interview with Peter Vale, September 8, 2010.
50. Interview with Peter Vale, September 8, 2010.
51. Interview with Peter Vale, September 8, 2010.
52. Interview with Peter Vale, September 8, 2010.
53. Interview with Garth Shelton, January 26, 2010.
54. Joseph Hanlon, 1986, *Beggar Your Neighbors: Apartheid Power in Southern Africa*, James Currey Ltd, p. 57.
55. Interview with Denis Venter, May 28, 2010.
56. Interview with Philip Nel, October 8, 2010.
57. Rhoodie, E., 1989, *PW Botha: The Last Betrayal*, SA Politics, Melville, p. 112.
58. Interview with Sara Pienaar, March 2, 2010.
59. Welsh, *The Rise and Fall of Apartheid*, p. 179.

60. Interview with Deon Fourie, May 25, 2010.
61. Interview with Derek Auret, June 7, 2010.
62. Interview with Niel Barnard, July 14, 2010.
63. Interview with Dave Steward, June 4, 2010.
64. Interview with Deon Geldenhuys, January 29, 2010.
65. Davies and O'Meara, 'Total Strategy', p. 190.
66. Hanlon, *Beggar*, p. 29.
67. Interview with Deon Geldenhuys, January 29, 2010.
68. Interview with Deon Geldenhuys, January 29, 2010.
69. Interview with Niel Barnard, July 14, 2010.
70. 'Apartheid Distabilisation: Pretoria's Regional Strategy', ANC Research Unit of the Department of Information and Publicity, November 1984, from Mayibuye Archive, University of Western Cape.
71. Interview with Peter Vale, September 8, 2010.
72. Interview with Peter Vale, September 8, 2010.
73. Interview with Sara Pienaar, March 2, 2010.
74. Interview with Anthoni van Nieuwkerk, February 26, 2010.
75. Vale, P., 2010, 'Thabo Mbeki and the Great Foreign Policy Riddle', in *Mbeki and After*, edited by Glaser, D., Wits Press, Johannesburg, p. 245.
76. Interview with Peter Vale, September 8, 2010.
77. Interview with John Daniel, July 29, 2010.
78. Interview with Peter Vale, September 8, 2010.
79. Interview with Anthoni van Nieuwkerk, February 26, 2010.
80. Interview with John Daniel, July 29, 2010.
81. Interview with Peter Vale, September 8, 2010.
82. Interview with Vasu Gounden, August 2, 2010.
83. Interview with John Daniel, July 29, 2010.
84. Interview with Peter Vale, September 8, 2010.
85. 'Foreign Policy in a New Democratic South Africa: A Discussion Paper', ANC Department of International Affairs, October 1993.
86. Mandela, N., 1993, 'South Africa's Future Foreign Policy', *Foreign Affairs*, Vol. 72, No. 5.
87. Interview with Peter Vale, September 8, 2010.
88. Interview with Peter Vale, September 8, 2010.
89. Interview with Peter Vale, September 8, 2010.
90. Interview with Roger Southall, January 26, 2010.
91. Interview with John Daniel, July 29, 2010.
92. Interview with Laurie Nathan, August 16, 2010.
93. Kenkel, *Whispering*, p. 149.
94. Shaw, M., 1994, 'Biting the Bullet: Negotiating Democracy's Defense', in *The Small Miracle: South Africa's Negotiated Settlement*, South African Review 7, edited by Friedman, S. and Atkinson, D., Ravan Press, Randburg, p. 233.
95. Kenkel, *Whispering*, p. 149.
96. Ibid., p. 153.

97. Interview with Willem Steenkamp, May 14, 2010.

98. Institute for Security Studies, 'History of ISS', www.iss.co.za.

99. Kenkel, *Whispering*, p. 175.

100. Interview with Jakkie Cilliers, July 22, 2011.

101. Interview with Jakkie Cilliers, July 22, 2011.

102. Interview with Jakkie Cilliers, July 22, 2011.

103. Interview with Aziz Pahad, January 28, 2011.

104. Van der Westhuizen, J., 1998, 'South Africa's Emergence as a Middle Power', *Third World Quarterly*, Vol. 19, No. 3, p. 446.

105. Black, 'Comparative Experiences', p. 85.

106. Interview with John Daniel, July 29, 2010.

107. Interview with Aziz Pahad, January 28, 2011.

108. Interview with Peter Vale, September 8, 2010.

109. Interview with Peter Vale, September 8, 2010.

110. Interview with Sara Pienaar, March 2, 2010.

111. Interview with Greg Mills, May 25, 2010.

112. Interview with Tim Hughes, February 7, 2010.

113. Vale, P., 1990 'Starting Over: Some Early Questions on a Post-Apartheid Foreign Policy', Southern Africa Perspectives, Center for Southern African Studies, Cape Town, p. 6.

114. Carlsnaes, W. and Nel, P., 2006, 'Introduction', in *In Full Flight: South African Foreign Policy After Apartheid*, edited by Carlsnaes, W. and Nel, P., Institute for Global Dialogue, Midrand, pp. 23–4.

115. Institute for Security Studies, 'History of ISS', www.iss.co.za.

116. Interview with Vasu Gounden, August 2, 2010.

117. Bentley, K. and Southall, R., 2005, *An African Peace Process: Mandela, South Africa, and Burundi*, HSRC Press, Pretoria, pp. 154–6.

118. Carlsnaes and Nel, 'Introduction', pp. 23–4.

119. Nantulya, P., 2003, 'South African NGOs: New Actors and Instruments in South African Foreign Policy', *South African Yearbook of International Affairs 2003/04*, South African Institute of International Affairs, Johannesburg, p. 24.

120. Ibid., pp. 27–8.

121. Carlsnaes and Nel, 'Introduction', pp. 23–4.

122. Interview with Anthoni van Nieuwkerk, February 26, 2010.

123. Interview with Siphamandla Zondi, May 27, 2010.

124. Interview with Anthoni van Nieuwkerk, February 26, 2010.

125. Interview with Garth le Pere, May 25, 2010.

126. Interview with Aziz Pahad, January 28, 2011.

127. Interview with Sara Pienaar, March 2, 2010.

128. Interview with Sara Pienaar, March 2, 2010.

129. Interview with Tim Hughes, February 7, 2010.

130. Interview with Aziz Pahad, January 28, 2011.

131. Author's private archive.

132. Interview with Greg Mills, May 25, 2010.
133. Interview with Adekeye Adebajo, March 3, 2011.
134. Interview with Aziz Pahad, January 28, 2011.
135. Interview with Garth le Pere, May 25, 2010.
136. Nathan, L., 2007, *Local Ownership of Security Sector Reform: A Guide for Donors*, University of Birmingham, Birmingham, pp. 104–5.
137. Vale, *Security*, p. 81.
138. Interview with Anthoni van Nieuwkerk, February 26, 2010.
139. Interview with Annette Seegers, February 23, 2010.
140. Interview with Garth le Pere, May 25, 2010.
141. Interview with Laurie Nathan, August 16, 2010.
142. Interview with Garth le Pere, May 25, 2010.
143. Carlsnaes and Nel, p. 25.
144. Interview with Laurie Nathan, August 16, 2010.
145. Interview with Willem Steenkamp, May 14, 2010.
146. Le Pere and Vickers, 'Civil Society and Foreign Policy', p. 68.
147. Interview with Garth Shelton, February 25, 2010.
148. Nantulya, 'South African NGOs', p. 20.
149. Interview with Aziz Pahad, January 28, 2011.
150. Interview with Roger Southall, January 26, 2010.
151. Interview with Garth le Pere, May 25, 2010.
152. Interview with John Daniel, July 29, 2010.
153. Interview with Garth le Pere, May 25, 2010.
154. Interview with Anthoni van Nieuwkerk, February 26, 2010.
155. Interview with Anthoni van Nieuwkerk, February 26, 2010.
156. Interview with Chris Landsberg, July 23, 2010.
157. Interview with Shadrack Gutto, May 27, 2010.
158. Interview with Laurie Nathan, August 16, 2010.
159. Interview with Mluleki George, October 28, 2010.
160. Interview with Henri Boshoff, January 25, 2010.
161. Interview with Garth le Pere, May 25, 2010.
162. Author's private archive.
163. Interview with Garth le Pere, May 25, 2010.
164. Interview with Tim Hughes, February 7, 2010.
165. Interview with Rok Ajulu, July 21, 2010.
166. Interview with Tim Hughes, February 7, 2010.
167. Interview with Mike Hough, July 21, 2010.
168. Interview with Annette Seegers, February 23, 2010.
169. Interview with Mills Soko, March 1, 2010.
170. Le Pere and Vickers, 'Civil Society and Foreign Policy', p. 68.
171. Nantulya, 'South African NGOs', p. 14.
172. Interview with Garth le Pere, May 25, 2010.
173. Interview with Garth Shelton, January 26, 2010.
174. Interview with Garth Shelton, January 26, 2010.

175. Interview with Henri Boshoff, January 25, 2010.
176. Nyuot Goh, J. 2005, 'South Africa's Policy Towards Sudan', *South African Yearbook of International Affairs 2005*, South African Institute of International Affairs, Johannesburg, p. 41.
177. Interview with Shadrack Gutto, May 27, 2010.
178. Interview with Elizabeth Sidiropoulos, May 26, 2010.
179. Interview with Mavivi Myakayaka-Manzini, November 19, 2010.
180. Interview with Karen Smith, September 23, 2010.
181. Author's private archive.
182. Interview with Mavivi Myakayaka-Manzini, November 19, 2010.
183. Interview with Boy Geldenhuys, September 6, 2010.
184. Nantulya, 'South African NGOs', p. 24.
185. Interview with Karen Smith, September 23, 2010.
186. Interview with Mavivi Myakayaka-Manzini, November 19, 2010.
187. Hughes, *Composers*, pp. 142–3.
188. Interview with Garth le Pere, May 25, 2010.
189. Interview with Garth le Pere, May 25, 2010.
190. 'State of the Nation Address by the President of South Africa, Thabo Mbeki to the Joint Sitting of the Houses of Parliament', February 8, 2002.
191. Interview with Garth le Pere, May 25, 2010.
192. Interview with Rok Ajulu, July 21, 2010.
193. Interview with Garth le Pere, May 25, 2010.
194. Interview with Rok Ajulu, July 21, 2010.
195. Van Nieuwkerk, 'South Africa's Post-Apartheid Foreign Policy Decision-making', pp. 188–9.
196. Alden and le Pere, 'South Africa's Post-Apartheid Foreign Policy', p. 74.
197. Interview with Tim Hughes, February 7, 2010.
198. Author's private archive.
199. Interview with Elizabeth Sidiropoulos, May 26, 2010.
200. Interview with Cunningham Ngcukana, May 24, 2010.
201. Interview with Chris Landsberg, July 23, 2010.
202. Interview with Garth le Pere, May 25, 2010.
203. Author's private archive.
204. Interview with Chris Landsberg, July 23, 2010.
205. Interview with Chris Landsberg, July 23, 2010.
206. Le Pere and Vickers, 'Civil Society and Foreign Policy', p. 69.
207. Interview with Laurie Nathan, August 16, 2010.
208. Interview with Karen Smith, September 23, 2010.
209. Interview with Rok Ajulu, July 21, 2010.
210. Interview with Laurie Nathan, August 16, 2010.
211. Quoted in Khoza, R., 2005, *Let Africa Lead*, Vezubuntu, Johannesburg, p. 51.
212. Interview with Adekeye Adebajo, March 3, 2011.
213. Le Pere and Vickers, 'Civil Society and Foreign Policy', p. 75.
214. Interview with Gerrit Olivier, January 20, 2010.

215. Le Pere and Vickers, 'Civil Society and Foreign Policy', p. 75.
216. Fourie, 'Machiavelli', p. 6.
*   Botha seems to have enjoyed a closer bond with American theoretician Samuel Huntington, whom he got to know while ambassador to Washington in the 1970s. Huntington, at Pik's urging, visited South Africa in 1981, addressing public gatherings and even meeting with PW Botha for several hours.
†   Fourie's timeline appears to be off, given Zimbabwe's February 1980 independence and the USSR's December 1979 invasion of Afghanistan, but the sentiment applies.
‡   Among academic interviewees, only one claimed he was offered a high-level position in government during this period.

Chapter 6   Business

1. Massie, *Loosing the Bonds*, p. 74.
2. Vale and Maseko, 'South Africa and the African Renaissance', p. 275.
3. Handley, A., 2008, *Business and the State in Africa: Economic Policy-Making in the Neoliberal Era*, Cambridge University Press, Cambridge, p. 81.
4. Ibid., p. 35.
5. Vale and Maseko, 'South Africa and the African Renaissance', p. 275.
6. Adebajo, A., 2010, *The Curse of Berlin: Africa After the Cold War*, UKZN Press, Scottsville, p. 221.
7. Bunting, B., 1986, *The Rise of the South African Reich*, International Defense and Aid Fund, London, p. 432.
8. Geldenhuys, D., 1984, 'South African Reactions to the Nkomati Accord: A House Divided', *Journal of Contemporary African Studies*, Vol. 4, No. 1/2, p. 201.
9. Nolutshungu, S., 1975, *South Africa in Africa: A Study in Ideology and Foreign Policy*, Manchester University Press, Manchester, p. 288.
10. Pfister, *Apartheid South Africa*, p. 96.
11. Ibid., p. 28.
12. Jaster, Mbeki, Clough, and Nkosi, *Changing Fortunes*, p. 60.
13. Wolvaardt, P.; Wheeler, T.; and Scholtz, W. (editors), 2010, *From Verwoerd to Mandela: South African Diplomats Remember, Volume 1*, Crink, Cape Town, p. 217.
14. Handley, *Business*, p. 51.
15. Dommisse, E., 2001, *Anton Rupert: A Biography*, Tafelberg, Cape Town, p. 28.
16. Welsh, *The Rise and Fall of Apartheid*, p. 261.
17. Interview with Niel Barnard, July 14, 2010.
18. Handley, *Business*, p. 57.
19. Relly, G., 1986, 'The Costs of Disinvestment', *Foreign Policy*, No. 63, p. 138.

20. Pretorius, L., 1994, 'The Head of Government and Organised Business', in *Leadership in the Apartheid State: From Malan to de Klerk*, edited by Schrire, R., Oxford University Press, Oxford, p. 242.
21. Carter, G., 1980, *Which Way is South Africa Going?* Indiana University Press, Bloomington, p. 90.
22. Bowman, *South Africa's Outward Strategy*, p. 8.
23. Interview with Jeremy Shearer, July 21, 2010.
24. *From Verwoerd to Mandela, Volume 1*, p. 178.
25. Munger, *Notes*, p. 56.
26. Pfister, *Apartheid South Africa*, p. 28.
27. Interview with Jeremy Shearer, July 21, 2010.
28. Gerber, L., 1973, *Friends and Influence: The Diplomacy of Private Enterprise*, Purnell, Cape Town, p. 17.
29. Ibid., p. 36.
30. Meiring, P., 1974, *Inside Information*, Howard Timmins Press, Cape Town, p. 141.
31. Interview with Neil van Heerden, June 24, 2010.
32. Munger, *Notes*, p. 57.
33. Bunting, 'South African Reich', p. 334.
34. Interview with Jeremy Shearer, July 21, 2010.
35. Interview with Neil van Heerden, June 24, 2010.
36. Hanlon, *Beggar*, p. 67.
37. Pfister, *Apartheid South Africa*, p. 21.
38. Interview with Neil van Heerden, June 24, 2010.
39. Adam, H.; Slabbert, F.; and Moodley, K., 1998, *Comrades in Business: Post-Liberation Politics in South Africa*, Tafelberg, Cape Town, p. 147.
40. Hanlon, *Beggar*, p. 68.
41. Ibid., p. 249.
42. Eglin, C., 2007, *Crossing the Borders of Power*, Jonathan Ball, Johannesburg, p. 210.
43. Bunting, 'South African Reich', p. 394.
44. Ibid., p. 395.
45. O'Meara, *Forty Lost Years*, p. 101.
46. Dommisse, *Anton Rupert*, p. 121.
47. Ibid., p. 282.
48. Geldenhuys, *Diplomacy*, p. 165.
49. Dommisse, *Anton Rupert*, p. 25.
50. Interview with Pik Botha, February 1, 2010.
51. Geldenhuys, *Diplomacy*, p. 160.
52. Simpson, G., 1989, 'The Politics and Economics of the Armaments Industry in South Africa', in *War and Society: The Militarization of South Africa*, edited by Cock, J. and Nathan, L., David Philip Publishers, Cape Town, p. 226.
53. Hanlon, *Beggar*, p. 9.
54. Ibid., p. 14.
55. Griffiths, 'The South African Military', p. 84.

56. Grundy, K., 1986, *The Militarization of South African Politics,* Indiana University Press, Bloomington, p. 48.
57. Pretorius, 'The Head of Government', p. 231.
58. Dommisse, *Anton Rupert*, p. 245.
59. Pottinger, B., 1988, *The Imperial Presidency: PW Botha, the First Ten Years*, Southern Book Publishers, Johannesburg, p. 122.
60. Geldenhuys, *Diplomacy*, p. 161.
61. Hanlon, *Beggar*, p. 10.
62. Ibid., p. 15.
63. Schrire, R., 1991, *Adapt or Die: The End of White Politics in South Africa*, Ford Foundation, New York, p. 62.
64. Hanlon, *Beggar*, p. 33.
65. O'Meara, *Forty Lost Years*, p. 330.
66. Schrire, *Adapt or Die*, p. 83.
67. Hanlon, *Beggar*, p. 54.
68. Interview with Barend du Plessis, May 22, 2010.
69. Munger, *Notes*, p. 54.
70. Eglin, *Crossing*, p. 93.
71. Interview with Renier Schoeman, November 2, 2010.
72. Interview with Dawie de Villiers, November 1, 2010.
73. Interview with Dawie de Villiers, November 1, 2010.
74. 'South African Trade By Region', www.dti.gov.za.
75. Hudson, J., 2007, 'South Africa's Economic Expansion Into Africa: Neo-Colonialism or Development?', in *South Africa in Africa: The Post-Apartheid Era*, edited by Adebajo, A.; Adedeji, A.; and Landsberg, C., UKZN Press, Scottsville, p. 131.
76. Vale and Maseko, 'South Africa and the African Renaissance', p. 279.
77. Adebajo, *Berlin*, p. 114.
78. Hudson, 'South Africa's Economic Expansion', p. 129.
79. Interview with Michael Spicer, October 11, 2010.
80. Daniel, J. and Bhengu, N., 2009, 'South Africa in Africa: Still a Formidable Player,' in *A New Scramble for Africa: Imperialism, Investment, and Development*, edited by Roger Southall and Henning Melber, UKZN Press, Scottsville, p. 140.
81. Qobo, M., 2006, 'Dilemmas in South Africa's Regional Strategy', in *The New Multilateralism in South African Diplomacy*, edited by Lee, D.; Taylor, I.; and Williams, P., Palgrave Macmillan, New York, p. 145.
82. Adebajo, A., 2007, 'South Africa and Nigeria in Africa: An Axis of Virtue?', in *South Africa in Africa: The Post-Apartheid Era*, edited by Adebajo, A.; Adedeji, A.; and Landsberg, C., UKZN Press, Scottsville, p. 230.
83. Alden and Soko, 'South Africa's Economic Relations with Africa', p. 374.
84. Naidu, S., 2004, 'South Africa and Africa: Mixed Messages?', in *Apartheid Past, Renaissance Future: South Africa's Foreign Policy 1994–2004*, edited by Sidiropoulos, E., South African Institute of International Affairs, Johannesburg, p. 211.

85. Hudson, 'South Africa's Economic Expansion', p. 144.
86. Nathan, L., 2009, 'Courting al-Bashir: South Africa, Sudan, and Darfur', in *Africa's Peacemaker: Lessons from South Africa's Conflict Resolution*, edited by Shillinger, K., South African Institute of International Affairs, Johannesburg, p. 83.
87. Sidiropoulos, E., 2008, 'Post-Mbeki, Post-Transition: South African Foreign Policy in a Changing World', *South African Journal of International Affairs, 2008/09*, South African Institute of International Affairs, p. 4.
88. Ahwireng-Obeng and McGowan, 'Partner or Hegemon,' p. 68.
89. Grobbelaar, N., 2005, 'South African Corporate Engagement with Africa: Unpacking Negative and Positive Perceptions', *South African Yearbook of International Affairs 2005*, South African Institute of International Affairs, Johannesburg, p. 68.
90. Sidiropoulos, 'Post-Mbeki', p. 9.
91. Interview with Mavivi Myakayaka-Manzini, November 19, 2010.
92. Adebajo, A., 2007, 'South Africa in Africa: Messiah or Mercantilist?', *South African Journal of International Affairs*, Vol. 14, No. 1, p. 41.
93. Interview with Aziz Pahad, January 28, 2011.
94. Author's private archive.
95. Interview with Michael Spicer, October 11, 2010.
96. Alden and Soko, 'South Africa's Economic Relations with Africa', p. 382.
97. Interview with Vincent Maphai, June 1, 2011.
98. Qobo, M., 2010, 'Refocusing South Africa's Economic Diplomacy: The 'African Agenda' and Emerging Powers', *South African Journal of International Affairs*, Vol. 17, No. 1, p. 19.
99. Interview with Whitey Basson, June 30, 2010.
100. Interview with Whitey Basson, June 30, 2010.
101. Handley, *Business*, p. 53.
102. Gevisser, *Mbeki*, p. 579.
103. Taylor, *Stuck In Middle GEAR*, p. 24.
104. Interview with Vincent Maphai, June 1, 2011.
105. Wilhelm, P., 2004, 'The 20 Most Influential People in SA Business: Thabo Mbeki', *Financial Mail*, December 24.
106. Hughes, *Composers*, pp. 39–40.
107. Hamman, R. and de Cleene, S., 2005, 'South Africa's Corporate Responsibility in Africa', *South African Journal of International Affairs*, Vol. 12, No. 2, p. 130.
108. Hughes, *Composers*, p. 38.
109. Interview with Peter Draper, October 14, 2010.
110. Interview with Neil van Heerden, June 24, 2010.
111. Dommisse, *Anton Rupert*, p. 296.
112. Gumede, W., 2003, 'Down to Business but Nothing to Show', in *Thabo Mbeki's World*, edited by Jacobs, S. and Calland, R., University of Natal Press, Durban, p. 206.
113. Interview with Michael Spicer, October 11, 2010.

114. Interview with Neil van Heerden, June 24, 2010.
115. Interview with Neil van Heerden, June 24, 2010.
116. Interview with Neil van Heerden, June 24, 2010.
117. Gumede, W., 2009, 'Delivering the Democratic Developmental State in South Africa', in *The Politics of Service Delivery*, edited by McLennan, A. and Munslow, B., Wits University Press, Johannesburg, p. 96.
118. Handley, *Business*, p. 88.
119. Interview with Michael Spicer, October 11, 2010.
120. Interview with Michael Spicer, October 11, 2010.
121. Interview with Vincent Maphai, June 1, 2011.
122. Quoted in Gevisser, *Mbeki*, pp. 688–689.
123. Ibid.
124. Interview with Reuel Khoza, October 25, 2010.
125. Interview with Essop Pahad, May 27, 2010.
126. Interview with Essop Pahad, May 27, 2010.
127. Interview with Smuts Ngonyama, March 2, 2010.
128. Handley, *Business*, p. 89.
129. Sidiropoulos and Hughes, 'The Challenge of South Africa's Africa Policy', p. 79.
130. Bond, P., 2006, *Talk Left, Walk Right: South Africa's Frustrated Global Reforms*, UKZN Press, Scottsville, p. 267.
131. McKinley, 'South African Foreign Policy Towards Zimbabwe', p. 359.
132. Khoza, *Let Africa Lead*, p. 141.
133. Ibid., p. 143.
134. Hughes, *Composers*, pp. 39–40.
135. Interview with Neil van Heerden, June 24, 2010.
136. Interview with Sam Motsuenyane, May 29, 2010.
137. Interview with Reuel Khoza, October 25, 2010.
138. Interview with Aziz Pahad, January 28, 2011.
139. Hughes, *Composers*, p. 38.
140. Interview with Michael Spicer, October 11, 2010.
141. Interview with Hermann Giliomee, February 24, 2010.

Chapter 7   Parliament

1. Norton, P., 2005, *Parliament in British Politics*, Palgrave Macmillan, London.
2. Frankel, *The Making of Foreign Policy*, pp. 16–17.
3. Hill, *The Changing Politics of Foreign Policy*, p. 254.
4. Frankel, *The Making of Foreign Policy*, p. 25.
5. Ibid.
6. Beloff, M., 1955, *Foreign Policy and the Democratic Process*, Johns Hopkins Press, Baltimore, p. 20.

7. South Africa Act of 1909, Section 17.
8. Cloete, J., 1985, *Parliaments of South Africa*, JL van Struik, Cape Town, p. 12.
9. Pienaar, *South Africa and International Relations*, p. 2.
10. Vandenbosch, *South Africa and the World*, p. 100.
11. Hancock, WK, 1968, *Smuts: The Fields of Force, 1919–1950*, Cambridge Press, Cambridge, p. 322.
12. Cloete, Parliaments, p. 45.
13. Ibid., p. 86.
14. Interview with Boy Geldenhuys, September 6, 2010.
15. Geldenhuys, *Diplomacy*, p. 9.
16. Interview with Japie Basson, June 15, 2010.
17. Interview with Colin Eglin, March 23, 2011.
18. Geldenhuys, *Diplomacy*, p. 10.
19. Calland, R., 1997, 'All Dressed Up with Nowhere to Go? The Rapid Transformation of the South African Parliamentary Committee System', UCT School of Government, Cape Town, p. 6.
20. Interview with Boy Geldenhuys, September 6, 2010.
21. Interview with Pik Botha, February 1, 2010.
22. Geldenhuys, *Diplomacy*, p. 50.
23. Seegers, *The Military in the Making of Modern South Africa*, pp. 228–9.
24. Slabbert, F., 1986, *The Last White Parliament*, Jonathan Ball, Johannesburg, p. 41.
25. Geldenhuys, *Diplomacy*, p. 60.
26. Interview with Renier Schoeman, November 2, 2010.
27. Geldenhuys, *Diplomacy*, p. 61.
28. Interview with Andre Fourie, August 16, 2010.
29. Interview with Andre Fourie, August 16, 2010.
30. Rotberg, R., 1988, 'The Process of Decision Making in Contemporary South Africa', in *South Africa in Transition: To What?*, edited by Kitchen, H., Center for Strategic and International Studies, Washington DC, p. 28.
31. O'Meara, *Forty Lost Years*, pp. 48–9.
32. Interview with Johan Steenkamp, May 18, 2010.
33. Kotze, H., 1997, 'Take Us to Our Leaders: The South African National Assembly and its Members', Konrad Adenauer Stiftung Occasional Paper, p. 2.
34. Interview with Dawie de Villiers, November 1, 2010.
35. Interview with Japie Basson, June 15, 2010.
36. Geldenhuys, 'The Head of Government', p. 263.
37. Interview with Johan Steenkamp, May 18, 2010.
38. Interview with Dawie de Villiers, November 1, 2010.
39. Barber and Barratt, *South Africa's Foreign Policy*, pp. 60–1.
40. Cockram, G., 1970, *Vorster's Foreign Policy*, Academica, Cape Town, p. 16.
41. Good, *UDI*, p. 22.
42. Cockram, *Vorster's Foreign* Policy, p. 178.

43. Graaff, D., 1993, *Div Looks Back: The Memoirs of De Villiers Graaff*, Human and Rousseau, Cape Town, p. 242.

44. Eglin, *Crossing*, p. 183.

45. Pottinger, *The Imperial Presidency*, p. 30.

46. Suzman, H., 1993, *In No Uncertain Terms*, Jonathan Ball Press, Johannesburg, p. 264.

47. Meiring, *Inside Information*, p. 134.

48. Sole, D., 1991, *'This Above All': Reminiscences of a South African Diplomat*, unpublished, p. 309.

49. Interview with Renier Schoeman, November 2, 2010.

50. Ahmed, A., 2009, 'The Role of Parliament in South Africa's Foreign Policy Development Process: Lessons from the United States' Congress', *South African Journal of International Affairs*, Vol. 16, No. 3, p. 292.

51. De Villiers, B., 1995, *Foreign Relations and the Provinces*, HSRC Press, Pretoria, pp. 171–2.

52. Ahmed, 'The Role of Parliament', p. 292.

53. Constitution of South Africa, 1996, Section 231.

54. Barkan, 'Emerging Legislature or Rubber Stamp?', p. 9.

55. Hughes, T., 2001, 'The Parliamentary Committee on Foreign Affairs', *South African Yearbook of International Affairs 2001/02*, South African Institute of International Affairs, Johannesburg, p. 98.

56. Nel, P.; van Wyk, J.; and Johnsen, K., 2004, 'Democracy, Participation, and Foreign Policy Making in South Africa', in *Democratizing Foreign Policy? Lessons from South Africa*, edited by Nel, P. and Van der Westhuizen, J., Lexington Books, Lanham, pp. 45–6.

57. Shubin, 'Flinging the Doors Open', p. 10.

58. Interview with Raymond Suttner (email), July 9, 2010.

59. Daniel, J., 1995, 'One China or Two? South Africa's Foreign Policy Dilemma', *Transformation*, Vol. 27, pp. 48–9.

60. Banjo, 'Parliament-Foreign Policy Nexus', p. 63.

61. Interview with Raymond Suttner (email), July 9, 2010.

62. Van der Westhuizen, 'South Africa's Emergence', p. 446.

63. Interview with Raymond Suttner (email), July 9, 2010.

64. Van Nieuwkerk, 'South Africa's Post-Apartheid Foreign Policy Decision-Making', p. 153.

65. Interview with Raymond Suttner (email), July 9, 2010.

66. Williams, P., 2006, 'Pragmatic Multilateralism? South Africa and Peace Operations', in *The New Multilateralism in South African Diplomacy*, edited by Lee, D.; Taylor, I.; and Williams, P., Palgrave Macmillan, New York, p. 192.

67. Mills, *The Wired Model*, pp. 275–6.

68. Van Wyk, J., 1997, 'Parliament and Foreign Affairs: Continuity or Change?', *South African Yearbook of International Affairs 1997*, South African Institute of International Affairs, Johannesburg, p. 194.

69. Nel, van Wyk, and Johnsen, 'Democracy', p. 48.
70. Van Wyk, J., 1998, 'Parliament and the Foreign Policy Process', *South African Yearbook of International Affairs 1998/99*, South African Institute of International Affairs, Johannesburg, p. 293.
71. Schraeder, P., 2001, 'South Africa's Foreign Policy: From International Pariah to Leader of the African Renaissance', *Round Table*, No. 359, p. 237.
72. Interview with Raymond Suttner (email), July 9, 2010.
73. Interview with Raymond Suttner (email), July 9, 2010.
74. Raymond Suttner, 1996, 'A Brief Review of South African Foreign Policy Since 1994', *Umrabulo*, Issue 1, Fall.
75. Mills, *The Wired Model*, pp. 275–6.
76. Interview with Raymond Suttner (email), July 9, 2010.
77. Nel, van Wyk, and Johnsen, 'Democracy', p. 46.
78. Interview with Aziz Pahad, January 28, 2011.
79. Interview with Aziz Pahad, January 28, 2011.
80. Feinstein, *After the Party*, p. 123.
81. Ibid.
82. Interview with Ben Turok, September 30, 2010.
83. Booysen, S., 2001, 'Transitions and Trends in Policy Making in Democratic South Africa', *Journal of Public Administration*, Vol. 36, No. 2, p. 134.
84. Interview with Albertina Luthuli, November 1, 2010.
85. Barkan, 'Emerging Legislature or Rubber Stamp?', p. 8.
86. Interview with Albertina Luthuli, November 1, 2010.
87. Interview with Mtikeni Sibande, September 1, 2010.
88. Interview with Albertina Luthuli, November 1, 2010.
89. Nel, van Wyk, and Johnsen, 'Democracy', p. 42.
90. Barkan, 'Emerging Legislature or Rubber Stamp?', p. 7.
91. Gevisser, *Mbeki*, p. 715.
92. Interview with Tim Hughes, July 7, 2010.
93. Interview with Albertina Luthuli, November 1, 2010.
94. Interview with Job Sithole, May 24, 2010.
95. Hughes, 'Parliamentary Committee', p. 99.
96. Interview with Tim Hughes, July 7, 2010.
97. Interview with Tim Hughes, July 7, 2010.
98. Interview with Raymond Suttner (email), July 9, 2010.
99. Ahmed, 'The Role of Parliament', p. 297.
100. Le Pere, G. and van Nieuwkerk, A., 2004, 'Who Made and Makes Foreign Policy', in *Apartheid Past, Renaissance Future: South Africa's Foreign Policy 1994–2004*, edited by Sidiropoulos, E., South African Institute of International Affairs, Johannesburg, p. 125.
101. Interview with Job Sithole, May 24, 2010.
102. Hughes, *Composers*, p. 30.
103. Interview with Pallo Jordan, June 25, 2010.
104. Interview with Tim Hughes, February 7, 2010.

105. Interview with Mewa Ramgobin, November 10, 2010.
106. Interview with Albertina Luthuli, November 1, 2010.
107. Interview with Aziz Pahad, January 28, 2011.
108. Interview with Albertina Luthuli, November 1, 2010.
109. Banjo, 'Parliament-Foreign Policy Nexus', p. 63, pp. 66–7.
110. Interview with Fatima Hajaig, September 21, 2010.
111. Interview with Job Sithole, May 24, 2010.
112. Ahmed, 'The Role of Parliament', p. 305.
113. Ibid., p. 302.
114. Interview with Fatima Hajaig, September 21, 2010.
115. Interview with Mewa Ramgobin, November 10, 2010.
116. Klotz, A., 2006, 'State Identity in South African Foreign Policy', in *In Full Flight: South African Foreign Policy After Apartheid*, edited by Carlsnaes, W. and Nel, P., Institute for Global Dialogue, Midrand, p. 78.
117. Gumede, *Thabo Mbeki*, p. 140.
118. Interview with Pallo Jordan, June 25, 2010.
119. Interview with Job Sithole, May 24, 2010.
120. Interview with Job Sithole, May 24, 2010.
121. Van Wyk, 'Parliament and the Foreign Policy Process', p. 297.

* Although from 1961 to 1983 the office of state president was ceremonial and separate from that of the prime minister, the latter office holder was the true decision maker and such powers were, de facto, invested in him.

† There was no committee that dealt with intelligence, which was an area considered off-limits to parliament. 'There was no liaison between NIS and parliament,' remembers Niel Barnard, who claimed that parliament 'was not important for us.' He adds, 'Because intelligence was a national matter, a party political fight would not be made of it. There was an understanding it was not for public debate.'

Chapter 8 Ruling Parties

1. Basson, J., 2008, *State of the Nation: As Viewed from the Front Bench in Parliament 1969–1981*, Politika, Camps Bay, p. 107.
2. O'Meara, *Forty Lost Years*, pp. 48–9.
3. Interview with Con Botha, June 9, 2010.
4. Interview with Renier Schoeman, November 2, 2010.
5. Interview with Dawie de Villiers, November 1, 2010.
6. Interview with Niel Barnard, July 14, 2010.
7. Meli, *South Africa Belongs to Us*, p. 151.
8. Ndebele, N. and Nieftagodien, N., 2005, 'The Morogoro Conference: A Moment of Self-Reflection', in *The Road to Democracy in South Africa, Volume 1*, South African Democracy Education Trust, Johannesburg, p. 587.

9. Ellis and Sechaba, *Comrades Against Apartheid*, p. 55.
10. Lodge, T., 1983, *Black Politics in South Africa Since 1945*, Longman, New York, p. 300.
11. Ellis and Sechaba, *Comrades Against Apartheid*, p. 61.
12. Interview with Ben Turok, September 30, 2010.
13. Mangcu, X., 2009, *The Democratic Moment: South Africa's Prospects Under Jacob Zuma*, Jacana Press, Johannesburg, p. 44.
14. Interview with Pallo Jordan, June 25, 2010.
15. Interview with Aziz Pahad, January 28, 2011.
16. Callinicos, *Oliver Tambo*, p. 450.
17. Interview with Pallo Jordan, June 25, 2010.
18. Interview with Sipho Pityana, May 25, 2010.
19. Interview with Ben Turok, September 30, 2010.
20. Thomas, *Diplomacy*, p. XXI.
21. Macmillan, 'The ANC in Zambia', p. 317.
22. Callinicos, *Oliver Tambo*, pp. 519–20.
23. Interview with Pallo Jordan, June 25, 2010.
24. Interview with Pallo Jordan, June 25, 2010.
25. Interview with Essop Pahad, May 27, 2010.
26. Scholtz, L., 2008, 'The ANC/SACP and the Crushing of the 1968 Prague Spring', *Die Burger*, August 22.
27. Interview with Pallo Jordan, June 25, 2010.
28. Interview with Pallo Jordan, June 25, 2010.
29. Asmal, K. and Hadland, A., 2011, *Politics in My Blood: A Memoir*, Jacana, Johannesburg, pp. 65–7.
30. Interview with Pallo Jordan, June 25, 2010.
31. Interview with Pallo Jordan, June 25, 2010.
32. 'Decisions and Suggestions From NEC/PMC Meeting', January 25, 1984, in Gerhart, G. and Glaser, C., 2010, *From Protest to Challenge: A Documentary History of African Politics in South Africa, Volume 6: Challenge and Victory, 1980–1990*, Indiana University Press, Bloomington, p. 536.
33. Ndebele and Nieftagodien, 'The Morogoro Conference', p. 592.
34. 'Second National Consultative Conference: Report of the Commission on Foreign Policy', June 1985.
35. Email from Pallo Jordan, April 7, 2011.
36. Pfister, 'Gateway', p. 56.
37. Lodge, 'State of Exile', p. 5.
38. Email from Pallo Jordan, April 7, 2011.
39. Interview with Aziz Pahad, January 28, 2011.
40. 'State of Organization', January 17, 1989, in ANC Mayibuye Archives, University of the Western Cape.
41. 'Proposed Meeting Between Representatives of the Zambian Government and ANC Leadership', memorandum dated October 21, 1988, in ANC Mayibuye Archives, University of the Western Cape.

42. Pfister, 'Gateway', p. 58.
43. Ndlovu, S., 2005, 'The ANC's Diplomacy and International Relations', in *The Road to Democracy in South Africa, Volume 1*, South African Democracy Education Trust, Johannesburg, p. 634.
44. Email from Pallo Jordan, April 7, 2011.
45. Gevisser, *Mbeki*, p. 385.
46. Gumede, *Thabo Mbeki*, p. 38.
47. Interview with Aziz Pahad, January 28, 2011.
48. Interview with Essop Pahad, May 27, 2010.
49. Interview with Essop Pahad, May 27, 2010.
50. Lyman, *Partner to History*, p. 53.
51. Landsberg, *Quiet Diplomacy*, p. 47.
52. Sampson, A., 2009, *The Anatomist: The Autobiography of Anthony Sampson*, Jonathan Ball, Johannesburg, p. 224.
53. Gevisser, *Mbeki*, p. 402.
54. African National Congress Constitution, 2007, Rule 10, www.anc.org.za.
55. African National Congress Constitution, 2007, Rule 16.1, www.anc.org.za.
56. African National Congress Constitution, 2007, Rule 12, www.anc.org.za.
57. Booysen, 'Transitions and Trends', p. 133.
58. Interview with Mavivi Myakayaka-Manzini, November 19, 2010.
59. Booysen, 'Transitions and Trends', p. 133.
60. Butler, A., 2005, 'How Democratic Is the African National Congress?', *Journal of Southern African Studies*, Vol. 31, No. 4, p. 729.
61. Sidiropoulos, 'Post-Mbeki', pp. 7–8.
62. Interview with Mosiuoa Lekota, March 25, 2011.
63. Hughes, *Composers*, p. 30.
64. Paruk, *The Transitional Executive Council*, p. 30.
65. Interview with Aziz Pahad, January 28, 2011.
66. Hughes, *Composers*, p. 25.
67. Interview with Mavivi Myakayaka-Manzini, November 19, 2010.
68. Interview with Mavivi Myakayaka-Manzini, November 19, 2010.
69. Interview with Pallo Jordan, June 25, 2010.
70. Interview with Mavivi Myakayaka-Manzini, November 19, 2010.
71. Hughes, *Composers*, p. 29.
72. Interview with Raymond Suttner (email), July 9, 2010.
73. Interview with Mosiuoa Lekota, March 25, 2011.
74. Interview with Fatima Hajaig, September 21, 2010.
75. Interview with Pallo Jordan, June 25, 2010.
76. Interview with Mosiuoa Lekota, March 25, 2011.
77. Interview with Mosiuoa Lekota, March 25, 2011.
78. Interview with Job Sithole, May 24, 2010.
79. Interview with Essop Pahad, May 27, 2010.
80. Interview with Job Sithole, May 24, 2010.
81. Interview with Mavivi Myakayaka-Manzini, November 19, 2010.

82. Interview with Job Sithole, May 24, 2010.
83. Interview with Mewa Ramgobin, November 10, 2010.
84. Gumede, *Thabo Mbeki*, p. 135.
85. Ibid.
86. Interview with Essop Pahad, May 27, 2010.
87. Interview with Mavivi Myakayaka-Manzini, November 19, 2010.
88. Interview with Pallo Jordan, June 25, 2010.
89. Interview with Renier Schoeman, November 2, 2010.
90. Interview with Job Sithole, May 24, 2010.
91. Interview with Mluleki George, October 28, 2010.
92. Herbst, J., 2005, 'Mbeki's South Africa', *Foreign Affairs*, Vol. 84, No. 6, p. 96.

Chapter 9   Government Departments

1. Allison, G. and Zelikow, P., 1999, *Essence of Decision: Explaining the Cuban Missile Crisis*, Longman, London, p. 143.
2. Pienaar, *South Africa and International Relations*, p. 8.
3. Grundy, *Militarization*, p. 8.
4. Van Wyk, A., 2005, 'Eric Louw: Pioneer Diplomat, 1925–37', in *History of the South African Department of Foreign Affairs 1927–1993*, edited by Wheeler, T., South African Institute of International Affairs, Johannesburg, p. 27.
5. Nothling, F., 2005, 'A Department in its Own Right, 1955–1966', in *History of the South African Department of Foreign Affairs 1927–1993*, edited by Wheeler, T., South African Institute of International Affairs, Johannesburg, p. 522.
6. Sole, D., 1994, 'South African Foreign Policy from Hertzog to De Klerk', *South African Journal of International Affairs*, Vol. 2, No. 1, p. 108.
7. Boulter, R., 1997, 'FC Erasmus and the Politics of South African Defense, 1948–1959', unpublished doctoral dissertation, Rhodes University, Grahamstown, p. 17.
8. Ibid., p. 109.
9. Seegers, *The Military in the Making of Modern South Africa*, p. 110.
10. Du Plessis, A., 1997, 'The Geopolitical Context: A Sea Change from Old to New Geopolitics', in *Change and South African Foreign Relations*, edited by Carlsnaes, W. and Muller, M., International Thomson Publishing, Johannesburg, p. 20.
11. Boulter, 'FC Erasmus', p. 84.
12. Pfister, *Apartheid South Africa*, p. 34.
13. Munger, *Notes*, p. 46.
14. Geldenhuys, *Diplomacy*, p. 23.
15. Sole, 'This Above All', p. 230.
16. *From Verwoerd to Mandela, Volume 2*, p. 26.

17. Sole, 'This Above All', p. 261.
18. Sole, 'Hertzog to de Klerk', p. 108.
19. Interview with Albert van Niekerk, July 5, 2010.
20. O'Meara, *Forty Lost Years*, p. 213.
21. Horwitz, *Communication*, p. 73.
22. Meiring, *Inside Information*, p. 137.
23. Barber and Barratt, p. 114.
24. Interview with Frikkie Botha, May 18, 2010.
25. Interview with Frikkie Botha, May 18, 2010.
26. O'Brien, *The South African Intelligence Services*, p. 13.
27. Sole, 'This Above All', p. 251.
28. Winter, G., 1981, *Inside BOSS: South Africa's Secret Police*, Penguin, London, p. 42.
29. International Defense and Aid Fund, 1975, 'BOSS: The First Five Years', London, p. 10.
30. O'Brien, *The South African Intelligence Services*, p. 25.
31. Rotberg, 'The Process of Decision Making', p. 14.
32. D'Olivera, J., 1977, *Vorster the Man*, Ernest Stanton Publishers, Johannesburg, pp. 241–2.
33. Sanders, *Apartheid's Friends*, p. 42.
34. Sole, 'This Above All', p. 262.
35. Boulter, 'FC Erasmus', p. 89.
36. O'Meara, *Forty Lost Years*, pp. 227–228.
37. Price, R., 1991, *The Apartheid State in Crisis: Political Transformation in South Africa 1975–1990*, Oxford University Press, Oxford, p. 43.
38. Geldenhuys, *Diplomacy*, p. 80.
39. Roherty, J., 1992, *State Security in South Africa: Civil-Military Relations Under PW Botha*, ME Sharpe, London, p. 73.
40. O'Meara, *Forty Lost Years*, p. 219.
41. Interview with Pik Botha, May 20, 1997, George Washington University Security Studies Archive.
42. Interview with Pik Botha, February 1, 2010.
43. Malan, M., 2006, *My Life with the South African Defense Force*, Protea Books, Pretoria, p. 173.
44. Grundy, *Militarization*, p. 36.
45. Batchelor, P., Dunne, P., and Lamb, G., 2002, 'The Demand for Military Spending in South Africa', *Journal of Peace Research*, Vol. 39, No. 3, p. 342.
46. Rees, M. and Day, C., 1980, *Muldergate: The Story of the Info Scandal*, Macmillan, Johannesburg, p. 67.
47. Interview with Herbert Beukes, June 16, 2010.
48. Interview with Gerrit Olivier, January 20, 2010.
49. Papenfus, *Pik Botha*, p. 431.
50. Interview with Louis Nel, October 11, 2010.
51. *From Verwoerd to Mandela, Volume 3*, p. 358.

52. Davies, 'The SADF's Covert War', p. 110.
53. Rotberg, 'The Process of Decision Making', p. 27.
54. Interview with Gerrit Olivier, January 20, 2010.
55. Griffiths, 'The South African Military', p. 86.
56. Interview with Pik Botha, February 1, 2010.
57. Interview with Denis Worrall, January 18, 2011.
58. *From Verwoerd to Mandela, Volume 3*, p. 338.
59. Interview with Jeremy Shearer, July 21, 2010.
60. Interview with Pik Botha, February 1, 2010.
61. Papenfus, *Pik Botha*, p. 789.
62. Interview with Dave Steward, June 4, 2010.
63. Leonard, *South Africa at War*, p. 15.
64. McCarthy, S., 1996, 'Challenges for the South African Intelligence Community', in *South Africa's Defense and Security Into the 21 st Century*, edited by Gutteridge, W., Dartmouth, Hanover, p. 65.
65. Weir, A. and Bloch, J., 1981, 'The Militarization of BOSS', *Covert Action*, No. 13, p. 32.
66. Interview with Tienie Groenewald, May 28, 2010.
67. Interview with Niel Barnard, July 14, 2010.
68. McCarthy, 'Challenges', p. 66.
69. Interview with Niel Barnard, July 14, 2010.
70. Pfister, *Apartheid South Africa*, p. 19.
71. Gevisser, *Mbeki*, p. 491.
72. Potgeiter, D., 2007, *Total Onslaught: Apartheid's Dirty Secrets Exposed*, Struik, Cape Town, p. 136.
73. Interview with Niel Barnard, July 14, 2010.
74. Interview with Jannie Roux, May 28, 2010.
75. Interview with Tienie Groenewald, May 28, 2010.
76. Potgeiter, *Total Onslaught*, p. 95.
77. Interview with Niel Barnard, July 14, 2010.
78. Seegers, *The Military in the Making of Modern South Africa*, p. 132.
79. Pottinger, *The Imperial Presidency*, pp. 42–43.
80. Geldenhuys, D. and Kotze, H., 1983, 'Aspects of Political Decision-making in South Africa', *Politikon*, Vol. 10, No. 1, p. 39.
81. Davies and O'Meara, 'Total Strategy', p. 193.
82. Selfe, J., 1989 'South Africa's National Management System', in *War and Society: The Militarization of South Africa*, edited by Cock, J. and Nathan, L., David Phillip Press, Cape Town, p. 152.
83. Interview with Pik Botha, February 1, 2010.
84. Interview with Niel Barnard, July 14, 2010.
85. Interview with Jannie Roux, May 28, 2010.
86. O'Meara, *Forty Lost Years*, p. 282.
87. Interview with Kent Durr, June 11, 2010.
88. Welsh, *The Rise and Fall of Apartheid*, p. 476.

89. De Klerk, F., 1998, *FW de Klerk, The Last Trek-A New Beginning*, MacMillan, New York, p. 273.
90. Interview with Dave Steward, June 4, 2010.
91. *From Verwoerd to Mandela: Volume 3*, p. 291.
92. De Klerk, *The Last Trek*, p. 122.
93. Batchelor, Dunne, and Lamb, 'The Demand for Military Spending', p. 343.
94. De Klerk, *The Last Trek*, p. 119.
95. Landsberg, C., 2010, 'South African Foreign Policy Formulation, 1989–2010', unpublished, p. 10.
96. Seegers, *The Military in the Making of Modern South Africa*, pp. 266–7.
97. De Klerk, *The Last Trek*, pp. 117–8.
98. Interview with Niel Barnard, July 14, 2010.
99. Landsberg, *Quiet Diplomacy*, pp. 61–2.
100. Mills, G., 1999, 'South African Foreign Policy: From Isolation to Respectability', in *South Africa in Southern Africa: Reconfiguring the Region*, edited by Simon, D., Ohio University Press, Athens, p. 78.
101. Nzo, 'Foreign Minister's Budget Vote Address', p. 225.
102. Asmal and Hadland, *Politics in My Blood*, p. 206.
103. Fabricius, P., 1999, 'Virtuosity Versus Bureaucracy', *South African Yearbook of International Affairs 1999/2000*, South African Institute of International Affairs, Johannesburg, p. 220.
104. Landsberg, 'In Search of Global Influence', p. 6.
105. Muller, 'South African Diplomacy', p. 605.
106. Sampson, *Mandela*, pp. 547–8.
107. Interview with Tom Wheeler, January 29, 2010.
108. Muller, M., 2000, 'Some Observations on South Africa's Economic Diplomacy and the Role of DFA', Institute for Global Dialogue Occasional Paper 27, p. 4.
109. Van Nieuwkerk, A., 2006, 'Foreign Policy Making in South Africa: Context, Actors, and Process', in *In Full Flight: South African Foreign Policy After Apartheid*, edited by Carlsnaes, W. and Nel, P., Institute for Global Dialogue, Midrand, p. 40.
110. Mills, *The Wired Model*, pp. 286–7.
111. Hughes, *Composers*, pp. 15–16.
112. Butler, 'How Democratic Is the African National Congress?', p. 722.
113. Booysen, 'Transitions and Trends', p. 133.
114. Chikane, F., 2000, 'Democratic Governance—a Restructured Presidency at Work', The Presidency.
115. Interview with Pallo Jordan, June 25, 2010.
116. Interview with Aziz Pahad, January 28, 2011.
117. Interview with Sydney Mufamadi, October 15, 2010.
118. De Jager, N., 2006, 'The South African Government and the Application of Cooptive Power', *Politikon*, Vol. 33, No. 1, p. 105.
119. Hughes, *Composers*, p. 17.

120. Nel, P. and van Wyk, J., 2003, 'Foreign Policy Making in South Africa: From Public Participation to Democratic Participation', *Politeia*, Vol. 22, No. 3, p. 62.
121. Interview with Aziz Pahad, January 28, 2011.
122. Calland, *Anatomy*, pp. 38–40.
123. Van Nieuwkerk, 'South Africa's Post-Apartheid Foreign Policy Decision-making', p. 150.
124. Author's private archive.
125. Author's private archive.
126. Mills, *The Wired Model*, p. 355.
127. Interview with Aziz Pahad, January 28, 2011.
128. Author's private archive.
129. Stober, P. and Ludman, B., 2005, *Mail and Guardian A-Z of South African Politics*, Jacana, Johannesburg, p. 114.
130. Interview with Sipho Pityana, May 25, 2010.
131. Hughes, *Composers*, p. 68.
132. Draper, P., 2005, 'Consultation Dilemmas: Transparency Versus Effectiveness in South Africa's Trade Policy', in *Reconfiguring the Compass: South Africa's African Trade Diplomacy*, edited by Draper, P., South African Institute of International Affairs, Johannesburg, p. 97.
133. Interview with Aziz Pahad, January 28, 2011.
134. Interview with Mills Soko, March 1, 2010.
135. Bertelsmann-Scott, T., 2004, 'The Democratization of Trade Policy', in *Democratizing Foreign Policy? Lessons from South Africa*, edited by Nel, P. and Van der Westhuizen, J., Lexington Books, Lanham, p. 126.
136. Gutteridge, W., 1996, 'The Transformation of the South African Military', in *South Africa's Defense and Security Into the 21st Century*, edited by Gutteridge, W., Dartmouth Press, Hanover, p. 9.
137. Barber, *Mandela's World*, p. 99.
138. Le Roux, L., 2003, 'The South African National Defense Force and its Involvement in the Defense Review Process', in *Ourselves to Know: Civil-Military Relations and Defense Transformation in Southern Africa*, edited by Williams, R.; Cawthra, G.; and Abrahams, D., Institute for Security Studies, Pretoria, p. 155.
139. Williams, R., 2003, 'Defense in a Democracy: The South African Defense Review and the Redefinition of the Parameters of the National Defense Debate', in *Ourselves to Know: Civil-Military Relations and Defense Transformation in Southern Africa*, edited by Williams, R.; Cawthra, G.; and Abrahams, D., Institute for Security Studies, Pretoria, p. 217.
140. Le Roux, 'SANDF', p. 165.
141. Neethling, T., 2004, 'The Defense Force and Peacekeeping: Linking Policy and Capability', in *Apartheid Past, Renaissance Future: South Africa's Foreign Policy 1994–2004*, edited by Sidiropoulos, E., South African Institute of International Affairs, Johannesburg, p. 145.

142. Interview with Henri Boshoff, January 25, 2010.
143. Author's private archive.
144. Author's private archive.
145. Author's private archive.
146. Green, P., 2008, *Choice Not Fate: The Life and Times of Trevor Manuel*, Penguin, New York, p. 473.
147. Interview with Mluleki George, October 28, 2010.
148. Interview with Mosiuoa Lekota, March 25, 2010.
149. Asmal and Hadland, *Politics in My Blood*, p. 206.
150. De Villiers, *Foreign Relations and the Provinces*, p. 154.
151. Van Wyk, J., 1998, 'The External Relations of Selected South African Subnational Governments', *South African Journal of International Affairs*, Vol. 5, No. 2, p. 37.
152. White, G., 1996, 'Grassroots Foreign Policy? A Case for Provincial Participation', *Indicator South Africa*, Vol. 13, No. 4, p. 26.

* The influence of the Ministry of Intelligence (established in 1999) nor its ministers—Joe Nhlanhla (1999–2002), Lindiwe Sisulu (2002–4) and Ronnie Kasrils (2004–8)—on Mbeki is not entirely clear, with interviewees lacking insight on the issue. Although few interviewees viewed those ministers as part of Mbeki's foreign policy 'inner circle,' even cabinet members acknowledged that they were not privy to most of those interactions. 'I'm sure Ronnie had more conversations with Thabo than any of us realize,' said one minister.

Chapter 10   The Prime Minister and President

1. Constitution of South Africa, 1961, Section 7.
2. Constitution of South Africa, 1983, Section 6.
3. Constitution of South Africa, 1996, Sections 84 and 231.
4. Hancock, WK, 1962, *Smuts: The Sanguine Years 1870–1919*, Cambridge University Press, Cambridge, p. 438.
5. Pienaar, *South Africa and International Relations*, p. 9.
6. Hancock, *The Fields of Force*, p. 267.
7. Spence, *Republic Under Pressure*, pp. 1–2.
8. Crafford, F., 1945, *Jan Smuts: A Biography*, Howard Timmins Press, Cape Town, p. 187.
9. Malherbe, E., 1981, *Never a Dull Moment,* Howard Timmins Press, Cape Town, p. 280.
10. Sole, 'Hertzog to de Klerk', p. 106.
11. Sole, *'This Above All'*, p. 67.
12. Curry G., 1961, 'Woodrow Wilson, Jan Smuts, and the Versailles Settlement', *The American Historical Review*, Vol. 66, No. 4, July 1961, pp. 968–70.

13. Van Wyk, A., 2005, 'The High Commissioner in Great Britain', in *History of the South African Department of Foreign Affairs 1927–1993*, edited by Wheeler, T., South African Institute of International Affairs, Johannesburg, p. 54.

14. Geldenhuys, *Diplomacy*, p. 9.

15. Neame, L., 1929, *Some South African Politicians*, Maskew Miller Limited, Cape Town, p. 9.

16. Muller, CFJ, 2005, 'The Creation of the Department of External Affairs', in *History of the South African Department of Foreign Affairs 1927–1993*, edited by Wheeler, T., South African Institute of International Affairs, Johannesburg, p. 7.

17. Barber and Barratt, *South Africa's Foreign Policy*, p. 15.

18. Interview with Donald Sole, May 22, 2010.

19. Interview with Donald Sole, May 22, 2010.

20. Geldenhuys, 'The Head of Government', p. 255.

21. Nel, *A Soviet Embassy in Pretoria?*, p. 2.

22. Adams, *The Unnatural Alliance*, p. 5.

23. Interview with Donald Sole, May 22, 2010.

24. Sole, *'This Above All'*, p. 143.

25. Sole, 'South African Foreign Policy', pp. 106–7.

26. Geldenhuys, 'The Head of Government', p. 255.

27. Munger, E., 1979, 'Foreward', *The Afrikaners*, edited by Edwin Munger, Tafelberg, Cape Town, p. 5.

28. Geldenhuys, *Diplomacy*, p. 21.

29. Sole, 'South African Foreign Policy', p. 108.

30. Interview with Donald Sole, May 22, 2010.

31. Barber and Barratt, *South Africa's Foreign Policy*, p. 29.

32. Dommisse, *Anton Rupert*, p. 41.

33. Adam and Giliomee, *Ethnic Power Mobilized*, p. 202.

34. O'Meara, *Forty Lost Years*, p. 112.

35. Stultz, 'The Politics of Security', p. 15.

36. Graaff, *Div Looks Back*, p. 186.

37. Barnard, F., 1967, *13 Years with Dr. HF Verwoerd*, Voortrekkerpers, Johannesburg, p. 18.

38. Hepple, *Verwoerd*, p. 110.

39. Sole, 'South African Foreign Policy', p. 109.

40. Interview with Pik Botha, February 1, 2010.

41. Interview with Tom Wheeler, January 29, 2010.

42. Geldenhuys, 'The Head of Government', p. 263.

43. Munger, *Notes*, p. 85.

44. Interview with Donald Sole, May 22, 2010.

45. Sole, 'South African Foreign Policy', p. 109.

46. Botha, *Verwoerd is Dead*, p. 49.

47. *From Verwoerd to Mandela, Volume 1*, p. 102.

48. Giliomee, H., 1983, 'BJ Vorster and the Sultan's Horse', Best of Frontline, p. 3.

49. D'Olivera, *Vorster the Man*, pp. 265–6.
50. Rotberg, 'The Process of Decision Making', p. 12.
51. O'Meara, *Forty Lost Years*, p. 206.
52. Munger, 'Foreward', p. 5.
53. Giliomee, 'Vorster', p. 3.
54. Barber and Barratt, *South Africa's Foreign Policy*, p. 113.
55. Interview with Pik Botha, February 1, 2010.
56. Grundy, *Militarization*, p. 88.
57. De Villiers, L., 1980, *Secret Information*, Tafelberg, Cape Town, p. 74.
58. Eglin, *Crossing*, p. 171.
59. Grundy, *Militarization*, pp. 34–5.
60. De Klerk, *The Last Trek*, pp. 66–7.
61. Interview with Dawie de Villiers, November 1, 2010.
62. De Klerk, *The Last Trek*, p. 67.
63. Interview with Jannie Roux, May 28, 2010.
64. Hamann, H., 2001, *Days of the Generals,* Zebra Press, Cape Town, p. 54.
65. Giliomee, H., 2008, 'The Rubicon Revisited', Politicsweb, August 20.
66. Interview with Tienie Groenewald, May 28, 2010.
67. Pottinger, *The Imperial Presidency*, p. 354.
68. Sole, *'This Above All'*, p. 483.
69. Interview with Pik Botha, February 1, 2010.
70. Schrire, R., 1994, 'The Head of Government and the Executive', in *Leadership in the Apartheid State: From Malan to De Klerk*, edited by Schrire, R., Oxford University Press, Oxford, p. 60.
71. Interview with Jannie Roux, May 28, 2010.
72. Interview with Jannie Roux, May 28, 2010.
73. Crocker, C., 1992, *High Noon in Southern Africa: Making Peace in a Rough Neighborhood*, Jonathan Ball, Johannesburg, p. 316.
74. Giliomee, 'The Rubicon Revisited'.
75. Interview with Niel Barnard, July 14, 2010.
76. Interview with Niel Barnard, July 14, 2010.
77. Barber, *Mandela's World*, p. 41.
78. De Klerk, W., 1991, *FW de Klerk: The Man in his Time*, Jonathan Ball, Johannesburg, p. 74.
79. Geldenhuys, D. and Kotze, H., 1991, 'FW de Klerk: A Study in Political Leadership', *Politikon*, Vol. 19, No. 1, p. 36.
80. Interview with Dawie de Villiers, November 1, 2010.
81. De Klerk, *FW de Klerk*, pp. 153–4.
82. Interview with Dave Steward, June 7, 2010.
83. Interview with Jannie Roux, May 28, 2010.
84. Interview with Barend du Plessis, May 22, 2010.
85. Interview with Pik Botha, February 1, 2010.
86. Interview with Dave Steward, June 7, 2010.
87. Interview with Dave Steward, June 7, 2010.

88. Interview with Aziz Pahad, January 28, 2011.
89. Alden, 'Solving South Africa's Chinese Puzzle', p. 133.
90. Interview with Aziz Pahad, January 28, 2011.
91. Schraeder, 'South Africa's Foreign Policy', p. 236.
92. Jhazbay, I., 2007, 'South Africa's Relations with North Africa and the Horn: Bridging the Continent', in *South Africa in Africa: The Post-Apartheid Era*, edited by Adebajo, A.; Adedeji, A.; and Landsberg, C., UKZN Press, Scottsville, p. 277.
93. Interview with Sydney Mufamadi, October 15, 2010.
94. Interview with Mangosuthu Buthelezi, August 3, 2010.
95. Fabricius, 'Virtuosity Versus Bureaucracy', p. 221.
96. Sampson, *Mandela*, p. 502.
97. Landsberg, 'South African Foreign Policy Formulation', p. 16.
98. Vale, 'Thabo Mbeki', p. 246.
99. Interview with Tom Wheeler, January 29, 2010.
100. Olivier, G., 2003, 'Is Thabo Mbeki Africa's Savior?', *International Affairs*, Vol. 79, No. 4, p. 815.
101. Landsberg, *Quiet Diplomacy*, pp. 159–60.
102. Olivier, 'Mbeki', p. 822.
103. Schoeman, M., 2001, 'Objectives, Structures, and Strategies: South Africa's Foreign Policy', *South African Yearbook of International Affairs 2001/02*, South African Institute of International Affairs, Johannesburg, p. 83.
104. Olivier, 'Ideology in South African Foreign Policy', pp. 180–1.
105. Author's private archive.
106. Gumede, *Thabo Mbeki*, p. 134.
107. Interview with Aziz Pahad, January 28, 2011.
108. Gevisser, *Mbeki*, p. 734.
109. Interview with Pallo Jordan, June 25, 2010.
110. Interview with Ben Turok, September 30, 2010.
111. Johnson, R., 2009, *South Africa's Brave New World: The Beloved Country Since the End of Apartheid*, Penguin Books, New York, p. 99.
112. Author's private archive.
113. Hadland, A. and Rantao, J., 2000, *The Life and Times of Thabo Mbeki*, Struik Books, Cape Town, p. 92.
114. Gevisser, *Mbeki*, p. 700.
115. Interview with Pallo Jordan, June 25, 2010.
116. Interview with Pallo Jordan, June 25, 2010.
117. Interview with Sydney Mufamadi, October 15, 2010.
118. Interview with Aziz Pahad, January 28, 2011.
119. Interview with Mosiuoa Lekota, March 25, 2011.
120. Interview with Aziz Pahad, January 28, 2011.
121. Interview with Smuts Ngonyama, March 2, 2010.
122. Calland, *Anatomy*, p. 43.

123. Lecoutre, D., 2009, 'South Africa's Mediation Efforts in Francophone Africa: Assessment of the Case of Cote d'Ivoire in the Context of a Stylistic Divide between Anglophone and Francophone Africa', in *Africa's Peacemaker: Lessons from South Africa's Conflict Resolution*, edited by Shillinger, K., South African Institute of International Affairs, Johannesburg, p. 159.
124. Gevisser, *Mbeki*, p. 247.
125. Author's private archive.
126. Hadland and Rantao, *Mbeki*, p. 102.
127. Feinstein, *After the Party*, pp. 115–6.
128. Author's private archive.
129. Interview with Aziz Pahad, January 28, 2011.
130. Interview with Aziz Pahad, January 28, 2011.
131. Interview with Sipho Pityana, May 25, 2010.
132. Interview with Sipho Pityana, May 25, 2010.
133. Interview with Essop Pahad, May 27, 2010.
134. Interview with Smuts Ngonyama, March 2, 2010.

Chapter 11   Conclusion—Room, But Not Willingness, for Engagement

1. Interview with Elizabeth Sidiropoulos, May 26, 2010.
2. Interview with Ben Skosana, September 21, 2010.
3. De St. Jorre, J., 1977, *A House Divided: South Africa's Uncertain Future*, Carnegie Endowment for International Peace, New York, p. 55.
4. Afrobarometer, 2009, 'Proportional Representation and Popular Assessments of MP Performance in South Africa: A Desire for Electoral Reform?', Afrobarometer Briefing Paper 76.

BIBLIOGRAPHY

Books, Press, Unpublished Dissertations, Presentations, and Journal Articles

Adam, H. and Giliomee, H., 1979, *Ethnic Power Mobilized: Can South Africa Change?*, Yale University Press, New Haven.

———— and Uys, S., 1988, 'Eight New Realities in Southern Africa', in *South Africa in Transition: To What?*, edited by Kitchen, H., Center for Strategic and International Studies, Washington DC.

————, van zyl Slabbert, F. and Moodley, K., 1998, *Comrades in Business: Post-Liberation Politics in South Africa*, Tafelberg, Cape Town.

Adams, J., 1984, *The Unnatural Alliance*, Quartet Books, London.

Adebajo, A., 2007, 'South Africa and Nigeria in Africa: An Axis of Virtue?', in *South Africa in Africa: The Post-Apartheid Era*, edited by Adebajo, A.; Adedeji, A.; and Landsberg, C., UKZN Press, Scottsville.

———— 2007, 'South Africa in Africa: Messiah or Mercantilist?', *South African Journal of International Affairs*, Vol. 14, No. 1, pp. 29–48.

———— 2010, *The Curse of Berlin: Africa After the Cold War*, UKZN Press, Scottsville.

Afrobarometer, 2009, 'Proportional Representation and Popular Assessments of MP Performance in South Africa: A Desire for Electoral Reform?', Afrobarometer Briefing Paper 76.

Ahwireng-Obeng, F. and McGowan, P., 2001, 'Partner or Hegemon: South Africa in Africa', in *South Africa's Foreign Policy: Dilemmas of a New Democracy*, edited by Broderick, J.; Burford, G.; and Freer, G., Palgrave Press, New York.

Ahmed, A., 2009, 'The Role of Parliament in South Africa's Foreign Policy Development Process: Lessons from the United States' Congress', *South African Journal of International Affairs*, Vol. 16, No. 3, pp. 291–310.

Ajulu, R., 2001, 'Thabo Mbeki's African Renaissance in a Globalizing World Economy: The Struggle for the Soul of the Continent', *Review of African Political Economy*, Vol. 28, No. 87, pp. 27–42.

Alden, C., 1996, *Apartheid's Last Stand: The Rise and Fall of the South African Security State*, Macmillan Press, London.

———— 2001, 'Solving South Africa's Chinese Puzzle: Democratic Foreign Policymaking and the Two Chinas Issue', in *South Africa's Foreign Policy: Dilemmas of a New Democracy*, edited by Broderick, J.; Burford, G.; and Freer, G., Palgrave Press, New York.

———— and le Pere, G., 2003, 'South Africa's Post-Apartheid Foreign Policy—From Reconciliation to Revival?', Adelphi Paper 362, Oxford University Press, Oxford.

———— and Soko, M., 2005, 'South Africa's Economic Relations with Africa: Hegemony and its Discontents', *Journal of Modern African Studies*, Vol. 43, No. 3, pp. 367–92.

———— and le Pere, G., 2010, 'Strategic Posture Review: South Africa', *World Politics Review*. (Available at: http://www.worldpoliticsreview.com/articles/5565/strategic-posture-review-south-africa, accessed March 11, 2014.)

Allison, G. and Zelikow, P., 1999, *Essence of Decision: Explaining the Cuban Missile Crisis*, Longman, London.

Alves, P.; Kalaba, M.; Wilcox, O.; Fundira, T.; and Williams, B., 2006, 'Deepening Integration in SADC: South Africa—SADC's Economic Engine', Friedrich Ebert Stiftung, Johannesburg.

Asmal, K. and Hadland, A., 2011, *Politics in My Blood: A Memoir*, Jacana, Johannesburg.

Banjo, A., 2009, 'A Review of Parliament-Foreign Policy Nexus in South Africa and Namibia', *Canadian Journal of Politics and Law*, Vol. 2, No. 3, pp. 61–70.

Barber, J. and Barratt, J., 1990, *South Africa's Foreign Policy: The Search for Status and Security 1945–1988*, Cambridge University Press, Cambridge.

————, 2004, *Mandela's World: The International Dimension of South Africa's Political Revolution 1990–99*, Ohio University Press, Athens.

Barkan, J., 2005, 'Emerging Legislature or Rubber Stamp? The South African National Assembly After Ten Years of Democracy', CSSR Working Paper No. 134, University of Cape Town Centre for Social Science Research.

Barnard, F., 1967, *13 Years with Dr. HF Verwoerd*, Voortrekkerpers, Johannesburg.

Barrell, H., 1992, 'The Turn to the Masses: The African National Congress' Strategic Review of 1978–79', *Journal of Southern African Studies*, Vol. 18, No. 1, pp. 64–92.

Barron, C., 2006, 'Alf Ries: Propagandist for the National Party', *Sunday Times*, November 5.

Basson, J., 2008, *State of the Nation: As Viewed from the Front Bench in Parliament 1969–1981*, Politika, Camps Bay.

Batchelor, P., Dunne, P., and Lamb, G., 2002, 'The Demand for Military Spending in South Africa', *Journal of Peace Research*, Vol. 39, No. 3, pp. 315–30.

BBC News, 2008, 'Zimbabwe Arms Ship Quits South Africa', April 19.

Beloff, M., 1955, *Foreign Policy and the Democratic Process*, Johns Hopkins Press, Baltimore.

Benjamin, L., 2001, 'South Africa and the Middle East: Anatomy of an Emerging Relationship', in *South Africa's Foreign Policy: Dilemmas of a New Democracy*, edited by Broderick, J.; Burford, G.; and Freer, G., Palgrave Press, New York.

Bentley, K. and Southall, R., 2005, *An African Peace Process: Mandela, South Africa, and Burundi*, HSRC Press, Pretoria.

Bertelsmann-Scott, T., 2004, 'The Democratization of Trade Policy', in *Democratizing Foreign Policy? Lessons from South Africa*, edited by Nel, P. and Van der Westhuizen, J., Lexington Books, Lanham.

Bischoff, P. and Southall, R., 1998, 'Early Foreign Policy of Democratic South Africa', in *African Foreign Policies*, edited by Stephen Wright, Westview Press, Boulder.

Black, D., 1995, 'Comparative Experiences for a New South Africa', in 'Parliaments and Foreign Policy: The International and South African Experience', conference report, Center for Southern African Studies.

Bond, P., 2006, *Talk Left, Walk Right: South Africa's Frustrated Global Reforms*, UKZN Press, Scottsville.

Booysen, S., 2001, 'Transitions and Trends in Policy Making in Democratic South Africa', *Journal of Public Administration*, Vol. 36, No. 2, pp. 125–44.

Botha, J., 1967, *Verwoerd is Dead*, Books of Africa, Johannesburg.

Boulter, R., 1997, 'FC Erasmus and the Politics of South African Defense, 1948–1959', unpublished doctoral dissertation, Rhodes University, Grahamstown.

Bowman, L., 1971, *South Africa's Outward Strategy: A Foreign Policy Dilemma for the United States*, Ohio University Center for International Studies, Athens.

Breuning, M., 2007, *Foreign Policy Analysis: A Comparative Introduction*, Palgrave Macmillan, New York.

Bunting, B., 1986, *The Rise of the South African Reich*, International Defense and Aid Fund, London.

Butler, A., 2005, 'How Democratic is the African National Congress?', *Journal of Southern African Studies*, Vol. 31, No. 4, pp. 719–36.

Calland, R., 1997, 'All Dressed Up with Nowhere to go? The Rapid Transformation of the South African Parliamentary Committee System', University of Cape Town School of Government.

——— 2004, *Anatomy of South Africa: Who Holds the Power?* Zebra Press, Cape Town.

Callinicos, L., 2004, *Oliver Tambo: Beyond the Engeli Mountains*, David Phillip Press, Cape Town.

Carlsnaes, W. and Nel, P., 2006, 'Introduction', in *In Full Flight: South African Foreign Policy After Apartheid*, edited by Carlsnaes, W. and Nel, P., Institute for Global Dialogue, Midrand.

Carter, G., 1980, *Which Way is South Africa Going?* Indiana University Press, Bloomington.

Clarke, D., 2010, *Africa: Crude Continent, The Struggle for Africa's Oil Prize*, Profile Books, London.

Cloete, J., 1985, *Parliaments of South Africa*, JL van Struik, Cape Town.

Cobbett, W. 1989, 'Apartheid's Army and the Arms Embargo', in *War and Society: The Militarization of South Africa*, edited by Cock, J. and Nathan, L., David Phillip Press, Cape Town.

Cockram, G., 1970, *Vorster's Foreign Policy*, Academica, Cape Town.

Conchiglia, A., 2007, 'South Africa and its Lusophone Neighbors: Angola and Mozambique', in *South Africa in Africa: The Post-Apartheid Era*, edited by Adebajo, A.; Adedeji, A.; and Landsberg, C., UKZN Press, Scottsville.

Crafford, F., 1945, *Jan Smuts: A Biography*, Howard Timmins Press, Cape Town.

Crocker, C., 1992, *High Noon in Southern Africa: Making Peace in a Rough Neighborhood*, Jonathan Ball, Johannesburg.

Curry G., 1961, 'Woodrow Wilson, Jan Smuts, and the Versailles Settlement', *The American Historical Review*, Vol. 66, No. 4, July 1961, pp. 968–86.

Dadoo, Y., 1997, 'Relations with the Middle East and Arab World', in *Change and South African Foreign Relations*, edited by Carlsnaes, W. and Muller, M., International Thomson Publishing, Johannesburg.

Dalcanton, C., 1976, 'Vorster and the Politics of Confidence, 1966–1974', *African Affairs*, Vol. 75, No. 299, pp. 163–81.

Danaher, K., 1984, *In Whose Interest: A Guide to US-South Africa Relations*, Institute for Policy Studies, Washington DC.

Daniel, J., 1995, 'One China or Two? South Africa's Foreign Policy Dilemma', *Transformation*, Vol. 27, pp. 35–49.

——— and Bhengu, N., 2009, 'South Africa in Africa: Still a Formidable Player,' in *A New Scramble for Africa: Imperialism, Investment, and Development*, edited by Roger Southall and Henning Melber, UKZN Press, Scottsville.

Davidson, B., 1974, 'South Africa and Portugal', *A Journal of Opinion*, Vol. 4, No. 2, pp. 9–20.

Davies, R. and O'Meara, D., 1985, 'Total Strategy in Southern Africa: An Analysis of South African Regional Policy Since 1978', *Journal of Southern African Studies*, Vol. 11, No. 2, pp. 183–211.

———, 1989, 'The SADF's Covert War Against Mozambique', in *War and Society: The Militarization of South Africa*, edited by Cock, J. and Nathan, L., David Phillip Press, Cape Town.

De Jager, N., 2006, 'The South African Government and the Application of Cooptive Power', *Politikon*, Vol. 33, No. 1, pp. 61–84.

De Klerk, F., 1998, *FW de Klerk, The Last Trek-A New Beginning*, MacMillan, New York.

De Klerk, W., 1991, *FW de Klerk: The Man in his Time*, Jonathan Ball, Johannesburg.

De St. Jorre, J., 1977, 'South Africa: Up Against the World', *Foreign Policy*, No. 28, pp. 53–85.

——— 1977, *A House Divided: South Africa's Uncertain Future*, Carnegie Endowment for International Peace, New York.

De Villiers, B., 1995, *Foreign Relations and the Provinces*, HSRC Press, Pretoria.

De Villiers, L., 1980, *Secret Information*, Tafelberg, Cape Town.

Diamond, L., Linz, J., and Lipset, S., 1988, *Democracy in Developing Countries, Volume One: Comparing Experiences with Democracy*, Lynne Rienner, Boulder.

Dlamini, K., 2002, 'Is Quiet Diplomacy an Effective Conflict Resolution Strategy?', in *South African Yearbook of International Affairs 2002/2003*, South African Institute of International Affairs, Johannesburg, pp. 171–8.

D'Olivera, J., 1977, *Vorster the Man*, Ernest Stanton Publishers, Johannesburg.

Dommisse, E., 1979, 'The Changing Role of the Afrikaans Press', in *The Afrikaners*, edited by Munger, E., Tafelberg, Cape Town.

——— 2001, *Anton Rupert: A Biography*, Tafelberg, Cape Town.

Draper, P., 2005, 'Consultation Dilemmas: Transparency Versus Effectiveness in South Africa's Trade Policy', in *Reconfiguring the Compass: South Africa's African Trade Diplomacy*, edited by Draper, P., South African Institute of International Affairs, Johannesburg.

Dugger, C., 2008, 'Zimbabwe Arms Shipped by China Spark an Uproar', *New York Times*, April 19.

Du Pisani, A., 1988, 'What do We Think? A Survey of White Opinion on Foreign Policy Issues No. 4', South African Institute of International Affairs.

Du Plessis, A., 1997, 'The Geopolitical Context: A Sea Change from Old to New Geopolitics', in *Change and South African Foreign Relations*, edited by Carlsnaes, W. and Muller, M., International Thomson Publishing, Johannesburg.

The Economist, 2008, 'The See-No-Evil Foreign Policy', November 15.

Eglin, C., 2007, *Crossing the Borders of Power*, Jonathan Ball, Johannesburg.

Ellis, S. and Sechaba, T., 1992, *Comrades Against Apartheid: The ANC and the South African Communist Party in Exile*, Indiana University Press, Bloomington.

Evans, G., 1996, 'South Africa in Remission: The Foreign Policy of an Altered State', *The Journal of Modern African Studies*, Vol. 34, No. 2, pp. 249–69.

Fabricius, P., 1999, 'Virtuosity Versus Bureaucracy', *South African Yearbook of International Affairs 1999/2000*, South African Institute of International Affairs, Johannesburg, pp. 217–24.

Feinstein, A., 2007, *After the Party: A Personal and Political Journey Inside the ANC*, Andrew Jonathan Ball, Johannesburg.

Fig, D., 1984, 'Theorizing South Africa's Foreign Policy: The Case of Latin America', unpublished doctoral dissertation, University of Cape Town.

The Financial Gazette (Harare), 2009, 'GDP Drops Sharply', April 17.

Fourie, D., 2009, 'What Happened to Machiavelli's Advice to the Prince? Experience in Teaching Strategic Studies', unpublished.

Frankel, J., 1963, *The Making of Foreign Policy: An Analysis of Decision Making*, Oxford University Press, Oxford.

Fritz, N., 2009, 'People Power: How Civil Society Blocked an Arms Shipment for Zimbabwe', SAIIA Occasional Paper 36.

Geldenhuys, D. and Kotze, H., 1983, 'Aspects of Political Decision-making in South Africa', *Politikon*, Vol. 10, No. 1, pp. 33–45.

———— 1984, *The Diplomacy of Isolation: South African Foreign Policy Making*, St. Martin's Press, London.

———— 1984, 'South African Reactions to the Nkomati Accord: A House Divided', *Journal of Contemporary African Studies*, Vol. 4, No. 1/2, pp. 179–213.

———— and Kotze, H., 1991, 'FW de Klerk: A Study in Political Leadership', *Politikon*, Vol. 19, No. 1, pp. 20–44.

———— 1992, 'The Foreign Policy of Transition in South Africa', in *Foreign Policy Issues in a Democratic South Africa*, edited by Venter, A., Papers from a Conference of Professors World Peace Academy, Johannesburg.

———— 1994, 'The Head of Government and South Africa's Foreign Relations', in *Leadership in the Apartheid State: From Malan to de Klerk*, edited by Schrire, R., Oxford University Press, Oxford.

———— 2006, 'South Africa's Role as International Norm Entrepreneur', in *In Full Flight: South African Foreign Policy After Apartheid*, edited by Carlsnaes, W. and Nel, P., Institute for Global Dialogue, Midrand.

Geldenhuys, J., 2009, *At the Front: A General's Account of the Border War*, Jonathan Ball, Johannesburg.

Gerber, L., 1973, *Friends and Influence: The Diplomacy of Private Enterprise*, Purnell, Cape Town.

Gerhart, G. and Glaser, C., 2010, *From Protest to Challenge: A Documentary History of African Politics in South Africa, Volume 6: Challenge and Victory, 1980–1990*, Indiana University Press, Bloomington.

Gevisser, M., 2007, *Thabo Mbeki: The Dream Deferred*, Jonathan Ball, Johannesburg.

Giliomee, H., 1983, 'BJ Vorster and the Sultan's Horse', Best of Frontline.
———— 2008, 'The Rubicon Revisited', Politicsweb, August 20.
Good, R., 1973, *UDI: The International Politics of the Rhodesian Rebellion*, Faber and Faber, London.
Gossman, A., 2010, 'The South African Military and Counterinsurgency: An Overview', in *South Africa and Contemporary Counterinsurgency: Roots, Practices, and Prospects*, edited by Deane-Peter Baker and Evert Jordan, UCT Press, Cape Town.
Graaff, D., 1993, *Div Looks Back: The Memoirs of De Villiers Graaff*, Human and Rousseau, Cape Town.
Green, P., 2008, *Choice Not Fate: The Life and Times of Trevor Manuel*, Penguin, New York.
Griffiths, R., 1991, 'The South African Military: The Dilemmas of Expanded Influence in Decision-making', *Journal of Asian and African Studies*, Vol. 26, No. 1, pp. 76–95.
Grobbelaar, N., 2005, 'South African Corporate Engagement with Africa: Unpacking Negative and Positive Perceptions', in *South African Yearbook of International Affairs 2005*, South African Institute of International Affairs, Johannesburg, pp. 65–74.
Grundy, K., 1986, *The Militarization of South African Politics,* Indiana University Press, Bloomington.
Gumede, W., 2003, 'Down to Business but Nothing to Show', in *Thabo Mbeki's World*, edited by Jacobs, S. and Calland, R., University of Natal Press, Durban.
———— 2005, *Thabo Mbeki and the Battle for the Soul of the ANC*, Zebra Press, Cape Town.
———— 2009, 'Delivering the Democratic Developmental State in South Africa', in *The Politics of Service Delivery*, edited by McLennan, A. and Munslow, B., Wits University Press, Johannesburg.
Gutteridge, W., 1996, 'The Transformation of the South African Military', in *South Africa's Defense and Security Into the 21st Century*, edited by Gutteridge, W., Dartmouth Press, Hanover.
Habib, A., 2005, 'State-Civil Society Relations in Post-Apartheid South Africa', *Social Research*, Vol. 72, No. 3, pp. 671–92.
Hadland, A. and Rantao, J., 2000, *The Life and Times of Thabo Mbeki*, Struik Books, Cape Town.
Hamann, H., 2001, *Days of the Generals,* Zebra Press, Cape Town.
Hamman, R. and de Cleene, S., 2005, 'South Africa's Corporate Responsibility in Africa', *South African Journal of International Affairs*, Vol. 12, No. 2, pp. 127–41.
Hancock, WK, 1962, *Smuts: The Sanguine Years 1870–1919*, Cambridge University Press, Cambridge.
———— 1968, *Smuts: The Fields of Force, 1919–1950*, Cambridge Press, Cambridge.
Handley, A., 2008, *Business and the State in Africa: Economic Policy-Making in the Neoliberal Era*, Cambridge University Press, Cambridge.
Hank, S., 2010, 'RIP Zimbabwe Dollar', Cato Institute, Washington DC, May 3.
Hanlon, J., 1986, *Beggar Your Neighbors: Apartheid Power in Southern Africa*, James Currey Ltd, London.
Henshaw, P., 1996, 'Britain, South Africa, and the Sterling Area: Gold Production, Capital Investment, and Agricultural Markets 1931–1961', *The Historical Journal*, Vol. 39, No. 1, pp. 197–223.

Hepple, A., 1967, *Verwoerd*, Penguin, Johannesburg.

Herbst, J., 2005, 'Mbeki's South Africa', *Foreign Affairs*, Vol. 84, No. 6, pp. 93–105.

Hill, C., 2003, *The Changing Politics of Foreign Policy*, Palgrave Macmillan, New York.

Holsti, O., 1992, 'Public Opinion and Foreign Policy: Challenges to the Almond-Lippmann Consensus', *International Studies Quarterly*, Vol. 36, No. 4, pp. 439–66.

Honey, P., 2007, 'African Migrants: Fewer that was Thought', *Financial Mail*, February 16.

Horwitz, R., 2001, *Communication and Democratic Reform in South Africa*, Cambridge University Press, Cambridge.

Hudson, J., 2007, 'South Africa's Economic Expansion Into Africa: Neo-Colonialism or Development?', in *South Africa in Africa: The Post-Apartheid Era*, edited by Adebajo, A.; Adedeji, A.; and Landsberg, C., UKZN Press, Scottsville.

Hughes, T., 2001, 'The Parliamentary Committee on Foreign Affairs', in *South African Yearbook of International Affairs 2001/02*, South African Institute of International Affairs, Johannesburg, pp. 97–104.

———— 2004, *Composers, Conductors and Players: Harmony and Discord in South African Foreign Policymaking*, Konrad Adenauer Stiftung, Johannesburg.

Huntington, S., 1996, *The Clash of Civilizations and the Remaking of the World Order*, Free Press, London.

Ilsley, L., 1940, 'The War Policy of South Africa', *The American Political Science Review*, Vol. 34, No. 6, pp. 1178–87.

Institute for Security Studies, 'History of ISS', www.iss.co.za.

International Defense and Aid Fund, 1975, 'BOSS: The First Five Years', London.

Jackson, G., 1993, *Breaking Story: The South African Press*, Westview Press, Boulder.

Jaster, R.; Mbeki, M.; Nkosi, M., and Clough, M., 1992, *Changing Fortunes: War, Diplomacy, and Economics in Southern Africa*, Ford Foundation, New York.

Jhazbay, I., 2007, 'South Africa's Relations with North Africa and the Horn: Bridging the Continent', in *South Africa in Africa: The Post-Apartheid Era*, edited by Adebajo, A.; Adedeji, A.; and Landsberg, C., UKZN Press, Scottsville.

Johnson, A., 2001, 'Democracy and Human Rights in the Principles and Practice of South African Foreign Policy', in *South Africa's Foreign Policy: Dilemmas of a New Democracy*, edited by Broderick, J.; Burford, G.; and Freer, G., Palgrave Press, New York.

Johnson, R., 2009, *South Africa's Brave New World: The Beloved Country Since the End of Apartheid*, Penguin Books, New York.

Jordaan, E., 2008, 'Barking at the Big Dogs: South Africa's Policy Towards the Middle East', *Round Table*, Vol. 97, No. 397, pp. 589–603.

Kenkel, K., 2005, 'Whispering to the Prince: Academic Experts and National Security Policy Formulation in Brazil, South Africa and Canada', unpublished doctoral dissertation, University of Geneva.

Khoza, R., 2005, *Let Africa Lead*, Vezubuntu, Johannesburg.

Klotz, A., 2006, 'State Identity in South African Foreign Policy', in *In Full Flight: South African Foreign Policy After Apartheid*, edited by Carlsnaes, W. and Nel, P., Institute for Global Dialogue, Midrand.

Kotze, H., 1997, 'Take Us to Our Leaders: The South African National Assembly and its Members', Konrad Adenauer Stiftung Occasional Paper.

Landsberg, C., 2004, *The Quiet Diplomacy of Liberation: International Politics and South Africa's Transition*, Jacana, Johannesburg.
———— 2005, 'In Search of Global Influence, Order and Development: South Africa's Foreign Policy a Decade After Political Apartheid', *Policy: Issues & Actors*, Vol. 18, No. 3.
———— and Monyae, D., 2006, 'South Africa's Foreign Policy: Carving a Global Niche', *South African Journal of International Relations*, Vol. 13, No. 2, pp. 131–45.
———— 2007, 'South Africa and the Making of the AU and NEPAD: Mbeki's "Progressive African Agenda"', in *South Africa in Africa: The Post-Apartheid Era*, edited by Adebajo, A.; Adedeji, A.; and Landsberg, C., UKZN Press, Scottsville.
———— 2010, *The Diplomacy of Transformation: South African Foreign Policy and Statecraft*, Macmillan, Johannesburg.
———— 2010, 'South African Foreign Policy Formulation, 1989–2010', unpublished.
Lecoutre, D., 2009, 'South Africa's Mediation Efforts in Francophone Africa: Assessment of the Case of Cote d'Ivoire in the Context of a Stylistic Divide between Anglophone and Francophone Africa', in *Africa's Peacemaker: Lessons from South Africa's Conflict Resolution*, edited by Shillinger, K., South African Institute of International Affairs, Johannesburg.
Leonard, R., 1983, *South Africa at War*, Lawrence Hill, Westport.
Le Pere, G. and Vickers, B., 2004, 'Civil Society and Foreign Policy', in *Democratizing Foreign Policy? Lessons from South Africa*, edited by Nel, P. and Van der Westhuizen, J., Lexington Books, Lanham.
Le Pere, G. and van Nieuwkerk, A., 2004, 'Who Made and Makes Foreign Policy', in *Apartheid Past, Renaissance Future: South Africa's Foreign Policy 1994–2004*, edited by Elizabeth Sidiropoulos, South African Institute of International Affairs, Johannesburg.
Le Pere, G.; Pressend, M.; Ruiters, M.; and Zondi, S., 2008, 'South Africa's Participation in the System of Global Governance: A Review Prepared for the Presidency's Fifteen Year Review', Institute for Global Dialogue, unpublished.
Le Roux, L., 2003, 'The South African National Defense Force and its Involvement in the Defense Review Process', in *Ourselves to Know: Civil-Military Relations and Defense Transformation in Southern Africa*, edited by Williams, R.; Cawthra, G.; and Abrahams, D., Institute for Security Studies, Pretoria.
Leysens, A. and Fourie, P., 1997, 'Relations with Latin America', in *Change and South African Foreign Relations*, edited by Carlsnaes, W. and Muller, M., International Thomson Publishing, Johannesburg.
Lodge, T., 1983, *Black Politics in South Africa Since 1945*, Longman, New York.
———— 1987, 'State of Exile: The African National Congress of South Africa, 1976–86', *Third World Quarterly*, Vol. 9, No. 1, pp. 1–27.
———— 1999, 'Policy Processes within the ANC and Tripartite Alliance', *Politikon*, Vol. 26, No. 1, pp. 5–32.
Lyman, P., 2002, *Partner to History: The U.S. Role in South Africa's Transition to Democracy*, US Institute of Peace, Washington DC.
Macmillan, H., 2009, 'The African National Congress of South Africa in Zambia: The Culture of Exile and the Changing Relationship with Home, 1964–1990', *Journal of Southern African Studies*, Vol. 35, No. 2, pp. 303–29.

Malan, M., 2006, *My Life with the South African Defense Force*, Protea Books, Pretoria.

Malherbe, E., 1981, *Never a Dull Moment*, Howard Timmins Press, Cape Town.

Mandela, N., 1993, 'South Africa's Future Foreign Policy', *Foreign Affairs*, Vol. 72, No. 5, pp. 86–97.

Mangcu, X., 2009, *The Democratic Moment: South Africa's Prospects Under Jacob Zuma*, Jacana Press, Johannesburg.

Maroleng, C., 2005, 'Cote d'Ivoire: Perils and Prospects', *South African Yearbook of International Affairs 2005*, South African Institute of International Affairs, Johannesburg, pp. 29–35.

Masiza, Z., 1999, 'Silent Citizenry: Public Participation and Foreign Policy-making', Center for Policy Studies, Policy Brief No. 15.

Massie, R., 1997, *Loosing the Bonds: The United States and South Africa In the Apartheid Years*, Doubleday, New York.

Mbeki, M., 2002, 'Towards a More Productive South African Foreign Policy', *South African Yearbook of International Affairs 2002/03*, South African Institute of International Affairs, Johannesburg, pp. 13–19.

Mbeki, T., 1994, 'South Africa's International Relations: Today and Tomorrow', in *From Pariah to Participant: South Africa's Evolving Foreign Relations, 1990–1994*, edited by Mills, G., South African Institute of International Affairs, Johannesburg.

McCarthy, S., 1996, 'Challenges for the South African Intelligence Community', in *South Africa's Defense and Security Into the 21st Century*, edited by Gutteridge, W., Dartmouth, Hanover.

McKinley, D., 2004, 'South African Foreign Policy Towards Zimbabwe Under Mbeki', *Review of African Political Economy*, Vol. 31, No. 100, pp. 357–64.

Meiring, P., 1974, *Inside Information*, Howard Timmins Press, Cape Town.

Meli, F., 1989, *South Africa Belongs to Us: A History of the ANC*, Indiana University Press, Bloomington.

Mervis, J., 1989, *The Fourth Estate: A Newspaper Story*, Jonathan Ball, Johannesburg.

Mills, G., 1999, 'South African Foreign Policy: From Isolation to Respectability', in *South Africa in Southern Africa: Reconfiguring the Region*, edited by Simon, D., Ohio University Press, Athens.

——— 2000, *The Wired Model: South Africa, Foreign Policy and Globalization*, Tafelberg, Cape Town.

Mlambo, A., 2000, 'Partner or Hegemon? South Africa and its Neighbors', in *South African Yearbook of International Affairs 2000/01*, South African Institute of International Affairs, Johannesburg, pp. 65–72.

Moodie, T., 1975, *The Rise of Afrikanerdom: Power, Apartheid, and the Afrikaner Civil Religion*, University of California Press, Berkeley.

Muller, CFJ, 2005, 'The Creation of the Department of External Affairs', in *History of the South African Department of Foreign Affairs 1927–1993*, edited by Tom Wheeler, South African Institute of International Affairs, Johannesburg.

Muller, M., 1999, 'South African Diplomacy and Security Complex Theory', *Round Table*, No. 352, pp. 585–620.

——— 2000, 'Some Observations on South Africa's Economic Diplomacy and the Role of DFA', Institute for Global Dialogue Occasional Paper 27.

Munger, E., 1965, *Notes on the Formation of South African Foreign Policy*, The Castle Press, Cape Town.

—— 1967, *Afrikaner and African Nationalism*, Oxford University Press, Oxford.

—— 1979, Foreward, *The Afrikaners*, edited by Edwin Munger, Tafelberg, Cape Town.

Naidoo, K., 2004, 'South African Civil Society and the Making of South African Foreign Policy', in *Apartheid Past, Renaissance Future: South Africa's Foreign Policy 1994–2004*, edited by Sidiropoulos, E., South African Institute of International Affairs, Johannesburg.

Naidu, S., 2004, 'South Africa and Africa: Mixed Messages?', in *Apartheid Past, Renaissance Future: South Africa's Foreign Policy 1994–2004*, edited by Sidiropoulos, E., South African Institute of International Affairs, Johannesburg.

Nantulya, P., 2003, 'South African NGOs: New Actors and Instruments in South African Foreign Policy', in *South African Yearbook of International Affairs 2003/04*, South African Institute of International Affairs, Johannesburg, pp. 11–32.

Nathan, L., 2007, *Local Ownership of Security Sector Reform: A Guide for Donors*, University of Birmingham, Birmingham.

—— 2009, 'Courting al-Bashir: South Africa, Sudan, and Darfur', in *Africa's Peacemaker: Lessons from South Africa's Conflict Resolution*, edited by Shillinger, K., South African Institute of International Affairs, Johannesburg.

Ndebele, N. and Nieftagodien, N., 2005, 'The Morogoro Conference: A Moment of Self-Reflection', in *The Road to Democracy in South Africa, Volume 1*, South African Democracy Education Trust, Johannesburg.

Ndlovu, S., 2005, 'The ANC's Diplomacy and International Relations', in *The Road to Democracy in South Africa, Volume 1*, South African Democracy Education Trust, Johannesburg.

Neame, L., 1929, *Some South African Politicians*, Maskew Miller Limited, Cape Town.

Neethling, T., 2004, 'The Defense Force and Peacekeeping: Linking Policy and Capability', in *Apartheid Past, Renaissance Future: South Africa's Foreign Policy 1994–2004*, edited by Sidiropoulos, E., South African Institute of International Affairs, Johannesburg.

Nel, P., 1990, *A Soviet Embassy in Pretoria?*, Tafelberg, Cape Town.

—— 1999, 'The Foreign Policy Beliefs of South Africans: A First Cut', *Journal of Contemporary African Studies*, Vol. 17, No. 1, pp. 123–46.

——, Taylor, I. and van der Westhuizen, J., 2000, 'Multilateralism in South Africa's Foreign Policy: The Search for a Critical Rationale', *Global Governance*; Vol. 6, No. 1, pp. 43–60.

—— and van Wyk, J., 2003, 'Foreign Policy Making in South Africa: From Public Participation to Democratic Participation', *Politeia*, Vol. 22, No. 3, pp. 49–71.

——, van Wyk, J. and Johnsen, K., 2004, 'Democracy, Participation, and Foreign Policy Making in South Africa', in *Democratizing Foreign Policy? Lessons from South Africa*, edited by Nel, P. and Van der Westhuizen, J., Lexington Books, Lanham.

Ngubentombi, N., 2003, 'South Africa's Foreign Policy Towards Swaziland and Zimbabwe', *South African Yearbook of International Affairs 2003/04*, South African Institute of International Affairs, Johannesburg, pp. 146–57.

Nolutshungu, S., 1975, *South Africa in Africa: A Study in Ideology and Foreign Policy*, Manchester University Press, Manchester.

Norton, P., 2005, *Parliament in British Politics*, Palgrave Macmillan, London.

Nothling, F., 2005, 'A Department in its Own Right, 1955–1966', in *History of the South African Department of Foreign Affairs 1927–1993*, edited by Tom Wheeler, South African Institute of International Affairs, Johannesburg.

Nyangone, E., 2008, 'South Africa's Relations with Gabon and the Ivory Coast: 1969–1994', unpublished doctoral dissertation, University of Stellenbosch.

Nyuot Goh, J. 2005, 'South Africa's Policy Towards Sudan', in *South African Yearbook of International Affairs 2005*, South African Institute of International Affairs, Johannesburg, pp. 37–45.

Nzo, A., 1999, 'Foreign Minister's Budget Vote Address', March 4, 1999, *South African Journal of International Affairs*, Vol. 6, No. 2, pp. 217–26.

O'Brien, K., 2010, *The South African Intelligence Services: From Apartheid to Democracy, 1948–2005*, Routledge, Milton Park.

Olivier, G., 2003, 'Is Thabo Mbeki Africa's Savior?', *International Affairs*, Vol. 79, No. 4, pp. 815–28.

––––––– 2006, 'Ideology in South African Foreign Policy', *Politeia*, Vol. 25, No. 2, pp. 168–82.

O'Meara, D., 1977, 'The Afrikaner *Broederbond* 1927–1948: Class Vanguard of Afrikaner Nationalism', *Journal of Southern African Studies*, Vol. 3, No. 2, pp. 156–86.

––––––– 1996, *Forty Lost Years*, Ravan Press, Randberg.

Owen, K., 1988, 'A Fundamental Shift in South African Politics?', in *South Africa in Transition: To What?*, edited by Kitchen. H., Center for Strategic and International Studies, Washington DC.

Papenfus, T., 2010, *Pik Botha and His Times*, Litera Publications, Pretoria.

Parsons, W., 1995, *Public Policy: An Introduction to the Theory and Practice of Policy Analysis*, Edward Elgar, London.

Paruk F., 2008, 'The Transitional Executive Council (TEC) As Transitional Institution to Manage and Prevent Conflict in South Africa (1994)', unpublished MA thesis, UNISA.

Peete F. and Bateman B., 2006, 'I Love the ANC, Says COSATU's Madisha', Independent Online, September 6.

Pelzer, A. (editor), 1966, *Verwoerd Speaks: Speeches 1948–1966*, APB Publishers, Johannesburg.

Pfister, R., 2003, 'Gateway to International Victory: The Diplomacy of the African National Congress in Africa, 1960–1994', *Journal of Modern African Studies*, Vol. 41, No. 1, pp. 51–73.

––––––– 2005, *Apartheid South Africa and African States: from Pariah to Middle Power, 1961–1994*, Tauris Academic Studies, London.

Phimister, I. and Raftopoulos, B., 2004, 'Mugabe, Mbeki & the Politics of Anti-Imperialism', *Review of African Political Economy*, Vol. 31, No. 101, pp. 385–401.

Pienaar, S., 1987, *South Africa and International Relations between the Two World Wars: The League of Nations Dimension*, Wits Press, Johannesburg.

––––––– 1997, 'Relations with Central and Eastern Europe', in *Change and South African Foreign Relations*, edited by Carlsnaes, W. and Muller, M., International Thomson Publishing, Johannesburg.

Pogrund, B., 2000, *War of Words: Memoirs of a South African Journalist*, Seven Stories Press, New York.

Polakow-Suransky, S., 2010, *The Unspoken Alliance: Israel's Secret Relationship with Apartheid South Africa,* Pantheon Books, New York.

Pollak, R., 1981, *Up Against Apartheid: The Role and Plight of the Press in South Africa,* Southern Illinois University Press, Carbondale.

Potgeiter, D., 2007, *Total Onslaught: Apartheid's Dirty Secrets Exposed,* Struik, Cape Town.

Potter, E., 1975, *The Press as Opposition: The Political Role of South African Newspapers,* Rowman and Littlefield, Totowa.

Pottinger, B., 1988, *The Imperial Presidency: PW Botha, the First Ten Years,* Southern Book Publishers, Johannesburg.

Pretorius, L., 1994, 'The Head of Government and Organised Business', in *Leadership in the Apartheid State: From Malan to de Klerk,* edited by Schrire, R., Oxford University Press, Oxford.

Price, R., 1991, *The Apartheid State in Crisis: Political Transformation in South Africa 1975–1990,* Oxford University Press, Oxford.

Prys, M., 2007, 'Regions, Power and Hegemony: South Africa's Role in Southern Africa', Paper presented at the Sixth Pan-European International Relations Conference, Turin, September 12–15.

Purkitt, H. and Burgess, S., 2005, *South Africa's Weapons of Mass Destruction,* Indiana University Press, Bloomington.

Qobo, M., 2006, 'Dilemmas in South Africa's Regional Strategy', in *The New Multilateralism in South African Diplomacy,* edited by Lee, D.; Taylor, I.; and Williams, P., Palgrave Macmillan, New York.

—— 2010, 'Refocusing South Africa's Economic Diplomacy: The 'African Agenda' and Emerging Powers', *South African Journal of International Affairs,* Vol. 17, No. 1, pp. 13–28.

Rall, M., 2003, *Peaceable Warrior: The Life and Times of Sol Plaatje,* Sol Plaatje Educational Trust, Kimberley.

Relly, G., 1986, 'The Costs of Disinvestment', *Foreign Policy,* No. 63, pp. 131–46.

Rees, M. and Day, C., 1980, *Muldergate: The Story of the Info Scandal,* Macmillan, Johannesburg.

Rhoodie, E., 1989, *PW Botha: The Last Betrayal,* SA Politics, Melville.

Roberts, R., 2007, *Fit to Govern: The Native Intelligence of Thabo Mbeki,* STE Publishers, Johannesburg.

Roherty, J., 1992, *State Security in South Africa: Civil-Military Relations Under PW Botha,* ME Sharpe, London.

Rotberg, R., 1988, 'The Process of Decision Making in Contemporary South Africa', in *South Africa in Transition: To What?,* edited by Kitchen, H., Center for Strategic and International Studies, Washington DC.

SAPA, 2006, 'COSATU Thanks Members for Swazi Blockade', April 13.

Sampson, A., 2000, *Mandela: The Authorized Biography,* Random House, New York.

—— 2009, *The Anatomist: The Autobiography of Anthony Sampson,* Jonathan Ball, Johannesburg.

Sanders, J., 2006, *Apartheid's Friends: The Rise and Fall of South Africa's Secret Service,* John Murray Press, London.

Schoeman, M., 2000, 'South Africa as an Emerging Middle Power', *African Security Review,* Vol. 9, No. 3, pp. 1–13.

——— 2001, 'Objectives, Structures, and Strategies: South Africa's Foreign Policy', in *South African Yearbook of International Affairs 2001/02*, South African Institute of International Affairs, Johannesburg, pp. 73–85.

——— and Alden, C., 2003, 'The Hegemon that Wasn't: South Africa's Policy Toward Zimbabwe', *Strategic Review for Southern Africa*, Vol. 23, pp. 1–28.

Scholtz, L., 2008, 'The ANC/SACP and the Crushing of the 1968 Prague Spring', *Die Burger*, August 22.

Schraeder, P., 2001, 'South Africa's Foreign Policy: From International Pariah to Leader of the African Renaissance', *Round Table*, No. 359, pp. 229–43.

Schrire, R., 1991, *Adapt or Die: The End of White Politics in South Africa*, Ford Foundation, New York.

——— and Silke, D., 1997, 'Foreign Policy: The Domestic Context', in *Change and South African Foreign Relations*, edited by Carlsnaes, W. and Muller, M., International Thomson Publishing, Johannesburg.

——— 1994, 'The Head of Government and the Executive', in *Leadership in the Apartheid State: From Malan to De Klerk*, edited by Schrire, R., Oxford University Press, Oxford.

Seegers, A., 1996, *The Military in the Making of Modern South Africa*, Tauris Publishing, London.

Selebi, J., 1999, 'South African Foreign Policy: Setting New Goals and Strategies', *South African Journal of International Affairs*, Vol. 6, No. 2, pp. 207–16.

Selfe, J., 1989 'South Africa's National Management System', in *War and Society: The Militarization of South Africa*, edited by Cock, J. and Nathan, L., David Phillip Press, Cape Town.

Serfontein, H., 1979, *Brotherhood of Power: An Expose of the Secret Afrikaner Broederbond*, Rex Collings Limited, London.

Shaw, G., 1999, *The Cape Times: An Informal History*, David Philip Publishers, Cape Town.

——— 2007, *Believe in Miracles: A Reporter's Story*, Ampersand Press, Cape Town.

Shaw, M., 1994, 'Biting the Bullet: Negotiating Democracy's Defense', in *The Small Miracle: South Africa's Negotiated Settlement*, South African Review 7, edited by Friedman, S. and Atkinson, D., Ravan Press, Randburg.

Shelton, G., 1986, 'Theoretical Perspectives on South African Foreign Policy Making', *Politikon*, Vol. 13, No. 1, pp. 3–21.

Shubin, V., 1995, *Flinging the Doors Open: Foreign Policy of the New South Africa*, Centre for Southern African Studies, University of the Western Cape.

———, 1996, 'The Soviet Union/Russian Federation's Relations with South Africa, with Special Reference to the Period since 1980', *African Affairs*, Vol. 95, No. 378, pp. 5–30.

——— 2008, *The 'Hot' Cold War: The USSR in Southern Africa*, Pluto Press, London.

Sidiropoulos, E. and Hughes, T., 2004, 'The Challenge of South Africa's Africa Policy', in *Apartheid Past, Renaissance Future: South Africa's Foreign Policy 1994–2004*, edited by Sidiropoulos, E., South African Institute of International Affairs, Johannesburg.

Sidiropoulos, E., 2008, 'Post-Mbeki, Post-Transition: South African Foreign Policy in a Changing World', in *South African Journal of International Affairs, 2008/09*, South African Institute of International Affairs, Johannesburg, pp. 3–10.

Simpson, G., 1989, 'The Politics and Economics of the Armaments Industry in South Africa', in *War and Society: The Militarization of South Africa*, edited by Cock, J. and Nathan, L., David Philip Publishers, Cape Town.

Slabbert, F., 1986, *The Last White Parliament*, Jonathan Ball, Johannesburg.

Snyder, R.; Bruck, H.; Sapin, B, Hudson, V.; Chollet, D.; and Goldgeier, J., 2003, *Foreign Policy Decision-making*, 2003, Macmillan Press, New York.

Sole, D., 1991, *'This Above All': Reminiscences of a South African Diplomat*, unpublished.

——— 1994, 'South African Foreign Policy from Hertzog to De Klerk', *South African Journal of International Affairs*, Vol. 2, No. 1, pp. 104–13.

Solomon, H., 2002, 'The Poverty of Pretoria's Preventative Diplomacy in the Great Lakes Region', in *South African Yearbook of International Affairs 2002/03*, South African Institute of International Affairs, Johannesburg, pp. 137–44.

Somerville, K., 1984, 'The USSR and Southern Africa since 1976', *The Journal of Modern African Studies*, Vol. 22, No. 1, pp. 73–108.

South African Institute of International Affairs, 'History of SAIIA', www.saiia.org.za.

Southall, R., 1999, 'South Africa In Africa: Foreign Policy Making During the Apartheid Era', Institute for Global Dialogue, Occasional Paper 20.

Spence, J., 1965, *Republic Under Pressure: A Study of South African Foreign Policy*, Oxford University Press, Oxford.

Stevens, R., 1970, 'South Africa and Independent Black Africa', *Africa Today*, Vol. 17, No. 3, pp. 25–32.

Stiff, P., 2002, *The Silent War: South African Recce Operations 1969–1994*, Galago, Germiston.

Stober, P. and Ludman, B., 2005, *Mail and Guardian A-Z of South African Politics*, Jacana, Johannesburg.

Stultz, N., 1969, 'The Politics of Security: South Africa Under Verwoerd, 1961–66', *The Journal of Modern African Studies*, Vol. 7, No. 1, pp. 6–20.

Suzman, H., 1993, *In No Uncertain Terms*, Jonathan Ball Press, Johannesburg.

Suttner, R., 1996 'A Brief Review of South African Foreign Policy Since 1994', *Umrabulo*, Issue 1.

——— 1997, 'South African Foreign Policy and the Promotion of Human Rights', in *South African Yearbook of International Affairs 1997*, South African Institute of International Affairs, Johannesburg, pp. 300–8.

Suzman, H., 1993, *In No Uncertain Terms*, Jonathan Ball Press, Johannesburg.

Taylor, I., 2001, *Stuck in Middle GEAR: South Africa's Post-Apartheid Foreign Relations*, Praeger Press, London.

——— 2006, 'Contradictions in South African Foreign Policy and NEPAD', in *In Full Flight: South African Foreign Policy After Apartheid*, edited by Carlsnaes, W. and Nel, P., Institute for Global Dialogue, Midrand.

Thomas, S., 1995, *The Diplomacy of Liberation: The Foreign Relations of the ANC Since 1960*, Tauris Publishing, London.

Vale, P., 1990 *Starting Over: Some Early Questions on a Post-Apartheid Foreign Policy*, Southern Africa Perspectives, Center for Southern African Studies, Cape Town.

——— and Maseko, S., 1998, 'South Africa and the African Renaissance', *International Affairs*, Vol. 74, No. 2, pp. 271–87.

————— 2003, *Security and Politics in South Africa: The Regional Dimension*, UCT Press, Cape Town.

————— 2010, 'Thabo Mbeki and the Great Foreign Policy Riddle', in *Mbeki and After*, edited by Glaser, D., Wits Press, Johannesburg.

Vandenbosch, A., 1970, *South Africa and the World: The Foreign Policy of Apartheid*, University of Kentucky Press, Lexington.

Van der Westhuizen, J., 1998, 'South Africa's Emergence as a Middle Power', *Third World Quarterly*, Vol. 19, No. 3, pp. 435–55.

Van Nieuwkerk, A., 2006, 'South Africa's Post-Apartheid Foreign Policy Decision-making on African Crises', unpublished doctoral dissertation, University of the Witwatersrand.

————— 2006, 'Foreign Policy Making in South Africa: Context, Actors, and Process', in *In Full Flight: South African Foreign Policy After Apartheid*, edited by Carlsnaes, W. and Nel, P., Institute for Global Dialogue, Midrand.

————— 2007, 'A Critique of South Africa's Role on the UN Security Council', *South African Journal of International Affairs*, Vol. 14, No. 1, pp. 61–77.

Van Wyk, A., 2005, 'Eric Louw: Pioneer Diplomat, 1925–37', in *History of the South African Department of Foreign Affairs 1927–1993*, edited by Wheeler, T., South African Institute of International Affairs, Johannesburg.

—————, 2005, 'The High Commissioner in Great Britain', in *History of the South African Department of Foreign Affairs 1927–1993*, edited by Wheeler, T., South African Institute of International Affairs, Johannesburg.

Van Wyk, J., 1997, 'Parliament and Foreign Affairs: Continuity or Change?', in *South African Yearbook of International Affairs 1997*, South African Institute of International Affairs, Johannesburg, pp. 189–213.

————— 1998, 'The External Relations of Selected South African Subnational Governments', *South African Journal of International Affairs*, Vol. 5, No. 2, pp. 21–59.

————— 1998, 'Parliament and the Foreign Policy Process', in *South African Yearbook of International Affairs 1998/99*, South African Institute of International Affairs, Johannesburg, pp. 291–306.

Venter, D., 2001, 'South African Foreign Policy Decision-making in the African Context', in *African Foreign Policies, Power and Process*, edited by Khadiagala, G. and Lyons, T., Lynne Rienner, Boulder.

Viljoen, G., 1979, 'An Afrikaner Looks Ahead', in *The Afrikaners*, edited by Munger, E., Tafelberg, Cape Town.

Wallace, W., 1971, *Foreign Policy and the Political Process*, Macmillan Press, New York.

Weir, A. and Bloch, J., 1981, 'The Militarization of BOSS', *Covert Action*, No. 13.

Welsh, D., 2009, *The Rise and Fall of Apartheid,* Jonathan Ball, Johannesburg.

White, G., 1996, 'Grassroots Foreign Policy? A Case for Provincial Participation', *Indicator South Africa*, Vol. 13, No. 4, pp. 25–30.

Wilhelm, P., 2004, 'The 20 Most Influential People in SA Business: Thabo Mbeki', *Financial Mail*, December 24.

Wilkins, I. and Strydom, H., 1980, *The Super Afrikaners*, Jonathan Ball, Johannesburg.

Williams, P., 2006, 'Pragmatic Multilateralism? South Africa and Peace Operations', in *The New Multilateralism in South African Diplomacy*, edited by Lee, D.; Taylor, I.; and Williams, P., Palgrave Macmillan, New York.

Williams, R., 2003, 'Defense in a Democracy: The South African Defense Review and the Redefinition of the Parameters of the National Defense Debate', in *Ourselves to Know: Civil-Military Relations and Defense Transformation in Southern Africa*, edited by Williams, R.; Cawthra, G.; and Abrahams, D., Institute for Security Studies, Pretoria.

Winter, G., 1981, *Inside BOSS: South Africa's Secret Police*, Penguin, London.

Wolvaardt, P.; Wheeler, T.; and Scholtz, W. (editors), 2010, *From Verwoerd to Mandela: South African Diplomats Remember, Volumes 1–3*, Crink, Cape Town.

ANC Documents

'Adopted Resolutions on Foreign Policy', ANC 48th National Conference, July 1991.

African National Congress Constitution, 2007.

'Apartheid Distabilisation: Pretoria's Regional Strategy', ANC Research Unit of the Department of Information and Publicity, November 1984, from Mayibuye Archive, University of Western Cape.

'Commission Reports and Draft Resolutions: International Relations', ANC National Policy Conference, June 2007.

'Decisions and Suggestions From NEC/PMC Meeting', January 25, 1984, in Gail Gerhart and Clive Glaser, *From Protest to Challenge: A Documentary History of African Politics in South Africa, Volume 6: Challenge and Victory, 1980–1990*, Indiana University Press, 2010.

'Foreign Policy in a New Democratic South Africa: A Discussion Paper', ANC Department of International Affairs, October 1993.

'Foreign Policy Perspective in a New South Africa', ANC, December 1994.

'Proposed Meeting Between Representatives of the Zambian Government and ANC Leadership', memorandum dated October 21, 1988, in ANC Mayibuye Archives, University of the Western Cape.

'Second National Consultative Conference: Report of the Commission on Foreign Policy', June 1985.

'State of Organization', January 17, 1989, in ANC Mayibuye Archives, University of the Western Cape.

Government Documents

Chikane, F., 2000, 'Democratic Governance—A Restructured Presidency at Work', The Presidency.

Constitution of South Africa, 1961.

Constitution of South Africa, 1983.

Constitution of South Africa, 1996.

Defense White Paper, Department of Defense, 1996.

Defense Review, Department of Defense, 1998.

South Africa Act of 1909.

'South African Trade By Region', www.dti.gov.

'State of the Nation Address by the President of South Africa, Thabo Mbeki to the Joint Sitting of the Houses of Parliament', February 8, 2002.

INDEX

Abacha, Sani, 34–35, 43, 116, 243
Adebajo, Adekeye, 117, 131
Afghanistan, 2, 102
Africa Institute of South Africa, 53, 92, 95–96, 100–101, 114, 126, 128
African Advertiser, 72
African Center for Constructive Resolution of Disputes, 114–115, 125
African Charter, 18, 233
African National Congress
Contacts with government while in exile, 26, 213
Department of Information and Publicity (DIP), 106, 189
Department of International Affairs (DIA), 8, 31, 54, 106–108, 188, 192–193, 245, 257
Department of International Relations, 8, 192–193, 199, 257
Foreign policy in exile, 15, 26–30, 185–187
Foreign policymaking in exile, 183–185, 187–189
Interactions with academics before transition, 106–108
Interactions with academics during transition, 108–112,
Kabwe conference, 184, 187–188
Mafikeng conference, 197
Morogoro conference, 28, 184, 187–189
National Executive Committee (NEC), 174, 177, 184–185, 187, 191–194, 252
NEC Subcommittee on International Relations, 8, 126, 193–196, 199
National Working Committee (NWC), 174, 191–193
Parliamentary caucus, 170–180
Polokwane conference, 45, 149
Post-transition decisionmaking structures, 3, 190–192
Relations with business community, 148–149, 151
Relations with civil society, 55
Relations with press, 83–84, 87
Relations with tripartite alliance partners, 6, 43, 61–65
Religious Affairs Committee, 137
Stellenbosch conference, 197
African Peer Review Mechanism, 39, 60
African Renaissance, 37–38, 43–44, 220
African Union, 39, 63
Afrikaanse Pers, 74
Afrikaner Party, 16
Afrobarometer, 259
Airports Company South Africa, 148

Ajulu, Rok, 123, 128–129, 131–132
Allison, Graham, 200
Anglo-American, 7, 93, 135–136, 138,
    141, 143, 145, 150–152
Angola, 34, 150, 194, 251
    Military involvement, 50, 53, 58,
        78–80, 82, 96, 165, 206–208,
        211, 215, 237
    Pre-1994 involvement, 21–22,
        24–26, 28, 136
Arafat, Yasser, 37
Arcelor Mittal, 155
Argentina, 22
Argus Group, 72
Arms sales, 36, 120, 165, 171, 244, 255
Asmal, Kader, 109, 119, 187, 219, 227
Association of Chambers of Commerce,
    135
Aung San Suu Kyi, 109
Auret, Derek, 49

Baker, James, 209
Balfour Declaration, 14, 16, 52,
    161–162, 201
Banjo, Adewale, 1
Barber, James, 20
Barlows (Barlow Rand), 143
Barnard, Niel, 13, 80–81, 94, 96,
    102, 105, 132, 182, 212–217,
    240–241
Barnato, Barney, 135
Barratt, John, 20, 93, 100, 107, 109,
    114, 116
Basson, Japie, 48, 164, 166
Basson, Whitey, 150
Basuto National Party, 20
Beaufre, Andre, 97–98
Beeld, 74–75, 77
Berlin Air Lift, 17
Beukes, Herbert, 209
BHP Billiton, 150
Big Business Working Group, 152
Biko, Steven, 23
Bizos, George, 107

Black Business Council, 151
Black Economic Empowerment, 149,
    152
Bloom, Tony, 138
Bodenstein, HD, 232
Boesak, Allan, 54
Boshielo, Simon, 62, 65
Boshoff, Henri, 50, 58, 125, 226
Botha, Con, 182
Botha, Frikkie, 204
Botha, Louis, 162, 230
Botha, Pik, 13, 25, 53, 80, 82, 95, 104,
    142, 164–169, 207–209, 211,
    215, 217, 235, 237, 239, 242,
Botha, PW, 23–26, 75–79, 86, 95,
    105, 141, 143–145, 165, 183,
    206–212, 228, 237–241
Botswana (Bechuanaland), 18, 20, 24,
    34–35, 183, 189, 211
Brazil, 22
Brazzaville Protocol, 25
Brenthurst Group, 152
Breuning, Marijke, 1, 10
British Broadcasting Corporation, 79
Broederbond, 6, 51–54, 141, 182,
    198, 205
Brussels Convention, 73
Bureau of State Security, 21, 23,
    205–206, 212–213
Burger, Albie, 235
Burma (Myanmar), 41, 86, 89, 128,
    177
Burundi, 39–40, 58, 88, 115, 225
Bush, George HW, 31
Business Day, 84, 87
Business Leadership South Africa, 7,
    147, 151, 256, 260
Business South Africa, 151
Business Unity South Africa, 7, 151,
    256, 260
Buthelezi, Mangosuthu, 244

Caetano, Marcelo, 22
Calland, Richard, 10, 249

Cameroon, 147
Cape Argus, 72
Cape Federation of Labor Unions, 54
Cape Times, 72, 78–79, 81, 89, 110
Cape Town Gazette, 72
Carlton conference, 141, 144
Cassinga attacks, 207
Castro, Fidel, 37
Cawthra, Gavin, 110
Center for Chinese Studies
　(Stellenbosch), 125
Center for Conflict Resolution, 115,
　117
Center for International Politics
　(Potchefstroom), 93
Center for Latin American Studies
　(UNISA), 93
Center for Policy Studies, 115–116
Center for South African Studies, 108,
　114
Central African Republic, 21
Central Intelligence Agency, 190, 206
Chamber of Mines, 135
Chase Manhattan Bank, 25
Chettle, John, 140
Chikane, Frank, 11–12, 54, 61, 87,
　156, 249
China, 32, 41, 54, 62, 124
　Chinese arms shipment, 2008,
　　66–67, 261
　'One China' policy, 37, 63, 66, 171,
　　194, 219–220, 243, 250, 252,
　　260
Cilliers, Jakkie, 111, 114
Cillié, Piet, 74, 76–77, 82–83
Citigroup, 155
Citizen, The, 207
Cock, Jacklyn, 110
Cockram, Ben, 92, 97–98
Coetsee, Kobie, 213
Colombia, 129
Commerzbank, 155
Committee on Security
　Management, 217

Commonwealth, 16, 32, 35, 60, 162,
　166, 195, 202, 232
　Eminent Persons Group, 210
　Trade preferences, 17–19, 145
　Withdrawal from, 14, 167, 203, 235,
　　259
Communist Party of South Africa,
　26, 28
Comoros, 139
Comprehensive Anti-Apartheid Act,
　25, 31
Congo-Brazzaville, 67
Congo-Kinshasa (Zaire), 34, 39–40,
　122, 137, 148, 202, 219, 225,
　244, 249. 251
Congress of South African Trade
　Unions, 6, 43, 61–67, 69,
　260–262
Constellation of Southern African
　States, 24, 142, 144
Coordination and Implementation
　Unit, 222
Cornelissen, Scarlett, 58
Crocker, Chester, 104, 240
Cuba, 22, 25, 65, 85, 195

Daniel, John, 108, 113, 121
Davies, Martyn, 124
Davies, Rob, 104, 106, 108–109, 114
De Beers, 135, 138
Defense Act of 1912, 201
Defense Advisory Council, 143
Defense Amendment Act, 78, 80–81
Defense Staff College, 97
De Klerk, FW, 30–31, 77, 111, 148,
　216–218, 228, 241–243
De Klerk, Willem, 82
Democratic Alliance, 86, 176, 179
Democratic Party, 115
Democratic Party (USA), 100, 190
Department of Defense, 9, 60, 96–99,
　119, 123, 164
　Pre-1994 role, 23–25, 201–203,
　　206–208

Post-1994 role, 39, 218, 224–228, 257
Department of External Affairs, 16, 173, 201, 204, 231–233
Department of Foreign Affairs, 32, 54, 56, 139, 172, 208, 215, 230, 257
Diplomatic Academy, 124
Interactions with academia, 95–96, 100–102, 104, 112, 117, 110, 124–125
Policy, Research, and Analysis Unit (PRAU), 125
Post-1994 challenges, 35, 218–220, 222–224, 249
Relations with business community, 148, 150, 156
Relations with Department of Defense, 202–203, 206–212
Relations with Department of Information, 203–204
Relations with Parliament, 170–173, 176, 178
Department of Home Affairs, 35
Department of Information, 9, 21, 93, 203–207
Department of National Security, 212
Department of Provincial and Local Government, 221
Department of Trade and Industry, 9, 118, 123–124, 150, 200, 218, 221, 224, 257
Development Bank of Southern Africa, 144
De Villiers, Dawie, 50, 145, 166, 182, 238, 242
Diamond, Larry, 4
Die Afrikaanse Patriot, 72
Die Burger, 72–77, 86, 89
Die Transvaler, 73–74, 76, 234
Dlamini-Zuma, Nkosazana, 58, 60, 87, 122, 176, 194, 223–224, 228
Dommisse, Ebbe, 75–76, 79, 81–82
Draper, Peter, 124, 152
Du Pisani, Andre, 94

Du Plessis, Barend, 52, 145, 242
Du Plessis, Jan, 99
Du Plessis, Wynand, 211
Durr, Kent, 215
Dutch Reformed Churches, 53–54

East Timor, 243
Ebrahim, Ebrahim, 171, 173, 176, 180, 193
Eduardo Mondlane University, 104
Eglin, Colin, 164, 168, 176, 180, 238, 256
Ehlers, Ters, 216, 240
Erasmus, FC, 202
Erwin, Alec, 123, 219
Eskom, 42, 127, 135, 148, 156
Esterhuyse, Willie, 96, 107, 213
European Community, 30
European Union, 2, 118, 219
Evans, Rusty, 113, 172, 176, 219

Fabricius, Peter, 76, 80, 82, 87–89
Fatah, 57
Federasie van Afrikaanse Kultuurverenigings (FAK), 51, 53
Federated Chambers of Industry, 135–136
Feinstein, Andrew, 173–174, 250
Ferreira, Jannie, 89
Financial Mail, 144
Fischer, Bram, 81
Fitzgerald, Niall, 155
Ford Foundation, 116
Ford, Gerald, 204
Foreign Affairs, 33, 109
Foreign Policy Analysis, 3
Fourie, Brand, 100, 103, 235, 237
Fourie, Deon, 92, 94, 97–99, 101, 133
France, 73, 97, 147
Frankel, Joseph, 2, 161
Fraser, Allan, 97–98
Freedom Charter, 27, 108
Frelimo, 57

Friedman, Steven, 156
Friedrich Ebert Stiftung, 115

G-8, 45
G-77, 32
Gadhafi, Muammar, 37, 244
Geldenhuys, Boy, 49, 54, 164, 176, 180, 256
Geldenhuys, Deon, 10, 32, 94–95, 103–105, 118, 163
Geldenhuys, Jannie, 13, 80, 99, 210
Gencor, 143
Genscher, Hans-Dietrich, 209
George, Mluleki, 122, 198, 226
Georgetown University, 212
Germany, 16, 32, 115, 168
Gerwel, Jakes, 244
Gevisser, Mark, 175, 247–248
Ghana, 18, 21, 233
Gibson, Rex, 81
Giliomee, Hermann, 52, 74, 158
Gingrich, Newt, 190
Ginwala, Frene, 108
Global Political Agreement, 45
Gounden, Vasu, 108, 114, 129, 132
Government Communication and Information System, 58
Graaff, De Villiers, 167
Great Britain, 16–18, 26, 29, 36, 48, 82, 136, 138, 161–162, 167, 187, 199, 202
Groenewald, Tienie, 214, 239
Growth for All, 154
Gumbi, Mojanku, 12, 156, 249
Gumede, Josiah, 38–39
Gumede, William, 196
Gutto, Shadrack, 122, 125, 132

Hajaig, Fatima, 57, 171, 178, 180, 194
Hamas, 57
Handley, Antoinette, 154
Hani, Chris, 111
Hanlon, Joseph, 104
Havana Conference, 29

Havenga, Nicholaas, 202, 232
Heard, Tony, 78–79, 86
Heitman, Helmoed Romer, 99, 111, 119
Herbst, Jeffrey, 199
Hertzog, JBM, 16, 52, 54, 135, 162, 230–232, 257
Hill, Christopher, 70, 160
Hirsch, Alan, 109
Hofmeyr, Jan, 231
Holsti, Ole, 5–6
Hough, Mike, 94, 99
Houphouet-Boigny, Felix, 21
Hughes, Tim, 114, 123, 128, 175–177, 222
Human Rights Council, 41
Huntington, Samuel, 4
Hussein, Saddam, 57
Huyser, John, 98

Independent Media Group, 155
Indonesia, 31
India, 31–32
Industrial Development Corporation, 135–136
Inkatha Freedom Party, 176
Institute for Defense Policy, 111, 114
Institute for Global Dialogue, 109, 116–118, 121–124, 127, 129–130
Institute for Justice and Reconciliation, 115, 126
Institute for Security Studies, 111, 116–117, 125
Institute for Strategic Studies (University of Pretoria), 93–94, 98–99, 114
Institute for the Study of Marxism (Stellenbosch), 93
Internal Security Act, 79
Inter-Congolese Dialogue, 40, 249
International Court of Justice, 235
International Institute of Strategic Studies, 100
International Monetary Fund, 25, 38, 42

International Relations, Peace, and
    Security cluster, 221–222
Iran, 22, 41, 129, 219
Iraq, 12, 40, 57, 192, 223
Irish Republican Army (Sinn Fein), 187
Israel, 22, 24, 40, 51, 57, 232
Israel-South African Friendship League,
    50
Ivory Coast, 21, 40

Jackson, Gordon, 78
Jele, Josiah, 107, 188
Jhazbhay, Iqbal, 125
Johannesburg Stock Exchange, 141,
    147
John Birch Society, 100
Johnson, Alexander, 3
Johnson, Lyndon, 100
Jonathan, Leabua, 20, 236
Jooste, GP, 235
Jordaan, Danny, 171
Jordan, Pallo, 13, 43, 65–66, 106, 177,
    179–180, 184–186, 194–195,
    197, 221, 247–248
Joubert, Jan-Jan, 86
Justice, Crime Prevention, and Security
    cluster, 221

Kabila, Joseph, 40
Kabila, Laurent, 34
Kahn, Calvin, 110
Kasrils, Ronnie, 119, 122, 195
Kaunda, Kenneth, 28, 141, 205
Kennedy, John F, 11
Kenya, 21, 136
Kerzner, Sol, 139
Khoza, Reuel, 155–157
Khumalo, Bheki, 45
Khumalo, Dumisani, 249
Killen, Rae, 211
Kimberley Process, 224
Kinkel, Klaus, 241
Kissinger, Henry, 104, 209
Kohl, Helmut, 115

Kohlhausen, Martin, 155
Korean War, 17, 233
Kotzé, Hennie, 105
Kunert, Dirk, 95
KWV, 137

Labour Party (Great Britain), 190
Landmines, campaign to ban, 60, 171
Landsberg, Chris, 115, 121, 123,
    127–132
League of Nations, 230–231
Lebanon, 40
Lekota, Mosiuoa, 13, 43, 122,
    194–195, 197, 226–227, 248
Leistner, Erich, 101
Leon, Tony, 179
Le Pere, Garth, 56, 116–117,
    119–123, 127–129, 131–132
Le Roux, Len, 225
Lesotho (Basutoland), 18, 20, 24,
    34–35, 57, 115, 142, 172, 220,
    236, 244
Liberia, 21, 115, 226
Liebenberg, Kat, 80, 111
Linz, Juan, 4
Lipset, Seymour, 4
Lockerbie bombings, 243–244
Louw, Eric, 53, 78, 201–203, 228,
    232–235
Luthuli, Albertina, 56, 174–175,
    177–178
Luthuli House, 174, 191, 196
Luyt, Louis, 143

Mabizela, Stanley, 108
Machel, Samora, 141
Macozoma, Saki, 155, 157
Madagascar, 21, 139
Madisha, Willie, 63–65, 69
Mafolo, Titus, 121
Maharaj, Mac, 107
Mail & Guardian, The, 87, 113
Makatini, Johnny, 185, 188–190
Makhanya, Mondli, 84–85, 87–88

Makoni, Simba, 127
Malan, Daniel F, 16–19, 73–75, 166,
  202–203, 228, 232–233, 252
Malan, Magnus, 102, 104, 143, 208,
  211–212, 216–217, 228,
  239–240
Malawi, 21–22
Malaysia, 31
Malcolm X, 186
Mali, 148
Mamabolo, Kingsley, 124
Mandela, Nelson, 8, 15, 30–38, 40,
  107, 115, 260–261
  Decisionmaking style, 194,
    218–220, 228, 243–246, 250,
    252–253
  Foreign Affairs article, 109, 113
  Relations with business community,
    84, 86, 90
  Relations with Parliament,
    170–172
  Release, 26, 106, 186, 213, 241,
Manuel, Trevor, 122, 226–227
Maphai, Vincent, 108, 150–151, 154
Markinor, 59
Maseko, Sipho, 108
Masire, Ketumile, 34
Masuku, Bongani, 64–66, 69
Matlhako, Chris, 62, 64, 69
Mbeki, Moeletsi, 127
Mbeki, Thabo
  Decisionmaking style, 9–11, 228,
    244–250, 252–253, 258, 261
  Foreign policy priorities as President,
    15, 30, 33, 35, 37–41
  Management of government, 32,
    113, 220–227
  Pre-transition ANC role, 29–31,
    129, 185, 188–190
  Relations with academics in office, 7,
    116, 120–123, 128, 133
  Relations with academics during
    transition, 106–108

Relations with ANC as President, 8,
  12, 45–46, 181, 192–193,
  196–199
Relations with business community,
  148–149, 151–156, 158
Relations with civil society and
  public, 58, 60–62, 260
Relations with Parliament, 170,
  172–178
Relations with press, 83–90
Relations with tripartite alliance
  partners, 6, 63–66
Zimbabwe policy, 41–45, 65, 128,
  156–157, 195, 250–252
Mboweni, Tito, 152, 174
McCuen, John, 98
Meiring, Kobus, 137
Meiring, Piet, 168
Menatsi, Richard, 61
Mercury, The, 78
Mervis, Joel, 73
Middle East, 6, 11, 37, 59, 61–62, 66,
  129, 180, 223
Military Intelligence, 94, 97, 111, 205,
  211–214
Military Research Group, 110–111
Mills, Greg, 114, 116–117, 224
Minty, Abdul, 172, 223
Mnangagwa, Emmerson, 180
Modise, Joe, 225
Mogoba, Stanley, 116
Morocco, 123, 194–195
Motlatsi, James, 63
Motsepe, Patrice, 155
Motsuenyane, Sam, 144, 157
Movement for Democratic Change, 41,
  44–45, 64, 127
Mozambique, 21–22, 24, 28, 104,
  107, 136, 141, 206, 210, 214,
  221–222, 244
MPLA, 22, 57, 194
Mufamadi, Sydney, 45, 58, 65–66, 68,
  122, 221, 244, 248–249

Mugabe, Robert, 24, 34, 43–44,
  63–64, 88–89, 127, 141, 157,
  179, 195, 244, 251
Mulder, Connie, 77, 204, 207, 228, 237
Muldergate, 93, 164, 207–208
Muller, Hilgard, 45, 58, 65–66, 68,
  122, 221, 244, 248–249
Munger, Ned, 10, 49, 52–53, 68, 92,
  95, 99, 145, 202, 233, 235
Murray & Roberts, 137
Myakayaka-Manzini, Mavivi, 108, 126,
  149, 193–194, 196–197

Namibia, 25–26, 34, 206, 210, 235,
  241, 251
Napier, Wilfrid, 61
Nasionale Pers (Naspers), 72–76, 84,
  89, 137
Nathan, Laurie, 110, 115, 119, 122,
  131
National Assembly, 169, 227
National Conventional Arms Control
  Committee, 67, 119, 261
National Council of Provinces, 169,
  227
National Economic Development and
  Labor Council, 152
National Intelligence Agency, 123, 127
National Intelligence Service, 26, 94,
  96, 102, 211–214, 217
National Intelligence Coordinating
  Council, 123
National Office for the Coordination of
  Peace Missions, 226
National Party, 3, 16, 102, 133, 201
  Influence on foreign policy, 8,
    181–183, 198
  Parliamentary caucus, 162,
    165–167, 238, 241, 256
  Relations with press, 74–77, 83, 87,
    90, 255
National Religious Leaders' Forum, 61
National Security Council, 223
National Union of Mineworkers, 63

Native Land Act, 26
Naude, Beyers, 54
Ndungane, Njongonkulu, 61
Nel, Louis, 209
Nel, Philip, 55–56, 93–96, 101
Netshitenzhe, Joel, 12, 122, 249
New Economic Partnership for Africa's
  Development, 39–40, 44, 60–61,
  63, 128, 152, 177, 246
New National Party, 176
New York Times, The, 79
Ngcukana, Cunningham, 65, 129
Ngonyama, Smuts, 13, 156, 249, 251
Nhlanhla, Joe, 122
Nhlapo, Welile, 124, 222–223
Nigeria, 32, 34–36, 43, 116, 121, 147,
  171, 189, 197, 233, 343–244,
  251–252
Nkobi, Thomas, 184
Nkomati Accord, 187, 210
Nkuhlu, Wiseman, 249
Nokwe, Duma, 27, 184, 187–188
Non-Aligned Movement, 29, 32
North Atlantic Treaty Organization,
  17, 21
Norton, Philip, 160
Nqakula, Charles, 171
Ntsaluba, Ayanda, 87, 124, 176
Nzimande, Blade, 63
Nzo, Alfred, 35–36, 170, 172, 184,
  190, 194, 219–220

Obasanjo, Olusegun, 34
Official Secrets Act, 79
Old Mutual, 137
Olivier, Gerrit, 55, 94, 96, 118, 132,
  209–210
Open Society Initiative for Southern
  Africa, 67
Operation Savannah, 22, 50, 79
Oppenheimer, Ernest, 135
Oppenheimer, Harry, 140–142, 144
Orange Free State, 15, 76
O'Reilly, Tony, 155

Organization of African Unity, 29, 32, 35, 38, 187, 194
Owen, Ken, 83

Pahad, Aziz, 13, 33, 36, 44–45, 59, 61, 64–65, 112, 149, 157, 172, 184, 188, 190, 192–195
  Relations with academics, 112–113, 116–120, 122–123, 127–129, 131
  Relations with Mbeki, 221–224, 228, 243–245, 247–251
  Relations with press, 87–88
Pahad, Essop, 13, 57, 154, 186, 189–190, 197
Palestine, 40, 57, 65, 195, 223
Palestinian Liberation Organization, 37, 57, 195
Pan-Africanist Congress, 29, 32, 116, 193, 203
Paraguay, 22
Parliamentary Monitoring Group, 175, 180
Parsons, Wayne, 70
Pearson, Peter John, 69
Perskor, 74–75
Phillip, Ruben, 67
Pienaar, Sara, 101, 107, 114, 116,
Pienaar, Schalk, 74
Pirow, Oswald, 232
Pityana, Sipho, 124, 176, 185, 224, 251
Pogrund, Benjamin, 73
Policy Coordination and Advisory Services, 222, 249
Polokwane conference, 45, 149, 196
Portfolio Committee on Foreign Affairs, 36, 64, 126, 170–180, 194, 253, 257
Portugal, 22, 206–207
Potchefstroom University, 93
Prague Spring, 82
Premier Milling, 138
Presidential Support Unit, 222

Progressive Federal Party, 141, 167–168
Project Coast, 24

Radebe, Hopewell, 84, 88
Rafsanjani, Akbar, 219
Ramgobin, Mewa, 177, 179–180, 196
Rand Afrikaans University, 93, 98, 101, 103, 108
Rand Daily Mail, 72–73, 78, 80–81, 207
Rand zone, 21
Rapport, 80, 82
Rautenbach, Billy, 85
Reagan, Ronald, 25, 190
Reddy, JN, 144
Rembrandt, 137, 140, 154
RENAMO, 24, 210, 214
Relly, Gavin, 138, 141
Republican Intelligence, 205
Republican Party (US), 190
Reuters, 155
Rhodes, Bill, 155
Rhodes, Cecil, 135
Rhodesia, 21–22, 28, 48, 53, 136, 167, 205, 220, 237, 259
Rhoodie, Eschel, 204, 228, 237
Ries, Alf, 76, 82, 255
Rothmans, 137
Roux, Jannie, 214–215, 225, 239–240, 242
Rubicon speech, 25, 142, 240
Ruiterwag, 51
Rupert, Anton, 137, 140–143, 152, 234
Rupert, Johann, 154
Russia, 31, 41, 93
Rwanda, 45, 115, 244, 251

SAFM, 89
Saloojee, Yusuf, 107–108, 193
Sanlam, 137, 143
Santam, 137
Sappi, 154

Saro-Wiwa, Ken, 34–35, 171, 243
Sasol, 42, 156, 187
Savimbi, Jonas, 22, 34
Schlebush, Alwyn, 213
Schoeman, Maxi, 108, 246
Schoeman, Renier, 49, 145, 168, 198
Sechaba, 184
Seegers, Annette, 118, 123
Selebi, Jackie, 38, 55, 124, 148, 171,
    220, 228, 249
Senegal, 21
Senghor, Leopold, 21
September 11 attacks, 123, 192
Serfontein, Hennie, 52
Sharpeville Massacre, 19, 21, 142,
    203, 235
Shaw, Gerald, 78, 82
Shearer, Jeremy, 100, 139–140
Shell House, 109–110
Shell Oil Company, 34
Shelton, Garth, 101, 120, 124
Shop Steward, 62, 69
Shoprite Checkers, 148–150
Shultz, George, 29, 190
Sibande, Mtikini, 175
Sidiropoulos, Elizabeth, 116, 125,
    129, 254
Silvermine base, 21
Sisulu, Lindiwe, 122, 127
Sisulu, Walter, 27, 250
Sithole, Job, 57–58, 176–179,
    195–196, 198
Skosana, Ben, 176, 180, 256–257
Small Business Development
    Corporation, 144
Smith, Ian, 48, 213, 251
Smith, Karen, 131
Smuts, Jan, 16, 27, 54, 115, 135,
    163, 230–232, 247, 252, 258
Soekor, 60
Sole, Donald, 95, 100, 104, 168,
    203, 231–233, 235, 239
Solomon, Hussein, 108
South Africa Act, 161–162

South Africa Foundation, 139–140,
    147, 151, 156
South African Agricultural Union, 135
South African Air Force, 17
South African Army, 16
South African Association of Political
    Studies, 94
South African Breweries, 136, 143, 147
South African Chamber of Business,
    151, 152
South African Chamber of Commerce
    and Industry, 151
South African Communist Party, 6, 28,
    61–64, 69, 81, 96, 183, 187, 190
South African Council of Churches,
    60–61
South African Defense Force, 22,
    80–81, 93, 96–97, 99, 110–111,
    143, 206–208, 210–211, 215,
    225
South African Foreign Trade
    Organization, 136, 151
South African Institute of International
    Affairs, 17, 49, 93–94, 99–101,
    103, 107–108, 114–117,
    123–125, 127, 129, 147,
    175–176, 254
South African National Defense Force,
    35, 39, 58, 169, 221, 225–226
South African National Editors Forum,
    85
South African Press Association, 73
South African Reserve Bank, 127, 152,
    174
South African Secret Service, 123, 127,
    220
South African Trades and Labor
    Council, 54
South African Treasury, 122, 200, 225
Southall, Roger, 109, 120
Southern African Catholic Bishops
    Conference, 60–61, 69
Southern African Customs Union,
    21, 216

Southern African Development Community, 32–36, 39, 42–43, 147–148, 222, 251
Southern African Development Coordination Conference, 24
Southern Africa Litigation Center, 67
Southwest Africa, 25–27, 168
Southwest African People's Organization, 211
Soviet Union/USSR, 17, 22, 26–29, 93, 98–99, 101–102, 107–108, 184, 187, 189, 206, 241
Sowetan, The, 84
Soweto massacre, 22, 28, 142, 186
Spicer, Michael, 147, 149, 153–155, 158
Standard Bank, 153
State Security Committee, 205
State Security Council, 80, 105, 210, 214–217, 220, 228, 238–239, 252
Steenkamp, Johan, 53, 166–167
Steenkamp, Willem, 79–80, 110–111, 119
Stellenbosch University, 57, 93, 96, 98, 101, 131, 213
Steward, Dave, 50, 102, 211, 216, 242–243
Steyn, Pierre, 111
Stiff, Peter, 50
Strauss, Conrad, 153
Sudan, 39–41, 50, 125–126, 148, 225
Sunday Times, 72, 84, 105
Suttner, Raymond, 36, 63, 170–173, 176, 194, 222, 257
Stalin, Joseph, 26
Star, The, 72, 78, 82, 89
Strijdom, Johannes, 17–19, 74–75, 142, 166, 203, 228, 233–234, 252, 258
Strydom, Hans, 52
Swart, Freek, 77
Swaziland, 6, 18, 20, 24, 63, 65, 145, 189, 222, 260
Sweden, 29, 117, 173

Taiwan, 22, 31, 37, 243
Tambo, Oliver, 9, 27–29, 79, 183–185, 189–190, 197, 248
Tanzania, 148, 183–184
Tata, 155
Terrorism Research Center, 98
Thatcher, Margaret, 29
Thompson, Robert, 98
Tolbert, William, 21
Total Strategy, 17, 23, 53, 97, 143
Traher, Tony, 155
Transitional Executive Council, 15, 31, 193
Transnet, 127, 147
Transvaal (republic), 15
Transvaal (province), 76, 182, 204, 233
Tsafendas, Dimitris, 236
Tsedu, Mathata, 84–86, 89
Tsele, Molefe, 61
Tsvangirai, Morgan, 44, 63–64, 127
Turok, Ben, 174, 184–185, 247
Tutu, Desmond, 54, 61, 66–67
Tyawa, Baby, 58
Tyson, Harvey, 78, 80, 82

Uganda, 34
Umkhonto we Sizwe (ANC armed wing), 28, 110–111, 183, 188, 190
Unilateral Declaration of Independence (Rhodesia), 48, 82, 136, 167, 236
UNITA, 22, 34, 206, 214
United Democratic Front, 65, 112, 186
United Nations, 14, 16, 19–20, 22–23, 27, 32, 38, 40, 60, 171, 188, 209, 220, 231
Security Council, 37, 125, 128, 172, 207
United Party, 16, 77, 141, 162, 167, 231, 239
United States of America, 14, 16, 20–21, 25, 29, 32–33, 50, 68, 100, 103, 116, 136, 147, 160, 175, 186, 189, 207
University of Free State, 212

University of Pretoria, 93, 124, 203
University of South Africa, 3, 93–94,
    97, 122, 125
University of the Western Cape, 108
University of the Witwatersrand,
    92–93, 95, 97, 101, 110, 116,
    125
Uruguay, 22
USS Independence, 19
Uzbekistan, 41

Vale, Peter, 94, 100–101, 107–109,
    113–114, 121, 131
Van den Bergh, Hendrik, 53, 205–208,
    213, 215, 228, 237, 240
Van der Merwe, Sue, 123, 176
Van der Reit, WR, 98
Van der Westhuizen, Theuns, 76–77,
    80
Van Deventer, Hennie, 52, 81, 83–84
Van Heerden, Neil, 96, 140–141,
    152–154, 156, 158, 210
Van Niekerk, Albert, 203
Van Niekerk, Anton, 96
Van Nieuwkerk, Anthoni, 56, 58, 108,
    115–116, 121, 127
Van Staden, Gary, 108–109
Van Wyk, Jo-Ansie, 180
Venter, Denis, 92, 101
Versailles Conference, 26, 230–231
Verwoerd, Hendrik, 18–20, 22, 68,
    73–75, 99, 142, 145, 166, 203–
    204, 234–236, 238, 247, 252
Vickers, Brendan, 56, 132
Victoria Falls conference, 141, 205
Viljoen, Constandt, 80, 97, 211
Viljoen, Piet, 216
Viviers, Jack, 240
Vlok, Adriaan, 216
Volksblad, 52, 72, 76
Voortrekker Pers, 74
Vorster, John, 20–23, 48–50, 53, 74–
    76, 78, 86, 90, 143, 164, 187,
    203–208, 215, 228, 236–238, 258

Vosloo, Ton, 75–77, 81–82, 84,
    87–88

Wankie campaign, 28
Warsaw Pact, 29
Washington Star, 204
Weber, Phil, 75
Western Sahara, 62, 65, 171, 194–195
Wheeler, Tom, 219, 235, 246
Wilkins, Ivor, 52
Williams, Rocky, 110
World Bank, 38, 150
World Trade Organization, 32–33
World War I, 48, 230
World War II, 48, 54, 73, 135–136,
    161–162, 203–205, 231, 259
Worrall, Denis, 169, 210

Xuma, AB, 27

Zambia, 136, 145, 148, 184, 188, 205,
    214
Zim, Lazarus, 156
Zimbabwe, 41, 102, 107
    Academic engagement on, 123,
        127–129, 132–133
    ANC debate on, 41–45, 176,
        179–180, 195, 250–252
    Independence, 24, 29, 210, 213
    Intervention in Congo-Kinshasa, 34,
        219
    Outside actor engagement on, 61,
        63, 65–67, 156–1158, 259–260,
        262
    Relations with South Africa and
        ANC during 1980s, 24, 214
Zimbabwe African National Union-
    Patriotic Front, 41, 44, 85, 127,
    195, 251
Zimbabwe African People's Union, 195
Zimbabwe Congress of Trade Unions,
    63
Zondi, Siphamandla, 115
Zuma, Jacob, 40, 42, 194

www.ingramcontent.com/pod-product-compliance
Lightning Source LLC
Chambersburg PA
CBHW070902080426
R18103500001B/R181035PG41932CBX00015B/9